First Citizens of the Treaty City:

The Mayors and Mayoralty of Limerick 1197-2007

Councillor Ger Fahy, Mayor of Limerick 2007-2008

First Citizens of the Treaty City:

The Mayors and Mayoralty of Limerick 1197-2007

by Matthew Potter

Published in 2007 by Limerick City Council

British Library Cataloguing in Publishing Data
A CIP catalogue record for this book is available from the British Library.
ISBN   0-905700-16-3
           978-0-905700-16-8

Design and production by Creative Inputs, Ireland.
Printed in Ireland by Graham and Heslip Ltd.

Contents

Limerick City Council 2007.
Seated (L-R): Cllr. Lily Wallace, Cllr. Joe Leddin, Cllr. Maria Byrne, Cllr. John Cronin, Cllr. Kieran O'Hanlon.
Standing (L-R): Cllr. James Houlihan, Cllr. Jim Long, Cllr. Pat Kennedy, Mayor Ger Fahy, Cllr. Michael Hourigan,
Cllr. Gerry McLoughlin, Cllr. Kevin Kiely, Cllr. Kieran Walsh. (Egleston Brothers Photographers)
Inset (L-R): Cllr. Kathleen Leddin, Cllr. John Ryan, Cllr. Diarmuid Scully, Cllr. John Gilligan.
(Inset photographs by Copper Reed Studio)

Limerick City Council Management Team 2007
Seated (L-R): John Field, Director of Service, Tom Mackey, Limerick City Manager, Pat Dromey, Director of Service.
Standing (L-R): Caroline Curley, Director of Service, Pat Dowling, Director of Service,
Kieran Lehane, Director of Service.
(Egleston Brothers Photographers)

Acknowledgements

Limerick City Council; Limerick City Gallery of Art; Limerick City Library; Jim Kemmy Municipal Museum, Limerick.

Councillor Ger Fahy, Mayor of Limerick; former Mayors of Limerick: Mr. Jack Bourke; Mr. Tony Bromell; Mr. Bobby Byrne; Mr. Clement Casey; Mr. Thady Coughlan; Councillor John Cronin; Mr. Joe Harrington; Councillor Michael Hourigan; Mrs. Terry Kelly; Councillor Patrick Kennedy; Mr. Paddy Kiely; Councillor Joe Leddin; Mr. Paddy Madden; Mr. Denis A. O'Driscoll; Councillor Kieran O'Hanlon; Ms. Jan O'Sullivan TD; Mr. Frank Prendergast; Mr. John Quinn; Councillor John Ryan; Mr. Dick Sadlier; Councillor Diarmuid Scully.

Staff of Limerick City Council: Mr. Tom Mackey, Limerick City Manager; Mr. Pat Dowling, Director of Service; Mr. Oliver O'Loughlin, Director of Service (on secondment to Department of the Environment, Heritage and Local Government); Ms. Geraldine Costello, FAS and Limerick City Library; Ms. Sheila Deegan, Arts Officer; Mr. Tony Dillon; Ms. Dolores Doyle, Limerick City Librarian; Mr. Mike Fitzpatrick, Director/Curator Limerick City Gallery of Art; Mr. Flann Haskett; Ms. Jacqui Hayes, Limerick City/County Archivist; Mr. Brian Hodkinson, Jim Kemmy Municipal Museum; Mr. Michael Maguire, Limerick City Library; Mr. Jason Murphy; Mr. Des Ryan; Mr. Larry Walsh, Curator of the Jim Kemmy Municipal Museum.

Former staff of Limerick City Council: Mr. Brendan Keating; Mr. Conn Murray and Mr. Flann O'Neill former City Managers and Ms. Marie Cantillon, former Administrative Officer.

Ms. Geraldine Begley, indexer; Mr. Tony Browne; Dr. Mark Callanan, Institute of Public Administration; Mr. Richard Carew; Mr. Joseph Coffey; Copper Reed Studio; Mr. John Curtin; Mr. Cyril de Courcy; Mr. Michael Donnellan; Mr. Tom Donovan; Egleston Brothers Photographers; Desmond Fitzgerald, the Knight of Glin; Mr. John Garrard, University of Salford; Ms. Judith Hill; History Department, Mary Immaculate College; History Department, University of Limerick; Mr. Liam Irwin, Head of the History Department, Mary Immaculate College; Mrs. Kay Joyce.

Mr. Denis M. Leonard, Director Limerick Civic Trust; Ms. Mae Leonard; Limerick Chamber of Commerce; Limerick Civic Trust; Dr. A.P.W. Malcomson; Dr. Muiris MacCarthaigh, Institute of Public Administration; Professor Anthony McElligott, University of Limerick; Mr. Eamonn McEneaney, Curator of Waterford Treasures at the Granary Museum; Mr. Bryan McHugh; Mr. Joe McMahon; Mrs. Sarah McNamara; Mary Immaculate College; Mr Tadhg Moloney; Fr. Brian Murphy, Glenstal Abbey; National Archives; National Gallery of Ireland; National Library of Ireland.

Mr. Eugene O'Callaghan; Mr. Gerald O'Carroll; Mr. Ciarán O'Gríofa; Dr. Desmond O'Grady; Professor Gearóid O'Tuathaigh, National University of Ireland,

Galway; Mr. Alan Phylan; Mr. John Power, former Librarian Mary Immaculate College; Press 22 Photographic Agency; Mr. Paddy Reidy; Sir David O'Grady Roche; Dr. Thomas Ryan, RHA; Shannon Heritage; Mrs. Angela South; Trinity College, Dublin; University of Limerick; Fr. Mark Tierney, Glenstal Abbey; Dr. Patrick Waldron.

John Gormley

Foreword of the Minister for the Environment, Heritage and Local Government

One of the most ancient titles commonly used in Ireland today is that of Mayor. Its origins can be traced back to Roman times, but it was the French-speaking Normans who first introduced it to Ireland in the thirteenth century. In the intervening 800 years, it has been used by several of our cities and towns as the official designation for the elected head of their governing bodies. In the past, the Mayoralty was sometimes criticised for being a foreign import, but it has become firmly embedded in our national consciousness and has even been adopted informally by several non-municipal towns and villages, a sure sign of its popularity. Indeed the Local Government Act of 2001 for the first time authorised all local authorities, including non-urban ones such as counties to adopt the title for their elected head. Consequently, there are now more Mayors in Ireland than at any time since the foundation of the State.

The ancient and historic city of Limerick has one of the oldest Mayoralties in Ireland and is justly proud of its long and distinguished tradition of municipal self-government. In 2006, Limerick City Council demonstrated its awareness and commitment to the study of this heritage by publishing, *The Government and the People of Limerick: The History of Limerick Corporation/City Council 1197-2006* by Matthew Potter, which was the first complete account of the government of an Irish urban area ever written. Now, they are following this up with a companion volume, the present work, *First Citizens of the Treaty City: The Mayors and Mayoralty of Limerick 1197-2007* by the same author.

This book consists of two parts. The first is a very full and comprehensive account of the evolution of the Mayoralty of Limerick, while the second is a chronicle of each individual Mayor since the 1840s. Both compliment each other very successfully, for the interaction of the office and the individual incumbents is a very significant and interesting aspect of the unfolding narrative. The Mayoralty is like a stream that flows onwards immutably, but each Mayor brings to it his or her own individual life history and experience, and in so doing alters the office to a greater or lesser degree. Matthew Potter has performed a masterly feat in interweaving these two strands into an interesting, readable and scholarly narrative.

Limerick is one of the most dynamic and cosmopolitan urban areas in Ireland and I am proud to say that I have strong associations with the city, having spent much of my childhood there. It has made tremendous progress in recent decades, but has retained an appreciation of its past and its heritage. Limerick has long been a centre of excellence, from its wonderful architectural legacy to its many literary, musical and sporting figures, and in *First Citizens of the Treaty City*, the reader is re-acquainted with much that is familiar as well as encountering some new and very interesting insights. One of the most striking of these is the manner in which for some 200 years in the fifteenth and sixteenth centuries, the Mayors administered Limerick as a virtually independent city-state, like modern Singapore or Hong Kong.

First Citizens of the Treaty City makes a very large and important contribution to our knowledge of both urban life and administrative structures in Ireland over a very long time span. As such, it is a work that will be of interest to a wide cross-section of the reading public, including teachers and scholars; local government staff; politicians; journalists and local historians. I wish to congratulate Limerick City Council for their visionary action in commissioning and publishing this work, which is both a window into the past and an act of faith in the future.

John Gormley, T.D., Minister for the Environment, Heritage and Local Government

Mayor's Foreword

Limerick was founded by the Vikings some 1100 years ago and since then has had a long, colourful and often dramatic history. Every citizen of Limerick is aware that he or she is living in a city that is the product of many centuries of continuous development, and that each generation has made a contribution to the heritage of the city. One need only recall the medieval splendour of St. Mary's Cathedral, the magnificent Georgian streetscapes of Newtown Pery, imposing Victorian churches such as St. John's Cathedral and, in our own time, the ultra-modern hotels and office buildings rising dramatically along the banks of the Shannon.

Since 1197, Limerick has been governed by a local government system at the head of which stands a chief officer, originally termed Provost but since the thirteenth century known as the Mayor. The role of the Provosts and Mayors in the life of the city has been a crucial one for over 800 years, and is now the subject of a major book, *First Citizens of the Treaty City: the Mayors and Mayoralty of Limerick 1197-2207* by Matthew Potter. This is a most wonderful and readable work, which takes the reader on a journey through time and allows him or her to experience what it was actually like to live in Limerick in the past. It is believed that, since 1197, around 580 individuals have held the office of First Citizen of Limerick and the reader gets to meet a great many of them along the way. And, what a varied set of people they were! Generals, peers, parliamentarians, newspaper proprietors, revolutionaries, merchants, writers, lawyers and schoolteachers are but some of the professions held by Limerick's Mayors and Provosts throughout the ages. Politically too, they have spanned the spectrum from arch-reactionaries to radical revolutionaries, with assorted Cromwellians, Whigs, Tories, Home Rulers, Progressives and Socialists in between.

Modern Limerick is a vibrant, dynamic and prosperous city and has enjoyed economic growth, a flourishing arts scene, outstanding sporting success and an enviable quality of life. In such circumstances, it can be easy to overlook the achievements of previous generations and to concentrate exclusively on the present. However, Limerick continues to be aware of its rich and ancient past and to celebrate its wonderful cultural heritage. The Mayors and Mayoralty form one of the most significant chapters in the city's history and they have probably had a greater impact on the history of Limerick than any other office holders. Therefore the modern city is as much a product of their activities as it of any other body of men and women.

As the latest in a line of Provosts and Mayors that extends back 811 years, I want to pay tribute to the enlightened and far-sighted action of the management team of Limerick City Council in commissioning a book that introduces a major part of the city's history and heritage to the general public. In so doing, it will be a companion volume to *The Government and the People of Limerick: The History of Limerick Corporation/City Council 1197-2006*, which was published by Limerick City Council in the summer of 2006. I am confident that, like this earlier volume, *First Citizens of the Treaty City* will become a standard work in its field and that it will be widely read and consulted for many years to come.

Cllr. Ger Fahy, Mayor of Limerick

City Manager's Foreword

The office of Mayor of Limerick is one of the oldest in Ireland and can trace its origins back to 1197 when Limerick received its first charter from John, Lord of Ireland. In 1197, Limerick was a small and peripheral town on the outer edge of Western Christendom, itself a civilisation that had yet to make a major impact on the rest of the world. By contrast, Limerick in 2007 is a rapidly growing and successful city with strong links to our European neighbours and also the USA. During the intervening 810 years, a succession of Provosts and Mayors has presided over the constantly changing city of Limerick and have made a remarkable contribution to its history and heritage.

Limerick City Council is justifiably proud of the enormous progress that Limerick has made over the past twenty years, but is also acutely aware of and committed to the city's proud history and ancient traditions. A country, city or institution that is without knowledge of its history is like a person without a memory. It is necessary to know about the past in order to understand the present. It is for this reason that *First Citizens of the Treaty City. The Mayors and Mayoralty of Limerick 1197-2007* has been published.

Like its companion volume, *The Government and the People of Limerick: The History of Limerick Corporation/City Council 1197-2006*, which was published in 2006, *First Citizens of the Treaty City* combines scholarly rigor and detail with an easy and readable style, which will make it accessible to everyone. The evolution of the Mayoralty as an institution is described in detail and the biography of every Mayor since the establishment of the modern Limerick Corporation/City Council in 1841-42 is set out in the concluding two chapters. It has been said that biography is the most accessible form of history and the chronicling of our Mayors over the past 165 years is a very significant and welcome feature of the book. Sadly, many of these had passed out of the public consciousness and had been largely forgotten but *First Citizens of the Treaty City* will restore them to the historical record and will re-introduce them to their rightful place in the collective memory of Limerick city.

The Irish local government network, of which the Mayoralty forms such a significant element, is the oldest institutional system in the country, with the exception of the Christian churches. It has served the nation well and continues to be a major force for good in Irish society. One need only think of the transformation of Limerick city over the past twenty years, through the process of Urban Renewal. Like the City Council itself, the Mayoralty of Limerick is a constantly changing and evolving institution, which has been re-invented on several occasions, but has always successfully adapted itself to the circumstances of the times. *First Citizens of the Treaty City* tells us the story of this process. It is a very significant book that contributes greatly to our understanding of the history and heritage of Limerick, a city that is both ancient and modern, while combining the best of both in a highly successful manner. I am confident that this volume will find a place on the shelf of Limerick people and indeed Irish people in general, at home and abroad for many years to come.

Tom Mackey, City Manager

The staff of Michael Donnelly, Mayor of Limerick 1903-04
(Jim Kemmy Municipal Museum)

Chapter One
Introduction

While the history of Limerick city has been the subject of many fine works over the past 250 years, this book is the first history of the mayors and mayoralty of Limerick ever published.[1] 'The distinguished English historian John Garrard has edited a major work on the institution of mayoralty worldwide which is entitled *Heads of the Local State: Mayors, Provosts and Burgomasters since 1800* which was published in autumn 2007. While describing Irish mayors as local heads of state may seem somewhat inaccurate, it will be argued in the present work that the mayors of Limerick (and their counterparts throughout the country) have in fact functioned as such since the office was established. For centuries, they were local kings who wielded great power and influence, but the introduction of the management system completed their transition to local presidents with a largely though not exclusively ceremonial role.'[2] Indeed, a number of works on the mayors of other towns and cities in Ireland have already been published.[3] However, the idea of writing a history of the mayors and mayoralty of Limerick originated with Gerry Joyce, who worked with Limerick Corporation for thirty years and who wrote a significant and well-received book on the street names of Limerick city, published in 1995.[4] He had already begun work on a history of the mayors of Limerick when he died at a comparatively young age in 1995 and the present book is in many respects a tribute to his memory.

Limerick Corporation was founded by John, Lord of Ireland in 1197, was renamed Limerick City Council in 2002 and at the time of writing, has administered the city for over 800 years. The mayors and mayoralty are of vital importance in the history of Limerick city for a number of reasons. Firstly, the role of local government was paramount in the administration of the country from the twelfth to the eighteenth centuries and in turn the role of the mayors was paramount in the local government system. Throughout these centuries, the Catholic Church was the other major institution that impacted on the lives of the populace, but the central government played only a relatively minor role. Secondly, while the corporation has lost some of its primacy since the eighteenth century, it still continues to be the most important institution in the city and it is no exaggeration to describe its history as a virtual history of Limerick city itself.[5] Thirdly, although the Limerick City Management Act of 1934 transformed the mayoralty into a predominantly ceremonial institution, this did not in any way result in a decline in its significance and glamour; the reverse would seem to be the case. In view of the antiquity, power and prestige of the institution, it can be argued that the mayors have probably had a greater impact on the history of Limerick than any other office holders, with the possible exception of the bishops.

The Origins of the Mayoralty in Ireland.

Local authorities have played an important role in Ireland for over 800 years.[6] The term 'local government' was invented in 1835 by Jeremy Bentham, the celebrated English philosopher and social reformer. It still remains the most usual term for what in recent decades is also commonly referred to as 'sub-national government' or 'the local state.' In 1982, Desmond Roche, one of the leading authorities on the Irish system wrote that 'local government is commonly defined as a system of administration in political sub-divisions of a state, by elected bodies having substantial control of local affairs, including the power to impose taxes'.[7] He also described them as having a clearly defined geographical area of operation, which is a sub-division of a state; as being governed by bodies elected in their own operational area and possessing a certain degree of autonomy, particularly in the fields of administration and taxation.[8] In 2003, Mark Callanan, one of the foremost contemporary experts on Irish local authorities wrote that modern local government has four main roles: 'an instrument of local democracy; a provider of services; an agent of central government and a local regulator'.[9]

The Irish system of local authorities was established by the Normans in the late twelfth and early thirteenth centuries.[10] Borough corporations in urban areas and counties or shires in non-urban areas were the principal units of the Norman local state. Cities and towns received charters, which were written constitutions setting out the basic machinery for their administration and which provided for the establishment of elected bodies, later known as corporations, to run their affairs. The office of mayor developed as part of this urban local government system.[11]

The title of mayor is derived from the Latin word maior meaning 'a greater man'. In the Roman Empire, great landowners often appointed a *major domus* or supervisor to administer their estates. The practice was later used by the Merovingian kings of France (who reigned between 476 and 751) and their estate manager, whose official title was *major palatii* or 'mayor of the palace', eventually, became a virtual prime minister and the real ruler of the country. The process was taken to its logical conclusion in 751, when the mayor of the palace overthrew the last of the Merovingians, and became king himself. In the eleventh and twelfth centuries, the title of mayor was used in France to describe the chief executive of a city or town and was later imported to both England and Ireland by the Normans. Consequently, it is to France that Ireland owes the mayoralty, and not to England, as is frequently believed.[12]

The Medieval Mayoralty of Limerick.

In the history of the local state, the Middle Ages can be said to have continued into the early nineteenth century, because the medieval system of administration survived into the 1830s and 1840s. Bearing this in mind, broadly speaking the history of Limerick's mayors and mayoralty may be divided into two periods, the medieval and the modern. During the medieval period (1197-1842), Limerick Corporation was an omni-competent authority, which filled the roles of sole representative assembly, service provider, agent of the central administration and local regulator. It provided for the city's defence, organised and controlled its economic life including markets, fairs, fisheries and the port, ran its legal system, organised the police, built and maintained its infrastructure and protected its environment. The citizens of Limerick had little contact with central government because most of its functions (such as the collection of some taxes, and the levying of men, money and supplies in wartime) were discharged on an agency basis by the corporation.[13]

In the medieval period, Limerick city was ruled by the mayor and city council. Like his modern counterpart, the mayor was the ceremonial head of the city but he was also the combined chief executive, chief justice and general, who governed the city with the assistance of the council and a small number of officials, in the absence of a professional bureaucracy. The mayor was similar to a local king in that he possessed executive, judicial and legislative powers (exercising the latter as leader of the council); was the ceremonial head of the local state; and possessed many of the trappings of kingship, such as impressive robes, a sceptre or wand, and a regal form of address (Your Worship).

In theory, the mayor was elected by the freemen, a large, though predominantly male and propertied minority of the population but in practice, he was usually chosen from among a tiny, exclusive clique of wealthy merchants. This process was given official recognition in 1672 when the right to elect the mayor was removed from the freemen and placed in the hands of the city council. In the sixteenth century, the Reformation introduced religious conflict to Limerick and eventually produced a Protestant ascendancy in the corporation, which lasted from 1651 to 1841. This resulted in the municipal authority becoming even more unrepresentative, as it was only the Protestants within the merchant elite who could exercise political power.[14] This process culminated in the eighteenth century when a single powerful ruling family (first the Roches and then the Smyth-Verekers) established a near absolute control over the corporation.

In theory, the mayor continued to be elected by the city council, but in practice he was often appointed by the ruling clique. Corruption was widespread and the corporation concentrated on its political role, particularly the returning of MPs to parliament, while its functions as service provider and local regulator were gradually abandoned. The resulting vacuum was filled by other agents, including the grand jury, parish vestries and improvement commissioners. However, this traditional picture of local government in eighteenth century Britain and Ireland as being incorrigibly corrupt and incompetent has been challenged by the modern urban historian Rosemary Sweet who, in her study of English towns between 1680 and 1840 has suggested that the apparent decay of English borough governments was in fact caused by the unprecedented demands made on them as a result of rapidly increasing population, the beginnings of the Industrial Revolution and the rising expectations of a much larger, better educated and more politically aware general public.[15] While Limerick did not experience an industrial revolution at this time, both the city's economy and population expanded rapidly between 1745 and 1815, and in consequence its local state was confronted with challenges similar to those experienced by British urban areas at this time.

The Modern Mayoralty of Limerick.

The modern age of Limerick's mayoralty began in 1842 with the election of the first mayor under the Municipal Corporations (Ireland) Act of 1840. In the 1840s, Irish local authorities declined in status and range of activities. Many of the functions abandoned in the eighteenth century were never regained and they also lost control over the local judicial and economic systems. The rise of Irish nationalism and democracy made successive British governments reluctant to give powers to local authorities which they feared might become centres of opposition to their rule.[16] The result was increasing centralisation and lack of autonomy, compared to the local state in Britain and the continent of Europe.

The period since 1842 has also been notable for the rise of the professional administrator in local government. The Act of 1840 provided for Limerick to be ruled by the mayor and council as before, but in succeeding decades, the powers and authority of senior fulltime officials such as the town clerk and city treasurer increased steadily, while those of the part-time mayor and councillors correspondingly declined. The transition from local king to local president had thus begun and culminated with the appointment of the first city manager in 1934. Henceforth a professional administrator ran the city on a day-to-day basis while the role of the mayor became largely ceremonial. In addition a relatively small number of officials had staffed the corporation in the nineteenth century but an increasingly large, complex and professional civic bureaucracy evolved in the second half of the twentieth century.

In the modern period, the mayoralty became a much more representative institution than ever before. Under the Act of 1840, only a tiny minority could vote in local elections and the mayor continued to be elected by the council and not directly by the electorate. Nevertheless, Protestant Ascendancy was ended in Limerick in the 1840s and the Catholic elite took control of the corporation. Later, the Local Government Act of 1898 introduced popular participation in local government and the transition to a completely democratic system was finally completed by the Local Government (Extension of Franchise) Act of 1935. In this manner, the mayoralty gradually became a democratic, though still indirectly elected institution.

The modern mayoralty also adapted itself very successfully to changing political circumstances. Although it had been a symbol of Protestant ascendancy for nearly 200 years, the Catholic elite that took power in Limerick in 1841 embraced the office and made it their own. Later the Home Rule party that rebuffed the British monarchy retained the mayoralty and turned it into a symbol of nationalism. The same pattern was to be repeated in 1899 with the election of the Labour Corporation and in 1920, when Sinn Féin gained control of the city council. In 1921, the killing of Mayors Clancy and O'Callaghan completed the transformation of the mayoralty into a nationalist symbol. Clearly, the unique and prestigious office of mayor was capable of endless reinvention and adaptability.[17]

The decline in the actual powers of the mayor, particularly after 1934 was mirrored in the reduction of the pomp and circumstance surrounding the office, which began in the decades after 1945. The use of the mayoral wand ceased in the 1950s, the style 'Your Worship' was increasingly replaced by the less formal 'Mayor', and many holders of the office even dispensed with the wearing of ceremonial robes. In an age that became increasingly democratic and informal, the mayor of Limerick completed the transition from king to president of the local state.

Endnotes

1   There are a number of major works on the history of Limerick city. The most notable are John Ferrar, *History of Limerick, Ecclesiastical, Civil and Military from the Earliest Records to the Year 1787*, (Limerick, 2nd ed. 1787); P. Fitzgerald and J.J. McGregor, *The History, Topography and Antiquities of the County and City of Limerick; with a Preliminary view of the History and Antiquities of Ireland*, 2 Vols, (Dublin, 1826-7); Maurice Lenihan, *Limerick, its History and Antiquities, Ecclesiastical, Civil and Military, From the Earliest Ages*, (Dublin, 1866. Reprinted Cork and Dublin 1991) and Rev. John Begley, *The Diocese of Limerick*, 3 Vols, (Dublin 1906-38).

2   John Garrard (ed.), *Heads of the Local State: Mayors, Provosts and Burgomasters since 1800* (Aldershot, 2007).

3   See Eamonn McEneaney, *A History of Waterford and its Mayors from the 12th Century to the 20th Century*, (Waterford, 1995); Antóin O'Callaghan, *The Lord Mayors of Cork 1900 to 2000*, (Cork, 2000) and William Henry, *Roll of Honour. The Mayors of Galway City 1485-2001*, (Galway, 2002). For the Mayors of Wexford, see Padge Reck, *Wexford - A Municipal History*, (Wexford, 1987), pp 13-63.

4   Gerry Joyce, *Limerick City Street Names*, (Limerick 1995).

5   For the history of local government in Limerick city, see Matthew Potter, *The Government and the People of Limerick. The History of Limerick Corporation/City Council 1197-2006*, (Limerick, 2006).

6   The best accounts of the Irish system of local government are Desmond Roche, *Local Government in Ireland*, (Dublin, 1982) and Mark Callanan and Justin F. Keogan (eds), *Local Government in Ireland Inside Out*, (Dublin, 2003). For municipal corporations see John J Webb, *Municipal Government in Ireland: Medieval and Modern*, (Dublin, 1918). See also John A. Garrard, 'The History of Local Political Power-Some Suggestions for Analysis' in *Political Studies*, Vol. 25, No.2, (1977).

7   Roche, *Local Government*, p. 1.

8   Ibid., p. 1.

9   Mark Callanan, 'The Role of Local Government' in Callanan and Keogan, *Local Government*, pp 4- 5.

10 For the local government system in medieval Ireland see A.J. Otway – Ruthven, *A History of Medieval Ireland*, (London, 1968), pp 173-87 and David B. Quinn, 'Anglo-Irish Local Government 1485-1534', in *Irish Historical Studies*, I (1938-9), pp 354-81.

11 For the mayoralty in Ireland, see Muiris MacCarthaigh and Mark Callanan, 'The Mayoralty in the Republic of Ireland' and Colin Knox, 'Mayoralty in Northern Ireland: Symbol or Substance?' both in Garrard, *Heads of the Local State* (forthcoming 2008).

12 See the *New Encyclopaedia Britannica*, Volume 7, Micropaedia, (London, 1988), pp 976-77.

13 Potter, *The Government and the People of Limerick*, pp 57-70.

14 For Limerick Corporation in the long eighteenth century see Eamon O'Flaherty, 'Urban Politics and Municipal Reform in Limerick 1723-62' in *Eighteenth Century Ireland*, VI, (1991), pp 105-20 and Jennifer Moore, 'Newtown Pery- the Antithesis to Corporation Corruption and the Birth of a New City in Eighteenth Century Limerick ' in *History Studies*, V, (2004), pp 28-49.

15 Rosemary Sweet, *The English Town, 1680-1840. Government, Society and Culture*, (Harlow, Essex, 1999), pp 141-50.

16 See Oliver McDonagh 'Ideas and Institutions 1830-45' in W.E. Vaughan (ed.), *A New History of Ireland Volume V Ireland Under the Union, I, 1801-70* (Oxford, 1989) pp 206-07.

17 For similar developments in England see John Garrard, 'The Mayoralty since 1835' in *Proceedings of the Lancashire and Cheshire Historical Society*, Volume 90, (1994).

This picture of the four principal mayors in Ireland is taken from the Great Charter Roll of Waterford, which dates to c. 1372. The mayors shown are: Dublin (top left), Waterford (top right), Cork (bottom left) and Limerick (bottom right) and are the earliest depictions of any Irish mayors. Interestingly, the mayor of Limerick is wearing the extremely short tunic fashionable at the time, while his colleagues are more soberly clad. (Waterford Treasures at the Granary Museum)

Chapter Two
The Mayoralty in the Medieval Period 1197-1534

Cities and Towns in Medieval Europe.

The origins of the mayoralty of Limerick can only be fully understood in the context of the history of urban life in Europe in the Middle Ages.[1] After the fall of the Roman Empire the so-called 'Dark Ages' (400 to 1000 AD) saw Western Europe fall far behind the great civilisations in the Middle East, India and China. The period was characterised by economic collapse, political chaos and widespread violence. Towns and cities declined sharply, even though they continued to prosper in Asia. However the dawn of the first millennium saw the fortunes of Western Europe begin to improve dramatically, and the period 1000 to 1300 was one of political, religious, economic and intellectual expansion. The eleventh century saw the beginnings of religious reform, the expansion of monasticism and the rise of the Papacy. The first universities were founded; Gothic art and architecture originated in France and spread all over Europe; the two great legal systems of the world, the Common Law of England and the Civil Law of mainland Europe came into existence and the growing power of the monarchy in England, France and Germany brought about increased stability. Western Europe, having closed most of the gap with the great Asian civilisations, also expanded its boundaries rapidly on every front. The Muslims were driven out of Spain, German settlers moved into Eastern Europe, Norman barons invaded England, Ireland and Wales, and crusaders conquered the Holy Land.[2]

The Establishment of the Medieval Local State.

Underlying all of these developments was an important economic revolution, characterised by population growth, the expansion of agriculture, trade and industry, the beginnings of capitalism and the consequent rise of a merchant and manufacturing class. Towns and cities were among the main beneficiaries of the revival of Europe and multiplied rapidly both in numbers and in size.[3] Between 1000 and 1300, most cities with a population of 20,000 at least doubled in size. New towns were also founded, particularly in frontier regions such as the Baltic, Eastern Europe, Scotland and Ireland. These foundations strengthened the hold of rulers on recently conquered territories by providing administrative and religious centres that promoted both colonisation and economic expansion.

Between 1150 and 1300, the growth of trade and industry in Western Europe gave birth to a movement by the merchant and manufacturing classes to take control of the government of the urban areas.[4] There were several reasons for this. Firstly, medieval Europe was the heir to two traditions of self–government and democracy, namely those of Greece and of the Germanic peoples. Secondly, the fall of the Roman Empire had resulted in the disappearance of efficient, bureaucratic government in Western Europe and as a result, the unsettled conditions of the Dark Ages helped foster local autonomy and initiative. The result was the feudal system, with its emphasis on localism, self-reliance and political fragmentation. Thirdly, the increasingly prosperous and confident cities and towns wanted self-government to enable their property rights to be protected, to control their local economies and to end the interference of often corrupt and unsympathetic feudal lords, bishops and monarchs.

In turn, the monarchs, bishops and feudal lords had various reasons for granting autonomy to the towns and cities. Firstly, kings sometimes formed alliances with the townspeople and granted charters to towns under the control of troublesome feudal lords, in order to promote the former and undermine the latter. Secondly some cities and towns were so large and powerful that the ruler had no choice but to grant them self-government. Thirdly, kings and lords raised money by selling privileges to wealthy towns.[5] Fourthly, expansionary rulers used the promise of urban liberties to attract colonists to the towns that they had founded in newly conquered territories in order to strengthen their grip on these lands, promote the culture and religion of the conquerors and create wealth that could be taxed by fostering economic prosperity, trade and manufacturing.[6]

The communal movement was of major significance to the growth of urban autonomy in medieval Europe.[7] It began in France in the tenth century and became widespread throughout Europe in the second half of the twelfth century. Communes were oath-bound associations of the inhabitants of a town originally established for mutual protection, but later progressed to demanding urban self-government. The title of mayor, originally used to describe powerful officials employed by the kings of France, was borrowed by the communal movement to denote the elected leader of a commune who administered it with the assistance of a council. Indeed, the office of mayor and the institution of a town council were characteristic of the communal movement and were imported into England (and later to Ireland) from France in the late twelfth and early thirteenth centuries.

Urban self-government was usually attained when a monarch, feudal lord or senior clergyman granted a charter (a document like a written constitution), giving the town a measure of self-rule and its citizens certain rights and freedoms. Charters in France and the Holy Roman Empire were usually given to the commune, putting its members in charge of the town and the mayor of the commune then became chief executive of the town or city in question. Later, the term commune was given to the actual unit of local government and is still used in this sense in modern France.

The movement for urban autonomy was very successful, and cities and towns all over Europe received varying degrees of self-government in the period 1150 to 1300. It is important to remember that it took very different forms in England and on the continent. Medieval England was a unified, highly centralised and well-run kingdom, ruled by powerful monarchs, who seldom allowed towns to have too much autonomy. On the other hand the Holy Roman Empire, consisting of modern Germany, the Netherlands, Belgium, Switzerland, Austria and all of Northern Italy was highly decentralised, and many urban areas within its borders eventually achieved *de facto* independence. Ireland's urban local state was a hybrid of both. Between 1171 and 1300, Irish towns achieved limited autonomy on the English model but from 1300 to 1600, the drastic decline of English rule resulted in their gradually achieving virtual independence like the cities of mainland Europe.

The Establishment of Limerick Corporation.

Limerick city had been founded by the Vikings in 922 AD and was captured by the Normans around the year 1195. To administer this latest Norman acquisition, Limerick Corporation was established by a charter issued by John, Lord of Ireland on 18 December 1197.[8] Written in Latin, the common literary language of medieval Western Christendom, this document was Limerick's first formal written constitution and it introduced the most modern local government system of its time, imported from England and France, the two most dynamic countries in thirteenth-century Europe.[9]

The civic constitution of medieval Limerick consisted of two parts: a written constitution set out under twelve charters issued by various English monarchs between 1197 and 1609 and an unwritten constitution that had evolved without explicit authorisation. The former included the hundred court, the gild merchant, the mayoralty and the bailiffs while the latter included the common council and the aldermen. There were three different representative bodies in the city. The freemen of Limerick constituted the civic electorate and met weekly in the hundred court to transact legal and administrative business. At a special annual meeting of the hundred court, they elected the mayor and (after 1413) the two bailiffs. The gild merchant was similar to the modern chamber of commerce. The common council, the most important of the three representative bodies was equivalent to the modern city council and consisted of aldermen and ordinary councillors. The mayor and the two bailiffs formed the executive of the city and were nominally elected by the freemen assembled in the hundred court, but in reality were chosen by the civic elite from amongst the membership of the common council. They served for one year but could be re-elected, and governed the city with the assistance of the common council and a small number of officials. Limerick city continued to be governed under the provisions of its medieval civic constitution until 1841.

The Establishment of the Mayoralty of Limerick.

The system of borough government in both England and Ireland evolved continuously between 1169 and 1300.[10] Similarly, Limerick's mayoralty gradually evolved during the century 1197 to 1292, so it is not possible to state exactly when it came into existence. Contrary to popular opinion, Limerick's first charter of 1197 did not establish or even mention the office of mayor. Indeed, Limerick enjoyed a very limited form of self-government under this charter, which mentioned only three elements of the city government: the prepositus, the bailiffs and the hundred court. The prepositus (usually translated as 'provost' the title still used by Scottish mayors) and his two deputies known as bailiffs, were civil servants appointed by central government in Dublin to administer the city, while the hundred court, consisting of the freemen, was a combined city council and law court with limited powers.[11] In addition, Limerick city was under the jurisdiction of the sheriff (or governor) of the county of Munster (after the 1250s the sheriff of the newly created county of Limerick) who was responsible for the collection of the annual rent of £40, known as the fee farm of the borough that was paid by the city to the king. The rule of the sheriffs which was often both overbearing and venal, was greatly resented by the townspeople, and fuelled their desire for self–government.[12]

The charter of 1197 also established the gild merchant, which was an association of the city's merchants, similar to the modern chamber of commerce. In the English boroughs, the gild merchant had large revenue from its membership fees, it elected its own officers and its chief executive was called an alderman, an Anglo-Saxon title, which literally meant the 'senior' or the 'elder' man.[13] Originally applicable to the governor of a shire, it became the official title of the head of a guild. The English historian James Tait claimed that the guild was an embryonic local authority and wrote that 'the gild alderman anticipated the elected mayor, or bailiffs, the gild organisation the borough assembly and town council and the gild purse the borough treasury'.[14] Similarly, the gild merchant of Limerick probably acted as a *de facto* local authority, due to the limited autonomy conceded in the first charter.

Silver penny of King John minted in Limerick
in the thirteenth century.
(Jim Kemmy Municipal Museum)

The next step in the process of civic emancipation occurred when the citizens of Limerick received the right to collect the fee farm rent themselves and pay it directly to the exchequer in Dublin. This ended the sheriff's role in the city's internal affairs.[15] It is not known when Limerick's citizens received the farm of the borough but it was probably at the same time that they were given the right to elect their first mayor as the two privileges were usually granted together.[16]

In the period 1189 to 1216, the communal movement spread from France to England bringing with it the characteristic institutions of the mayoralty and city council.[17] The mayor superseded both the appointed provost, and the alderman of the gild merchant as the elected and legally recognised head of the borough. For nearly 200 years, the question of when Limerick received its first mayor has been the subject of a number of popular and enduring myths. It has been proudly asserted and popularly believed that the city's first elected mayor took office under the provisions of the charter of 1197, was the first such elected mayor in Ireland and even that Limerick had an elected mayor before London itself.[18] Then in 1997, Larry Walsh, curator of Limerick's Jim Kemmy Municipal Museum, published an important article that clarified the matter for the first time. In it, he stated that in 1215, London became the first city in England and in 1229, Dublin the first city in Ireland to elect a mayor. Furthermore, Walsh wrote that Limerick's chief executive under the first charter of 1197 was an appointed provost, not an elected mayor.[19]

Walsh demonstrated that the first charter of 1197 had specified that the citizens of Limerick should 'have all the liberties and free customs through all Ireland which the citizens of Dublin have', making it possible after 1229 for Limerick to follow Dublin in having an elected mayor.[20] He thinks that it is possible that the right was simply assumed following Dublin's example, or it may be that the future King Edward I, as Lord of Ireland (1254 – 72) granted the right, as he is believed to have done in both Cork and Waterford. What is known is that Limerick's first citizen at the accession of Edward I in 1272 was officially called the mayor.[21] Limerick's constitutional status was clarified in 1292. In 1274, the citizens of Limerick petitioned the king for an enumeration of their liberties under John's charter of 1197 and in reply Edward I directed his justiciar (chief governor of Ireland, later termed lord lieutenant, lord deputy or viceroy) to 'inquire what liberties the citizens of Dublin enjoy; whether the citizens of Limerick enjoy the same liberties; which of them they have used and which not; and whether it would be to the king's detriment that he should grant to the latter citizens his charter specifying the liberties as prayed'.[22] The justiciar found that Limerick was indeed entitled to all of Dublin's privileges, but it was not until 1292 that Edward I acted on this recommendation when he granted Limerick its second charter.[23] In it, the citizens of Limerick were explicitly given the right to 'each year elect from amongst themselves a mayor discreet, proper, faithful to the king, and fit for the rule of the city'.[24] The mayor was elected for a term of one year by the freemen assembled in the hundred court and on election had to be 'presented to the king, or the justiciar if the king is not present and swear fealty to the king'.[25] As no English king visited Ireland between 1210 and 1394 it was to the chief governor in Dublin that the mayor always tendered his oath of loyalty, until the charter of 1413 abolished the practice.

The Establishment of Limerick City Council.

As with the mayoralty, it is not possible to pinpoint an exact date for the establishment of Limerick City Council. The first charter had established two representative assemblies in the city's constitution - the gild merchant and the hundred court - but both were large and unwieldy and were eventually superseded by the city council. City and town councils in England and Ireland seemed to have evolved from three sources.[26] Firstly, they probably emerged from the hundred court either as a jury to adjudicate in legal cases or as a smaller advisory body to the mayor. Secondly they may have evolved from the gild merchant. Thirdly, the concept was introduced from France as part of the communal movement. Councils were originally established to provide the mayor with legal advice and to enable him to consult with the citizens, but later they acquired both a legislative and an administrative role.

Limerick's city council probably came into existence in the thirteenth century.[27] London was the first city in England and Dublin was the first city in Ireland to establish a city council. In 1229, Dublin elected a council of twenty-four to assist the newly elected first mayor.[28] Other Irish cities soon acquired elected councils, which quickly supplanted the gild merchant and the hundred court as the leading legislative and representative body.[29] Most councils established at this time had twelve or twenty-four members and it is likely that Limerick conformed to this pattern. Some councils in medieval England and Ireland were elected by the freemen, others filled vacancies by co-option and there were others that combined the two methods. In practice, the difference between the three modes of selection was slight for in virtually all urban authorities, the mayor and council tended to be chosen from among a small wealthy clique with little involvement from the general public or even the freemen. While it is not known what the method of selection was in medieval Limerick, it was definitely by co-option in the seventeenth and eighteenth centuries. By 1300, Limerick had borrowed from the French communal movement 'the full conception of a self governing urban community, presided over by a chief magistrate and council of its own choice, and with all the component parts cemented together by binding oaths which inculcated a high ideal of civic loyalty and service'.[30]

Medieval English towns were almost always ruled by small elites and the same seems to have been true in Ireland.[31] Obviously, this was frequently due to the desire of the wealthy oligarchy to monopolise power, but the historian Gearóid MacNiocaill in his research into the government of medieval Irish boroughs, concluded that the number of potential office-holders was often very limited for a number of more benign reasons.[32] Firstly, the mayor and bailiffs were virtually always selected from the ranks of the wealthiest merchants, but a major disincentive was that they had to suspend trading for their terms of office, which could put their businesses in jeopardy. Secondly, the population of medieval Limerick was never more than 3,000-3,500, of which the elite would have only formed a small proportion.[33] Thirdly, in periods of economic decline, there was a corresponding decrease in the number of wealthy potential candidates for civic office. Finally, many candidates were reluctant to become involved in city government for a variety of personal reasons, such as apathy, diffidence or family and business commitments.[34] Recent research has indicated that the mayoralty in Limerick in the Middle Ages and after was dominated by

Map, bird's eye view of Limerick in 1691 by Richard Ahern, 1991, sponsored by Treaty 300 and Power Whiskey. The hourglass shape of medieval Limerick is clearly depicted.
(Jim Kemmy Municipal Museum)

eight prominent families, such as the Arthurs (who held the office of mayor on sixty-one occasions between 1218 and 1608), the Creaghs (thirty-one times between 1216 and 1787), and the Comyns (twenty-nine times between 1407 and 1648). Even more strikingly, between 1440 and 1494, thirty-four out of the fifty-four who held office were Arthurs.[35] This process of consolidation continued into the sixteenth century by which time a mayoral elite of twenty-four merchant families, similar to the much more famous fourteen tribes of Galway, monopolised the government of the city.[36]

In the fourteenth and fifteenth centuries, there were revolts in towns all over Europe, particularly in Flanders, France, Germany and Italy, caused by the desire of the citizens for a greater share in the government of the local state. In general the result was a widening of the ruling elite to include wealthy craftsmen as well as merchants, but most of the inhabitants were not admitted and the urban areas of Europe continued to be ruled by small exclusive oligarchies until the nineteenth century.[37] In both England and Ireland, the movement for more inclusive urban government was less violent and was marked by the institution of common councils.[38] Originally established to widen participation in the municipal government, they also came under the control of the ruling oligarchies within a short time.[39] The common council was often double the size of the existing council and the members of the latter were then renamed aldermen.[40] Sometimes the two councils were collectively called the common council, and other times, the name was just applied to the larger of the two. Some urban areas retained a two-tier system of councils while others eventually merged them into one. Limerick's common council was probably established in the fifteenth century but there is no record of how it was selected. Limerick did not retain a two-tier system like Dublin, and the original city council was subsumed into a single common council. Its senior members (such as former mayors) came to be known as the aldermen as a reminder of the time when there had been two councils. The title of alderman, borrowed from the gild merchant, was first adopted in the late Middle Ages in Limerick, but was not mentioned in a charter until James I's charter of 1609.[41] It is not known how many members the common council had in the Middle Ages, but in 1833, there were sixty-nine, including the mayor and fifteen aldermen.[42] Throughout its existence, the common council of Limerick was nearly always under the firm control of the mayoral elite.

In medieval Limerick, the freemen constituted the politically active section of the community and receiving the freedom of the city was not an honorary distinction such as it is has been since the late nineteenth century. They met in the hundred court on a weekly basis and had the right to elect the mayor and later the two bailiffs. Later they received the right to vote in elections to the Irish Parliament. Originally, the freemen were simply those who held burgages or plots of land within the city boundary. Later it was extended to other categories and eventually, it was possible to become a freeman by being (1) the eldest son of a freeman; (2) marrying the daughter of a freeman; (3) completing a seven-year apprenticeship with a freeman (4) receiving the freedom as a gift from the common council; (5) purchasing the privilege, and (6) the mayor gained the right to appoint two freemen.[43] The first three were considered to be the traditional and legitimate road to the freedom of the city. Nevertheless, the freemen always constituted a privileged, disproportionately prosperous and almost entirely male minority of the city's inhabitants.

Limerick Becomes a City-State.

The civic constitution of Limerick continued to evolve until the seventeenth century. Incorporation meant that the mayor and city council collectively formed a borough corporate and constituted a separate legal entity from the individual members. There were five main characteristics of borough incorporation: (1) Perpetual succession, which meant that the corporation had a continuous existence; (2) the right to own, rent or lease lands and property; (3) the use of a corporate seal; (4) the right to make bye-laws; and (5) the right to sue and be sued in a court of law.[44] Incorporation evolved gradually in most urban areas and existed in practice long before it was formally granted. The first formal grant of incorporation in England was Coventry in 1345 while the first Irish town to receive it was Drogheda in 1412.[45] Limerick probably enjoyed corporate status for many years before formally receiving it from Queen Elizabeth I in her charter of 1583 which also gave the term 'Limerick Corporation' official recognition for the first time.

The highest possible official status attainable by an urban area in England and Ireland was to be erected into a county in its own right. As with incorporation it was usually a gradual and informal process which culminated in an official grant that merely confirmed an existing state of affairs. In the town so honoured, the office of bailiff was abolished and replaced by that of sheriff, as the latter title was only used in an administrative county. The first English urban area to receive county status was Bristol in 1373 while in Ireland the first was Drogheda which received it in 1412.[46] Limerick city became an administrative county under the charter issued by James I in 1609.

However, several urban areas in late medieval Ireland attained a higher, though unofficial, status when they became virtual city-states, like their counterparts in contemporary Germany, Italy and Flanders. In eighteenth-century England, the constitution of the borough corporation was sometimes compared to that of the kingdom itself, with the mayor analogous to the king, the common council to the House of Lords and the freemen in their assembly such as the hundred court to the House of Commons.[47] It was a particularly striking analogy in the case of Limerick between 1413 and 1603, when the city was a *de facto* independent state.

In the thirteenth century, approximately two-thirds of Ireland was conquered by the Normans and the Anglo-Norman colony enjoyed great prosperity and efficient government. However, conditions changed dramatically in the first half of the fourteenth century due to the Bruce invasion, a revival of the power of the Gaelic Irish, the Great European Famine of 1314-20 and the Black Death of 1348-51. The cumulative result of these events was the collapse of effective English rule in Ireland and a prolonged economic recession, which lasted for over 150 years. In the fourteenth and fifteenth centuries, the country gradually fragmented into a mosaic of lordships that nominally owed allegiance to the king, but often ignored his authority and that of his Irish administration. The only part of Ireland remaining under direct rule was the Pale, an area around Dublin, about thirty miles long, and twenty miles wide, although most of Munster and Leinster, plus the towns remained very loyal to the English government. Ireland moved away from the highly organised and centralised English model, to the system in Germany and Italy, where urban areas and the great lords became *de facto* independent rulers.[48] In the fifteenth century the kings of England granted charters to the principal Irish towns that vastly increased their autonomy, and gave them a degree of independence unknown to English towns.[49] However, this was done, not to empower them, but as recognition that central government was unable to assist them, protect them or even communicate with them on a regular basis.[50] In consequence, they became virtual city-states.

King Henry V of England has achieved immortality due to his great victory at the Battle of Agincourt and the eponymous play by Shakespeare. However, it is not widely known that he also played a vital role in the history of Limerick, because his charter of 1413 granted the city virtual independence.[51] Under its provisions, the two bailiffs were to be elected by the citizens, not appointed by central government as heretofore, and the incoming mayor was to be sworn in by the previous mayor, or by the citizens, not before the king or justiciar. Both of these innovations recognised that communications between Dublin and Limerick had been effectively cut as a result of the collapse of central control outside the Pale. The most important article of the charter stated that 'no justiciar, escheator, inquisitor, clerk of market or other servant of the king, justice of the peace or of labourers shall enter or interfere in any matter within the city, except concerning felonies'.[52] Instead, the mayor and his successors were allowed to exercise the full powers of all these officers. In effect, the mayor had become king of Limerick and the only temporal superior that he now acknowledged was the king of England in his capacity as Lord of Ireland.

Limerick was a city-state for nearly two centuries (1413 – 1603) and the status of the mayor of Limerick approached that of a king in miniature more than at any time before or since. The results were mixed. On the one hand, the city escaped from the jurisdiction of the justiciar and his officials, who were often both venal and inept. Also, the corporation also stopped paying both the annual fee farm rent of £40 and the customs revenue to the crown.[53] Henceforth and for the next 200 years, little or no customs revenue was remitted by Limerick Corporation to the exchequer in Dublin except for a brief period in the late fifteenth and early sixteenth centuries.[54] As a result, Limerick became financially as well as politically independent of the Dublin government. On the other hand, *de facto* independence had been neither sought nor desired by the citizens of Limerick, who would have much preferred to be secure in the enjoyment of their privileges as English subjects and protected from their formidable Irish enemies. Limerick's two principal neighbours were the

The walls of Fethard, County Tipperary are among the best preserved in Ireland and convey some idea of the appearance of the walls of Limerick in medieval and early modern times. (Jim Kemmy Municipal Museum)

Fitzgerald, Earls of Desmond, who ruled all of modern County Limerick, North Cork, and North Kerry and the O'Briens of Thomond, who ruled over all of modern County Clare.[55]

In consequence, Limerick city endured a precarious existence for much of the fifteenth and sixteenth centuries. In 1427, the mayor and burgesses sent an appeal to King Henry VI asking that they be given custody of King John's Castle, as the city 'stands immediately in Irish enemy land' so that 'the Irish enemies may come to the doors of the said city some time or the other'.[56] They lamented that if the 'Irish enemies or the English rebels were to capture the castle, the city and its hinterland for forty miles would be entirely destroyed, because the Irish enemies are so strong'.[57] The corporation were duly given custody of the castle for a time. In 1450, Limerick was so completely cut of by the 'Irish rebels' and the 'English rebels', that all supplies had to be brought in by sea.[58] Limerick merchants had to pay tribute (equivalent to protection money) to the local lords in order to allow free passage of their goods along the River Shannon.[59]

The Role of the Medieval Mayor of Limerick.

If a borough corporation was like a kingdom, then medieval Limerick was governed by a king (the mayor), and a parliament (the council).[60] The medieval mayor of Limerick was a powerful semi-regal figure, who combined the modern roles of city manager, judge and general. He possessed legislative, judicial and executive powers, presided over meetings of the city council and served as chief magistrate in the civic courts. He organised the building and maintenance of the city walls, bridges, and other public works, and organised the paving of the streets. He enforced the corporation's control over the city's economic life and organised the collection of taxes. In times of war, he was supreme military commander of the city militia (which consisted of all able-bodied men) and in peacetime, he was ceremonial head of the local state.[61] Like the king in his kingdom, the mayor was the embodiment of Limerick city and recognising no superior except the justiciar, and after the granting of Henry V's charter of 1413, the king himself.[62]

Two incidents serve to illustrate the many-sided role of the medieval mayor of Limerick. In 1332, a number of the Earl of Desmond's retainers seized King John's Castle, where they had been imprisoned, and killed the governor. Mayor Thomas Bambery gathered an army of the townspeople, captured the castle and executed all of the rebels, 'irrespective of rank or quality'.[63] In 1435, there was a serious legal dispute between the mayor, Richard Arthur, and the bishop John Mothel, which culminated when the latter excommunicated the mayor and the two bailiffs. The mayor and corporation took their case to the pope himself, who eventually overruled the bishop.[64] Clearly the modern mayor's role is much less challenging, not to say less dangerous than that of his medieval predecessors!

The power of the mayor was limited by two important considerations, which to a large extent mitigated the overweening nature of the office. Firstly, his term of office only lasted for one year and while mayors often served on more than one occasion, they hardly ever served consecutive terms, except in the fifteenth century. This meant that no individual mayor was in office long enough to establish an effective or long-lasting power base. Secondly, the office of mayor tended to be rotated within a tightly-knit group of well-to-do and intermarried families, which resulted in the incumbent acting as a *primus inter pares* rather than as a dominant autocrat.

Next in rank to the mayor came the two bailiffs, who were effectively two deputy mayors. Originally appointed by the Dublin government, they were elected by the citizens annually from 1413 onwards under the provisions of Henry V's charter while in 1609, the charter of James I changed their title to 'sheriff,' the appropriate designation for the senior official of a county.[65] Limerick Corporation also employed a small number of other officials, who were usually appointed by the mayor and city council. In 1460 Limerick Corporation employed a public assistant clerk of the court; a collector of tolls; a collector of market dues; a caretaker for the public clock; a number of Mayor's sergeants (who acted as policemen) and two porters.[66] The most senior of these was the public assistant clerk, later known as the town clerk. Other positions created in succeeding decades included the recorder (legal advisor), the chamberlain (treasurer) and the water bailiff (who administered the port).[67]

In 1460, the mayor of Limerick received an annual salary of fifty shillings and each bailiff got twenty shillings.[68] The municipal officials also added to their income by receiving various fees. Fines and legal costs went to the civic courts, to be divided between the mayor and bailiffs. The mayor and councillors, who were not professional administrators, did a lot of the routine work themselves and the English historian Susan Reynolds wrote of medieval English boroughs: 'to modern English eyes, the boundary between elected and paid, voluntary and professional, officers looks very unclear'.[69] Not surprisingly, there were incidences of corruption and inefficiency and a Limerick byelaw of 1512 stipulated that all those convicted of bribery or perjury were to be debarred from holding office and deprived of the right to vote at the election of city officers.[70]

This photograph from the 1950s gives an idea of the massive scale of the walls of King John's Castle.
(Jim Kemmy Municipal Museum)

The Beginning of Limerick's Civic Traditions.

Whatever their shortcomings, the mayor and council always enjoyed the status of a local king and parliament, as can be seen in the byelaws of various Irish borough corporations. In both Dublin and Waterford a person who insulted the mayor outside the city hall had to pay a fine of forty shillings, while to do so in court cost £10. In Cork, a person who claimed in court that the mayor was showing bias, or was exceeding his powers could be fined £1. In Dublin and Waterford, a person who injured the mayor had to pay a fine of £40. If his blood was spilt, the penalties increased to a fine of £100, loss of the right hand, or jail for life. In 1384, a man who verbally abused the mayor of Kilkenny was obliged to pay a barrel of wine, or £10 for a second offence.[71]

The practice of wearing special ceremonial robes also developed to emphasise the special status of the mayor. The wealthy gentleman of the fifteenth century wore a formal gown called a houppelande, which was ground length, with hanging sleeves, a hood, and fur trimmings, but when it went out of fashion for every day wear, it survived in a fossilised form as the academic, legal and civic gown.[72] In 1543, the mayor of Limerick was given the right to carry a staff or wand by King Henry VIII.[73] The corporation also possessed a ceremonial mace by the 1550s. One of the earliest references to the mayor and council of Limerick wearing ceremonial robes can be found in a description of the official visit of the Earl of Sussex, lord deputy of Ireland to the city on 20 June 1558.[74] The mayor's fur-trimmed gown and wand were the equivalent of a king's ermine robes and sceptre and in an age when royalty and aristocracy were expected to dress splendidly, did much to exalt both the mayoralty and the local state of which he was head.

Any self-respecting king and parliament must have a home. It is not known where the corporation carried on its business in the first 250 years of its existence but the Tholsel built between 1449 and 1451 on Mary Street was the first purpose built municipal headquarters in Limerick city.[75] The word 'tholsel' is derived from the Anglo-Saxon words 'toll' meaning a tax and 'sael' which means a hall. Limerick's tholsel was a combined city hall, custom house, courthouse and chamber of commerce. It was a two-story building, with the ground floor open to the street, and used to hold markets while the upper floor contained the council chamber.[76] The building of the Tholsel played a major role in enhancing the power and dignity of the local state in Limerick.

The Functions of Limerick Corporation.

The functions of central government in medieval Ireland were to maintain the king's rule, suppress disorder, administer the legal system and collect taxes. Some of the chief preoccupations of modern governments, such as education, health and social welfare, were under the control of the church. Almost all the other functions of government were delegated to local authorities, which were the shires in rural areas and the borough corporations in urban areas. Consequently, the corporation in the Middle Ages had far greater powers than its present-day successor.

Its functions can be grouped under the following broad headings: defence; law and order; control of trade and industry; environment and infrastructure. The mayor and council were responsible for building and maintaining the walls of the city and of organising the male population into a kind of civic militia. They administered the police and night watch, controlled the legal system and the courts and meted out punishment to criminals. The economic life of the city, including fairs and markets, the port and fisheries, quality control and trade practices, prices and rates of pay were also part of their remit. The mayor and corporation regulated the environment, including refuse collection, street cleaning, fire fighting and prevention and the regulation of wandering animals. The building and maintenance of infrastructure, including bridges, streets, quays and public buildings was also the responsibility of the municipal authority.[77] When the Irish parliament came into existence in the late thirteenth century Limerick city received the right to return two MPs, who were probably chosen by the mayor and council to begin with, but were later returned by a restricted electorate, of whom the freemen of the city formed the largest category.[78]

From medieval times until the 1760s, the walled city of Limerick was in the shape of an hourglass, and consisted of the Englishtown where King John's Castle, the Tholsel and St. Mary's Cathedral were situated and the Irishtown.[79] By modern standards, it was very small with a total area of fifty-seven acres, but the jurisdiction of the mayor and corporation extended much further, as in 1216, King John granted lands to the city that probably totalled at least 5,000 acres.[80] Even allowing for the vagueness of medieval units of measurement, the King's grant gave Limerick Corporation control over an area that was at least the same as its modern counterpart.[81]

The Mayoralty in the Fifteenth Century.

Between 1300 and 1470, Limerick in common with the rest of Ireland, endured the Bruce invasion, the Great European Famine of the Middle Ages (1314 - 20), several visitations of the bubonic plague or Black Death, a sharp reduction in population, political fragmentation leading to endemic warfare, and prolonged economic recession. Not surprisingly, the Anglo-Irish colony was depleted by large-scale emigration to England and in 1435 the mayor and corporation of Limerick complained to the Dublin government that this was causing them severe economic difficulties.[82] The city's population fell sharply, its economy remained stagnant and the Earls of Desmond and the O'Briens of Thomond posed a constant threat.

Consequently, it was difficult to find candidates willing to serve as mayor.[83] The result was that Limerick became even more oligarchic in the fifteenth century than ever before. Between 1400 and 1500, forty-one Arthurs and fifteen Comyns held the post of mayor and the city's two longest serving mayors held office at this time; Thomas Arthur (mayor on seven occasions between 1460 and 1489); and Thomas Comyn (mayor on six occasions between 1407 and 1417).[84] In an attempt to reverse this trend, legislation was enacted to force the Irish municipal elites to do their duty. In 1461, Waterford imposed a fine of 100 shillings on any eligible person who stayed away from the meeting to elect a new mayor. A person refusing to be mayor was fined nine marks and for refusing to be bailiff the fine was four marks. Although documentation is lacking, it is reasonable to suppose that Limerick enacted similar byelaws.[85]

This crisis also contributed to an improvement in the status of the Gaelic Irish in the urban areas of Ireland. Like all of the towns of the Anglo-Norman colony, Limerick was a bastion of English rule and was very loyal to the crown. A large proportion of the population and nearly all of the mayors were of Anglo-Norman descent and would have considered themselves to be English. Under the Statutes of Kilkenny (1366), the English community were forbidden to marry Irish people, to use the Irish language or to adopt any aspects of Irish culture, and no ethnic Irish could be appointed to civil or ecclesiastic office.[86] In Limerick city, these regulations were reinforced by the 1413 charter which stated that 'no one of Irish blood or nation (the word Irish to be understood as usually understood in Ireland) should be mayor or exercise any office within the city; and that no person should take or maintain any man or child of Irish blood and nation as apprentice, on pain of losing his franchise' (i.e. his citizenship).[87] In 1512, the Limerick byelaw which outlawed corruption also stipulated that no-one could receive the freedom of Limerick unless they could speak English fluently and wore 'English apparel'.[88] On paper there existed a fully-fledged system of institutional discrimination against the Gaelic Irish of Limerick city.

In practice, the ethnic Irish played a major role in Limerick, which was dependent on its Gaelic and Gaelicised hinterland for trade, and to provide immigrants to replenish the population, particularly after the Black Death. It was even possible for families of Gaelic Irish extraction to be assimilated into the mayoral elite, the most prominent example being the Creaghs, who provided Limerick with thirteen mayors between 1216 and 1534.[89] This process culminated in 1535, when Edmund Sexten became the first ethnic Irishman to serve as mayor of Limerick.[90]

Limerick shared in the economic recovery of late fifteenth century Europe and after 1500, the building or stone houses on Limerick's main streets became much more common.[91] By the second half of the sixteenth century, Limerick had emerged as the third largest city in Ireland, after Dublin and Galway.[92] However, the Earls of Desmond and the O'Briens of Thomond continued to be a threat to the city. To take one example, in 1461 Limerick Corporation began paying an annual tribute of sixty marks to the O'Briens as a kind of protection money.[93] Relations with Galway were also poor and in 1524 war broke out between the two cities, occasioned according to Lenihan by the jealousy felt by the Limerick elite of the superior trade and prosperity of their Galway counterparts.[94] Hostilities were sparked off when the wealthy Limerick merchant and ex-mayor David Comyn, kidnapped and held to ransom a citizen of Galway, on the ground that 'he could have no justice administered to him in Galway'. A brief and inconclusive war followed and was concluded by a formal treaty of peace signed on 7 May 1524.[95]

Mayor Nicholas Arthur (1405-1465).

The first mayor of Limerick whose life is documented to any significant extent is Nicholas Arthur, who served on three separate occasions as first citizen of the city: 1436, 1446 and 1452.[96] A successful merchant who exported horses, falcons, hounds furs and other products to England, he counted among his customers high ranking members of the English elite including the royal family and even King Henry VI himself. In June 1428 while sailing from Limerick to England with a cargo of merchandise, he was captured by pirates from the French duchy of Brittany, which was then at war with England, and along with the ship's crew brought a prisoner to the Breton port of St. Malo. There all of his merchandise was sold and he was kept prisoner in the renowned Mont St. Michel for two years until his family paid a huge ransom. On obtaining his freedom, Nicholas travelled to London to meet his friend and customer King Henry VI and obtained permission to recover his losses by seizing the property of any Bretons living in the king's dominions. He was successful in doing so, both 'by land and sea' and recovered all that he had lost 'even to the last farthing.'[97] Clearly Nicholas was a formidable, determined and hard-headed individual.

Returning to Limerick Nicholas got married in 1431 to Catherine, daughter and heiress of John Skiddy, a senior member of Cork City Council and they had a large family. Three of his sons became members of Limerick City Council and another served as bailiff of the city. His son Thomas served as bishop of Limerick between 1472 and 1486. Nicholas himself died at the age of sixty and was buried in St. Mary's Cathedral, having devoted his life 'to the increase of his property'.[98] He can be regarded as the archetype of the wealthy, powerful and closely-knit mayoral elite that ruled Limerick in the medieval period.

Endnotes

1   The most comprehensive account of cities and city life in medieval Europe is David Nicholas's massive two volume survey: *The Growth of the Medieval City from Late Antiquity to the Early Fourteenth Century*, (London, 1997) and *The Late Medieval City 1300-1500*, (London, 1997).

2   The most comprehensive modern account of Europe between 1000 and 1300 is found in David Luscombe and Jonathan Riley-Smith (eds), *The New Cambridge Medieval History Volume 4, c 1024-c 1198*, Parts 1 and 2, (Cambridge 2004) and David Abulafia (ed.), *The New Cambridge Medieval History. Volume 5 c1198-c1300*, (Cambridge, 1998). For medieval Ireland, see Art Cosgrove (ed.), *A New History of Ireland, Volume II, Medieval Ireland 1169-1534*. (Oxford, 1987) ; Otway-Ruthven, *A History of Medieval Ireland*, and J.F. Lydon, *The Lordship of Ireland in the Middle Ages*, (Dublin 1972).

3   Nicholas, *The Growth of the Medieval City*, pp 87-100.

4   Ibid., pp 141-68, 228-321.

5   See James Tait, *The Medieval English Borough. Studies on its Origins and Constitutional History*, (Manchester, 1936), pp 162-83, 252-56.

6   For the local government system in medieval Ireland see Otway –Ruthven, *A History of Medieval Ireland*, pp 173-87 and Quinn, 'Anglo-Irish Local Government 1485-1534', pp 354-81. Details of the functions of Irish borough corporations in the Middle Ages can be found in Gearoid MacNiocaill, *Na Buirgeisi, XII-XIV Aois*, 2 Vols, (Charraig Dhubh, 1964), Vol. 2. Two

very important works on English towns in the Middle Ages are Colin Platt, *The English Medieval Town*, (London, 1976) and Susan Reynolds, *An Introduction to the History of English Medieval Towns*, (Oxford, 1977). Both are very useful on the development of urban local government and can thus be used, albeit with caution, in relation to contemporary developments in Ireland.

7   For the communal movement see Nicholas, *The Growth of the Medieval City*, pp 146-52, 230-34, and 290-93.

8   'Lord of Ireland' was the title borne between 1177 and 1541 by the kings of England as rulers of Ireland. The only time that it was held separately was by the future King John between 1177 and 1199 and by the future King Edward I between 1254 and 1272.

9   For Limerick Corporation in the Middle Ages see Potter, *The Government and the People of Limerick*, pp 18-94.

10 Eamonn McEneaney, 'Origins' in Eamonn McEneaney (ed.), *A History of Waterford and its Mayors from the Twelfth to the Twentieth Century*, (Waterford, 1995), pp 27-29 and Reynolds, *English Medieval Towns*, pp 118-39.

11 For the provisions of Limerick's first charter see E. Curtis and R. B. MacDowell (eds), *Irish Historical Documents*, (London, 1943), pp 24-27.

12 See R. Dudley-Edwards, 'The Beginnings of Municipal Government in Dublin' in Howard Clarke (ed.), *Medieval Dublin. The Living City*, (Dublin, 1990), pp 146-47.

13 Juliet Gardiner and Neil Wenborn (eds), *The History Today Companion to British History*, (London, 1995), pp. 16-17, 254-55.

14 Tait, *Medieval English Borough*, p. 231.

15 For the farm of the borough see Platt, *English Medieval Town*, pp 154-57 and Reynolds, *English Medieval Towns*, pp 102-11.

16 Tait, *Medieval English Borough*, pp 185-6.

17 Ibid., pp 290-96.

18 For an example of these assertions appearing in an official publication see *Limerick. Official Guide to the City of Limerick*, (Limerick, 1976), p. 12.

19 Larry Walsh, 'The Mayoral Myth' in David Lee (ed.), *Remembering Limerick. Historical Essays Celebrating the 800th Anniversary of Limerick's First Charter granted in 1197*, (Limerick, 1997), pp 39-45.

20 Lenihan, *History of Limerick*, p. 47.

21 Eamonn McEneaney, 'Mayors and Merchants in Medieval Waterford City, 1169-1495', in William Nolan, Thomas P. Power and Des Cowman (eds), *Waterford History and Society*, (Dublin, 1986), p. 148.

22 H.S. Sweetman, *Calender of Documents Relating to Ireland*, Vol. 2, 1252-84, (London, 1877), no. 1056, p. 186.

23 Ibid., no. 1041, pp 461-63.

24 Ibid., p. 462.

25 Ibid., p. 462.

26 See Tait, *Medieval English Borough*, pp 264-5, 296, 350-52; Platt, *English Medieval Town*, pp 157-61 and Reynolds, *English Medieval Towns*, pp 121-23.

27 Most English borough councils seem to have established councils in the thirteenth century. See Platt, *English Medieval Town*, p. 161.

28 For Dublin see Dudley-Edwards, '*Beginnings of Municipal Government in Dublin*' p. 149.

29 For the establishment of the town council of Kilkenny see A. J. Otway-Ruthven, *Liber Primus Kilkenniensis*, (Kilkenny, 1961), pp 2-3.

30 Tait, *Medieval English Borough*, p. 294. For the vagueness of our knowledge concerning the methods of choosing officials and councillors at this time see Reynolds, *English Medieval Towns*, pp 122-23.

31 See Platt, *English Medieval Town*, pp 142-50 and Reynolds, *English Medieval Towns*, pp 171-77.

32 MacNiocaill, *Na Buirgeisi*, II, pp 345, 350-51. For a fuller discussion of the issue see Gearóid MacNiocaill, 'Socio-Economic Problems of the Late Medieval Irish Town' in David Harkness and Mary O'Dowd (eds), *The Town In Ireland*, (Belfast, 1981), pp 7-21.

33 For an estimate of the population of Medieval Limerick, see Brian Hodkinson, 'The Medieval City' in Liam Irwin, Gearóid O'Tuathaigh and Matthew Potter (eds) *Limerick History and Society* (forthcoming 2008).

34 MacNiocaill, '*Socio-Economic Problems of the Late Medieval Irish Town*' pp 7-22.

35 Denis Leonard, 'Provosts and Mayors of Limerick, 1197-1997, in Lee, *Remembering Limerick*, pp 378-92.

36 Colm Lennon, *The Urban Patriciates of Early Modern Ireland: A Case-Study of Limerick*, (Dublin, 1999), p. 6.

37 For a general account of these developments see Nicholas, *The Later Medieval City*, passim.

38 Tait, *Medieval English Borough*, pp 302-38 and Reynolds, *English Medieval Towns*, pp 173-77.

39 Tait, *Medieval English Borough*, p. 302.

40 Ibid., pp 321-22.

41 Its usage from 1841 to 2004, denoting the councillor who received the most votes in each electoral ward, was not established until the Municipal Corporations (Ireland) Act of 1840 reformed the whole machinery of Irish urban government.

42 See *Reports of the Commissioners Appointed to Enquire into Municipal Corporations in Ireland. H.C.* 1835(27), (hereafter referred to as *Municipal Corporations Report*) p. 351.

43 See *Municipal Corporations Report* pp 352-53.

44 The standard work on the subject is Martin Weinbaum, *The Incorporation of Boroughs*, (Manchester, 1937). For the five characteristics of incorporation see pp 18-22.

45 Weinbaum, *Incorporation of Boroughs*, pp 47-68.

46 Ibid., pp 54-57.

47 Sweet, *The English Town*, p. 36.

48 Otway-Ruthven, *A History of Medieval Ireland*, pp 339-94.

49 R.A. Butlin, 'Irish Towns in the Sixteenth and Seventeenth Centuries,' in R.A.Butlin (ed.), *The Development of the Irish Town*, (London, 1977), pp 64-65 and Webb, *Municipal Government*, pp 59-60.

50 For the experience of Waterford, see McEneaney, 'Mayors and Merchants in Medieval Waterford, pp 158-60.

51 *Municipal Corporations Report*, p. 345.

52 Ibid.

53 Otway-Ruthven, *A History of Medieval Ireland*, pp 371-74.

54 See Stephen G. Ellis, *Ireland in the Age of the Tudors 1447-1603. English Expansion and the End of Gaelic Rule*, (Harlow, 1998), pp. 179-80 and Victor Treadwell, 'The Establishment of the Farm of the Irish Customs 1603-13' in *The English Historical Review*, Vol. XCIII, (1978), p. 588. For the temporary revival of centralised control see Steven G. Ellis, 'Historical Revision XIX: The Irish Customs Administration under the Early Tudors' in *Irish Historical Studies*, Vol. XXII, No. 87, (March, 1981), pp 271-77.

55 For an account of the situation in Munster see D.B. Quinn, ' 'Irish' Ireland and 'English' Ireland' in Cosgrove, *A New History of Ireland*, II, pp 627-30 and Kenneth Nicholls, *Gaelic and Gaelicised Ireland in the Middle Ages*, (Dublin, 1972), pp 154-69.

56 *Calender of Patent Rolls*, (London 1891-1971).

57 Ibid.

58 Fitzgerald and McGregor, *History of Limerick*, II, p. 407. Begley, *The Diocese of Limerick*, Vol. 1, p. 316.

59 Lenihan, *History of Limerick*, p. 91.

60 For the role of the medieval Irish mayor see Webb, *Municipal Government*, pp 5-8 and MacNiocaill, *Na Buirgeisi*, II, pp 338-43.

61 Kenneth Wiggins, *Anatomy of a Siege. King John's Castle, Limerick, 1642*, (Bray, Co. Wicklow, 2000), p. 8 and Otway-Ruthven, *A History of Medieval Ireland*, pp 247-51.

62 *Municipal Corporations Report*, p. 345.

63 Lenihan, *History of Limerick*, p. 61. See also Fitzgerald and McGregor, *History of Limerick*, II, p. 74.

64 MacNiocaill, *Na Buirgeisi*, II, p. 411.

65 See Webb, *Municipal Government*, pp. 8-11.

66 Lenihan, *History of Limerick*, p. 696.

67 For municipal bureaucracy in the Middle Ages, see Reynolds, *English Medieval Towns*, pp 120-21; MacNiocaill, *Na Buirgeisi*, II, p. 344 and Webb, *Municipal Government*, p. 47.

68 Lenihan, *History of Limerick*, p. 696.

69 Reynolds, *Medieval English Towns*, p. 121.

70 Fitzgerald and Mcgregor, *History of Limerick*, II, pp 410-11.

71 MacNiocaill, *Na Buirgeisi*, II, pp 352-53.

72 For an account of the evolution of civic ceremonial dress see Alan Mansfield, *Ceremonial Costume*, (London, 1980), pp 245-65.

73 Fitzgerald and McGregor, *History of Limerick*, II, p. 416.

74 For the description of Sussex's visit, see *Calender of the Carew Manuscripts Preserved in the Archiepiscopal Library at Lambeth*, (6 Vols.), (London, 1867-73), 1515-74, pp 275-76.

75 British Library (hereafter BL), Additional Mss. 31886: The annals of the city and diocese of Limerick (from the earliest times) to 1768, compiled by the Rev. James White. A transcript of the original manuscript by Maurice Lenihan, 1865.

76 For a description of the Tholsel see Judith Hill, *The Building of Limerick*, (Cork, 1991), pp 51-52.

77 The best general accounts of the functions of urban local authorities in medieval Ireland are MacNiocaill, *Na Buirgeisi*, II, and Webb, *Municipal Government*, pp 21-58. For contemporary English borough government see Platt, *English Medieval Town*, pp 93-178 and Reynolds, *English Medieval Towns*, pp 126-30, 177-81.

78 Potter, The *Government and the People of Limerick*, pp 71-72.

79 Celie O'Rahilly 'Medieval Limerick: The Growth of Two Towns' in Howard B. Clarke (ed.), *Irish Cities*, (Cork and Dublin, 1995), p 172.

80 Frank Prendergast, 'Medieval Borough Boundaries' in Lee, *Remembering Limerick*, pp 45-49.

81 At the time of writing Limerick City Council administers an area of 5155 acres. I am indebted to Brian Hodkinson for drawing to my attention the inexact nature of medieval units of land measurement.

82 Maria Kelly, *A History of the Black Death in Ireland*, (Stroud, Gloucestershire, 2001), pp 131-32.

83 MacNiocaill, *Na Buirgeisi*, II, pp 345-47.

84 Leonard, ' *Provosts and Mayors of Limerick*' pp 378-92.

85   MacNiocaill, *Na Buirgeisi*, II, pp 345-47.

86   Ellis, *Ireland in the Age of the Tudors*, pp. 22-24 and Otway-Ruthven, *A History of Medieval Ireland*, pp 291-94.

87   *Municipal Corporations Report*, p. 345.

88   Fitzgerald and McGregor, *History of Limerick*, II, pp 410-11.

89   Lennon, *Urban Patriciates*, pp 5-6, 12.

90   For accounts of his life see Brian Hodkinson, 'Edmund Sexten: The First Irish Mayor of Limerick', in Lee, *Remembering Limerick*, pp 107-11.

91   Hill, *The Building of Limerick*, pp 38-42.

92   Anthony Sheehan, 'Irish Towns in a Period of Change 1558-1625' in Ciaran Brady and Raymond Gillespie, (eds.), *Natives and Newcomers. Essays on the Making of Irish Colonial Society 1534-1641*, (Dublin, 1986), pp 94-97.

93   Begley, *The Diocese of Limerick*, I, p. 317.

94   Lenihan, *History of Limerick*, p.73.

95   Ibid.

96   Lenihan, *History of Limerick*, pp 367-69.

97   Ibid., p. 367.

98   Ibid., p. 369.

The Royal coat-of-arms placed over the entrance to the council chamber
in the Exchange by Mayor William York
(Jim Kemmy Municipal Museum)

Chapter Three
The Mayoralty in the Tudor and Stuart Periods. 1534-1691

The End of the Medieval Ireland.

The years 1534-43 marks the end of the Middle Ages in Ireland.[1] Among the innovations that marked this decade were the introduction of the Reformation in the years 1534-6, the dissolution of the monasteries between 1539 and 1542 and a 'constitutional revolution' in the relationship between the English crown and the Irish political system, the most important aspect of which was the assumption of the title 'King of Ireland' by Henry VIII.[2] Perhaps most importantly, the English government in Ireland determined to bring the whole country under its control, although a definite policy to conquer the whole country by military force was only arrived at in the 1560s and 1570s.[3] The increasing emphasis on extending effective English rule by force, the introduction of the Reformation and the beginning of the policy of plantation (or colonisation) in the 1550s alienated the Anglo-Irish community in the Pale and the towns, for it was to result in their increasing exclusion from their accustomed role as allies of, and participants in the Dublin government.[4] Large numbers of Protestant settlers, hostile to both the Anglo-Irish and the Gaelic Irish (both of which groups remained Catholic) began coming to Ireland. These settlers came to be known as the 'New English' while the Anglo-Irish became known as the 'Old English'. The government tended to regard the Protestant New English as reliable allies compared to the Catholic Old English, causing the latter to feel angry and excluded from a share in running the country. The mayoral elite of Limerick continued to be almost entirely Old English and Catholic in composition until the 1650s. After nearly seventy years of warfare, the crown eventually conquered all of Ireland and in 1603, the country was united under one government for the first time ever, but in general the period 1534 to 1603 was one of endemic warfare, destruction and economic decline.[5]

Limerick in the Sixteenth Century.

However the government pursued a conciliatory policy towards the cities and towns of Ireland because they were the mainstay of English rule, were loyal to the crown, and staunchly English in culture.[6] They were also a major asset to the government in its declared aim of extending effective rule throughout the country, as they could be used as military bases.[7] The crown did little to upset their *de facto* independence, even though this resulted in it receiving little or no revenue from them. The townspeople supported the government's policy of extending its control over the entire country as they wanted to be protected from their ethnic Irish enemies and hoped that the imposition of English rule would result in the peaceful conditions necessary for economic growth.[8] However, these hopes were not to be realised as the endemic warfare of the period 1534 to 1603 and the resultant distress and disease, led to a decline in the prosperity and population of the towns.[9]

Limerick city was one of the most important urban areas in Ireland and with a population of between 2,400 and 3,600, ranked third after Dublin (5,000) and Galway (4,000-4,200) and was larger than Cork and Waterford (2,400 each).[10] In 1536, an English visitor described Limerick as 'a wonderous proper city and strong and standeth environed with the river of Shenon (sic) and it may be called little London for the situation and the plenty'[11] while in 1574, the Limerick born Jesuit Fr. David Wolfe wrote that 'Limerick is the mightiest and most beautiful of all the cities of Ireland'.[12] Other commentators also pronounced Limerick to be one of the finest town in Ireland, or at least the finest in Munster.[13] In view of this significance, it was inevitable that Limerick would feature prominently in the major events of the sixteenth century.

Mayor Edmund Sexten (1486-1555).

The election of Edmund Sexten (later the family changed the spelling of the name to 'Sexton') as mayor in 1535 marked the beginning of the new era in Limerick.[14] He was the first Gaelic Irishman to hold the office and one of the most significant and controversial figures in the entire history of Limerick. Sexten owed his prominence to the patronage of King Henry VIII. Although theoretically ineligible for any office in the city under the provisions of successive charters issued since 1413, he and his relatives received the freedom of Limerick on the direct orders of the King in 1534 and he was elected Mayor in 1535.[15] Intelligent, unscrupulous and cunning, Sexten played a far bigger role than most mayors of Limerick and acted as the main contact between the crown and the great Munster lords. Indeed, during his mayoralty he spent several months staying at the royal household in London, advising the king on Irish affairs.[16]

During Sexten's mayoralty, the Dublin government took a much greater interest in Limerick and its hinterland than it had done for centuries. Between 1536 and 1540, Lord Leonard Grey served as lord deputy and worked closely with Sexten.[17] Grey asserted his authority over Limerick Corporation but also campaigned against the city's enemies. The citizens of Limerick were pleased to see the government intervene to protect them from their local foes and initially did not resent his intervention in their affairs.[18] At the beginning of 1536, Grey attacked the Lordship of Pubblebrien, a territory that includes the modern villages of Mungret, Clarina, Patrickswell and Crecora and which was ruled by a cadet branch of the O'Briens of Thomond. The Lords of Pubblebrien were long standing enemies of the city of Limerick, whose territories adjoined theirs.[19] Grey and his army, accompanied by Mayor Edmund Sexton and a contingent of the local municipal militia, captured Carrigogunnell Castle, which was the principal stronghold in Pubblebrien. Mayor Sexton was given the privilege of carrying the King's standard into the fallen stronghold. After the O'Briens recovered the castle by a trick, Grey captured it a second time in August 1536, and had the entire garrison hanged in Limerick city. When Grey and Sexten followed this up by capturing O'Briens Bridge, a major stronghold of the O'Briens of Thomond, the mayor and about thirty others were accidentally thrown into the water, when the bridge suddenly collapsed. Two people were killed, but Sexten managed to escape injury.[20]

After Sexten's mayoralty had ended, the Reformation was introduced to Limerick by Lord Leonard Grey on a later visit to the city.[21] He arrived on 28 July 1537, and in a letter to Henry VIII, he described what happened: 'I called the mayor and his brethren (the city council) before me and had them sworn to you according to the statute of supremacy, and sworn further to refuse the usurped power of the Bishop of Rome. I commanded the mayor to have all the commonalty of the said city likewise sworn, and to certify their oaths into your Chancery. Then, I had the bishop of Limerick sworn, and commanded him to have all his clergy sworn'.[22] Grey was thus acting in the tradition of medieval central government, by delegating all powers and responsibilities to the mayor of Limerick. However, the citizens of Limerick remained loyal to the old faith and the Reformation was ignored by both the mayoral elite and the general population.[23]

The dissolution of the monasteries and friaries in Limerick soon followed and Edmund Sexten obtained the bulk of their forfeited lands. In 1537, he was granted the lease on the lands of the Augustinians and the Crutched Friars and in 1542, he received the property of the Franciscans. Only the Dominicans' property eluded him, for it was granted to the Earl of Desmond in 1544.[24] Sexten believed that he had earned this huge amount of land by serving the crown with loyalty and diligence during his mayoralty. Along with his involvement in the capture of Carrigogonnell and O'Briens Bridge, he had captured a ship belonging to the O'Briens of Thomond, and burnt towns in their territory. He also claimed to have saved Limerick city on two occasions. Firstly, he had brought about the assassination of one of the greatest Gaelic lords, O'Conor Sligo, whom he asserted had threatened to burn Limerick.[25] Secondly Sexten claimed credit for preventing Lord Leonard Grey from destroying the city.[26] The historian Sarah Johnson thinks that Grey had intended allowing his mutinous troops to plunder Limerick in lieu of paying them and if this is correct, then Sexten really did the city a great service.[27]

However, he received no gratitude from the citizens of Limerick. The mayoral elite hated and envied him, regarding him as an upstart Irishman, who had supported the Reformation and had enriched himself at the expense of the monasteries. When the Lord Deputy, Sir Edward Bellingham wrote to the city council of Limerick in 1548, asking that Sexten be again elected mayor, they flatly refused his request.[28] Sexten died in 1555 aged sixty-nine and soon after his corpse was taken from its tomb in St. Mary's Cathedral and hung by the heels from the roof where it remained undiscovered for three years. This deed was perpetrated by three members of the mayoral elite, Alderman Christopher Creagh, Piers White and Edward White supposedly because of Sexten's support of the Reformation.[29]

Mayor Edmund Sexten had a major impact on the future history of Limerick city. His land acquisitions were later described as 'the greatest transfer of stolen property ever in the city'.[30] The whole of his vast estate eventually passed by marriage into the hands of the Pery family, from Devonshire who settled in Limerick in the seventeenth century and later used these lands as the basis for establishing a major political role for themselves locally and nationally.[31] The former lands of the Augustinian Friars were known as South Prior's Land and in the eighteenth century, the Perys would build a new Georgian city of Limerick there, which would eventually eclipse the medieval city, centred on Englishtown and Irishtown.

Queen Elizabeth I and Limerick.

During the reign of Queen Elizabeth I (1558-1603), the whole of Ireland was brought under effective English rule for the first time. An important aspect of this process was the establishment of provincial governments in the outlying parts of Ireland. While it had been originally intended that Munster, Connaught and Ulster would each be ruled by a governor called a lord president, appointed by the Queen, Ulster was eventually excluded from the scheme and it was implemented in Connaught in 1569 and in Munster in 1571. The lord president of Munster was to play a major role in extending English rule and was to prove to be a formidable enemy of Limerick's municipal autonomy on a number of occasions.[32]

Throughout her reign, Elizabeth I also tried to impose the Reformation on Ireland, though she usually lacked the means to do so effectively. All of the principal civil and religious office-holders were supposed to take the Oath of Supremacy to the Protestant Church of Ireland while attendance at divine service was made compulsory, on pain of payment of a substantial fine. In the towns and cities, the mayors were given the task of enforcing this legislation.[33] As before, passive conformity continued to be the norm and the mayor and city councillors of Limerick circumvented the legislation.[34] On 9 June 1564, the mayor and recorder of Limerick were among the commissioners appointed by the queen 'with power to correct heresies and other offences…and to administer to all persons there, as may seem good to them, the Oath of Supremacy' in the counties of Carlow, Waterford, Kilkenny, Cork, Kerry, Limerick and Tipperary.[35] This policy was a total failure and when the staunchly Protestant Lord Deputy Sir Henry Sidney paid an official visit to Limerick in March 1567, he was disgusted to have to endure Catholic religious ceremonial including a *Te Deum* in St. Mary's Cathedral.[36] Things did not change much in the next quarter of a century. On 23 May, 1594, the mayor of Limerick was again appointed as one of the commissioners to enforce the Acts of Supremacy and Uniformity, this time in the dioceses of Limerick, Cork, Cloyne and Ross, but seven months later, the Anglican bishop John Thornburgh wrote to the English Privy Council, urging them to force the mayor and aldermen of Limerick to bring their families and servants to his church services.[37]

However, the government's contradictory policies towards the towns were to hinder more vigorous enforcement of the Reformation legislation. The queen and her advisors wanted to promote the Church of Ireland but simultaneously, continued to promote the autonomy of the boroughs.[38] This produced two major absurdities. Firstly, responsibility for enforcement of the legislation lay with the mayors of the town, who were themselves usually at the forefront in disregarding the Oath of Supremacy. Secondly, a successful prosecution for any breaches of the Reformation legislation by the citizens, including the mayor and city councillors would result in a fine being paid to the corporation, not to central government. The prospect of the corporation paying a fine to itself was not a serious deterrent to the flouting of the law, and not surprisingly, the Reformation made little headway in Limerick city until the 1650s.

The Charters of 1575 and 1583.

Limerick's tenth charter (dated 28 October 1575) included the grant of a sword of state to be carried before the mayor on ceremonial occasions.[39] Sir Henry Sidney himself made an official visit to Limerick in 1575, and presented the sword to the mayor, Richard Everard. The civic sword signified that the mayor possessed the power of life and death over his citizenry and thus symbolically reinforced his authority. It is both the oldest surviving item of the city insignia, and the oldest Irish civic sword in existence and is kept in Limerick's Jim Kemmy Municipal Museum.[40] The charter further stipulated that the mayor, bailiffs and recorder in their legal capacity could now try felonies, which was a power that they had not previously possessed. All fines and forfeitures or other financial penalties arising from any act of parliament could now be

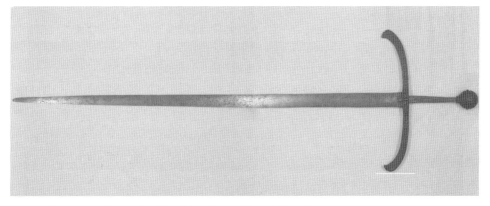

The civic sword granted to Limerick by Queen Elizabeth I in 1575. (Jim Kemmy Municipal Museum)

retained by the corporation for its own use. The mayor and bailiffs could not be summonsed to appear before any court of law, except in cases of contempt, felony or treason.[41]

On the 24 April, 1578 Queen Elizabeth I granted Limerick Corporation jurisdiction over Scattery Island (which has an area of 166 acres and is situated in the Shannon Estuary about sixty miles from Limerick city) at an annual rent to the crown of £3-12s-12d.[42] While it may be a far-fetched comparison, it can be argued that in an age of colonial expansion, the 'local kingdom' of Limerick, headed by its quasi-monarchical mayor, acquired an overseas possession like Spain, Portugal and other contemporary kingdoms.[43]

Since the creation of the title in 1329, successive Earls of Desmond had been traditional enemies of Limerick Corporation and the city's mayors usually looked to the government to protect them from this danger. In the reign of Elizabeth I, the thirteenth Earl of Desmond rebelled against the government twice: in 1569-73 (when the rebellion was actually led by his cousin James Fitzmaurice Fitzgerald) and 1579-83. The outbreak of the second Desmond Rebellion in 1579 precipitated one of the most terrible wars in Irish history. Limerick city remained loyal to the Queen, and served as a major base for operations against the rebels as well as providing municipal troops for the government's army. The mayor of Limerick, Nicholas Stritch presented a force of 1,000 armed citizens of Limerick to the English commander, Sir William Pelham, to assist him in the war against Desmond.[44] Limerick's municipal army fought with the government forces until the rebellion was finally crushed in 1583.[45]

Limerick did not have to wait long for its loyalty to be rewarded as the city's eleventh charter was granted on 19 March 1583.[46] Under its most important provision, 'our city of Limerick shall be, and remain forever hereafter shall remain one body corporate and politic, in deed, fact and name by the name of Mayor, Bailiffs and Citizens of the City of Limerick'.[47] This granting of corporate status made of Limerick's civic authority a separate legal entity, distinct from its members, so that it is only from 1583 that we can correctly refer to the government of the city as 'Limerick Corporation'.

The Loyalty of the Mayoral Elite to the English Crown.

The dogged loyalty of Limerick's staunchly Catholic and Old English mayoral elite to the Protestant English crown may seem puzzling, but it was grounded in a coherent political ideology. Since the 1530s, the Reformation had created a gulf between the Old English on the one hand and the Dublin government and the New English settlers on the other.[48] In response, the Old English developed a coherent ideology which informed their actions until their final overthrow in the 1650s. Firstly, they considered themselves to be the English nation in Ireland, a middle nation between the native Irish and the Protestant New English and that the kingdom of Ireland was a separate sister kingdom, equal in status to England, while sharing the same monarch. Secondly, the Old English wanted a sort of 'Home Rule' centred on the Irish parliament and wanted to be actively involved in governing the country in partnership with the government. Thirdly and most controversially, they believed that they could combine loyalty to the crown in civil matters with loyalty to the Pope and the Catholic Church in matters of religion. This contention was anathema in the sixteenth and seventeenth centuries and was never accepted by the English authorities in Ireland, although they were unable to do much to suppress it until the 1650s.[49]

Following the conclusion of the second Desmond Rebellion, the Plantation of Munster and the activities of the lord presidency transformed the province, placing it more firmly under English rule than at any previous time in its history. Despite the increasingly Protestant nature of the crown's administration, Limerick remained stubbornly loyal to both queen and pope. England and Spain were at war from 1585 to 1604, and although Spain claimed to be champion of the Catholic Church, the mayoral elite remained loyal to the English connection. Successive mayors of Limerick gathered intelligence from merchants newly arrived from Spain and its dominions (trade was continued throughout the war) and passed it on to the authorities.[50] The civic elite was afraid that the Spanish Armada might succeed in conquering England and in the autumn of 1588, they were horrified when seven Spanish ships anchored within their territory at Scattery Island. After they left, Mayor George Fanning of Limerick wrote to his Waterford counterpart describing 'the happy news of the departure of the Spaniards.'[51]

The Mayoralty during the Nine Years War.

The outbreak of the Nine Years War in 1594 presented the mayors of Limerick with a major new challenge. The crushing defeat of the English army at the Battle of the Yellow Ford (14 August, 1598) resulted in the rebellion spreading throughout Ireland, and English rule came close to being completely overthrown. In Limerick city, there was a constant fear of a Spanish landing.[52] Limerick's municipal soldiers fought throughout the war in the service of the government and even took part in the campaigns in Ulster itself.[53] After the Battle of the Yellow Ford, the Plantation of Munster collapsed, the whole province rose in rebellion, and the English settlers were forced to flee for their lives. A large number made their way to Limerick city, where in the words of an English officer, 'they were received and well used by the mayor and city, for which they deserve great thanks.'[54]

Limerick city had not had a regular garrison of government troops stationed there for many decades. In response to the threat posed by the rebels, the government appointed the staunchly Protestant and loyal Donough O'Brien, fourth Earl of Thomond (1560-1624), head of the O'Briens of Thomond, as commander of the garrison of Limerick city, which consisted of his ethnic Irish troops from County Clare.[55] The citizens of Limerick

were disgusted at having an army of their traditional Gaelic enemies within their walls.[56] Not surprisingly, tensions soon arose, and letters of complaint were sent to London. On 14 January 1600, the Earl of Thomond wrote to Sir Robert Cecil describing how 'the mayor pulls off the hats of lieutenants and gentlemen and treads the same under his feet. The townsmen threaten to make an end of them all in one day'.[57] He also complained that the mayor and corporation themselves imprisoned soldiers who had allegedly committed crimes, instead of handing them over to him for court martial.[58] In response, the mayor of Limerick, William Stritche, sent a petition on behalf of the citizens of Limerick to the queen, in which he alleged that Thomond's troops were both disloyal and ineffective.[59] After further complaints by both sides, Thomond and his troops were eventually withdrawn from Limerick.[60]

Between 1600 and 1603, Sir George Carew (1555-1629) served as lord president of Munster.[61] A stern and autocratic figure, he suppressed the rebellion in the province and took measures to reduce the autonomy of the towns.[62] As part of this policy, Carew picked a fight with the mayor of Limerick, Geoffrey Galway in November 1600. One of the Earl of Thomond's soldiers had been imprisoned on the orders of the mayor for stealing a hatchet and Carew ordered the man to be handed over to be tried by a military court. The

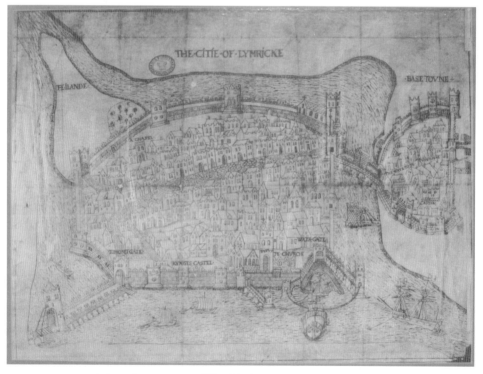

A sixteenth-century map of Limerick city. (Jim Kemmy Municipal Museum)

mayor and council refused to comply, and in response, Carew deposed Mayor Galway and fined him £400. No duly elected mayor of Limerick had been dismissed by the government in centuries but the citizens did not resist out of fear of Carew's soldiers and the threat posed by the rebels. The high-handed action of the lord president indicated the direction that government strategy would take when peace was imposed, and all Ireland was under effective English rule for the first time.[63]

The Battle of the Mayors and the End of Limerick's Independence.

The Nine Years War ended in 1603 with the complete defeat of the Gaelic lords and the establishment of effective English rule over all of Ireland for the first time. These dramatic events coincided with the accession of King James VI of Scotland to the English throne under the name James I. The government's policy towards the towns was now twofold: firstly, religious conformity had to be enforced and secondly, their *de facto* independence was to be ended.[64]

Sir Henry Brouncker, who served as lord president of Munster from 1604 to 1607 attempted to put these policies into action.[65] In 1606, the mayor of Limerick, Edmund Fox, who had served eleven months of his twelve month term refused to take the Oath of Supremacy, and also declined to attend divine service.[66] He was deposed by Brouncker, and replaced by Andrew Creagh, who only served for one month. Nevertheless, this brief term marked a historical milestone, for Creagh was the first Protestant mayor of Limerick.[67] He was succeeded by Edmund Sexton, who was also a Protestant and who was a grandson of the notorious Mayor Edmund Sexten of the 1530s.[68] However, King James, who feared rebellion, and was anxious for good relations with Spain following the conclusion of the war in 1604, ordered the campaign to be discontinued after he had received complaints from the Old English community in Munster against Brouncker 's heavy-handed rule.[69]

During the presidency of Brouncker's successor, Henry Lord Danvers, the government returned to the attack and thus precipitated what Maurice Lenihan later described as 'the Battle of the Mayors' in Limerick.[70] It began in October 1611 when Mayor David Comyn and one of his sheriffs, David Rice were deposed after only a month in office, for refusing to take the Oath of Supremacy and to go to church. The new mayor was Edmund Sexton who had previously held office in similar circumstances in 1606-7. In 1612, Mayor William Meade and both sheriffs were deposed after four months in office, but the new mayor, Christopher Creagh merely took the Oath. He did not attend church, but was still allowed to finish out his term as mayor. In 1613, the mayor and both sheriffs were deposed after three months, and their successors served out the rest of their terms in office. In 1614-15, two successive mayors were deposed but the third remained in office. In the same year, Limerick had three sets of sheriffs, of whom the first two pairs were deposed and the last pair resigned.[71]

At this point, the fourth Earl of Thomond, an old adversary of the corporation, succeeded Danvers as president of Munster and proceeded to reduce the mayoralty to obedience during his term of office.[72] In 1615-16, Limerick had five successive mayors. The first two were deposed, the third resigned, the fourth was deposed, and the fifth, Christopher Creagh was fined £100 and briefly imprisoned. Of the eight sheriffs who served that year, all but one was deposed, for non-conformity. The resistance of the mayoral elite was finally broken in 1616, when the mayor and two sheriffs all conformed to the Church of Ireland. There was a brief resumption of the conflict in 1620 when Henry Barkley was elected mayor in October, but he was deposed by Thomond on the same day, without ever getting a chance to take office.[73] The Battle of the Mayors ended in victory for the government and Limerick returned an unbroken succession of Protestant mayors from 1616 to 1625.[74] However, it proved to be only a temporary success, and the death of Lord Thomond on 6 September 1624, saw the collapse of his policy. In June 1625, two Catholic sheriffs were elected to serve alongside a Protestant mayor, in 1626, all three office holders elected were Catholic, and publicly attended Mass and subsequently, Limerick's mayors and sheriffs were all Catholics until 1651.[75]

Limerick's mayoral elite had shown considerable astuteness in this crisis and Colm Lennon has written that 'civic government was held together by the juggling of the principal offices among those eligible' including the Protestant Edmund Sexton.[76] By contrast a similar 'battle of the mayors' in Waterford resulted in the city temporarily losing both its charter and its mayoralty when the corporation were abolished between 1618 and 1625.[77]

Limerick City Becomes a County.

Between 1608 and 1609, most of the principal Irish towns including Dublin, Waterford, Cork, Limerick, Drogheda, Galway, Wexford, New Ross, Youghal and Kinsale received new charters.[78] Their independent status was ended, but their powers and responsibilities were not otherwise reduced.[79] Limerick's twelfth and final charter, issued by James I on 3 March 1609, is typical of this policy.[80] It promoted Limerick city to being an administrative county in its own right, under the official title of 'the County of the City of Limerick'.[81] This represented the culmination of the corporation's evolution into a completely autonomous local authority, independent of the neighbouring administrative counties which, ironically and paradoxically occurred at the same time as the city's unwanted 'independence' was being brought to an end.[82] The city was to continue to elect a mayor, but the two bailiffs were now to be promoted to be two sheriffs.[83] The title of alderman was mentioned for the first time in a charter, although Limerick had been electing aldermen for two hundred years.[84] The charter also conferred on Limerick Corporation exclusive admiralty jurisdiction over the Shannon from a point three miles

Northeast of the city to the mouth of the Shannon. The mayor of Limerick was now termed 'the admiral of the Shannon' which gave him control over maritime affairs within this area.[85] The mayor, recorder and four of the aldermen were appointed justices of the peace for the new county of the city of Limerick. Any three or more of them (of which two had to be the mayor and recorder) could sit as a law court, and hear all felonies and other crimes, except treason and murder.[86]

In accordance with the provisions of the charter the boundary of the new county of the city of Limerick was declared to extend three miles from the exterior of the city walls, East, West, and South. Thus, from 1609 to 1841, the total area under the jurisdiction of the corporation was between 25,400 and 25,700 acres, compared to 5,155 acres today. As it is difficult to estimate the area of the city and its Liberties between 1216 and 1609, it is impossible to know if this represented an extension of the city boundary, although it is likely that it was. Under the 1609 charter, the mayor and corporation had the power to 'perambulate', or travel around the city boundary to assert their validity, while large stones (later known as mayor stones) were erected to mark the boundaries.[87]

View of Kilmallock in the early nineteenth century showing town houses similar to Limerick's 'stone castles' in the Tudor and Stuart era. (Jim Kemmy Municipal Museum)

As a result of becoming a county, Limerick city was given the right to have its own grand jury, consisting of twenty-three individuals chosen by the sheriffs to appear at the law courts to determine if there were sufficient grounds to proceed with a prosecution.[88] However, in the early seventeenth century, the grand juries began to acquire administrative functions and eventually evolved into local authorities in their own right. The parish vestry also emerged as a local authority in this period.[89] Each parish was under the control of the Church of Ireland and was administered by a vestry or assembly consisting of all Anglican ratepayers. Both bodies were given the right to levy a form of taxation called cess (later to be known as rates). In Limerick city, neither the grand jury nor the parish vestry assumed a major administrative role until the eighteenth century.[90]

Mayor Dominick Fanning and the Rebellion of 1641.

The charter of 1609 granted Limerick city important new powers, particularly county status which it retains to the present. Between 1606 and 1616, the city was deprived of its *de facto* independence after 200 years, but the increased security enjoyed after the establishment of effective English rule throughout the island was more than adequate compensation. Nevertheless, within a few decades, Limerick was to find itself in open rebellion against the English crown for the first time since 1197.

On 23 October 1641, rebellion broke out in Ulster, and by December, the Old English landowners of Leinster, Munster, and Connaught had joined the revolt. The rebels soon controlled most of Ireland and the Confederation of Kilkenny, a kind of parliament, which met from 1642 to 1649, was their *de facto* headquarters. Their aim was to establish an independent kingdom of Ireland, ruled by the Catholics, answerable to the king alone, and, with no interference from the English parliament, which, from 1642 was at war with the crown. They also wanted Catholic landowners and property owners in general to be left in undisputed possession of their holdings and complete and open religious toleration for the Catholic Church. These demands represented the culmination of the attempts by the Old English to reconcile their loyalty to the crown with their Catholicism.[91]

Between October 1641 and October 1642 the mayor of Limerick was the Old English merchant Dominick Fitzsimon Fanning. He supported the Confederation of Kilkenny, and was prepared to use mob violence to this end.[92] He was the most prominent mayor that Limerick had produced since the time of Edmund Sexten and his name is commemorated in Fanning's Castle on Limerick's Mary Street, which is reputed to have been his residence.[93] Soon after the outbreak of the rebellion, Fanning visited King John's Castle and having discovered that the supply of arms and munitions there was very low, decided to help the rebels capture the city. From February to May 1642, Mayor Fanning organised a campaign of violence, pillage and murder against the English people living in Limerick and in May, he allowed a rebel army into the city, over the protests of many of the townspeople, including even some aldermen. King John's Castle was then besieged and captured by the rebel army, assisted by Fanning and his supporters.[94] Limerick was now free from English rule for the first time in 450 years and while maintaining a nominal allegiance to the king, remained so for nearly ten years (1642-51).

Stony Thursday: Limerick's Mayoral Coup D'Etat.

Limerick sent representatives to the Confederation of Kilkenny, and the divisions within the city mirrored those among the Confederates (as the Catholic rebels were known).[95] There were two main parties in the ranks of the rebels. The Old English wanted a quick reconciliation with the king, and concentrated on securing religious toleration, about which they were prepared to be flexible. The Gaelic Irish were more intransigent, in that they wished to reverse the Ulster Plantation and wanted to hold out for full religious freedom in Ireland. The Catholic clergy tended to take the side of the latter party. Both the Old English and the Gaelic Irish professed continuing loyalty to King Charles I, though the latter did so without great enthusiasm.[96] In Limerick, the mayor and council represented the moderate Old English faction while the more extreme party was led by ex-mayor Alderman Dominick Fanning, and consisted of the majority of the common people, including the native Irish, who did not normally participate in the political life of the city.[97]

In the summer of 1646, these disputes escalated into a major revolutionary crisis in Limerick. On 5 June, the Confederate army in Ulster, led by Owen Roe O'Neill won a great victory over the Scottish army, fighting on the side of Protestantism and parliament, at the Battle of Benburb. Soon after Archbishop Rinuccini who was the Papal nuncio to the Confederation of Kilkenny and a supporter of the extreme party, arrived in Limerick, accompanied by the supreme council of the Confederation. On Sunday, 16 June, there was a great procession in Limerick to celebrate the victory. It was led by the whole of the army stationed in Limerick, followed by thirty-two standards captured from the Scots at Benburb, and brought to Limerick by a Jesuit priest. They were followed by Rinuccini, accompanied by four Irish bishops, the members of the supreme council, and lastly the mayor and council in their red robes. A large crowd watched the procession as it made its way to St. Mary's Cathedral, for a *Te Deum*.[98]

In 1646, James Butler, twelfth Earl and first Marquis of Ormond, who was the King's lord deputy of Ireland, concluded an agreement with the Confederation of Kilkenny known as the 'Ormond Peace' which was vague on religious toleration, but provided for the role of the Old English in Irish public life being safeguarded. This was not acceptable to the native Irish, nor to the extreme Catholic party led by Rinuccini, but was favoured by the Old English, including most of Limerick's mayoral elite. The supreme council returned to Kilkenny, while Rinuccini went to Waterford to attend a national synod of the Catholic clergy, where the Ormond Peace was strongly condemned and its supporters threatened with excommunication. In Limerick, tensions between the moderate and extreme parties had been brought to their highest level by the great procession of 16 June.[99] On 20 August, the herald-at-arms William Roberts and his colleagues arrived in Limerick to proclaim the Ormond peace, and although the gates of the city were shut in their faces, they were grudgingly admitted the next day.[100] The Mayor, John Bourke, and city council supported Roberts and his mission as they had already voted in favour of the peace.[101]

On Thursday 21 August 1646, the crisis finally developed into a full scale revolution. Dressed in his elaborate ceremonial costume and accompanied by the mayor and aldermen in their scarlet robes, together with some of the leading townspeople, the herald began to proclaim the peace at the junction of John Street, Broad Street and Mungret Street in the Irishtown.[102] However, they were attacked by a mob of 500 armed citizens led by ex-mayor Dominick Fanning. The mob showered the official party with a volley of stones (thus christening the riot 'Stony Thursday') and throwing themselves on the dignitaries, proceeded to assault them.[103] The herald's costume was torn off him, and the mayor and some of the aldermen severely beaten. The mayor was 'dragged through the gutter as a dead man in his scarlet gown', the herald also left for dead in the street, and many of the official party sustained serious injuries.[104] The dignitaries fled to a nearby house, and the herald and his colleagues were given refuge by their arch-enemy, Fanning, the only person capable of protecting them from the mob.[105] The crowd then proclaimed Fanning and two of his supporters mayor and sheriffs of Limerick respectively, without the formality of an election. This was the first time ever that the mayor of Limerick had been overthrown in a coup d'etat, but as Liam Irwin has written, 'it might be argued that it was the first time that a mayor had been directly chosen by the people, as the various charters had disingenuously allowed.'[106]

The Abolition of the Mayoralty (1651-56).

The Stony Thursday coup d'etat solved nothing and Limerick continued to be plagued by internal strife even after the arrival of the parliamentary army, under Cromwell, at Ringsend, County Dublin, on 15 August 1649.[107] Between June and October 1651, Limerick was besieged by the parliamentary army led by Cromwell's son-in-law, Henry Ireton. Mayor Peter Creagh, a moderate, was sidelined by the extreme party, led by Fanning, Sir Geoffrey Galway (son of the mayor who had quarrelled with Carew), and the bishop of Emly, Terence Albert O'Brien. They led the defence of the city and initially refused to treat with Ireton, holding out for increasingly unrealistic terms. The mayor was excluded when negotiations finally begun and the corporation was represented by Fanning, who was an alderman and by the recorder, one Mr. Stackpoole. Negotiations broke down, due to the stubbornness of both sets of negotiators.[108] After huge loss of life, the moderate party finally triumphed and on 29 October 1651, the keys of Limerick were handed over to Ireton.[109] The articles of surrender were negotiated and signed by some corporation members along with military officers, but not by the mayor, whose role throughout the siege, had been a marginal one. The chief negotiator for the Corporation was in fact Recorder Stackpoole.[110] Shortly afterwards, the Cromwellians captured Fanning while he was hiding in his family vault in St. Francis Churchyard and he was hanged, drawn and quartered.[111]

Limerick was transformed forever under Cromwellian rule in Limerick over the next nine years.[112] The historian Eamon O'Flaherty wrote that 'the 1650s represent the real turning point in early modern Irish history, and the events of the late 1680s and early 1690s were merely a dramatic and symbolic sequel; a final attempt to reverse the changes of the 1650s.'[113] Limerick Corporation was abolished in 1651, and the city ruled by a military governor until June 1656. Two years after the abolition of the Stuart monarchy, the local Limerick monarchy, the mayoralty, was also overthrown and the city was without a mayor from 1651 to 1656.[114] This is the only break in the continuity of the office between the thirteenth century and the present.

The Old English mayoral elite of the Arthurs, Creaghs, Roches, Comyns, Fannings, Stritchs and Whites was also overthrown and replaced by a New English Protestant ruling class. Historian Toby Barnard rightly pointed out that 'the removal of Catholic property owners from the towns was of an equal importance with the transplantation of Catholic landed proprietors, yet it has received little attention.'[115] It was the biggest change in the history of the mayoralty and corporation between 1197 and 1841.[116] There was also a huge influx of English people into Limerick city. In 1659, the population of the walled city was only 1,367, with a further 1,738 living in the Liberties, according to the census of that year, the first ever taken in Ireland. Of those in the walled city, 720 (52.7%) were English and only 647 (47.3%) were Irish.[117] Some Dutch immigrants also came to the city, the most prominent of whom were Laurence de Geer and Abraham van Hoegarden.[118]

The Dutch Mayors of Limerick.

Limerick Corporation and the mayoralty were restored in June 1656. The government reinstated the charter of 1609, and twelve aldermen were elected, who in turn selected as mayor the military governor of the town, Henry Ingolsby.[119] However, there was no restoration of the displaced Catholic oligarchy and the Protestant settlers formed a new mayoral elite. Indeed Catholics were rigorously excluded from local government and suffered institutional discrimination.[120]

Four years after the 'local monarchy' was restored, King Charles II was restored to the throne of the three kingdoms. Between 1660 and 1672, Roger Boyle, Earl of Orrery (1621-79) served as the last lord president of Munster, until the abolition of the office in August 1672.[121] Ambitious, able and arrogant, he represented the New English desire to exclude Catholics from any position of authority, or from any role in the economic life of the country.[122] However, he also promoted the economic development of Limerick especially by encouraging Dutch immigration to the city. Orrery wanted to tap into the skills of the Dutch Republic, the most prosperous and successful economic power of the seventeenth century, to promote the city's economic growth and on 26 June 1663 he wrote that 'I have already got above eighty Dutch thither who have set up considerable manufactures and trade by sea.'[123] They soon attained a significant role in the government of the city. Samuel Foxon was the first of the Dutch mayors (1666-67) and was succeeded by E. Werenooght (1669-70), R. Studdenooght (1670-71) and William York (1673-74; 1674-75 and 1678-79).[124]

Unfortunately for Orrery, the Dutch imported their tradition of political independence and activism, as well as their entrepreneurial skills. Mayor Samuel Foxon who held office in 1666-67 and Orrery quarrelled bitterly over the composition of the membership of City Council. After the restoration of the monarchy, James, Marquis of Ormond, who had served as lord deputy in the 1640s was created a duke and appointed lord lieutenant of Ireland. Ormond disliked Orrery, but in 1666 he granted him the right

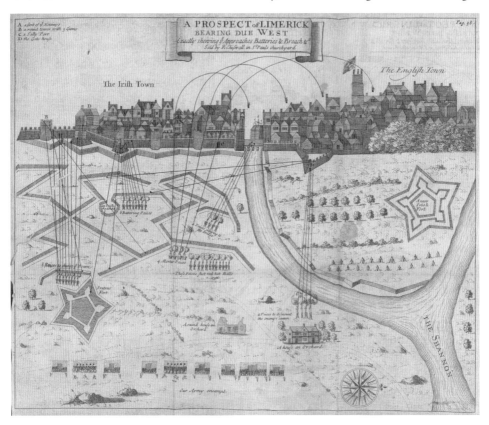

A Dutch print of Limerick under siege in 1690.
(Jim Kemmy Municipal Museum)

to name the members of the councils in the chartered towns of Munster, including Limerick, as part of a review of all of their charters. Orrery asked for a list of nominees from Mayor Foxon. A number of these were Protestants belonging to sects outside the Church of Ireland, and Orrery excluded these from the list. The mayor pretended to agree to this, but then reported the matter to Ormond, and asked him to restore the original list. Ormond agreed to Foxon's request, as a means of humiliating Orrery. Orrery was furious and had his revenge by preventing Foxon from ever again serving as mayor of Limerick.[125]

The greatest of the Dutch mayors was William York (1637-79), who served three terms in 1673-74; 1674-75 and 1678-79. York was a very active mayor, who ordered that Thomond and Baal's Bridges should be repaired, and moved the city market, from Johns Gate to Mungret Street, near the site of the modern market. In 1673, Mayor York ordered the construction of a new civic headquarters on Nicholas Street that became known as the Exchange. He contributed £400 from his own private resources to pay for it and in consequence, the new town hall was known as 'York Exchange', for some time afterwards. It consisted of a covered market surrounded by an arcade on the ground floor, and the council chamber, which took up the full length of the first floor. York also donated a large royal coat of arms, which was hung over the entrance to the council chamber.[126]

Mayor York also contributed to the provision of a new set of bells for St. Mary's Cathedral. On 14 March 1674, they were rung for the first time to mark the end of the Third Anglo-Dutch War of 1672-74 and as part of the celebrations, the mayor and corporation rode through the streets in their scarlet robes, escorted by the local militia. York died on 1 April 1679 aged forty-two while serving a third term as mayor and a splendid monument was erected to his memory in St. Mary's Cathedral by his son, also called William.[127]

The New Rules of 1672.

In 1672, the government introduced the New Rules in order to prevent Catholics from recovering any of their former political influence in the borough corporations.[128] The New Rules varied from town to town and in Limerick had four main provisions. Firstly, the approval of the lord lieutenant and his council was necessary for the appointment of the mayor, sheriffs, recorder and town clerk, within ten days of their election. Secondly, all such officers had to take the Oath of Supremacy, or lose their positions. Thirdly, the election of all corporate officers, including the mayor, sheriffs, recorder and town clerk, was taken away from the general body of freemen, meeting in the court d'oyer hundred (formerly known as the hundred court and pronounced 'deer hundred'), and vested in the common council. Henceforth the election of these officers was to take place on the first Monday after Midsummer Day in June, and they would continue to take up office on the first Monday after Michaelmas. The three-month interval between election and assumption of office was to allow sufficient time for the obtaining of the approval of the lord lieutenant and his council and to elect new officers if some were not approved. Also, nothing was permitted to be discussed in the court d'oyer hundred, which had not been already passed by the common council. The penalty for breach of this stipulation was to be disenfranchisement. Fourthly, the admission of foreigners and Protestants to the freedom of the city was provided for.[129]

The New Rules had several important results. Firstly, the Protestant Ascendancy established in the 1650s was greatly strengthened. Secondly municipal autonomy was reduced in theory, although in practice, the borough corporations continued to be left to their own devices so long as they adhered to the Rules. Thirdly the tendency towards oligarchy that was always present in municipal government was now given statutory recognition, with the concentration of all real power in the hands of the common council (a body whose members were chosen by co-option) at the expense of the court d'oyer hundred (a body representing the freemen of the city). Fourthly, the latter disappeared completely between the 1680s and the 1820s, except for a brief and unsuccessful revival between the 1720s and 1760s.[130] Fifthly, the removal of the election of the mayor from the citizens to the council instituted a system that has endured to the present (and survived an abortive initiative to restore the direct election of mayors in 2001-03).

Sir William King.

One of the most significant mayors of the Restoration period was Sir William King, who acquired a great deal of land in County Limerick as a result of the Cromwellian plantation and played a major role in both Limerick city and county for some fifty years. A staunch Protestant, he was elected one of the two MPs for County Limerick in the only parliament of Charles II's reign which sat from 1661 to 1666. He first held office as mayor of Limerick from 1665 to 1666 and in that capacity welcomed the lord lieutenant, the Duke of Ormond with great ceremony when he made an official visit to the city in 1665. On the death of Mayor William York, King was elected to serve out the remainder of his term of office, from April to September 1679 and he served a third and final term from September 1679 to September 1680. King inaugurated an unpleasant tradition during his final mayoralty by quartering troops exclusively on Catholic householders while exempting Protestants from this onerous exaction. He also served as military governor of Limerick until his dismissal following the accession of the Catholic King James II. In 1690, at the time of the first Williamite siege of Limerick, he was imprisoned but soon escaped and made his way to the army of William of Orange, to whom he gave valuable information. After the Treaty of Limerick, King prospered in the 1690s and was one of the officials appointed to grant licences to carry arms to the citizens of Limerick city and county. King resided in a mansion in Kilpeacon, about five miles from Limerick city and built a church there which contained an impressive monument to him. He died on 10 September 1706, and his large estates passed into the hands of his great-nephews.[131]

The Temporary Catholic Restoration in Limerick.

The death of Charles II on 6 February 1685 ushered in a new period of crisis for Limerick. His successor, James II was a devout Roman Catholic, but nevertheless the Protestant dominated corporation of Limerick greeted his accession warmly. On Sunday, 13 February, his official proclamation as king in the city was marked by great pageantry, when the mayor, the sheriffs, the governor, the Protestant bishop and clergy, and the city council in their ceremonial robes rode through the streets in procession, followed by the trade guilds and the militia on foot.[132]

However, within a few months, a Catholic restoration was in progress throughout Ireland. Although the civic government in the whole of Ireland had been in Protestant hands since the 1650s, many of the wealthy Catholics merchants and traders had regained much of their social and economic (though not their political) power and had benefited from the general prosperity.[133] In Limerick, the military governor, Sir William King, was dismissed by the Dublin administration, and replaced by Anthony Hamilton, a Catholic, who went to Mass publicly, the first holder of the post to do so since 1651.[134] Under his direction, the garrison of the city began the practice of public attendance of Mass. Limerick Corporation rapidly threw off its Protestant character. Twelve Catholic merchants were made freemen and the recorder, William Turner embraced Catholicism. Soon after, the Catholic and Old English Earl of Tyrconnell, who had been appointed Lord Lieutenant by James II deposed the mayor and two sheriffs who were Protestants and replaced them with a Catholic mayor, Robert Hannon, and two new sheriffs, one Protestant and one Catholic. The common council formally elected them, and they took office on 8 April 1687. Soon after, the mayor, governor, recorder and one of the sheriffs went publicly to Mass. Limerick Corporation was to remain under Catholic control for the next four years.[135]

In the meantime, James II was overthrown by his Protestant son-in-law, William of Orange. In March 1689, James arrived in Ireland with a French army, and over the next two years the largest war ever fought on Irish soil was to engulf the whole country.[136] Although Limerick's role in this conflict was a major one, the mayors had a limited role in both of the great sieges of the city. During the first siege, Limerick's military governor was a French general, Boisseleau, and during the second, Sarsfield was the *de facto* commander.[137] The mayors of Limerick Thomas Harrold (1689-90) and John Power (1690-91) were completely overshadowed, although they supported the garrison defending the city. The main result of these terrible years for Limerick was the utter destruction of the city. The Treaty of Limerick, which was signed on 2 October 1691 restored the Protestant Ascendancy and Limerick was not to have a Catholic mayor again until 1842.

Endnotes

1   The second volume of *A New History of Ireland* which deals with the medieval period terminates in 1534. See also, Nicholas Canny, *From Reformation to Restoration: Ireland 1534-1660*, (Dublin, 1987), p. 1.

2   Brendan Bradshaw, *The Irish Constitutional Revolution in the Sixteenth Century*, (Cambridge, 1979).

3   The classic work on the Tudor conquest of Ireland is Nicholas Canny, *The Elizabethan Conquest of Ireland: A Pattern Established 1565-76*, (Hassocks, 1976).

4   Bradshaw, *Irish Constitutional Revolution*, pp 258-63 and Ellis, *Ireland in the Age of the Tudors*, p. 265.

5   These developments are discussed in Ellis, *Ireland in the Age of the Tudors*, pp 218-309.

6   For Irish towns in the sixteenth century see Colm Lennon, *Sixteenth-Century Ireland. The Incomplete Conquest*, (Dublin 1994), pp. 20-40; Sheehan, 'Irish Towns in a Period of Change' and Butlin, 'Irish Towns in the Sixteenth and Seventeenth Centuries'.

7   See Eamon O'Flaherty, 'The Urban Community and the State 1590-1690' in Bernadette Whelan (ed.), *The Last of the Great Wars. Essays on the War of the Three Kings in Ireland 1688-91*, (Limerick, 1995), pp 161-62.

8   Sheehan, 'Irish Towns in a Period of Change', pp 105-06.

9   Butlin, 'Irish Towns in the Sixteenth and Seventeenth Centuries, pp 90-92. See also *Ellis, Ireland in the Age of the Tudors*, pp 352-3.

10   L.M. Cullen, 'Economic Trends, 1660-91' in T.W. Moody, F.X. Martin and F.J. Byrne, (eds), *A New History of Ireland, Vol.III, Early Modern Ireland 1534-1691*, (Oxford, 1991), p. 390.

11   *Carew Manuscripts*, 1515-74, p. 105.

12   Brendan Bradshaw, 'Fr. Wolfe's Description of Limerick City, 1574' in *North Munster Antiquarian Journal*, Vol. XVII, (1975), p. 49.

13   Hill, *The Building of Limerick*, p. 29.

14   For accounts of his life see Hodkinson, 'Edmund Sexten', in Lee, *Remembering Limerick*, pp 107-11; Clodagh Tait, 'A Trusty and Well-beloved Servant. The Career and Disinterment of Edmond Sexton of Limerick, d.1554' in *Archivium Hibernicum*, Vol. 56, (Maynooth, 2002), pp 51-64 and Sarah Johnson, 'By Crafty Means: Edmund Sexton and the Politics of Patronage in Sixteenth Century Ireland', (Unpublished MA thesis, St.Hugh's College, Oxford, 2005). See also Lennon, *Urban Patriciates*, passim.

15   Hodkinson, 'Edmund Sexten', pp 107-08.

16   Ibid., p. 108.

17   Ellis, *Ireland in the Age of the Tudors*, pp 148-49 and Lennon, *Sixteenth-Century Ireland*, pp 145-52.

18   For the attitude of the townspeople in Ireland to the prospect of greater government intervention see Bradshaw, *Irish Constitutional Revolution*, pp 35-36.

19   For an account of this campaign see Lenihan, *History of Limerick*, pp 75-77.

20   Hodkinson, 'Edmund Sexten', p. 109.

21   The best account of the Reformation in sixteenth century Limerick is to be found in Brendan Bradshaw, S.M., 'The Reformation in the Cities: Cork, Limerick and Galway, 1534-1603' in John Bradley, (ed.), *Settlement and Society in Medieval Ireland*. Studies presented to F. X. Martin, O.S.A., (Kilkenny, 1988), pp 445-76.

22   *Carew Manuscripts*, 1515-74, p. 146.

23   Bradshaw, 'The Reformation in the Cities', pp 459-60.

24   For Sexten's acquisitions see Hodkinson, 'Edmund Sexten', pp 109-11 and Lenihan, *History of Limerick*, pp 642-57.

25   For Sexten's supposed achievements see *Carew Manuscripts*, 1515-74, pp 152-53.

26   Lenihan, *History of Limerick*, pp 80-81.

27   Johnson, 'Edmond Sexten', pp 23-24.

28   *Calendar of State Papers*, 1509-73, pp 88-89.

29   Lennon. *Urban Patriciates*, pp 5-6, 23.

30   Kevin Hannan, 'The Rich Inheritance of a Limerick Mayor' in Lee, *Remembering Limerick*, pp 111-12.

31   Lennon, *Urban Patriciates*, pp 17-18.

32   For the Lord Presidencies, see Liam Irwin, 'Lords President of Munster and Connacht, 1569-1672' in T. W. Moody, F. X. Martin and F. J. Byrne, (eds), *A New History of Ireland, Volume IX, Maps, Genealogies, Lists. A Companion to Irish History, Part 2*, (Oxford, 1984), pp 534-36 and Liam Irwin, 'The Suppression of the Irish Presidency System', in *Irish Historical Studies*, XXII, (1980-81), pp 21-33. For the Munster presidency see also Liam Irwin, 'The Lord Presidency of Munster 1625-72' (Unpublished MA thesis, University College Cork, 1976).

33   Lennon, *Sixteenth-Century Ireland*, pp 307-08.

34   Bradshaw, 'The Reformation in the Cities', p. 465.

35   *The Irish Fiants of the Tudor Sovereigns during The Reigns of Henry VIII, Edward VI, Philip and Mary, and Elizabeth I*, 3 Vols, (Dublin 1994), Vol. 2, p. 76.

36   Bradshaw, 'The Reformation in the Cities', p. 462.

37   *Calendar of State Papers*, 1592-96, p. 288.

38   Sheehan, 'Irish Towns in a Period of Change', pp 105-06 and O'Flaherty 'The Urban Community and the State' p. 162.

39   *Municipal Corporations Report*, p. 346.

40   Robert Herbert, 'The Antiquities of the Corporation of Limerick' in *North Munster Antiquarian Journal*, Vol. 4, No. 3, (Spring, 1945), p. 93.

41   *Municipal Corporations Report*, p. 346.

42   *Carew Manuscripts*, 1575-1588, p. 26; *Irish Fiants*, Vol. 2, pp 444-45.

43   For the history of Scattery see Jeremiah Newman, Bishop of Limerick, 'Scattery: an Unknown Part of the Diocese of Limerick' in *North Munster Antiquarian Journal*, Vol. 34 (1992), pp 13-29.

44   Lenihan, *History of Limerick*, p. 102.

45   Ellis, *Ireland under the Tudors*, p. 317.

46   Sheehan, 'Irish Towns in a Period of Change', p. 109.

47   Lenihan, *History of Limerick*, p. 739.

48   Ellis, *Ireland under the Tudors*, pp 282-83, 352-58.

49   For the development of this ideology see D. George Boyce, *Nationalism in Ireland*, (London, 1982), pp 46-93.

50   For examples of same, see *Calendar of State Papers*, 1574-85, p.468; 1586-88, p.30; 1588-92, p. 38.

51   Ibid., p. 38.

52   Fitzgerald and McGregor, *History of Limerick*, II, pp 186-90.

53   *Municipal Corporations Report*, p.346.

54   *Calendar of State Papers*, 1598-99, p.347.

55   For the Earl of Thomond, see Sir Leslie Stephen and Sir Sidney Lee (eds), *The Dictionary of National Biography*, (London, 1908-09), 23 vols, Vol. 14, pp 757-59.

56   O'Flaherty, 'The Urban Community and the State', pp 165-66.

57   *Calendar of State Papers*, 1599-1600, pp 402-03.

58   Ibid.

59   Ibid., pp 419-20.

60   O'Flaherty,' The Urban Community and the State', p. 166; Calendar of State Papers, 1601-03, p. 2.

61   Irwin, 'Lords President of Munster and Connacht', p. 535.

62   Sheehan, 'Irish Towns in a Period of Change', pp 108-09.

63   Good accounts of this important episode can be found in O'Flaherty ' The Urban Community and the State', pp 166-67 and Sheehan, ' Irish Towns in a Period of Change', pp 108-09.

64   O'Flaherty, 'The Urban Community and the State', pp 168-70.

65   Irwin, 'Lords Presidents of Munster and Connacht', p. 535.

66   Irwin, 'Seventeenth Century Limerick', in Lee, *Remembering Limerick*, p. 116.

67   Ibid., pp 115-16.

68   Lennon, *Urban Patriciates*, p. 23.

69   Irwin, 'Seventeenth Century Limerick', p. 116.

70   This term was coined by Maurice Lenihan in his *History of Limerick*, pp 133-37.

71   These events are described in Lenihan, *History of Limerick*, pp 133-37 and 700-01.

72   Irwin, 'Lords President of Munster and Connacht', p. 535.

73   Ibid., p. 701.

74   Ibid., pp 701-02.

75   Ibid., p. 702.

76   Lennon, *Urban Patriciates*, pp 8-9.

77   McEneaney, *A History of Waterford and its Mayors*, pp 123-32.

78   *Carew Manuscripts*, 1603-1624, pp 22-23.

79   This is evidenced by the granting of county status to the cities of Cork, Limerick and Kilkenny and the town of Galway between 1608 and 1610.

80 The full text of the 1609 charter is reproduced in Ferrar, *History of Limerick*, pp 297-318.

81 Ibid., p. 300.

82 Ibid., pp 301-02.

83 Ibid., pp 302-03.

84 *Municipal Corporations Report*, p. 346.

85 Ferrar, *History of Limerick*, pp 305-11.

86 Ibid.

87 Ferrar, *History of Limerick*, p. 302. The district of Limerick city known as Mayorstone takes its name from one of these boundary marks.

88 Joseph Byrne, *Byrne's Dictionary of Irish Local History*, (Cork, 2004), p. 138.

89 Ibid., pp 318-19.

90 For a comprehensive account of the role of the parish in local government, see Elizabeth Fitzpatrick and Raymond Gillespie (eds), *The Parish in Medieval and Early Modern Ireland. Community, Territory and Building*, (Dublin, 2006), pp 41-48; 228-41; 277-324.

91 For a general account of this period, see Micheal O'Siochru, *Confederate Ireland, 1641-1649. A Constitutional and Political Analysis*, (Dublin, 1998).

92 Wiggins, *Anatomy of a Siege*, pp 55-57.

93 Hill, *The Building of Limerick*, pp 40-42.

94 For a detailed description of the siege, see Wiggins, *Anatomy of a Siege*, pp 67-224.

95 Lenihan, *History of Limerick*, p. 149.

96 Irwin, 'Seventeenth Century Limerick', pp 116-17.

97 Lenihan, *History of Limerick*, pp 153-55.

98 Ibid., p. 158.

99 O'Flaherty, 'The Urban Community and the State', p. 174.

100 Irwin, 'Seventeenth Century Limerick', p. 117.

101 Ibid.

102 Ibid.

103 Ibid.

104 *Calendar of State Papers, 1660-1662*, p. 371.

105 O'Flaherty, 'The Urban Community and the State', p. 175.

106 Irwin, 'Seventeenth Century Limerick', p. 118.

107 These disputes are detailed in Lenihan, *History of Limerick*, pp 165-70.

108 Wiggins, *Anatomy of a Siege*, p. 233. See also Lenihan, *History of Limerick*, pp 171-79.

109 Wiggins, *Anatomy of a Siege*, p. 233.

110 Irwin, 'Seventeenth Century Limerick', pp 118-19.

111 Lenihan, *History of Limerick*, pp 179-81.

112 See T.C. Barnard, *Cromwellian Ireland, English Government and Reform in Ireland 1649-1660*, (Oxford, 1975) for a good account of Ireland in the 1650s.

113 O'Flaherty, 'The Urban Community and the State', p. 176.

114 Ibid., p. 177.

115 Barnard, *Cromwellian Ireland*, p. 51.

116 Ibid., pp 50-89 for an account of the Cromwellian regime's policy towards the Irish boroughs.

117 Seamus Pender (ed.), *Census of Ireland*, c. 1659, (Dublin, 1939), pp 263-65.

118 Barnard, *Cromwellian Ireland*, pp 58-60.

119 Ibid. See also Lenihan, *History of Limerick*, p. 191.

120 Barnard, *Cromwellian Ireland*, pp 71-76.

121 Irwin, 'Lords President of Munster and Connacht', p. 535.

122 Irwin, 'The Suppression of the Irish Presidency System,' pp 26-27.

123 *Calendar of State Papers*, 1663-1665, pp 152-53.

124 Ibid., p. 119 and Lenihan, *History of Limerick*, pp 703-04.

125 Irwin, 'Seventeenth Century Limerick', pp 119-21.

126 Fitzgerald and McGregor, *History of Limerick*, II, pp 579-80.

127 Lenihan, *History of Limerick*, pp 207-08.

128 Webb, *Municipal Government*, p. 149.

129 The full text of the New Rules can be found in *A True State of the Present Affairs of Limerick Shewing the Rise and Progress of the Disputes in that City with Some Remarks on the Dangerous Consequences which must Attend the Investing Military Men with the Civil Powers of Corporations, (London, 1726), pp 67-72. See also Municipal Corporations Report*, p. 347.

130 A *True State of the Present Affairs of Limerick*, pp 33, 37-38 and *Municipal Corporations Report*, p. 356.

131 Ibid., pp 193, 203, 208-10, 292, 306.

132 Lenihan, *History of Limerick*, p. 210.

133 David Dickson, 'Catholics and Trade in Eighteenth-Century Ireland: an Old Debate Revisited' in T.P. Power and Kevin Whelan (eds), *Endurance and Emergence: Catholics in Ireland in the Eighteenth Century*, (Dublin, 1990), pp 85-100.

134 Ibid., p. 210.

135 Ibid., p. 211.

136 For this war, see Richard Doherty, *The Williamite War in Ireland, 1688-1691*, (Dublin, 1998).

137 For an excellent modern account of Sarsfield, see Liam Irwin, 'Sarsfield: The Man and the Myth' in Whelan, *The Last of the Great Wars*, pp 108-26.

Charles Smyth (1698-1784) who was mayor of Limerick in 1732-33 and MP for the city from 1731 to 1776.
To date he is the longest serving MP or TD in the history of Limerick city.
(APW Malcomson)

Chapter Four
The Mayoralty in the Age of the 'Corrupt Corporation'. 1691-1841

The Era of Municipal Misgovernment.

It has often been asserted that the most inglorious period in the history of Irish borough corporations was the 'long eighteenth century' (1691-1841). John J. Webb called this period 'the era of municipal misgovernment', and described it as 'one long sordid story of misgovernment, corruption, jobbery and intolerance.'[1] R.B. McDowell wrote that 'a highly complex and archaic structure, mismanagement and inertia characterised Irish municipal administration in the eighteenth century.'[2] In Limerick the municipal body of this period is often referred to as the 'Corrupt Corporation' and has long had obloquy heaped on it.[3] Maurice Lenihan claimed that 'in the history of the world, there has been seldom heard of such malversation, spoliation and unblushing plunder'[4] while Eamon O'Flaherty has described the eighteenth-century corporation as 'a corrupt and self-electing political oligarchy.'[5]

The municipal corporations in this period were afflicted by five major problems. Firstly, the Penal Laws enacted between 1695 and 1727 reinforced the New Rules of 1672 in excluding Catholics from local government. Secondly, the corporations became increasingly oligarchic, and ceased to represent the interests even of the Protestant citizens of the towns. Thirdly, municipal governments devoted themselves more and more to political activities. Fourthly, corruption of all kinds flourished. Fifthly, the boroughs abandoned many of their functions as local regulators and service providers. Indeed, Limerick Corporation was not conspicuously corrupt by the standards of the period, just merely typical of municipal government all over Europe in the eighteenth century.[6] The long eighteenth century was an age of reform and of revolution and in consequence corruption and abuses that would have been tolerated in earlier centuries were now judged much more harshly. In such circumstances, it was inevitable that the hopelessly archaic borough corporations should have been subject to continuous criticism throughout the period and were eventually completely reformed in the 1840s.[7]

The English urban historian Rosemary Sweet advanced a counter-argument in her study of English towns in the long eighteenth century, which may have equal validity for Irish urban areas.[8] She suggested that the apparent decay of English borough governments in this period was in fact caused by the unprecedented demands made on them as a result of rapidly increasing population, the beginnings of the Industrial Revolution and the rising expectations of a much larger, better educated and more politically aware general public. English towns underwent an 'urban renaissance' at this time and outgrew their medieval constitutions and administrative machinery, which had never been intended to cope with such unprecedented demands and duties.[9] Limerick did not undergo an industrial revolution but she did experience significant urban growth amounting to an 'urban renaissance.'

Limerick Corporation under the Protestant Ascendancy.

The Treaty of Limerick saw the re-imposition of Protestant supremacy and in 1691, George Roche became the city's mayor, the first in a continuous succession of Protestant holders of the office until 1841. In 1704, Catholics were banned from holding any position in a borough corporation, including membership of the common council; in 1710 they were debarred from serving on a grand jury and in 1727, they were deprived of the vote at municipal elections.[10] Some sixty years later, the Catholic Relief Act of 1793 permitted Catholics to vote at both parliamentary and municipal elections, and to become members of corporations and of grand juries. In theory, Protestant domination of the corporations was thus removed but in practice it continued in nearly all cases until 1841. No Catholic at all was admitted to any municipal office or membership of the common council in Limerick until after 1841.[11] This was because the common council, which was dominated by the most reactionary and sectarian elements among the Protestant population, selected new councillors by co-option, elected the mayor and sheriffs, appointed all officers and decided who should and should not be admitted as freemen.

The freemen theoretically comprised the electorate in the borough, but had no function in electing officers or replacements to the municipal council. Instead, their significance was due to their comprising the vast majority of the electorate for parliamentary elections, which is why the mayoral elite were so anxious to control entry to the roll of freemen.[12] Before 1800, Limerick city returned two MPs to the Irish parliament and one to the British parliament after the Act of Union. The three traditional rights to freedom were 1- being the eldest son of a freeman; 2-being married to the

Freedom box, Limerick silver; engraved with city arms and inscribed that it was presented to William Brown, 2 October 1693. The certificate of freedom was usually presented to distinguished recipients in a ceremonial freedom box.
(Jim Kemmy Municipal Museum)

daughter of a freeman and 3- having served an apprenticeship of seven years with a freeman. In addition, the right to the freedom could be granted as a gift of the common council, and it was this latter provision that led to the most widespread abuses as it enabled the councillors to grant the franchise to unlimited numbers of persons and to swamp the numbers eligible under the traditional three rights.[13]

Later, the manipulation of the roll of freemen was taken two steps further. Firstly, the practice grew up of allowing persons neither living nor working within the city boundaries to become freemen. These non-resident freemen came to dominate the electoral roll and consequently the resident freemen and freeholders were reduced in status. Secondly, from the 1770s onwards the common council began to systematically exclude those who claimed freedom as of right, under the traditional three headings.[14] In consequence, between 1794 and 1820, the non-resident freemen comprised more than half the electorate of the county of the city of Limerick, outnumbering the resident freemen, while in contemporary Dublin, only 10% of the electorate was non-resident. Indeed, non-residency spread to the common council itself and in 1833 the total membership was sixty-nine of whom nineteen (27% of the total) were not resident.[15] In consequence, at the beginning of the nineteenth century, Limerick Corporation was probably the most unrepresentative of all the city governments in Ireland.[16]

The New Rules of 1672 had introduced statutory limits to the authority of the freemen for the first time by firstly removing their right to elect the mayor and other officers and vesting it instead in the common council and secondly forbidding the court d'oyer hundred from discussing any issue that had not been already passed by the common council.[17] Consequently, the court d'oyer hundred, the most representative body in Limerick Corporation, disappeared between the 1680s to the 1720s, and again from the 1760s to 1823, although it was never formally abolished.[18] Even when it actually came back into existence between the 1720s and the 1760s it was usually a rubberstamp because firstly, the mayor and common council, as freemen, also had the right to membership of the court d'oyer hundred and as they formed a solid and disciplined block were able to dominate it completely and secondly they controlled entry into the roll of freemen, and therefore the actual membership of the court. [19]

The other major local authorities in Limerick were also sectarian bodies. The grand jury of the city was appointed by the two sheriffs of the corporation and while theoretically chosen from 'the most respectable, intelligent and opulent inhabitants of the city, without reference to local or political connection' was in fact 'confined exclusively to the aldermen, burgesses, freemen and friends of the corporation.'[20] Catholics were rarely chosen, and the jurors, like the corporation, weren't even representative of the Protestant inhabitants of the city. Although the corporation and grand jury were separate institutions, they were usually composed of the same individuals, and co-operation between them was extremely close. The functions of the grand jury included the building and maintenance of infrastructure such as roads, bridges, courthouses and prisons.[21] The parish vestries, consisting of the Anglican ratepayers, were more representative than the corporation or grand jury, but were also sectarian. Their main functions lay in the area of night watch, fire safety and the cleaning and lighting of streets.

The corrupt practices of Limerick Corporation have long enjoyed legendary status, mainly due to the writings of Maurice Lenihan. Among the most notorious were the exclusion of Catholics and most Protestants from the local government system, the appointment of unfit persons to municipal offices, manipulation of the freeman vote in order to control the parliamentary franchise, and the neglect of the corporation's functions as a local service provider and regulator.[22]

After 1692, the Irish parliament, which had only met periodically between the fourteenth and seventeenth centuries, became a permanent institution that met continually. In consequence, the status of MPs was greatly enhanced. In addition, the practice of politicians becoming members of parliament while continuing to sit as members of local authority evolved into a common practice in the long eighteenth century. Later known as the 'dual mandate', it remained a feature of the Irish political system until its abolition in 2003. Between 1691 and 1841, five mayors of Limerick were also members of parliament: George Roche, Thomas Pierce, Charles Smyth, the second Lord Southwell and Thomas Smyth.

The Corporation Roches 1715-61.

The most significant development in the political life of eighteenth century Limerick was the emergence of political dynasties that successively dominated the corporation and the political life of the city.[23] This trend represented the culmination of the oligarchic system that had prevailed for many centuries and led to a further narrowing of the mayoral elite, which was already reduced by the Penal Laws.

The first of these political dynasties were the Roches, usually known as 'the Corporation Roches'.[24] The first politically prominent member of the family, George, served as Limerick's first Protestant mayor after the Treaty of Limerick (1691-2).[25] The leading member of the family was George Roche (1677-1740), who was twice elected mayor of Limerick (1702-03, 1721-22) and at various times held the office of alderman, town clerk and recorder in the corporation. From 1713 to 1714 and again from 1715 to 1727, he represented the city in parliament along with his ally William Foord. In 1721-22 Roche became the first person in modern times to be simultaneously an MP and mayor of Limerick. He was married to Alice Vincent, whose family were the Roches' staunchest allies.[26] Despite his prominence, little is known about George Roche. His brother Tock Roche who served as mayor in 1705-06 and 1723-25 seems to have been the dominant force in the family's control of the corporation and was described by Lenihan as a 'bigot and a firebrand' and as 'the civic autocrat.'[27]

General Pierce (1667-1739): Mayor or Military Dictator?

In 1726, the ascendancy of the Roches was temporarily overthrown in a very dramatic fashion, when the military governor of the city, Lieutenant-General Thomas Pierce became mayor. An Englishman, he belonged to a politically active military family. Both he and his brother Edward were veteran professional soldiers who had served with distinction in the wars with France between 1689 and 1713.[28] Thomas's daughter Anne was married to his nephew, the famous architect, Sir Edward Lovett Pierce (1699-1733) who designed the Irish parliament building in College Green.[29]

Thomas Pierce sat as MP for Coleraine from 1703 to 1713, but was been absent on campaign for most of this time. Between 1715 and 1738, he served as military governor of Limerick, and seeing an opportunity for advancement due to the resentment felt by the citizenry towards the corrupt Roches, became involved in the politics of the city.[30] Pierce was already a member of the common council, and in 1726, a mob entered the council chamber at his instigation and demanded the right to vote in the mayoral election, contrary to the New Rules of 1672. Although this was not allowed and the mob withdrew before the election, the fear of a riot induced the common council to elect Pierce as mayor, though by a small majority.[31] To many this seemed to be a coup d'etat, not unlike Stoney Thursday eighty years before.

Soon after General Pierce revived the court d'oyer hundred to provide a platform for his supporters, who were drawn from the mass of the citizens.[32] One of his opponents alleged that 'there had not any such court been held within the memory of man', and denied that it was a properly constituted meeting, claiming instead that it was merely 'a confused assembly of people, irregularly and illegally met together.'[33] However, the court d'oyer hundred continued to be a regular part of the civic constitution until the 1760s. After vacating the mayoralty, Pierce sat as MP for Limerick city between 1727 and 1739. His combination of the positions of military governor, mayor and MP caused great unease among many in the mayoral elite and he was widely regarded as a potential military dictator.[34] Consequently, the Corporation Roches were able to rebuild their power base, and following the death of Pierce in 1739, they re-established their ascendancy in Limerick.

The Revival of the Roches 1739-1761.

From 1739 to the early 1760s, the Corporation Roches again dominated the corporation.[35] The leading figure in the family was now Arthur Roche, son of the late MP George, who was mayor of Limerick on three occasions (1743-4), (1756-7) and (1760-1), while his brother David was also mayor in 1749-50.[36] Their regime in these decades is often considered to be the culmination of the 'Corrupt Corporation.'[37] In 1761, Arthur Roche, the most powerful member of the family, told the House of Commons committee of enquiry into Limerick Corporation that 'he believed that no citizen of Limerick could now get a lucrative office without his consent, or any person be admitted an alderman, burgess or freeman of the said city, without his consent'.[38] The most notorious abuse occurred in 1747 and 1748, when some two-third of the corporation's property was leased to the Roches and their allies for terms of 999 years at very low rents. The corporation's finances suffered a mortal blow, for these properties were effectively lost forever. The Roches also quartered soldiers on Catholic merchants in a sectarian manner while local charities were neglected and even robbed by the corporation.[39]

The regime of the Roches did not result in the family monopolising the mayoralty for between 1702 and 1772, they held the office of mayor for a total of only nine years while their relatives the Vincents served for a total of seven years.[40] However, John Vincent became chamberlain (financial controller) in 1740, and Arthur Roche became town clerk in 1743. Like the mayoralty, appointments to these positions were made annually by the common council, but unlike the mayor, the recorder and town clerk usually served for several years in succession and were regarded as virtually permanent officials rather than annual office-holders.[41] Thus the regime was consolidated by its grip on these two vital civic offices. Nevertheless, the mayoralty continued to be the leading office in the corporation in fact as well as in appearance and was held by some of the most prominent political figures in the city including a number of MPs and even one peer.

Mayor Charles Smyth (1698-1784)

The Smyths were one of the most powerful families in eighteenth-century Limerick. The founder of the dynasty was Thomas (1654-1725), a native of Dundrum in County Down who served as Church of Ireland bishop of Limerick from 1695 to 1725.[42] His son Charles Smyth (1698-1784) served as mayor from 1732 to 1733. He was originally returned as one of the two MPs for Limerick city in 1731 as an ally of General Pierce and an opponent of the Corporation Roches but later became one of their closest political allies. This political suppleness enabled him to become the longest serving MP in the history of Limerick city, sitting from 1731 to 1776 and during these decades he consolidated the family grip on the constituency, which was not to be ended until 1820.[43]

The Smyths were a very well connected and powerful dynasty. One of Charles' brothers Arthur, was successively bishop of Clonfert, Down and Meath, before serving as archbishop of Dublin from 1766 to 1772, while another, George (1705-72) was MP for Blessington from 1759 to 1768.[44] In 1728, Charles Smyth married Elizabeth Prendergast, sister of Sir Thomas Prendergast (1700-60), owner of the town of Gort, and other large estates in County Galway.[45] On the death of Sir Thomas Prendergast, his property came into the possession of his nephew, John Smyth, (son of Charles), who consequently took the name of Prendergast.[46]

A barrister who never practiced, Smyth was described by contemporaries as being 'an easy quiet man' and as 'a gentleman of universal good character'.[47] He was the second person since 1691 to be simultaneously an MP and mayor of Limerick (1732-33). Smyth was fairly active politically and sat on forty-three parliamentary committees between 1731 and 1760. He opposed Catholic relief but was relatively enlightened in his attitude to municipal reform as it was he who brought the first improvement commission to Limerick, when he introduced legislation in 1757, providing for the establishment of the Baal's Bridge Commissioners.[48] Smyth died at his home in Kildare Street, Dublin on 18 August 1784 at the advanced age of eighty-six.[49] His sons Thomas (1732-85) and John (1742-1817) successively served as MP for Limerick city between 1776 and 1797. Charles' impact was a major one for a number of reasons. Firstly, a Smyth represented Limerick city in the Irish parliament without a break from 1731 to 1797. Secondly, they were succeeded by their kinsmen the Verekers in both the Irish and British parliaments from 1797 to 1820. Thirdly, the family was to control Limerick's civic government from 1776 to 1841.

Mayor Richard Maunsell (1684-1767).

Charles Smyth's constituency colleague, Richard Maunsell (1684-1767) was also remarkable for his longevity. An alderman for many years, he served as mayor of Limerick from 1734 to 1735, sheriff of County Limerick in 1743 and MP for Limerick city from 1741 to 1761. Although already in his late fifties when he was first returned as MP, he served on seventy-two parliamentary committees between 1741 and 1759.[50] One of his sons Richard was also an alderman of the corporation and served as mayor from 1788 to 1789. Another son Thomas was MP for Kilmallock from 1769 to 1776 and resided at Plassey near Limerick city (later the site of the University of Limerick). Thomas's son, another Thomas was MP for Thomastown, County Kilkenny from 1768 to 1776 and for Granard, County Longford from 1776 to 1783 and with his brother Robert founded the Bank of Limerick (better known as Maunsell's Bank) in 1798.[51] The brothers had made a fortune while serving in India and used some of it to establish the bank which was situated in Bank Place, Limerick. In 1820, Maunsell's Bank collapsed and with it the family's fortune and prosperity.[52] The Maunsells should not be confused with the Monsells of Tervoe, who were a prominent landed family in the Clarina area for some three hundred years and to whom they were only distantly related.

Thomas Southwell, second Baron Southwell of Castle Matrix (1698-1766).

Although the Southwells had settled in Ireland in the early seventeenth century, it was Sir Thomas Southwell (1665-1720) who made them a major landed family.[53] Following the Treaty of Limerick he acquired some 7,000 acres in the vicinity of the town of Rathkeale in County Limerick and introduced 130 Palatine families of German origins to the area.[54] Sir Thomas also became a major political figure and was MP for County Limerick from

1695 to 1699, 1703 to 1713 and 1715 to 1717.[55] He was created the first Baron Southwell in 1717 so his son Thomas succeeded him as MP for County Limerick from 1717 to 1720. On the death of his father, the younger Thomas became the second Lord Southwell. He resided at Castle Matrix, near Rathkeale but also had interests in Limerick city. In 1730 he was allowed to hold fairs at Singland and he also served as constable of King John's Castle. Lord Southwell was the only peer ever to be mayor of Limerick and served from 1737 to 1738. One of the richest and best-connected mayors in the history of the city, he married a high-born wife, Mary Coke who was a Lady of the Bedchamber to Queen Caroline, wife of King George II. The Southwell family had a strong connection with freemasonry and in 1743 the second Baron Southwell was appointed Grand Master of the Grand Lodge of Irish Freemasons. His brother Henry (1700-58) was MP for County Limerick from 1729 to 1758 and was mayor of Limerick from 1750 to 1751 while his son and successor Thomas (1720-80) was MP for Enniscorthy from 1747 to 1760 and for County Limerick from 1761 to 1766.[56]

The Smyths and the Verekers.

The most powerful political empire ever built in Limerick city was that of the Smyths and the Verekers. In 1761, a committee of the Irish parliament censured the Roches for their corrupt and selfish rule in Limerick, and their regime came to an end. However, their ally Charles Smyth continued to sit as MP for Limerick until his resignation in 1776, when he was succeeded by his son Thomas.[57] In the same year as he became MP, Thomas Smyth took control of the city government and thus established a regime that lasted sixty-five years. Describing this virtual coup d'etat, John Ferrar wrote: 'there was a revolution in the corporation when the direction of the common council fell into the hands of Thomas Smyth Esq.'[58] The large estates of the Prendergast family in County Galway had given the Smyths the financial resources to rival the Perys and to take over the corporation.

When Thomas died unmarried in 1785, he was succeeded by his brother John Prendergast Smyth (1742-1817), who sat as MP for Limerick city from 1785 until 1797 and controlled the corporation from 1785 to 1817.[59] In 1810, John was created Baron Kiltartan, and in 1816, Viscount Gort, both titles being taken from his Galway properties.[60] However, the first Lord Gort was also a life long bachelor, so with his death in 1817, the Smyth family of Limerick city became extinct, and their properties and political empire passed into the hands of their nephew Charles Vereker.

The Verekers were of Dutch ancestry and settled in Limerick in the reign of Queen Anne. In 1759, Thomas Vereker married Juliana Smyth, daughter of Charles Smyth and eldest sister of Thomas and John. Thomas Vereker was himself a man of property and political influence and served as sheriff of Limerick in 1762-3 and mayor 1767-8. His brother John was sheriff in 1763-4 and mayor 1769-70. Thomas and Juliana's son Charles was born in 1768 during his father's mayoralty, which presaged his future role as dictator of Limerick Corporation for twenty-five years.[61] Indeed, Charles Vereker (1768-1842) became the most powerful political boss ever seen in Limerick. He controlled the combined property and influence of the Prendergast, Smyth and Vereker families and sat for Limerick city in the Irish parliament (1794-1800) and at Westminster (1802-17). In the latter year, he succeeded his uncle as Lord Gort, and passed the family seat to his son John (1790-1865) who sat from 1817 to 1820. Charles Vereker not only dominated Limerick Corporation, and grand jury from 1817 to 1841 but as colonel of the city militia he also controlled the military in the city.[62]

The power of the Smyths and Verekers culminated between 1794 and 1797, and again from 1802 to 1820, when they monopolised the parliamentary representation of the city. Their combination of military and civil authority was similar to that held by General Pierce but while he had only controlled the corporation for a short time and later had to share power with the Roches, the Smyth-Verekers had absolute control for sixty-five years. Their political machine was far more sophisticated and pervasive than anything previously seen in Limerick city and was built around the extensive use of the non-freeman vote. During their ascendancy, the court d'oyer hundred was almost continuously in abeyance, leaving the common council in complete control of municipal affairs.[63]

Other abuses practiced during the Smyth-Vereker period included the following: the head of the Smyth-Vereker family, like Arthur Roche appointed all mayors, aldermen, sheriffs, recorders, common councillors, freemen and justices of the peace. As a result, many corrupt, unqualified and inept persons were appointed to positions in the corporation. The city charities were again the target of municipal rapacity and the second Lord Gort himself took £796 from one of them. Corporation properties were also alienated to members of the mayoral elite and were lost forever to the local authority. By 1841, virtually all of the corporation's properties had been lost in this manner.[64]

The three successive members of the family who controlled Limerick, namely Thomas Smyth (in 1776-85), his brother John Prendergast Smyth, later first Lord Gort (in 1785-1817) and the latter's nephew, Charles Vereker, second Lord Gort (in 1817-41), each held the key position of chamberlain (financial controller) of Limerick Corporation for long periods, while family members or allies held other municipal offices. A Vereker was mayor of Limerick on eight occasions between 1815 and 1841 and in 1833 no fewer than ten out of a total of sixty-nine members of the common council were members or connexions of the family.[65]

Mayor Thomas Smyth (1732-1785).

One of the most dynamic and popular figures in eighteenth century Limerick, Thomas Smyth as the eldest son and heir of the long serving Charles, succeeded to the family seat in Limerick city on the latter's retirement in 1776. He had briefly served as MP for Ballyshannon from 1775 to 1776 as he was a close ally of Thomas Conolly, Ireland's richest man who resided in Ireland's largest house Castletown House, and owned the town of Ballyshannon. Thomas Smyth served as mayor on two occasions, from 1764 to 1765 and from 1776 to 1777. During the first of these, he rode the bounds of Limerick city and its liberties with great ceremony and during his second term he held a great civic jubilee. It was also during his second mayoralty that he took control of the corporation and inaugurated the sixty-five year hegemony of the Smyth-Vereker connexion. During his second mayoralty, he emulated his father by serving as MP and mayor simultaneously. However it was not as mayor but as chamberlain that he effectively controlled the corporation for nearly a decade (1776-85).[66]

In the long eighteenth century, Limerick Corporation was seldom headed by far-sighted or able mayors, but Thomas Smyth was a rare exception. By reducing the mayor's salary and other economies he began an ambitious programme of public works, although his premature death prevented him from realising most of his plans.[67] His greatest achievement was the rebuilding of the Exchange. In 1702, the civic headquarters, which had been severely damaged during the sieges of 1690-91, was rebuilt during the mayoralty of William Davis, but in 1761, the parliamentary committee investigating Limerick Corporation

The beautiful and historic Exchange from a painting of 1820.
It was the headquarters of Limerick Corporation from 1673 to 1846.
(Jim Kemmy Municipal Museum)

reported that 'the tholsel and market house (the Exchange) of the said city are in a ruinous condition.'[68] Thomas Smyth had the Exchange entirely rebuilt in 1777-78 at a cost of £1500. The dean and chapter of St. Mary's Cathedral had donated a part of the churchyard to the corporation, so the new Exchange was larger than the old, and unlike the latter, it did not project onto the street. Ferrar wrote that 'it is supported by seven stone columns in the Tuscan order; the front is composed of cut stone, the windows trimmed with stone architraves and cornices, with a Tuscan entablature at the top. The council chamber is forty feet in length, thirty in breadth, and fifteen feet high, finished in the Ionic order.'[69] The Exchange, as rebuilt by Smyth, served as Limerick's town hall between 1778 and 1846.

In 1720, Limerick Corporation had built an official residence for the mayor, which was known as the mayoralty house and was situated in the churchyard of St. Mary's Cathedral, across Bridge Street from the city courthouse. In 1782 it was vacated by Smyth who intended to replace it with a more impressive residence, but his death resulted in the project being abandoned, and the mayor of Limerick was never again to enjoy the use of an official residence. The old mayoralty house was eventually demolished.[70]

Smyth was a supporter of the Volunteer movement and formed the citizens of Limerick into a militia regiment called the Limerick Union which was later superseded by the Loyal Limerick Volunteers of which he became commander with the rank of colonel. His brother John formed and commanded another regiment called the Limerick Independents. On 28 July 1783, Thomas Smyth as reviewing general presided at a review of several Volunteer regiments of cavalry and infantry from Counties Limerick and Clare at Loughmore near Mungret in County Limerick.[71]

Smyth never married but was reputed to be the father of four illegitimate children who for some unknown reason, were given the surname of Stuart. The most distinguished of these was Major-General Charles Stuart (1758-1828) who went to India at a young age and lived there all his life. Unusually for a European of his time, he became an enthusiastic devotee of Indian culture and customs. He wore Indian clothes, collected Indian sculpture and is even believed to have practiced Hinduism. In consequence he opposed the activities of Christian missionaries in India and was nicknamed 'Hindoo Stuart'.[72] Thomas Smyth himself died on 14 January 1785 in Bordeaux and in accordance with his express instructions, his body was brought back to Limerick and interred in St Munchin's Church.[73] According to Ferrar, Smyth was 'possessed of an excellent heart and amiable manners, he exercised his power without authority, and Limerick never enjoyed more peace and happiness than during the few years he represented it in parliament'.[74]

Mayor Andrew Watson (c. 1762-1832).

Andrew Watson was born and reared in Limerick city and according to his obituary in the *Limerick Herald* 'from infancy to the last stage of his existence he resided among his fellow-citizens'.[75] In 1781, he took over the ownership of the *Limerick Chronicle* from

John Ferrar the distinguished historian who had founded it in 1766, and continued to publish it until 1810. As a staunch ally of the Smyths and Verekers, Andrew Watson stoutly supported their political hegemony and was a member of the common council for most of his adult life. Indeed, he played a major role in the corporation, serving as sheriff in 1796 and 1798 and mayor from 1812 to 1813.[76]

One of Watson's most notable roles in Limerick city was as treasurer of the house of industry or workhouse, which had been built in 1774 on the North (now Clancy) Strand to serve both Limerick city and county. The governing body consisted of the mayor, recorder and charter justices of Limerick city, the magistrates of County Limerick, the Protestant bishop, and individual subscribers who became either annual or life governors, depending on the size of their donations.[77] The inmates of the workhouse consisted of the old and infirm, beggars, widows and orphans, abandoned children, destitute females, and the mentally handicapped.[78] There was also a house of correction for women, and two schools, one for the boys and one for the girls living in the institution. In the 1820s, it housed 450 inmates in conditions of gross overcrowding, for it was built to house only 200. Discipline was strict, food plain, and conditions spartan, but it was well run by the standards of the time, and attracted praise from the renowned prison reformer Elizabeth Fry when she visited it in 1827. The treasurer was actually the manager rather than merely financial controller and in this role Watson administered the workhouse in what was described as a 'judicious and economical' manner' for over forty years.[79] Indeed it was believed that it was his ability to operate the institution within a very tight budget that enabled it to remain in existence for so long a period. Andrew Watson can be described as the archetypical 'insider' whose multi-faceted involvement in the life of Limerick city made him one of its leading citizens for some fifty years. His son Henry was to serve as mayor of Limerick on four occasions: 1823-24, 1824-25, 1825-26 and 1854.[80]

John Prendergast Vereker, third Viscount Gort (1790-1865).

In view of the fact that he was born in the mayoralty house during the period when his father served as mayor, it is somewhat ironic that Charles Vereker, second Lord Gort never served as mayor of Limerick. However, his eldest son and heir John did so for two successive terms, 1831-32 and 1832-33.[81] Previously, John Vereker had sat as MP for Limerick city from 1817 to 1820 before losing his seat to Thomas Spring Rice in the general election of the latter year. John was unfortunate in that he presided over the decline of the power and wealth of the Verekers. He was the last of his family to represent Limerick in parliament and he succeeded his father as Lord Gort in 1842, shortly after the ending of the Verekers' control of Limerick Corporation. Indeed his brother Charles was the last mayor of Limerick under the old corporation (1841-42).[82] During the 1840s, the family became bankrupt as a result of the Famine and in 1851 Lough Cutra Castle and the entire estate in County Galway, including the town of Gort was sold.[83] However, the Verekers continued to own a large estate in the parish of Donoughmore near Limerick city until 1906.[84]

The Perys.

From 1761 to 1800, the Smyth-Vereker connection shared the parliamentary representation of Limerick city with the Perys.[85] Although they were the largest landowners in Limerick city and its liberties, the Perys did not become politically prominent until the time of Edmund Sexton Pery (1719-1806). Elected to the common council in 1748, Pery sat as MP for Limerick city from 1761 to 1785 and served as Speaker of the Irish House of Commons from 1771 to 1785, before being raised to the peerage as Viscount Pery of Newtown Pery.[86] He was succeeded as MP for the city by his nephew, Edmond, (1758-1844), who sat from 1786 to 1794 and in 1803 became the first Earl of Limerick.[87] Despite their great wealth and political prominence, no Pery ever held the office of mayor of Limerick, which is indicative of the iron grip on the corporation held by the Smyth-Vereker connexion.

Nevertheless, the Smyth-Verekers and the Perys, with one seat each, shared the city's parliamentary representation fairly amicably for most of the period 1761 to 1800. However, the Act of Union reduced Limerick's parliamentary representation to one seat for which the two dynasties fought furiously from 1800 to 1820. During these years the Verekers controlled the corporation, the grand jury, the military, the parliamentary and local electorate and the seat at Westminster. At the general election of 1820, Thomas Spring-Rice, son-in-law of Lord Limerick, won the seat from John Vereker only because a select committee of the House of Commons disallowed the votes of the non-resident freemen.[88] From 1820 to 1832, Spring-Rice held Limerick city in the Pery interest and the Verekers never regained it but they continued to control the corporation until 1841.[89]

The Emergence of Alternative Local Authorities.

Although after 1603, central government had extended its rule over the whole country, and Limerick had ceased to be a city-state, the corporation continued to provide the city with the vast bulk of its public services until the beginning of the eighteenth century. In 1672, Mayor George Ingoldsby had told the Lord Lieutenant of Ireland that the corporation's functions in the area of infrastructure were 'to maintain the walls of both divisions of the city, four drawbridges, two great stone bridges, one with five and the other with fourteen arches, twelve gates or posterns in the city walls, above ten bridges in the liberties, and in the several ways leading to and from the city, at least twelve miles of paved causeway.'[90] However, as the eighteenth century progressed, the role of the corporation declined steadily, due to both increasing inefficiency and emphasis on political activity and the unprecedented demands made by an expanding and developing city.[91]

In consequence, new service providers emerged including existing institutions, which had evolved into local authorities (the grand jury and the parish vestries); new institutions established by Act of Parliament; central government and private enterprise. Of these, the most important were the new statutory authorities, known as 'statutory bodies for special purposes,' that were established and given taxing and borrowing powers in order to provide a range of services either abandoned by or never provided by the corporation.[92] They included stand-alone statutory bodies such as turnpike trusts (which built and maintained roads), corporations of the poor (which built and administered workhouses) and improvement commissions.[93]

Improvement commissions were alternative local authorities consisting of a body of appointed or elected commissioners charged with the provision of services.[94] In 1757, ex-mayor Charles Smyth MP introduced them to Limerick city when he promoted the establishment of the Baal's Bridge Commission.[95] The function of this body was to widen and repair, or alternatively to rebuild Baal's Bridge, but they did not succeed in doing so.[96] Two other improvement commissions were later appointed in the city and enjoyed much greater success. In 1807, the Commissioners of St. Michael's Parish were established to administer Newtown Pery and the Limerick Bridge (later the Harbour Commissioners) were set up in 1823 to administer Limerick port.[97]

By 1841, the monolithic role of Limerick Corporation had been superseded by the activities of a wide variety of agencies. The seven main service providers were now the corporation, the grand jury, the parish vestries, the improvement commissioners, the stand-alone institutions, central government and the private sector. Defence was now under the control of central government. The corporation, the parish vestries, improvement commissions, and central government provided police and the night watch. The prison service was under the control of the corporation and the grand jury. The local legal system and control of the economy were under the corporation's control. The lax weir was leased to a private company while the port came under the control of an improvement commission. Street cleaning and water supply were provided by the private sector. Street lighting and the fire service were under the control of the parish vestries and the private sector. Infrastructure was built and maintained by all the service providers except the stand-alone bodies. Finally, all seven were involved in varying degrees in the provision of social welfare, education and health.[98]

Corporation Ceremonial and Regalia.

Nevertheless, the mayor of Limerick remained a figure of great power and prestige and continued to behave like a local king. On 5 and 6 September 1765, Mayor Thomas Smyth rode the bounds of the city and its liberties, in accordance with the 1609 charter. On this occasion, it was a huge procession, led by servants, bailiffs, and the mayor's sergeants, followed by a military band, the sword bearer and water bailiff, the two sheriffs, the mayor, then the members of the corporation, and finally the representatives of the trade guilds. All were on horseback, all richly dressed, and many carried ceremonial banners. On the 10 September, the mayor and his party sailed to Scattery Island where he held a court of admiralty. Then, he dropped a dart into the water at the mouth of the Shannon. This was a ceremony similar to those carried out by the lord mayor of Dublin, the mayor of Cork, and other civic magistrates who possessed admiralty jurisdiction. These pageants were based on the spectacular annual ceremony held by the doge (chief executive) of the Republic of Venice, when he sailed out to the Adriatic Sea, accompanied by a huge entourage and threw a gold dart into the water, as a symbol of his sovereignty over the sea. In 1765, the mayor of Limerick used the occasion of his riding the bounds to entertain his municipal colleagues and the representatives of the trade guilds in a lavish banquet where vast amounts of food were consumed and wine flowed freely.[99]

In 1776, Thomas Smyth was again elected mayor of Limerick, was elected MP for the city and also seized control of the corporation. He decided to commemorate his annus *mirabilis* by holding a civic jubilee in Limerick city, which began on 12 August with the most splendid riding of the bounds ever staged up to that time. That same night a fancy dress ball was held, and over the next few days there followed a series of glittering events attended by the elite of the city and the neighbouring counties: a play in the city's theatre; a 'Venetian breakfast' and regatta; an oratorio in St. Mary's Cathedral; a grand ball in the city assembly rooms on Charlotte's Quay; and a concert of vocal and instrumental music.[100]

The Crescent, one of Limerick's most striking Georgian streetscapes.
(Jim Kemmy Municipal Museum)

On the 5 June 1755, the Marquess of Hartington, lord lieutenant of Ireland arrived in Limerick for an official visit and stayed for a number of days. He later served as prime minister of Great Britain from 1756 to 1757 under the title of Duke of Devonshire.[101] Other lords lieutenant to make official visits included Lord Townsend in 1768, the Duke of Rutland in 1785 and the Duke of Richmond in 1807.[102] All were received by the mayor and corporation with appropriate and elaborate ceremonial, in accordance with the grandiose expectations of the period.

The corporation continued to accumulate civic regalia and acquired four silver maces in 1739 to replace the existing ones.[103] The maces were carried in procession on ceremonial occasions by four richly attired mace-bearers. Mayoral chains were uncommon in Britain and Ireland before the eighteenth century and there is no reference to the wearing of ceremonial chains by the mayor and sheriffs of Limerick Corporation before 1820, which would seem to indicate that the custom only commenced in that year.[104] In 1820 four gold chains of office were purchased, two were for the mayor and the others for the two sheriffs. The Mayor's principal chain was only worn on major ceremonial occasions due to its great weight. From 1822 onwards many of the mayors added extra links to the chain inscribed with their name, year of office and (after 1841) details of the events of their mayoralty. The practice continues to the time of writing. However, the mayor generally used the second chain, which consisted of fifty-one plain links and was much easier to wear. After the establishment of the reformed corporation in 1841, the two sheriffs' chains were worn by the town clerk and the city treasurer.[105]

The wearing of civic gowns by the mayor, sheriffs and aldermen dated back to the Middle Ages although the councillors did not start wearing them until a later period. In addition, the mayor's serjeants and constables, the sheriffs' bailiffs and the sword-bearer also wore ceremonial costumes.[106] In 1543, the mayor had been given the right to carry a wand of office. In the long eighteenth century, which was an age of monarchy and monarchical splendour, the mayor of Limerick, wearing his scarlet robes and carrying his ceremonial wand like a sceptre, appeared to be every inch a local king.

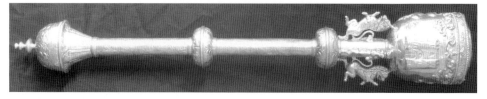

One of the four silver civic maces made for Limerick Corporation in 1739
(Jim Kemmy Municipal Museum)

Limerick's Economic and Spatial Revolution.

Although Ireland outside North-East Ulster did not experience an industrial revolution, it did experience an economic revolution between 1747 and 1815. The Irish economy grew by 400% during this unprecedented boom and in 1815 was five times bigger than it had been in 1730.[107] After 1750 Limerick also underwent an economic revolution. The tonnage of shipping that used the port increased by nearly 75% between 1751 and 1775 and almost doubled again between 1776 and 1800.[108] Customs receipts increased from £16,000 in 1751 to £32,000 in 1764 and £70,000 in 1821.[109] Limerick city's population increased from 11,000 in 1706 to 32,000 in 1776, and 48,000 in 1841.[110] Indeed between 1700 and 1841, the population of Limerick grew faster than that of any other Irish city except Belfast.[111]

The economic boom resulted in the creation of Newtown Pery, the most important development in Limerick between 1691 and 1841 and one of the most spectacular examples of Ireland's urban renaissance at this time.[112] Between 1770 and 1840, a whole new Georgian city was created which as early as 1822 contained 2,000 houses and 16,000 inhabitants, including within its boundaries 'all the wealth and trade of the city.'[113] Henceforth Limerick was to consist of an 'old town' in decline and a glittering 'new town' in the ascendancy.[114]

The enormous expansion of Limerick in wealth and population at this time lends credence to Rosemary Sweet's thesis that the medieval constitutions and administrative structures of the borough corporations were completely inadequate to cope with the rapid changes of the long eighteenth century. Interestingly, this economic and spatial transformation brought about a revival of the fortunes of the Catholic elite that had lost political control of the city in the 1650s. The families of Arthur, Roche and Comyn were among the significant merchant dynasties of the city whose wealth increased rapidly in this period.[115]

Because of the perceived inadequacy of the corporation, the Commissioners of St. Michael's Parish, consisting of twenty-one members, some of whom were elected and others appointed for life, were established in 1807 to govern Newtown Pery. Like the modern Vatican City, St. Michael's Parish became an independent enclave, in the centre of the area administered by Limerick Corporation. The commissioners maintained and cleaned the streets, provided street lighting and established a night watch (in effect a local police service). In the 1820s and 1830s, they introduced gas lighting and a piped water supply to Newtown Pery by entering into contracts with private companies to provide these services.[116] In general, the administration of the commissioners was somewhat more efficient and innovative than that of the corporation. The latter continued to administer the old city (Englishtown and Irishtown) and the liberties, so that there were effectively two rival corporations in Limerick until the abolition of St. Michael's Parish Commissioners in 1853.

The First Attempt to Reform the Corporation.

In 1761, a committee of the Irish House of Commons chaired by Edmond Sexton Pery investigated the abuses of the Corporation Roches, produced a report that severely condemned them, and recommended legislation to reform the Corporation.[117] The result was the 'Bill for better regulating the Corporation of the City of Limerick' introduced in the Irish Parliament in 1762. The election of the mayor was to be placed in the hands of both the court d'oyer hundred and the common council. The freemen, meeting in the court, were to choose four candidates by lot from their own ranks, and the common council would then elect one of the four to be mayor. The election of the two sheriffs was to be conducted as follows: the mayor and common council were to choose three candidates, and the court d'oyer hundred would elect one of these, while the process would be reversed in selecting the second sheriff.[118]

While the Bill revived the role of the court d'oyer hundred in electing the mayor, it did not exclude members of the common council from sitting in it, and thus their control over it would still have continued. However, even this flawed Bill did not become law. It passed the various stages of the Irish Parliament and was approved by the Lord Lieutenant and the Irish Privy Council, but was voted down by the British Privy Council and in consequence lapsed. The British privy councillors feared that the Bill would give excessive powers of the court d'oyer hundred, and thus create the danger that Catholic mobs might bring pressure to bear on the freemen and undermine the Protestant ascendancy in the city. They believed that the end result could be a return to the revolutionary 1640s and Catholic domination of the city. [119]

The Second Attempt to Reform the Corporation.

In the 1820 general election, the sitting MP for Limerick city representing the 'Corrupt Corporation', John Prendergast Vereker, was defeated by Thomas Spring Rice representing the Perys and the reformers, due to the fact that the votes of the non-resident freemen were disallowed. In 1822, Spring Rice acted as chairman of a select committee of the British House of Commons, which examined the entire local government system in Limerick and recommended that legislation be enacted to bring about its reform.[120]

The result was the Limerick Regulation Act of 1823, commonly known as Spring Rice's Act, in honour of its author.[121] Its main provision was the restoration of the court d'oyer hundred, consisting of the whole body of the freemen. It was chaired by the common speaker, who was

Thomas Spring Rice
(Limerick Chamber of Commerce.
Photograph by Egleston Brothers
Photographers)

elected by the court every two years. All acts of the corporation, having been passed at common council, were now required to be approved by the court. The election of officers was the only function still in the exclusive hands of the common council. This act contained most of the improvements that had been included in the Bill of 1762, but was for that very reason a failure. The mayor, and common council as freemen, took part in the proceedings of the court d'oyer hundred, and were able to control it, as had previously happened between the 1720s and the 1760s. Worst of all, the constitution of the common council was left untouched and it continued to be self-selecting and to control the election of the mayor and sheriffs. To the intense annoyance of the reformers the 'Corrupt Corporation' continued to govern Limerick city for the next twenty years.[122]

Endnotes

1   Webb, *Municipal Government*, p. 154.

2   R. B. Mc Dowell, 'Ireland in 1800' in T.W. Moody and W.E. Vaughan (eds), *A New History of Ireland, Vol. IV, Eighteenth-Century Ireland 1691-1800*, (Oxford, 1986), p. 705.

3   For Limerick Corporation see William Patrick Mulligan, 'The Enemy Within; The Enemy Without. How the Wealthier Class Manipulated Local Government in Nineteenth Century Limerick'. (Unpublished MA thesis, University of Limerick, 2005), which, despite its name, deals extensively with the eighteenth as well as the nineteenth centuries.

4   Lenihan, *History of Limerick*, p.447.

5   O'Flaherty, 'Urban Politics and Municipal Reform in Limerick,' p. 106.

6   The most comprehensive account of the local government system in eighteenth century Irish urban areas is Kenneth Milne, 'The Irish Municipal Corporations in the Eighteenth Century', (Unpublished Ph.D. thesis Trinity College, Dublin, 1962).

7   See also Sweet, *The English Town*, pp 27-161.

8   Sweet, *The English Town*, pp 141-50.

9   For England's urban renaissance see Peter Borsay, *The English Urban Renaissance, Culture and Society in the Provincial Town, 1660-1770*, (Oxford, 1989).

10   Milne, 'Irish Muncipal Corporations', pp 23-24, 145.

11   *Municipal Corporations Report*, pp 356-58.

12   Jennifer Ridden, ' Making Good Citizens': National Identity, Religion and Liberalism among the Irish Elite, c. 1800-1850 (Unpublished Ph.D. thesis, London University, 1998), pp 157-58.

13   *Municipal Corporations Report*, pp 352-53.

14   Ibid., p. 353.

15   Webb, *Municipal Government*, pp 168-70. For non –resident members of Limerick Common Council see *Municipal Corporations Report*, pp 361-62.

16   Ridden, 'Making Good Citizens', pp 156-58.

17   *Municipal Corporations Report*, p. 347.

18   *A True State of the Present Affairs of Limerick*, pp 33, 37-38 and *Municipal Corporations Report*, p. 356.

19   Anonymous (but the author was actually Dean Charles Massy), *A Collection of Resolutions, Queries, &c. Wrote on Occasion of the Present Dispute in the City of Limerick*, (Limerick, 1726), *passim* and *Municipal Corporations Report*, pp 352-55.

20   *Report of the Committee of 1822*, pp 4-5.

21   Ibid., p. 8.

22   Potter, *The Government and the People of Limerick*, pp 235-37.

23   The political situation in early eighteenth century Limerick is well described in Toby Barnard, *The Abduction of a Limerick Heiress. Social and Political Relations in Mid-Eighteenth Century Ireland*, (Dublin, 1998), pp 11-17, 40-47.

24   For the succession list of the Roches see Charles Mosley (ed.), *Burke's Peerage and Baronetage*, 2 Vols. (106th edition, Crans, Switzerland, 1999), Vol. 2, p. 2429.

25   Lenihan, *History of Limerick*, p. 704.

26   E. M. Johnston-Liik, *History of the Irish Parliament 1692-1800: Commons, Constituencies and Statutes 1692-1800*, 6 vols, (Belfast, 2002), Vol. VI, p. 172.

27 Lenihan, *History of Limerick*, p. 323.

28 For a brief profile of Pierce see Johnson-Liik, *History of the Irish Parliament*, VI, pp 35-36.

29 Ibid., pp 33-35.

30 Barnard, *Abduction of a Limerick Heiress*, p. 41.

31 *A True State of the Present Affairs of Limerick*, pp 18-29.

32 Ibid., pp 33-39.

33 Ibid., p. 33.

34 *A True State of the Present Affairs of Limerick*, *passim*.

35 O'Flaherty, ' Urban Politics and Municipal Reform', p. 109.

36 Lenihan, *History of Limerick*, p. 705.

37 A full account of the regime of the Roches in the 1740s and 1750s can be found in *Report from a Committee of the Irish House of Commons, on Petition from Freemen of Limerick, &c. 23rd December, 1761*, H.C. 1820 (270), (hereafter referred to as *Report of the Committee of 1761*).

38 Ibid., p. 9.

39 The best accounts of corruption under the Roches are to be found in *A Collection of Resolutions, and Report of the Committee of 1761*.

40 Lenihan, *History of Limerick*, pp 704-05.

41 Potter, *The Government and the People of Limerick*, pp 197-98.

42 Bishop Smyth's career is described in Lenihan, *History of Limerick*, pp 223-24 and Begley, *The Diocese of Limerick*, III, pp 135-42.

43 Johnson-Liik, *History of the Irish Parliament*, Vol. VI, pp 293-94.

44 Lenihan, *History of Limerick*, pp 223-25.

45 Johnson-Liik, *History of the Irish Parliament*, VI, pp 116-17.

46 Ibid., pp 115-16.

47 Ibid., p. 294.

48 Ibid.

49 Ibid.

50 Ibid., Vol. V, pp 217-18.

51 Ibid., pp 218-20.

52 For Maunsell's Bank see Hannan, *Limerick Historical Reflections*, pp 123-24.

53 Southwell is pronounced 'suddle.'

54 See Patrick J O'Connor, *All Ireland is in and about Rathkeale*, (Newcastle West, County Limerick, 1996) pp 70-74.

55 Johnson-Liik, *History of the Irish Parliament*, VI, pp 308-13.

56 Ibid.

57 Ibid., Vol. VI, pp 298-99.

58 Ferrar, *History of Limerick*, pp 91-92.

59 Johnson-Liik, *History of the Irish Parliament*, VI, pp 115-16.

60 Ibid.

61 Lenihan, *History of Limerick*, pp 224-25 and Mosley, *Burkes Peerage*, Vol. I, pp 1181-84.

62 For Charles Vereker, see Viscount Gort, Notes on the Gort Family (unpublished manuscript in the possession of the Knight of Glin, Glin Castle, County Limerick), pp 300-13; *Limerick Chronicle*, November 16, 1842; *Limerick Reporter*, November 15, 1842; *Dictionary of National Biography*, Vol. XX, pp 247-48.

63 Potter, *The Government and the People of Limerick*, pp 198-99.

64 The most comprehensive accounts of corruption under the Smyth-Verekers are to be found in *Report from the Select Committee on the Limerick Election Together with the Special Report from the Said Committee*, H.C. 1820 (229), iii (hereafter referred to as *Report of the Committee of 1820*); *Report of the Committee of 1822* and *Municipal Corporations Report*, pp 343-412.

65 *Municipal Corporations Report*, pp 357-58.

66 For Thomas Smyth, see Johnson-Liik, *History of the Irish Parliament*, VI, pp 298-99.

67 Ferrar, *History of Limerick*, pp 91-92.

68 *Report of the Committee of 1761*, p. 24.

69 Ibid., p. 201.

70 Ibid., p. 202.

71 Lenihan, *History of Limerick*, pp 383-86.

72 For Stuart, see Liz Wood, 'Charles Stuart' in Colin Matthew, Brian Harrison and Laurence Goldman (eds), *Oxford Dictionary of National Biography* (Oxford, 2004-07) consulted online at www.oxforddnb.com and William Dalrymple, *White Mughals*, (London, 2002), pp 36,42-44, 48-49, 372, 433, 496.

73 Lenihan, *History of Limerick*, p. 225.

74 Ferrar, *History of Limerick*, p. 92.

75 *Limerick Herald*, 17 September 1832.

76 Mulligan, 'The Enemy Within: The Enemy Without', pp 153-54.

77 Lenihan, *History of Limerick*, pp 496-98.

78 *Municipal Corporations Report*, p. 377.

79 Fitzgerald and McGregor, *History of Limerick*, II, p. 597.

80 *Limerick Chronicle*, 14 March 1860.

81 For John Prendergast Vereker, see Mosley, *Burkes Peerage*, I, pp 1181-83.

82 Lenihan, *History of Limerick*, pp 496-98.

83 Mark Bence-Jones, *A Guide to Irish Country Houses,* (London, 1988), p.192.

84 Thomas Toomey and Harry Greensmyth, *An Antique and Storied Land. A History of the Parish of Donoughmore, Knockea, Roxborough and its Environs in County Limerick,* (Limerick, 1991), pp 120-23.

85 The best account of the Perys in the long eighteenth century is A. P. W. Malcomson , 'Speaker Pery and the Pery Papers' in *North Munster Antiquarian Journal*, Vol. XVI, (1973-74), pp 33-60.

86 Johnston-Liik, *History of the Irish Parliament*, VI, pp 55-59.

87 The Pery succession list can be found in Mosley, *Burkes Peerage*, II, pp 1709-11.

88 For the events leading up to Spring Rice's triumph, see Ridden, 'Making Good Citizens', pp 162-69.

89 Ibid., pp 176-77.

90 *Report from the Select Committee on Petitions Relating to the Local Taxation of the City of Limerick, H.C.1822* (617), vii. (hereafter known as *Report of the Committee of 1822*), p. 7.

91 For an account of the functions of Limerick Corporation in the long eighteenth century see Potter, *The Government and the People of Limerick*, pp 202-35.

92 For a definitive account of alternative local bodies in England at this time see Sidney and Beatrice Webb, *Statutory Bodies For Special Purposes*, (London, 1922). See also Sweet, *The English Town*, pp 44-56.

93 For the increase in local legislation see Sir David Lindsay Keir, *The Constitutional History of Modern Britain Since 1485*, (9th Edition, London, 1968), p. 316. A modern account of the growth of local acts is Joanna Innes, 'The Local Acts of a National Parliament: Parliament's Role in Sanctioning Local Action in Eighteenth-Century Britain', in *Parliamentary History*, Vol. 17, No. 1, (1998).

94 Sweet, *The English Town*, pp 44-56.

95 Johnson-Liik, *History of the Irish Parliament*, VI, p. 293.

96 For the Baal's Bridge Commissioners see 31 Geo. II. C. 20.

97 For the Harbour Commissioners see Kevin Donnelly, Michael Hoctor and Dermot Walsh, *A Rising Tide. The Story of Limerick Harbour*, (Limerick, 1994). For St Michael's Parish Commission, see Mulligan, 'The Enemy Within; The Enemy Without', *passim*.

98 Potter, *The Government and the People of Limerick*, pp 202-35.

99 These ceremonies are described in Lenihan, *History of Limerick*, pp 355-56.

100 Ibid., pp 365-66.

101 Ibid., p. 344.

102 Ibid., pp 361, 392 and 417-18.

103 Herbert, 'Antiquities of the Corporation', pp 94-95.

104 Mansfield, *Ceremonial Costume*, p. 269.

105 Ibid., pp 96 and 101.

106 Heather Cunningham, 'Civic Peacocks' in Lee, *Remembering Limerick*, p. 335.

107 L. M. Cullen, 'Economic Development, 1750-1800' in Moody and Vaughan, *A New History of Ireland*, IV, pp 185-87.

108 David Dickson, ' Large-Scale Developers and the Growth of Eighteenth-Century Irish Cities' in P. Butel and L. M. Cullen, (eds), *French and Irish Perspectives on Urban Development, 1500-1900*, (Dublin, 1986), p. 109.

109 Patrick J. O'Connor, *Exploring Limerick's Past. An Historical Geography of Urban Development in County and City*, (Newcastle West, Co. Limerick, 1987), p. 42.

110 Ibid., p. 50.

111 Ibid., p. 36.

112 For Ireland's urban renaissance at this time see L.J. Proudfoot, ' Spatial Transformation and Social Agency: Property, Society and Improvement. 1700 to c. 1900' in Graham and Proudfoot, *An Historical Geography of Ireland*, pp 234-42; B. J. Graham and L. J. Proudfoot, *Urban Improvement in Provincial Ireland, 1700-1840*, (Athlone, 1994) and l. J. Proudfoot, *Property Ownership and Urban and Village Improvement in Provincial Ireland, ca. 1700-1845*, (London, 1997).

113 *Report of the Committee of 1822*, p. 4.

114 For a detailed description of the development of Newtown Pery, see Hill, *The Building of Limerick*, pp 90-141.

115 Dickson, 'Catholics and Trade in Eighteenth-Century Ireland', pp 85-100.

116 *Municipal Corporations Report*, pp 374-75.

117 See *Report of the Committee of 1761*.

118 The main provisions of the Bill are set out in *Report of His Majesty's Attorney and Solicitor General upon the Bill for better regulating the Corporation of Limerick*, (Dublin, 1762).

119 Ibid., pp 7-8.

120 *Report of the Committee of 1822*.

121 4 Geo. IV. c. 126.

122 Potter, *The Government and the People of Limerick*, pp 273-75.

The Mayoralty in the Age of the 'Corrupt Corporation'. 1691-1841

The Town Hall in Rutland Street, built in 1805 as the Commercial Buildings and
headquarters of Limerick Corporation from 1846 to 1990.
(Jim Kemmy Municipal Museum)

Chapter Five
The Mayoralty in the Modern Age.
1842 to the Present

The Establishment of the Modern Mayoralty in the UK and Europe.

In the Western world, the eighteenth and early nineteenth centuries was an age of Enlightenment, of reform and of revolution.[1] The historian Eric Hobsbawm coined the term 'the dual revolution' to describe the impact of the French and Industrial Revolutions on world history.[2] In Britain and Ireland, there were three major intellectual trends behind the movement for administrative and political reform. One was liberalism which wanted to extend civil and religious rights to a larger proportion of the population. The second was utilitarianism, which was founded by Jeremy Bentham (1749-1832) and whose followers believed that all human institutions should serve 'the greatest good of the greatest number'. The third was the classical school of economics which advocated the theory of *laissez-faire* which argued that government should have a very limited role in economic life. Sir David Kier wrote of the reformers of the period 1782-1867 (the high point of all three intellectual movements) that they believed that 'the administrative system needed to be overhauled and stripped of its antiquated survivals and useless accretions'.[3]

All over the Western world, local government, including the mayoralty, was transformed, reformed and modernised as a result of the 'Dual Revolution'. In France, the modern mayoralty was created in 1789 as part of the major administrative changes of the revolutionary era.[4] The modern German mayoralty traces its origins back to the municipal reforms introduced in Prussia in 1808 by Heinrich Friedrich Stein as part of his policy of reviving a kingdom that had been humiliatingly defeated by Napoleon.[5] In Spain, the modern mayoralty was founded in 1836 as part of a widespread programme of administrative and political modernisation.[6] As part of the creation of a united Italy, the Rattazzi Law of 1859 established a new system of local government, including the modern mayoralty.[7] For most of the decade 1830 to 1841, the Whigs ruled the United Kingdom and carried out a general overhaul of the political and administrative system in both Britain and Ireland. Municipal reform was a significant part of the Whig programme. The borough corporations were remodelled in Scotland in 1833 and in England in 1835 and in each case the modern mayoralty can be said to have been created.[8]

The Establishment of the Modern Mayoralty of Limerick.

Between 1836 and 1840, the local government system in Ireland was profoundly transformed by a reform programme which was embodied in three pieces of legislation:

the Grand Jury (Ireland) Act of 1836 which was chiefly applicable to the counties; the Poor Relief (Ireland) Act of 1838, which established the modern health and social welfare systems; and the Municipal Corporations (Ireland) Act of 1840, which transformed the borough corporations.[9]

Under the Municipal Corporations Act the number of boroughs in Ireland was reduced from sixty-eight to ten, in each of which the old corporation was abolished and replaced by a new one.[10] The judicial role of the corporations, including Limerick Corporation, was greatly reduced but the mayor *ex officio* continued to be a justice of the peace and to preside over the mayor's court of conscience. Limerick Corporation lost one of its two sheriffs, and the remaining one was no longer elected by the council, but appointed by the lord lieutenant. In 1876, this provision was to be modified. The corporations were allowed to nominate three persons, and the lord lieutenant then appointed one of these as the sheriff. In the nineteenth and early twentieth century, the sheriff was frequently known as the high sheriff. Control of the grand jury of Limerick city (which was selected by the sheriff) thus passed out of the hands of the corporation. The ineffectual court d'oyer hundred was also abolished a mere eighteen years after its restoration.[11]

The modern Irish mayoralty was created by the Municipal Corporations Act.[12] In Limerick, the common council, a self-electing body of indeterminate number, was replaced by a city council consisting of forty councillors elected by the burgesses (all adult males, in possession of property worth £10 or more per annum). One unintentionally comic consequence of the Act was that the mayor and council were often referred to in succeeding decades as 'Ali Baba and the Forty Thieves!' The city was divided into five electoral districts or wards, each of which was to return eight members to the council. The candidate receiving the greatest number of votes in each ward was to be an alderman, a provision that was not abolished until 2004. However, as the act stipulated that one fourth of the councillors were to be aldermen, three of the wards returned two aldermen each, and the other two one each, making a total of eight aldermen and thirty-two councillors. There was no general election of the council every few years. Instead, one third of the councillors went out of office annually and one half of the aldermen went out of office every three years, in a system similar to the modern United States Senate. In practice this meant councillors were elected for three-year periods and aldermen for six years.[13]

The mayor continued to be indirectly elected by the council, rather than directly by the voters. Annual elections to the council were held on 25 October and of the mayor on 1 November. He held office for one year, starting on 1 January of the following year, and was eligible to stand for re-election. The business of the new corporation continued to be transacted by the mayor and city councillors themselves, in the same manner as it had been in the old. However, the Act of 1840 provided for the appointment of committees of councillors, to oversee particular aspects of municipal business, and in this manner the mayor and councillors supervised the work of the corporation on a day-to-day basis until the appointment of the first city manager in 1934. [14]

The powers given to the new corporations were very limited compared to those of their English and Scottish counterparts. Their main functions under the 1840 Act were to make byelaws for the good government of the borough and the prevention and suppression of nuisances (dangerous or unsanitary buildings, or places).[15] The Act of 1840 also set out the city's new boundaries. In accordance with these recommendations, Limerick Corporation lost control over the liberties and Scattery Island and the area under its jurisdiction dropped from 25,700 acres to 2,395 acres, while the corresponding decline in population was from 66,000 to 44,000. Under the provisions of the Limerick Improvement Act of 1865 and Section 198 of the Public Health (Ireland) Act of 1878 a total of 365 acres was to be added to the city bringing the total area under its control to 2,760 acres.[16] In 1841, the north and south liberties were absorbed into Counties Clare and Limerick.

The Beginning of the Modern Mayoralty of Limerick, (1841-42).

On the 10 August 1841, the Lord Lieutenant issued a proclamation declaring the Act of 1840 operational in Limerick city. Although, the new corporation had few powers, had lost 90% of its territory and was chronically short of money, its establishment was greeted with joy in Limerick as it marked the end of the Protestant ascendancy. The people of Limerick celebrated the downfall of the 'Corrupt Corporation' by holding a huge procession through the city, which took the form of a mock funeral, with a hearse drawn by black-plumed horses containing a huge coffin for the 'remains' of the old corporation. The high point of the ceremony was the burning of the coffin, to the delight of the vast crowd.[17] On 11 November 1841, the new city council unanimously selected Martin Honan to be the first mayor under the Act of 1840. He took office on 1 January 1842 and was the first Catholic mayor since the Treaty of Limerick.[18]

However, the old corporation refused to accept that its time was up.[19] Seizing on the fact that the Lord Lieutenant's proclamation of 12 August was technically in breach of the Act of 1840, the last mayor elected by the old corporation, Charles Smyth Vereker, (second son of Lord Gort) obtained a court order declaring that the workings of the Act in Limerick, including the election of the new mayor and council, were null and void. As a result, there were two corporations and two mayors in operation in Limerick throughout the first half of 1842. Mayor Vereker refused to give possession of the Exchange, or the records, books and property of the corporation to the new body until amending legislation was enacted in July 1842, legalising the acts of the reformed corporation and declaring it to be the rightful local authority. The first real meeting of the new or Second Corporation eventually took place on 3 August 1842 and the old corporation finally disappeared. [20]

The New Town Hall.

Symbolically the new corporation soon acquired a new town hall. In the 1840s, the Exchange was regarded as being too small, too old-fashioned and to be situated in too peripheral a location for a municipal authority that hoped to re-establish its control over Newtown Pery. In 1805, the Commercial Buildings had been built on Rutland Street to house the merchants' association that later became the chamber of commerce. The Commissioners of St. Michael's Parish also used it as their headquarters. In 1833, both bodies moved out when the chamber of commerce moved to its present headquarters at 96 O'Connell Street, and the commissioners moved to their new purpose-built 'town hall' (now the Athenaeum building) on Cecil Street.[21] After a period of decline, during which it was rented out to various tenants, the Commercial Buildings were purchased by the corporation in 1846, and became the new town hall.[22] The first meeting of the city council was held there on 21 January 1847, during the Mayoralty of Thomas Wallnutt.[23]

The new town hall was to serve as the headquarters of the corporation until 1990, but the fate of the old Exchange was to be a sad one. It was abandoned by the corporation and after falling into ruins, was demolished in 1884 and the site absorbed into the burial ground of St. Mary's Cathedral. Only the colonnade from the façade escaped destruction and was incorporated into the wall of the burial ground, where it can still be seen.[24]

The Limerick Improvement and Corporation Acts, 1853.

By 1850, it was clear that three of the principal local authorities in Limerick city were in need of drastic reform. The new corporation was finding it difficult to administer the city, due to its lack of powers under the Act of 1840 and its extremely precarious finances. The Commissioners of St. Michael's Parish were widely perceived to be an anomaly and the grand jury of Limerick city was regarded as being both unrepresentative and unnecessary. Only the Limerick Poor Law Union, established in 1838, was working successfully. The result was the enactment of two important pieces of local legislation in 1853.

The Limerick Improvement Act became law on 15 August 1853.[25] Under its provisions the Commissioners of St. Michael's Parish were abolished and all of their assets and staff transferred to Limerick Corporation. The powers of the commissioners to pave, clean, light and watch were transferred to the corporation, which thus acquired explicit powers to discharge the functions omitted from the 1840 Act. The Act also abolished the financial and administrative role of the grand jury of Limerick city, and transferred these powers to the corporation, which inherited from it responsibility for providing and funding infrastructure, including the construction and repair of roads, bridges and quays, the maintenance of courthouses and jails and contributing to the cost of the district lunatic asylum. In order to provide the corporation with the means to discharge its many new functions, its financial base was radically changed. The 1840 Act had been the first to authorise it to levy rates, but this power had never been availed of. Now, under the

1853 Act, Limerick Corporation was authorised to raise two further types of rates: the general purposes rate to replace grand jury cess and the improvement rate to be used for all other purposes.

The Limerick Corporation Act became law on 28 June.[26] Under its provisions, the city was divided into eight electoral wards, instead of the previous five and the term of office of a councillor was increased from three to four years. Each of the eight wards was to return an alderman to the council. These two Acts came into effect on 1 January 1854. The only other change made in succeeding decades was the abolition of the parish vestry as a local government unit in 1864.[27]

In consequence of these two Acts, the Corporation of Limerick was placed in full control of the city's administration for the first time since 1609 and its obsolete rivals, the Commissioners of St. Michael's Parish and the grand jury abolished. The new 'Third Corporation' formally came into existence on 1 January 1854 following the local elections of the previous November. At the same time, the financial base of Limerick Corporation had been transformed and from 1854 onwards, rates were to be the mainstay of the city's finances.[28]

The Corporation Acquires New Functions 1878-99.

The terrible social problems that afflicted Britain and Ireland in the nineteenth century caused many to doubt the ability of the *laissez faire* economic system and the liberal political system to grapple effectively with the needs of society. One response to this problem was the growth of the various strands of socialism while another was the expansion of the activities of the state in a pragmatic and non-ideological fashion. One of the most widespread examples of the latter was the increasing municipilisation of various services which became known in Britain as 'gas and water socialism'. The provision of gas and electricity, the creation of a good, clean and reliable water supply, slum clearance, and inner city renewal were all features of the activities of British borough corporations at this time, and thereafter. 'Gas and water socialism' was not socialism but a pragmatic response to the huge social changes and many problems caused by the Industrial Revolution. The movement spread to Ireland, for although outside Ulster, the country did not experience the Industrial Revolution, the immense social problems that afflicted Irish towns were similar to those in Britain.[29]

Limerick Corporation embraced 'gas and water socialism' and in consequence expanded its activities considerably in the last twenty-two years of the century. In 1878, it established a municipal fire brigade and in 1879 it purchased the remaining private gas company in Limerick. In 1883, it bought the water supply network. In 1887, it began the building of social housing in the city, and in 1893 it established the first public library in Limerick.[30]

The Local Government Board.

The Local Government Board (LGB) was established in 1872, and was the first central authority to supervise local government in Ireland. Hitherto, local authorities in Ireland had always enjoyed wide autonomy but the LGB was given wide powers over the borough corporations and grand juries. Among its powers were the appointment of auditors, alteration of local government boundaries, transfer of powers between local authorities, and the granting of permission to raise new forms of rates, or to borrow extra monies. The degree of central control over local authorities exercised by the LGB was small by the standards of the modern Department of the Environment and Local Government, but throughout its fifty years in existence, its powers increased steadily. In the 1920s, the LGB was replaced by the Department of Local Government.[31]

The Role of the Mayor of Limerick 1842-99.

Between 1842 and 1899, the mayor of Limerick was elected by the council to serve a one-year term that coincided with the calendar year. From 1841 to 1853, the election of the mayor was held on 1 November, but under the Limerick Corporation Act of 1853, it was changed to 1 December. The mayor was a much more powerful figure than his modern counterpart, combining the ceremonial role of the present position with the powers and authority of the city manager. However, his effectiveness was hampered by the fact that the position was usually held on a part-time basis by a substantial professional or businessman and by the term of office being only for a year, although several mayors served more than one term.

Despite the rise of nationalism and democracy after 1842, the mayoralty continued to be the focus of civic pride and ambition. The importance of the office was due to a number of factors. Firstly, the mayor was the chief executive of the corporation and as such a figure of real power. Secondly, the office carried great prestige and visibility. The mayor was a virtual local monarch, the embodiment of the city, who wore a fur robe and carried a ceremonial rod, like a real king. He was also addressed as 'Your Worship' and referred to as 'The Right Worshipful the Mayor of Limerick', a quasi-regal style that survived well into the twentieth century. The ceremony of inaugurating a new mayor involved the chain of office being placed around his neck and the ceremonial rod being placed in his hands. Thirdly, the mayor was the leader of the social and political life of Limerick and his activities received virtually constant coverage in the local newspapers. He was also regarded as the embodiment of the society of which he was the head, and as such fulfilled a role similar to that of a powerful landed gentleman or peer. In short, the attainment of the mayoralty was a major status symbol.

Although in theory, it would have been possible to regard the mayoralty as a symbol of Protestant ascendancy (before 1841) or of British rule in Ireland (after 1871 and the rise of Home Rule), this did not in fact happen. The Catholic and Repeal elite that took power in Limerick in 1841 embraced the office of mayor and made it their own. Later the Home Rule party that rebuffed the British monarchy took a similar attitude and made the mayoralty into a symbol of nationalism. The same pattern was to be repeated in 1899 with the election of the Labour Corporation and in 1920, when Sinn Féin gained control of the city council. In 1921, the killing of Mayors Clancy and O'Callaghan completed the transformation of the Mayoralty into a nationalist symbol.[32]

Before the City Management Act of 1934, the mayor and city council administered the city themselves. The council met once a month, but transacted most of its business through a series of committees established under the Municipal Corporations Act of 1840. Many of the councillors were wealthy businessmen, and were able to devote a certain proportion of their time to the administration of the city. Initially, four committees were established but their number increased with the growing amount of services provided by the corporation.

Working under the direction of the mayor and council was a team of permanent officers.[33] The most senior of these was the town clerk, whose role as day-to-day chief executive was similar to that of the modern city manager. Next in rank came the treasurer, the rate collector, the city surveyor (renamed city engineer in 1935), the manager of the gas undertaking, the secretary of the gas committee, the gas engineer and the law agent. The mayor and councillors, who were all part-time, did not have the time to devote to full time administration and as the activities of the corporation expanded and became more complex in the last decades of the nineteenth century, they became increasingly reliant on their permanent officials. This was particularly the case in complex and technical areas such as gas production. The senior officials were not at the head of a local bureaucracy, as the number of white-collar staff was very small.[34] Nevertheless, more and more power and authority came into their hands and the role of the council was correspondingly reduced. The mayor was gradually transformed from a powerful local king into a ceremonial local president.

The senior bureaucrats were as much members of the municipal elite as the councillors and it was common practice for mayors and city councillors to take up senior administrative positions. Some prominent examples of this were William Spillane (1838-97) (mayor 1870), who served as manager of the gas undertaking from 1875 to 1897; Bryan O'Donnell (1848-1940) (mayor in 1893, 1894 and 1895), who served as rate collector from 1895 to 1935 and William Nolan (1855-1941) (mayor 1895 and 1896), who served as town clerk from 1896 to 1932.[35] Some of these held office for very long periods, and retired at an advanced age. William Nolan retired in 1932 at the age of seventy-seven having served as town clerk for thirty-six years.[36] Bryan O'Donnell was rate collector for forty years and retired at the age of eighty-eight in 1935.[37] The distinction between the political and administrative functions continued to be blurred until the 1934 Management Act.

Poster of the byelaws concerning the Peoples Park, Limerick dated April 1906
(Jim Kemmy Municipal Museum)

The Municipal Corporations Act of 1840 had drastically reduced the corporation's role in the judicial system, except for two exceptions. Firstly, the mayor's court of conscience continued to exist and was used to recover small debts (under £2). Its role continued to be similar to that of the modern small claims court. Secondly, the mayor was *ex officio* a justice of the peace for the borough, and as such was a judge of the courts of both quarter and petty sessions.[38] The appointment of the sheriff of Limerick city was in the hands of the Lord Lieutenant from 1841 to 1876, but in the latter year, the corporation was given the power to submit three names to him, from which he picked the sheriff.[39] In turn, the sheriff appointed the city grand jury, which after 1853 had a merely judicial role.

The Politics of the Mayoral Elite 1842-99.
In 1841, the population of Limerick city was 48,391 but the municipal electorate only numbered 1,227 of whom only 595 voted in the first local election held in the city in that year. However, the Tory and Protestant monopoly was decisively broken in 1841, and was never to be restored. Twenty-five of the forty councillors elected in 1841 were Catholics.[40] Henceforth, Catholics dominated the city council, although a significant Protestant and Conservative minority continued to be active until the end of the century. In the 1840s, the majority of the city council was staunchly O'Connellite and in 1843 petitioned the British parliament for the Act of Union to be repealed. This was the first time in its entire history that the corporation espoused a nationalist policy in the modern sense of the word.[41]

The collapse of the Repeal movement in 1848-50 transformed the composition of Limerick City Council, which was dominated by the Catholic Whigs from 1850 to 1871. These were usually wealthy, moderate, Liberal, unionist, loyal to the crown and opposed to physical force nationalism, such as Fenianism. Many of them were former Repealers, and after 1871, a lot of them switched over to supporting Home Rule.[42] After 1842, there was always a strong Protestant and Conservative party on the city council and in 1877, they comprised about one quarter of the total membership.[43] On 1 December 1856, the city council voted to adopt the 'rotatory system', by which every second mayor would be a Catholic or a Protestant. While this resolution was rescinded on 10 December 1857, the practice continued until 1864.[44] There were several Protestant mayors in this period, both Liberal and Conservative, including William Lane Joynt (mayor in 1862), Sir Peter Tait (mayor for three successive terms 1865-68) and James Spaight (mayor, 1856 and 1877), the last ever Conservative mayor of Limerick.[45]

The 1870s was marked by a nationalist revival and on 11 May 1871, the city council carried a resolution stating they approved 'the principle of Home Rule.'[46] However, a definite and committed nationalist majority only took control of Limerick City Council in the 1880s. The 1880s saw the apogee of Parnellism and in Limerick Stephen O'Mara (1844-1926) (mayor 1885-86) and Francis O'Keeffe (1856-1909) (mayor 1887-89) were both staunch nationalists. In the 1890s, the corporation was beset by fierce disputes between Parnellites and anti-Parnellites and mayors were drawn from both parties.

However, the 1880s represented a turning point in the political history of Limerick Corporation. Since 1197, with only brief exceptions, the corporation had always been loyal to the connection with England, but from the mid 1880s onwards, it became a permanently nationalist body.

The dual mandate was less common in this period in Limerick than it was to become after 1922 and only three mayors of Limerick also sat as MPs between 1842 and 1899. James Spaight was the first mayor of Limerick since John Prendergast Vereker to be also an MP and sat for Limerick city for a short period in 1858-59, in the interval between his two mayoralties of 1856 and 1877. Stephen O'Mara became the first mayor of Limerick to be simultaneously an MP since Thomas Smythe in 1776-77, when he held office in 1885 and 1886 and sat as MP for Queen's County for a few months in 1886. Francis O'Keeffe became the first serving mayor of Limerick to be simultaneously MP for Limerick city since Thomas Smythe in 1776-77 when he held office between 1887 and 1889 and sat in parliament from 1888 to 1900.

Limerick's mayoral elite were a wealthy, concentrated and well-resourced body of merchants and professional men, who combined social, economic and political leadership. They were an 'urban squirearchy' as defined by the English historian John Garrard, in that they resembled the country gentry both in their lifestyle and in their manner of exercising authority. They played a major role in the economic and commercial life of the city, dominated municipal politics and office and exercised a visible and social ascendancy through charitable, philanthropic and other activities.[47]

Wealthy dynasties produced successive generations of councillors and mayors. Notable examples of close family members who served as mayor were Andrew Watson (1812-13) and his son Henry (1823-26, 1854); Edmond Fitzgerald Ryan (1846) and his brother Michael (1859); John Boyse (1849) and his son Thomas (1869) and Stephen O'Mara (1885-86) and his sons Alphonsus (1918-20) and Stephen (1921-23). Intermarriage between members of the elite was also frequent. Martin Honan (mayor 1842-3) was married to a sister of Dr. Thomas Kane (mayor 1852 and 1857). Bryan O'Donnell (mayor 1893-4) was married to Alice Scanlon, whose father had been a city councillor. Alice's sister was married to a son of Robert Potter, the first law agent and MP for the city (1854-6). One of O'Donnell's daughters married a son of Michael Spain, who was high sheriff in 1893. John Quin (high sheriff 1869 and member of the city council for many years) was father to James and Stephen, both councillors while the latter was mayor (1916-18).[48]

Mayoral Pageantry and Traditions.

In England, the Municipal Corporations Act of 1835, which resulted in the emergence of much more representative borough councils than hitherto, was followed by the widespread reduction or even abolition of civic robes. For example, Hull City Council voted in 1836 to do away with 'gowns and the other paraphernalia of office', although later in the century there was a revival of civic ceremonial costume in English boroughs.[49] Interestingly, Irish borough corporations were much more traditional in their attitudes and retained nearly all of the old pageantry. In Limerick, despite dramatic changes in the political composition of the city council, the corporation's civic traditions underwent few major changes and the mayor and council continued to wear elaborate fur-trimmed red robes. In addition the mayor often wore Court dress, consisting of a coat, waistcoat, knee breeches, silk stockings, buckled shoes, bicorne hat and sword. His attendants such as the serjeants-at–mace also wore splendid uniforms.[50] In addition, the mayor continued to carry his sceptre-like wand on ceremonial occasions.

It was at this period also that the civic motto first appeared. It is in Latin and reads: *Urbs Antiqua Fuit Studiisque Asperrima Belli* which means 'an ancient city well versed in the arts of war'.[51] It is an adaptation of the description of the ancient North African city of Carthage in Virgil's epic poem the *Aeneid*, which was written in 19 BC. This motto had been quoted in respect of Limerick at the time of the sieges in the seventeenth century but was only adopted as the official civic motto in the mid nineteenth century.

Limerick Corporation also claimed that Limerick should be officially classified as the second city of Ireland after Dublin, which would allow representatives of the city, such as the mayor or deputations travelling to meet the queen or the viceroy, to take precedence immediately after their Dublin counterparts at official processions and ceremonies. This claim was hotly disputed by Cork on a number of occasions and resulted in acrimonious correspondence between the two corporations.[52]

Under the Municipal Privileges (Ireland) Act, of 1876, the council of each Irish borough was given the authority to elect and admit individuals to the honorary freedom of the city.[53] This conferred honorary citizenship, and was the highest accolade in the gift of the city. It superseded the ancient concept of the freedom of boroughs, obsolete since the Municipal Corporations Act of 1840, which had conferred full citizenship, and in particular, the right to vote and trade. The freedom of the city was conferred at a splendid ceremony at which the mayor, council and other civic personnel wore full ceremonial costume.

Nevertheless, the granting of the freedom became a highly political action from the start, and was used by the corporation to demonstrate its support for Home Rule. Thus, the first honorary freemen of Limerick were the city's two Home Rule MPs, Isaac Butt and Richard O'Shaughnessy, who both received it on 1 January, 1877. Charles Stewart Parnell became the third recipient on 14 July 1880, and was followed by Michael Davitt (who was not an MP at this time) and two other Home Rule MPs on 14 April 1884. On 4 October 1886 it was the turn of William Ewart Gladstone, the seventy-seven year old British prime minister (who was then out of office) and champion of Home Rule. Because he was too old to come to Limerick to receive it, the mayor and representatives of the corporation travelled to his residence, Hawarden Castle, in North Wales, accompanied by representatives from the corporations of Cork, Waterford and Clonmel. There Gladstone received the freedom of the four cities at a joint ceremony. It was a unique occasion in the history of the conferring of the freedom of Limerick for three reasons: firstly it was the only time that it was granted jointly with other local authorities, secondly it was the only time that it was conferred at the recipient's residence and thirdly Gladstone is the only British prime minister to be have been given the freedom.[54]

The Labour Corporation 1899-1902.

The Local Government (Ireland) Act, which became law on 12 August 1898, and was implemented in 1899, established democratically elected councils to run the counties, instead of the grand juries, whose functions were henceforth to be strictly judicial.[55] These changes were not applicable to Limerick city, which had received an elected council in 1841, and had seen the end of the administrative role of the grand jury in 1853. Nonetheless, the Act did have far-reaching effects in the city. Firstly, the £10 qualification introduced in the Act of 1840 was replaced by the granting of the vote to all householders and occupants of a portion of a house. Secondly, the local government franchise was also extended to women, who satisfied the same criteria as men. However women were not allowed to become members of the county and city councils until 1911 and did not receive the right to vote in national elections until 1918.[56] As a result of this dramatic reform, the local electorate in Limerick city increased by 768%, from 709 to 5,521 voters.[57]

Thirdly, the modern system of local elections came into being, as they were to be held every three years (every five years after 1953) instead of annually. All councillors and half of the aldermen were to go out of office every three years, except in the 1899 local elections, the first under the new system, where all aldermen and councillors were to be elected simultaneously. The term of office of an alderman continued to be six years, and that of a councillor was reduced from four to three years.[58] After independence, a most regrettable tendency to postpone local elections became increasingly common. This was done by act of the Oireachtas until 1973 and by ministerial order thereafter until the practice was abolished in 1999.[59] Fourthly, the term of office of the mayor, while remaining one year, now began in the middle of January rather than the first day of the calendar year. However, he continued to be elected by the city council, not directly by the voters.[60]

The first local election under the new Act was held in Limerick on 15 January 1899. The results appeared to be revolutionary, for the new mass electorate returned what came to be known as the 'Labour Corporation' or 'People's Parliament'. Twenty-seven of the old council had stood again for election but only eleven were returned. Among the sixteen who lost their seats were Mayor Michael Cusack and two former mayors, John J. Cleary and Ambrose Hall. The new council consisted of twenty-four Labour, five newly elected Mercantile (representing the business community) and eleven re-elected members. Half of the new aldermen were Labour.[61]

The 1899 election was the most dramatic in the history of Limerick Corporation as it was widely believed at the time that the city government had undergone revolutionary change, and that the old ruling class had been driven from power forever. Certainly, the election did mark the beginning of participation by the mass of the people in the election of the city council, which, for the first time ever, appeared to represent the common people and not merely the prosperous elite.[62] Also, in the 1899 local elections, Labour recorded a far greater success in Limerick than in any other city in Ireland.[63] Finally, the election as Mayor on 23 January 1899 of John Daly, a life long Fenian, and veteran of both the 1867 Rising and the dynamiting campaign of the 1880s caused consternation in many circles. He was an unapologetic advocate of the use of physical force to bring about an independent Ireland, and had served twelve years (1884-96) in an English prison for alleged revolutionary activities.[64]

However, the changes wrought in 1899 proved to be far from revolutionary in the long term. Firstly, the membership of the Labour Corporation were not socialists, and while some of them were more interested in social issues than their predecessors on the council, there was to be no organised Labour Party in Ireland until the foundation of the modern party in 1912. In consequence, the great victory of 1899 proved to be ephemeral and the Labour members elected to councils all over Ireland ceased to behave as if they were members of an organised party.[65] The Labour group on Limerick City Council soon disintegrated and the old mayoral elite gradually regained control.[66] Indeed, many of the mayors of Limerick in the period before and after Independence continued to be drawn form the ranks of the elite. A real and permanent Labour representation on city councils throughout Ireland began between 1911 and 1914, at the time of the founding of the Labour Party.[67] Secondly, the administrative structures, functions, procedures and financial base of the corporation underwent no significant changes as a result of the supposed political revolution of 1899. Thirdly, the permanent officials remained in office and continued to direct the affairs of the corporation on a day-to-day basis. The most senior of these was former mayor William Nolan, who was town clerk from 1896 to 1932. John J. Peacocke was city surveyor from 1899 to 1932; Bryan O'Donnell was rate collector (the most highly paid of all the officials) from 1895 to 1935, while John Dundon was law agent from 1894 to 1915 (when he was succeeded by his son, who served until 1955).[68]

The Mayoralty 1899-1914.

When Queen Victoria visited Ireland in April 1900, she promoted the mayor of Cork to be lord mayor. Rumours circulated at the time and since, that the mayor of Limerick was to be similarly honoured. This did not happen, and various theories have been put forward to account for this lack of promotion. One is that the Fenian Mayor Daly would have declined such a royal honour. Another is that the offer was never made, due to the insult directed at the Prince and Princess of Wales on their fleeting visit to Limerick in 1885, when the corporation had refused to accord them an official welcome.[69] Whatever the truth of the matter, Cork's first citizen gained precedence over his Limerick counterpart as a result of the royal visit, and Limerick's claim to be the second city in the country, which had been advanced periodically in the nineteenth century, was finally dismissed.

The election of a new council in January 1902 marked the end of the colourful mayoralty of John Daly, and also of the Labour Corporation. From 1902 to 1918, the dominant figure in the civic and political life of Limerick was Michael Joyce who sat as MP for the city from 1900 to 1918 and served two consecutive terms as mayor, from January 1905 to January 1907. He was the first mayor to be simultaneously an MP since Francis O'Keeffe in 1889.[70]

On 12 January 1904, the Redemptorist Fr. John Creagh director of the Arch-Confraternity of the Holy Family, a society of laymen that had a membership of 6,000, attacked the Jewish community in Limerick in a sermon delivered to a packed congregation in the Redemptorist Church and called on them to have no commercial dealings with Jewish business people, on grounds of their alleged usurious practices. The result was a boycott of the Limerick Jews, which greatly damaged their businesses and caused them to suffer sporadic violence and insult.[71] On 15 April 1904, a fifteen-year-old boy named John Raleigh was sentenced to one month in prison for throwing a stone at the Limerick rabbi. In response a special meeting of the city council was called for 20 April by Mayor Michael Donnelly, 'to adopt a memorial to the Lord Lieutenant' on Raleigh's behalf, and also to counter the bad publicity that Limerick was receiving owing to the boycott. A resolution was passed unanimously calling on the Lord Lieutenant to have the boy released. Members of the council denied that there was any boycott or violence being carried on against the Limerick Jews, but were quick to condemn Jewish 'usurious methods of dealing' and to lament the fact that Irish people had to emigrate to America, while 'Jews come in here and make a living.'[72] It was a low point in the history of the mayoralty and council of Limerick.

The Mayoralty and the 1916 Rising.

When the First World War began in the summer of 1914, John Redmond, the leader of the Home Rule party, called on Irishmen to join the British army and support the war effort. Limerick Corporation was almost entirely Redmondite in its composition, and supported both the leader and Irish participation in the war. Public opinion in the city was also strongly supportive of this stance, as large numbers of Limerick men were serving in the British armed forces.[73] However, there continued to be a section of public opinion and a minority on the city council opposed to the Redmondite position, both on politics and the war. When the Irish Volunteers (a paramilitary organisation established in 1913) split over the question of participation in the war, 7,000 of the Limerick branch supported Redmond and the war effort, but 500 were opposed.[74]

During the mayoralty of the moderate nationalist, Philip O'Donovan (1876-1953) from January 1913 to January 1916, support for the war held up in the corporation and in the city. His successor, Stephen Byrne Quin (1860-1944) who was mayor from January 1916 to January 1918, was a wealthy wine-merchant who described himself as a Home Ruler, but was in fact one of the most pro-unionist politicians to emerge in Limerick since the 1899 local elections. It was a singular irony that the 1916 Rising should have occurred during his mayoralty. Limerick city remained peaceful during the rising, but as in the rest of Ireland, public opinion was initially overwhelmingly hostile to the rebels.[75] Limerick Corporation made no official statement throughout this crisis but Mayor Quin won widespread praise for his role in orchestrating the disarmament of the Irish Volunteers in Limerick. After the rising, Sir John Maxwell, Commander-in-Chief of the British Army in Ireland, ordered that the various nationalist movements be disarmed, but the Limerick battalion of the Irish Volunteers refused to comply. Mayor Quin defused the situation by agreeing to accept the arms from the Volunteers, and then pass them onto the British garrison in Limerick.[76] The mayor was regarded by both sides as an honest broker, and a resolution was passed unanimously by the city council on 1 June 1916, expressing the 'fullest and most grateful appreciation' of all of the aldermen and city councillors for the efforts of the first citizen in successfully preserving 'the peace, good order and safety of the city during the recent crisis'.[77]

However, public opinion had already begun to move in favour of the rebels, following the execution of their leaders in May 1916. In Limerick, the fierce condemnation of the executions by the Catholic bishop, Edward Thomas O'Dwyer, played a major role in influencing the reaction both of the public and of the city council.[78] On 1 June, 1916, the council held its first meeting since the Easter Rebellion and while the mayor was thanked for his role in defusing tensions in the city, one of his principal opponents, Councillor John Dalton, proposed that Bishop O'Dwyer be congratulated for 'his spirited condemnation of the wantonly cruel and oppressive treatment of the surrendered Irish Volunteers', and that the council 'compare the inhuman conduct of militarism and its abettors in Ireland with the humane and kindly manner in which the Turks treated the surrendered British forces at Kut' (a sarcastic reference to the notorious cruelty of the Turks to British prisoners-of-war in the Middle East).[79] Although Mayor Quin disliked the resolution, it was passed anyway. Within a few months and at the instigation of Councillor Dalton, Bishop O'Dwyer was made a freeman of Limerick at a ceremony held in the Town Hall on 14 September 1916, and used the occasion to condemn both British rule, and what he regarded as the craven policies of the Redmondite majority on the city council.[80]

The First Sinn Féin Mayor of Limerick.
Although Quin was re-elected mayor in January 1917, the tide of public opinion was now running against him. In 1917, the Sinn Féin party was reorganised, with Eamon de Valera as its leader. Its aims were to bring about independence through the secession of the Irish

members from the British parliament, and the establishment of an Irish parliament in Dublin, in defiance of the authorities. Passive resistance to British rule would follow, and Irish delegates were to be sent to the peace conference that would be held at the end of the war. In the next mayoral election, held on 18 January 1918, Quin was defeated by Alphonsus O'Mara, whose father Stephen had been mayor in 1885 and 1886 and who now became the first Sinn Féin mayor of Limerick.

Both militant nationalism and militant labour were expanding in Limerick at this time and provided the background to the two general strikes, which occurred in the city during O'Mara's mayoralty.[82] The first was brought about by the decision of the British government to extend conscription to Ireland in April 1918. All the major nationalist political parties, the trade union movement and the Catholic Church united in a concerted campaign against this move and meetings were held throughout the country at which thousands signed an anti-conscription pledge. Mayor O'Mara called one such meeting in the Town Hall, thus putting himself at the head of the anti-conscription movement in Limerick. On Tuesday 23 April 1918, a twenty-four hour general strike was held throughout Ireland, during which Limerick city closed down for the day, and a huge procession of about 10,000 people marched through the streets. Nationwide, the campaign was a success, and the British government dropped the conscription plan for Ireland.[83]

The second Limerick general strike was caused by the fatal shooting of an RIC man by the IRA, during a failed attempt to rescue Robert (Bobby) Byrne, a local trade union and Sinn Féin activist from police custody. In response, the British authorities proclaimed martial law in Limerick city. Military checkpoints were to be set up on all roads into the city, and everyone had to obtain permits from the local military commander which had to be displayed whenever the holder entered or left the city.[84]

The Limerick Trades and Labour Council, which was the supreme administrative body of the trade union movement in the city called a general strike to express their outrage at British military rule. Between 14 and 26 April 1919, a general strike, known as the Limerick Soviet, won universal backing from the city's workforce. Limerick was governed during this fortnight by the strike committee of the trades council, nicknamed the Soviet, which controlled prices, distributed food, organised the provision of essential services, published a newspaper and even printed its own paper money.[85] Eventually, Mayor O'Mara and the Catholic bishop, Dr. Denis Hallinan brought the strike to an end. They met with the local military commander, who agreed to lift martial law, in return for the ending of the strike.[86] The Soviet achieved its aim of ending British military rule in the city, but in its aftermath, the labour and trade union movement in Limerick and in Ireland as a whole took a secondary place to the nationalist and Sinn Féin movement. The manner in which the mayor and the bishop took the initiative in bringing the crisis to an end clearly showed the unease that they had felt at such a display of trade union power.[87]

The general election of December 1918 resulted in Sinn Féin winning a landslide victory in Ireland outside Ulster. In Limerick city, the sitting Home Rule MP, ex-mayor

Michael Joyce, decided not to stand, and was replaced by the prominent Sinn Féin figure Michael Colivet.[88] On 21 January 1919, the War of Independence began, at Soloheadbeg, near Tipperary town, when the Irish Republican Army (IRA) as the Irish Volunteers were now called, killed two policemen. The Local Government (Ireland) Act of 1919, introduced proportional representation (PR) into the local electoral system and provided for all aldermen and councillors to go out of office simultaneously at the time of a local election.[89] The first local elections held under this legislation were in 1920 and apart from the 1899 elections, were the most important and decisive held in Limerick city since 1841, for several reasons. Firstly, PR was used for the first time. Secondly, the entire membership of the council was elected on the one day for the first time ever, except for the unique elections of 1899. Thirdly, Sinn Féin took control of the council winning twenty-six seats, compared to six for Labour, four for a local Ratepayers party and four Independents. Fourthly, the Sinn Féin majority included the first woman ever elected to Limerick City Council, Mrs. Emily Crowe of Sarsfield Street.[90]

The Murdered Mayors of Limerick.

On 30 January, 1920 the new council met and Michael O'Callaghan, who was a leading member of Sinn Féin and had served with the Irish Volunteers, was elected mayor.[91] The council voted to 'hereby acknowledge Dáil Eireann as the lawful government of Ireland', and to tender 'its full allegiance.'[92] This was the first time in its entire history that Limerick Corporation had voted in favour of a complete severance with the British connection. It was also decided not to put forward the names of three persons, one of which would be appointed high sheriff by the Lord Lieutenant, as provided for by the 1876 Act. This effectively brought the shrievalty (office of sheriff) to an end, although it was not to be formally abolished until 1926.

The Limerick delegation, led by Mayor George Clancy, at the funeral of Terence McSwiney in Cork city.
(Jim Kemmy Municipal Museum)

Michael O'Callaghan was succeeded as mayor by another prominent Sinn Féin activist, Alderman George Clancy, who was elected on 31 January 1921.[93] Five weeks later, the most brutal and violent event in history of Limerick's mayoralty since the 1650s occurred. At 1:00 a.m, on Monday morning the 7 March 1921, ex-Mayor O'Callaghan was shot dead in the presence of his wife in his own house. Half an hour later, Mayor Clancy was also murdered, as his wife looked on, in his residence in Castleview Gardens. A third man named Joseph O'Donoghue had been killed in Janesboro a few hours earlier. These 'curfew murders' horrified Limerick, and indeed the whole of Ireland. O'Callaghan and Clancy were the first mayors of Limerick to die as a result of political violence since the execution of Dominick Fanning by the Cromwellians in 1651. Their slaying followed on the killing of the lord mayor of Cork, Tomás McCurtain, on 20 March 1920, and the death of his successor Terence McSwiney on hunger strike seven months later. British security forces killed the 'murdered mayors of Limerick' in order to help destroy the Sinn Féin leadership cadre in Limerick. The killing of the two mayors completed the process of making the mayoralty of Limerick a thoroughly nationalist institution and helped to ensure its survival in an independent Ireland.[94]

After the killing of Mayor Clancy, James Casey, a Labour borough councillor who had been one of the leaders of the Limerick Soviet, served as acting first citizen of Limerick from 7 to 22 March 1921. His official title was deputy mayor. As such, he was the first member of the Labour Party to head the municipal authority. During his brief tenure in office, he organised the funerals of the three victims of the curfew murders, which were attended by very large crowds.[95]

The first female mayor of Limerick.

On 22 March 1921, Stephen O'Mara, was elected mayor of Limerick to serve out the remainder of George Clancy's term, and held office until October 1, 1923. His father had been mayor in 1885 and 1886 and his brother had been mayor from 1918 to 1920. In 1922, he spent a lot of time in the USA raising funds for Dáil Éireann, and in consequence was absent from Limerick for much of his mayoralty.[96] On 21 May, Mayor O'Mara appointed 'Alderman Mrs. O'Donovan as his locum tenens during his absence from the borough on and after that date'.[97] In 1921, she had become the second female member of Limerick City Council, but now made history by becoming the first female mayor, a position that she retained until 30 January 1922.[98] Her title was variously described as being deputy mayor (which had been the title used by James Casey) and locum tenens mayor.

The Mayoralty during the Civil War.

The War of Independence came to an end on 9 July 1921, when the British Government and the IRA agreed a truce. This was followed by the signing of the controversial treaty between representatives of the British government and Dáil Eireann on 6 December 1921. However, the serious disagreements that the Treaty caused in the ranks of both Sinn Féin and the IRA eventually led to the outbreak of civil war in Ireland in the Summer of 1922. In Limerick city, both pro- and anti-Treaty forces occupied various prominent strongholds in the city. Mayor Stephen O'Mara averted the outbreak of fighting by brokering an agreement, under which the pro and anti-Treaty IRA forces would withdraw from the city. The agreement was successfully put into operation, and was completed by the end of March 1922. The city was effectively demilitarised, and the prospect of fighting there postponed for the time being.[99] Limerick's respite from civil war was to be a brief one as both pro- and anti-Treaty forces soon returned to Limerick. Mayor O'Mara unsuccessfully tried to negotiate a second peace deal, and between 11 and 21 July 1922, the fourth siege of Limerick saw the pro-Treaty forces besiege and capture the city.[100]

Mayor O'Mara, whose sympathies lay with the anti-Treaty side, was imprisoned for four months, from December 1922 until March 1923, the first time that a serving mayor had been jailed in centuries. Following his release, O'Mara continued in office until 17 October 1923.[101] His successor took office in very unusual circumstances for Robert (Bob) de Courcy was unanimously elected as the new mayor while he was on hunger strike in prison in Dublin, having been jailed, early in 1923 for being in possession of loaded guns. He spent the first eight months of his mayoralty in prison and was only released on 26 June 1924 as part of an amnesty for anti-Treaty prisoners.[102]

The Change in the Terms of Office of the Mayor of Limerick.

Under the provisions of the Local Government Act of 1898, local elections were due to be held in the urban areas in January 1923. However, the Local Elections Postponement Act of 1922, 1923 and 1924 allowed the Minister for Local Government to put them off to a more convenient time and they were repeatedly postponed over the next two years.[103] It was this which allowed for the terms of office of Mayors Stephen O'Mara and Bob de Courcy to be extended indefinitely. The situation was somewhat regularised by the Local Government Act of 1925.[104] This provided for local elections being held not later than 26 June 1925.

On 23 June 1925, local elections were finally held. At this time, the political situation was somewhat fluid. The pro-Treaty group had formed the Cumann na nGaedheal Party in 1923, while the anti-Treaty group were known as Republicans, and in 1926 most of them joined the new Fianna Fáil Party. There was also a Progressive Party in Limerick, which was descended from the old Ratepayers group, but many of its members were aligned with Cumann na nGaedheal. The Labour Party had been founded in 1912, and had returned members to the city council since then. Finally there were also Independents. The new Limerick city council met on 30 June, and elected Councillor Paul A. O'Brien as mayor, to hold office until the next mayoral election which under the Local Government Act of 1898 was due to be held in January, 1926.[106] Later the Local Elections Postponement Act of 1925 provided for mayors of boroughs to remain in office until 30 June 1926. The Local Elections Act of 1927 finally put things on a permanent footing by providing that local and mayoral elections were to take place in June.[107] Since then, mayors of Limerick have always been elected in June.

The Limerick City Management Act of 1934.

The end of the civil war saw the emergence of a new Free State committed to reducing the powers of local authorities, a policy which met with the acquiescence of the general public, who had scant regard for local government. The most important aspect of the Free State's reform of local government in the 1920s was the introduction of the management system. The idea arose in the USA as part of the Progressive Movement that swept the country in the years 1890 to 1914.[108] The first manager in Ireland was appointed in Cork city under the Cork City Management Act of 1929. The next city to receive a manager was Dublin in 1930, followed by Limerick in 1934, Waterford in 1939 and all of the counties in 1942.

During, the 1920s, a pressure group emerged in Limerick that sought the abolition of the corporation and its replacement by one or more commissioners. This group, known as the Limerick Citizens and Ratepayers Society was supported in their demand by the local chamber of commerce and employers federation. Perhaps more surprisingly, there was also considerable support for the idea from within the ranks of the city council itself. In the 1920s and 1930s a Progressive Party (which took is name from the American Progressive movement), linked to the Ratepayers Society, emerged in Limerick city, which demanded retrenchment in public expenditure and vaguely defined social reform, but in particular campaigned for the introduction of the management system to the city.[109] In the 1925 local elections, twelve Progressives were returned to the forty-member council, while in the 1934 local elections to the fifteen-member council, the party secured six seats, the same as Fianna Fáil.[110] Many of the Progressives were associated with Cumann na nGaedheal and its successor Fine Gael, and after the introduction of the management system to Limerick city in 1934, the party lost its principal *raison d'etre* and consequently disappeared, while its membership became largely absorbed into Fine Gael.

The campaign for the introduction of the management system to Limerick eventually resulted in the enactment of the Limerick City Management Act, which became law on 6 September 1934.[111] The government of Limerick city was transformed forever by this piece of legislation. Before 1934 the mayor and council had administered the city on a day-to-day though part-time basis for some 740 years. After 1934 the routine management of civic affairs was placed in the hands of a full-time manager at the head of an increasingly large and professional bureaucracy. The mayor was no longer the local king but was transformed into the local president, a largely ceremonial head of state.

The Act provided for the appointment of a manager by the city council, though he was to be actually selected by the Local Appointments Commission. The functions of the corporation were divided into two categories in the Act: reserved and executive.[112] This division had been first set out in the Cork City Management Act of 1929 and was included in all subsequent legislation governing the management system.[113] The reserved functions were those of the council and included the making of the rate and the borrowing of monies; the making, amending or repeal of bye-laws; appointment or election of members to other bodies; the admission of persons to the freedom of the city;

election of the mayor; appointment of a city manager; appointment of committees and application for an extension of the borough boundary.[114] All functions that were not reserved were described as executive functions and were performed by the city manager. He was the day-to-day chief executive who drew up the annual budget, transacted all routine business and had exclusive control over the work-force of the local authority. The manager had the right to attend meetings of the council and 'to take part in discussions …as if he were a member' but not to vote.[115]

The membership of the city council was reduced from forty to fifteen of whom four were to be aldermen. When in 1950, Limerick city received its only significant boundary extension since 1841, the number of councillors was increased to seventeen, which remains unchanged at the time of writing. The electoral wards set up under the Acts of 1840 and 1853 were abolished and the whole of the city formed one electoral area until 1967 when the city was again divided into electoral wards. The election of the mayor was to take place each year at the first council meeting held after 22 June.[116] A proposal by Limerick Corporation that the title of lord mayor be conferred on the city's first citizen was rejected by the Department of Local Government and consequently was not included in the legislation.[117]

The election for the new city council was held on 8 November and the Act came into operation on 22 November 1934. The term of office of the incumbent mayor, Patrick F. Quinlan was terminated prematurely and Councillor James Casey (who had served as acting mayor in 1921) was elected to serve until the following June. On the same day, James P. Geraghty was appointed the first city manager.[118]

Limerick City Hall
(Copper Reed Studio)

The Mayoralty since 1934.

The 1960s and 1970s saw a radical transformation of Irish life. Industrialisation, urbanisation, population increase, the impact of free secondary education, the changes in the Catholic Church as a result of Vatican Two, the influence of television, membership of the EU and the greater participation of women in the workforce all played a role in this process which effectively brought an end to the social system created a century before in the aftermath of the Great Famine. An increasingly complex and sophisticated society demanded better and more comprehensive services and this in turn resulted in the role of local government becoming more challenging, with additional functions and greater expenditure being the end result. The role of government at both local and national level in managing the economy grew rapidly in the twentieth century and particularly in the decades after 1945.

Local authorities were no longer run by a few individual bureaucrats as in the nineteenth and early twentieth centuries but by large and many-layered bureaucracies. Limerick Corporation shared in all of these general trends. The increasing size and complexity of its operations can be gauged from the increase in its annual expenditure. In 1945 this amounted to £243,000 but by 1975 had increased to £4.7 million, while in 2005 it exceeded 67 million euro (equivalent to around £52 million).[119] From the 1930s onwards, the corporation took on new functions, and by the early twenty-first century, provided the following services: social housing; roads; water supply and sewerage; planning and development control; protection of the environment; sport and the arts (which includes libraries, museums and art galleries); fire safety; and community and enterprise.[120]

Although the Management Act of 1934 had transferred the day-to-day administration of the corporation to the city manager, the mayoralty continued to be an office of great importance and prestige. The mayor was chairman of the city council, and ceremonial head of the local state. If the eighteenth-century mayor had been regarded as a local king, equipped with fur robe and sceptre, then the twentieth-century mayor was a local president, a highly respected, omnipresent, ceremonial figure who symbolised and personified Limerick both within and outside the city. One of the most widely beloved and best remembered customs was for the mayor to visit the schools in the city and to mark the occasion, either a half day or a dispensation from homework was announced, thus guaranteeing that the mayor always enjoyed massive popularity with the children of Limerick, if not always with the parents!

However, since 1945, there has been a marked reduction in the pageantry of the mayoralty, aptly symbolising the transformation of the office from local king to local president. As late as the 1930s and 1940s, the mayor of Limerick still travelled on ceremonial occasions in a horse-drawn carriage, but this ceased after the war.[121] The use of a mayoral 'wand of jurisdiction' was discontinued in the 1950s and the civic maces are now only used on the occasion of the conferring of the freedom of the city.[122] On all but the most formal occasions, the mayor is no longer addressed as 'Your Worship' and instead is called simply 'Mayor'. The practice of wearing ceremonial red robes still continues, although since the 1970s they are lined with gold braid rather than the more lavish and expensive fur, as had previously been the case.[123] However, some of the councillors ceased to wear even the simplified robes as they regarded them as anachronistic and elitist. Nowadays, the mayoral chain is the most visible and frequently used item of civic regalia.[124]

Mayoral Facts and Figures.

The practice of mayors of Limerick serving consecutive terms seems to have been uncommon before the fifteenth century, but that of serving three consecutive terms was extremely rare until the nineteenth century, the solitary exception being Thomas Comyn between 1407 and 1410. John Prendergast Vereker inaugurated a brief trend when he served as mayor between 1815 and 1818 and was closely followed by Henry Watson, between 1823 and 1826. However, the practice reached its zenith between 1866 and 1957, with eleven mayors each serving for three years in succession and another one for a unique five consecutive terms. Peter Tait begun the trend when he served in 1866, 1867 and 1868, and was followed by John J. Cleary (1872-74), but neither served for a full three years. However, Francis A. O'Keeffe (1887-89) became the first to do so since Henry Watson. Michael Cusack came next (1896-99), but did not serve three full terms. John Daly (1899-1902), Timothy Ryan (1910-13), Philip O'Donovan (1913-16), Stephen O'Mara (1921-23) and Bob de Courcy (1923-25) all served three consecutive terms. The last two were unusual in that their mayoralties were artificially prolonged under the Electoral Postponement Acts, and neither served for a full three years. Patrick Donnellan served three full terms (1930-33) and the practice culminated when Dan Bourke served for an incredible five years in succession (1936-41), the only instance of its kind in the entire history of Limerick. The last mayor of Limerick to serve three consecutive terms

Mayor Ted Russell and fifteen former Mayors of Limerick in 1956. Back row Stephen Coughlan, Patrick O'Connell, John Carew, Gerard B.Dillon, Michael Hartney, John C. Hickey, James McQuane, Kevin Bradshaw, Michael B. O'Malley. Front Row. Patrick Donnellan, James Reidy, Michael J. Keyes, Mayor Ted Russell, Stephen O'Mara, Patrick F. Quinlan, Desmond O'Malley. (Jim Kemmy Municipal Museum)

was George E. (Ted) Russell (1954-57) although he also served on two subsequent occasions, in 1967-8 and 1976-77.[125] Indeed the practice of mayors serving for just two consecutive terms has become increasingly rare and has only occurred twice since the 1950s: Frances Condell in 1962-64 and Bobby Byrne in 1978-80.[126]

Frances Condell made history by becoming the first female to be elected mayor of Limerick in her own right in 1962 (Mrs. Mary O'Donovan had been locum tenens mayor in 1921-22).[127] To date Mrs. Condell is the only female mayor to serve two terms but there have been two others who served one term each: Terry Kelly (1983-84) and Jan O'Sullivan (1993-94).[128] The last mayor of Limerick to resign before the completion of his term was Donogh O'Malley who did so in November 1961 after serving for just five months. His resignation was caused by his being appointed Parliamentary Secretary (the equivalent of Minister of State) at the Department of Finance.[129]

The dual mandate, which had been comparatively rare in the nineteenth century, flourished between the attainment of Independence in 1922 and the statutory abolition of the practice in 2003. During this period, eight mayors of Limerick were simultaneously TDs: Dan Bourke who was mayor in 1936-41 and TD in 1927-52; James Reidy who was mayor in 1944-45 and TD in 1932-37 and 1938-54; John Carew who was mayor in 1953-54 and 1959-60 and TD in 1952-61; Ted Russell who was mayor in 1954-57, 1966-67 and 1976-77 and TD in 1957-61; Donogh O'Malley who was mayor in 1961 and TD from 1954-68; Steve Coughlan who was mayor in 1951-52 and 1969-70 and TD in 1961-77; Frank Prendergast who was mayor in 1977-78 and 1984-85 and TD in 1982-87 and Jim Kemmy who was mayor in 1991-92 and 1995-96 and TD in 1981-82 and 1987-97. Another three were elected TDs while not mayor: Michael Keyes who was mayor in 1928-30 and TD in 1927 and again in 1933-57; Michael Lipper who was mayor in 1973-74 and TD in 1977-81 and Jan O'Sullivan who was mayor in 1993-94 and has been a TD since 1998.[130]

Three mayors have simultaneously served in the Senate: Ted Russell who was mayor in 1954-57, 1966-67 and 1976-77 and senator in 1969-77; Patrick Kennedy who was mayor in 1974-75 and 1985-86 and senator in 1981-82 and 1983-92; and Jan O'Sullivan who was mayor in 1993-94 and senator in 1993-97. Four other mayors sat in the Senate after leaving office: Stephen O'Mara who was mayor in 1885 and 1886 and senator in 1925-26; James Reidy who was mayor in 1944-45 and senator in 1954-57; Gerard Dillon who was mayor in 1949-50 and senator in 1960-61 and Tony Bromell who was mayor in 1982-83 and senator in 1988-89. Stephen O'Mara is the only mayor of Limerick to have sat in both the British House of Commons and the Irish Senate. James Reidy, Ted Russell and Jan O'Sullivan are the only mayors of Limerick to have sat in *both* Houses of the Oireachtas. Ted Russell is the only person to have been *both* simultaneously mayor and TD (for a few months in 1957) and simultaneously mayor and senator (in 1976-77). Two former mayors of Limerick were later members of the cabinet; Michael Keyes who was Minister for Local Government (1949-1951) and for Posts and Telegraphs (1954-57); and Donogh O'Malley who was Minister for Health (1965-66) and for Education (1966-68).[131]

Since the 1920s there have been many city councillors belonging to either a political party other than the big three of Fianna Fáil, Fine Gael and Labour or else of independent status. In the 1920s and 1930s, there were four mayors aligned to the Progressive Party, though at least three of them were also connected to Cumann na nGaedheal. In the 1950s the Clann na Poblachta Party returned a few councillors in Limerick the most prominent of whom were mayors Steve Coughlan (who later joined Labour) and Ted Russell (who later joined Fine Gael). The most significant new party in the 1980s and 1990s was the Progressive Democrat Party which had three of its representatives elected to the council in 1991, all of whom later served as mayor. Independents were always more prominent in local than in national politics but have become more numerous in recent times. In 1991 the number of non-party councillors elected was to Limerick City Council was two but in 1999 it increased to three and the 2004 election resulted in six independents being returned, making them the largest single category of councillor. Two Independents have served as mayor of Limerick since 1934, Frances Condell (1962-64) and Joe Harrington (1998-99).

The Building of Limerick City Hall.

Since the late nineteenth century, Limerick Town Hall had been considered to be both unsuitable and inadequate. In 1986 Limerick Corporation made the decision to build a new headquarters in the historic Merchants' Quay area of the city's Englishtown. Designed by Burke-Kennedy Doyle and Partners Architects and built between 1988 and 1990 by McInerney Properties at a cost of £6 million, it was the first purpose built headquarters for Limerick Corporation since the construction of the Exchange over 300 years previously. It came into use on 14 February 1990 and was officially opened by the Taoiseach, Charles Haughey on 1 June 1990. The city was again being governed from the Englishtown, from which successive mayors had ruled Limerick from the thirteenth to the early nineteenth centuries and the period in Newtown Pery could now be regarded as an interval, albeit a 150-year one, in the corporation's continuous association with that area.[132]

The Proposal to have Mayors Directly Elected.

The Local Government Act of 2001 became law on 21 July 2001 and has been described as 'the basic legislation governing local government structures, operations and functions'.[133] Under its provisions, all county borough corporations became city councils, borough corporations became borough councils and both urban district councils and town commissioners became town councils. Thus Limerick Corporation became Limerick City Council with effect from 1 January 2002. In addition, under the Act, the ancient title of alderman was abolished after the 2004 local elections.[134]

One of the most controversial provisions of the Act was that from 2004 each cathaoirleach (chairperson) of a county and mayor of an urban area was to be directly

Mayor Joe Leddin photographed with fourteen former mayors of Limerick in the Council Chamber of Limerick City Hall on 27 April 2007. Seated (L-R) Frank Prendergast, John Cronin, Kieran O'Hanlon, Mayor Joe Leddin, Michael Hourigan, Jan O'Sullivan, Clem Casey, Paddy Madden. Standing (L-R) Dick Sadlier, Bobby Byrne, Tony Bromell, Gus O'Driscoll, Paddy Kiely, John Quinn, Jack Bourke.
(Press 22 Photographic Agency)

elected for a five year term by the voters rather than by the council and would be able to serve for a maximum of two consecutive terms. The elections to these posts were to be held every five years in conjunction with the local elections. This new system of direct elections was designed to redress what some commentators took to be the excessive power of the executive arm of local authorities and to provide for a greater level of democratic accountability.[135]

Had it been implemented this measure would have represented a major and historic change for three reasons; firstly, the term of office of mayors has always been one year since the establishment of the system in the twelfth and thirteenth centuries; secondly the right to elect the mayor had been removed from the citizens and vested in the councils by the New Rules of 1672 and thirdly the creation of this powerful new position would have had the potential to upset the checks and balances of the existing system. The result was a vigorous public debate on the issue, which was accompanied by a discussion on the merits of abolishing the dual mandate, a measure that had been included in the Act of 2001 but had been dropped in the face of strong opposition from many national and local politicians. The Local Government (Number 2) Act of 2003 represented a compromise in that it abolished the dual mandate while simultaneously repealing the clause in the 2001 Act that provided for the direct election of mayors.[136]

However the issue was restored to the political agenda four years later when, following the general election of 2007 a new coalition government was formed consisting of Fianna Fáil, the Progressive Democrats and (for the first time ever in Ireland) the Green Party. The latter party was committed to local government reform and in particular to the empowerment of local authorities. The prominent Green TD John Gormley, was appointed Minister for the Environment and Local Government on 14 June 2007 and a few weeks later announced the beginning of a process of consultation that would lead to the publication of proposals at the end of the year to establish a directly elected mayoralty in Dublin by 2011. He also suggested that directly elected mayors might also be introduced in other urban areas. At the time of writing, the process of consultation is only beginning.[137]

The Mayoralty of Limerick Today.

At the time of writing, the mayoralty continues to be a vigorous and thriving institution, which enjoys a high degree of popularity and visibility in Limerick city and its environs. The mayor is a local president with limited powers but great prestige and the office is eagerly sought after by the members of the city council. While it is commonplace to contrast the lack of power wielded by Irish mayors compared to their counterparts in Europe and North America, it can be argued that the mayor of an Irish city or town enjoys prestige precisely because of not being involved in the routine decision-making process. Often a constitutional monarch or ceremonial president commands more universal respect and loyalty than an active head of government. Like his or her colleagues throughout the state, the mayor of Limerick continues to function effectively as a ceremonial local president and is likely to continue doing so for many years to come. However, if John Gormley's proposals are successfully implemented in the next few years, the local presidency of Limerick is likely to move from the largely ceremonial Irish model to the powerful American or French model.

Endnotes

1   For the origins of the age of revolution and reform, see M. S. Anderson, *Europe in the Eighteenth Century*, (Oxford, 1979); William Doyle, *The Old European Order 1660-1800*, (Oxford, 2nd edition, 1992); Eric Hobsbawm, *The Age of Revolution*, (Oxford, 1962); and George Rudé, *Europe in the Eighteenth Century*.

2   Hobsbawm, *Age of Revolution*, passim.

3   Sir David Lindsay Keir, *The Constitutional History of Modern Britain Since 1485*, (9th Edition, London, 1968), p. 369.

4   Alan Norton, *International Handbook of Local and Regional Government. A Comparative Analysis of Advanced Democracies*, (London, 1994), pp 121-23.

5   Ibid., pp 236-37.

6   Raymond Carr, *Spain 1808-1975*, (second edition Oxford, 1982), p. 159.

7   Norton, *International Handbook of Local and Regional Government*, pp 190-92.

8   For developments in Britain in the 1830s see Alexander Llewellyn, *The Decade of Reform: the 1830s* (New York, 1971). For Ireland see Gearóid O'Tuathaigh, *Ireland Before the Famine 1798-1848,* (Dublin 1972).

9   For general surveys of the local government system in Ireland in the nineteenth century see William F. Bailey, *Local and Centralised Government in Ireland. A Sketch of the Existing Systems,* (Dublin, 1888); Virginia Crossman, *Local Government in Nineteenth Century Ireland,* (Belfast, 1994) and R. B. McDowell, *The Irish Administration, 1801-1914,* (London, 1964).

10 3 & 4 Vict. c. 108.

11 Ibid.

12 Ibid.

13 Ibid.

14 Ibid.

15 Ibid.

16 28 Vict. c. 8 and 41 & 42 Vict. c. 52.

17 Lenihan, *History of Limerick,* p. 497.

18 Minute Books of Limerick City Council (Limerick Archives), hereafter CCM, 11th November 1841.

19 This episode of the two corporations is described in Lenihan, *History of Limerick,* pp 497-98.

20 For the first meeting of the new corporation see Mulligan, 'The Enemy Within; The Enemy Without', p. 71.

21 For the history of the Commercial Buildings, see Lenihan, *History of Limerick,* p. 414.

22 Ibid.

23 CCM, 21 January 1847.

24 Anonymous, *A Descriptive and Historic Guide Through St. Mary's Cathedral, Limerick,* (3rd edition, Limerick, 1887), p. 61.

25 16 & 17 Vict. c. 194.

26 16 & 17 Vict. c. 73.

27 R. B. McDowell, 'Administration and the Public Service, 1800-70' in Vaughan, *A New History of Ireland Volume V.,* p. 560.

28 Potter, *The Government and the People of Limerick,* pp 314-16.

29 For 'gas and water socialism' in Britain, see Barry M. Doyle, 'The Changing Functions of Urban Government: Councillors, Officials and Pressure Groups' and Robert Millward, 'The Political Economy of Urban Utilities' in Martin Daunton (ed.), *The Cambridge Urban History of Britain.* Volume III, 1840-1950, (Cambridge, 2001), pp 287-313 and pp 315-49 respectively.

30 For 'gas and water socialism' in Limerick see Potter, *The Government and the People of Limerick,* pp 324-31.

31 For the LGB, see Mary E. Daly, *The Buffer State. The Historical Roots of the Department of the Environment,* (Dublin, 1997), pp 18-46.

32 For similar developments in England see John Garrard, 'The Mayoralty since 1835' in *Proceedings of the Lancashire and Cheshire Historical Society,* Volume 90, (1994).

33 For the staff of Limerick Corporation at the beginning of the twentieth century see *County Borough Council of Limerick. Return of the Average Weekly Expenses of the Different Departments of the Corporation,* (Limerick, 1902), hereafter known as *Limerick Corporation Return of 1902.*

34 See John Garrard, *Bureaucrats Rather Than Bureaucracies: The Power of Municipal Professionals 1835-1914.* Occasional Papers in History and Politics No.33, (Salford, 1993).

35 Information from Mr. Bryan McHugh.

36 For William Nolan and his family see Padráig de Bhaldraithe and Padráig Og de Bhaldraithe, 'The Nolans and Costelloes of Listowel, Limerick and Calgary' in *The Old Limerick Journal,* No. 27, (Autumn, 1990), pp 13-19. See also his obituary in *Limerick Chronicle,* 22 March 1941.

37 Information from Mr. Bryan McHugh.

38 Potter, *The Government and the People of Limerick,* p. 319.

39 39 & 40 Vict. c.76.

40 Mulligan, 'The Enemy Within; The Enemy Without', p. v, viii.

41 For the motion in favour of Repeal see CCM, 1 May 1843.

42 The Catholic Whigs are described at length in Matthew Potter, 'A Catholic Unionist: the Life and Times of William Monsell, first Baron Emly of Tervoe 1812-1894,' (Unpublished Ph.D thesis, National University of Ireland, Galway, 2001), *passim.*

43 *Report from the Select Committee on Local Government and Taxation of Towns (Ireland); together with the Proceedings of the Committee, Minutes of Evidence and Appendix,* H.C. 1877 (357), xii., hereafter referred to as *Report of the Committee of 1877,* p. 57.

44 Lenihan, History of Limerick, p. 517.

45   For an interesting insight into Spaight's personality and political outlook see minutes of his evidence in *Report of the Committee of 1877*, pp 18-37. For Tait see John C. Waite, Peter Tait. *A Remarkable Story*, (Little Norton, 2005).

46   CCM, 11 May 1871.

47   See John Garrard, 'Urban Elites, 1850-1914: The Rule and Decline of a New Squirearchy?' in *Albion*, Vol. 27, No.3, (Autumn, 1995) and John Garrard, *Leadership and Power in Victorian Industrial Towns 1830-80*, (Manchester, 1983), pp 13-35.

48   Information from Mr. Bryan McHugh.

49   Mansfield, *Ceremonial Costume*, pp 266-68. See also Simon Gunn, 'Ritual and Civic Culture in the English Industrial City, c. 1835-1914' in Morris and Trainor , *Urban Governance*, pp 226-241.

50   Heather Cunningham, 'Civic Peacocks' in Lee, *Remembering Limerick*, p. 335.

51   Laurence Walsh, *Historic Limerick, The City and Its Treasures*, (Dublin, 1984), p. 13.

52   For examples, see CCM, 30 March 1865; 23 February and 20 April 1871.

53   39 & 40 Vict. c. 76.

54   *Limerick Chronicle*, 5 October 1886.

55   61 & 62, Vict. c. 37.

56   Roche, *Local Government*, p. 47.

57   Ciarán O'Gríofa, 'Structures of Municipal Government in Limerick 1841-1934,' in Lee, *Remembering Limerick.*, p. 285.

58   61 & 62, Vict. c. 37.

59   Diarmaid Ferriter, *'Lovers of Liberty?'Local Government in 20th Century Ireland*, (Dublin, 2001), p. 66.

60   61 & 62, Vict. c. 37.

61   For the 1899 election in Limerick city see Enda McKay, 'The Limerick Municipal Elections, January 1899' in *The Old Limerick Journal*, No. 36, (Winter, 1999), pp 3-10. See also *Limerick Leader*, 18 January 1899.

62   Ciarán O'Gríofa, 'John Daly, the Fenian Mayor of Limerick', in Lee, *Remembering Limerick*, pp 200-01. For a detailed account of ther period, see Pat Collins, 'Labour, Church and Nationalism in Limerick 1893-1902', (Unpublished MA thesis, University College Cork, 1984).

63   *Freeman's Journal*, 19 January 1899.

64   A good account of the Fenian mayor is O'Gríofa, 'John Daly', pp 197-204. See also Collins, 'Labour, Church and Nationalism', pp 158-204, 249-96.

65   Arthur Mitchell, *Labour in Irish Politics. The Irish Labour Movement in an Age of Revolution*, (Dublin, 1974), pp 18-20.

66   Collins, 'Labour, Church and Nationalism', pp 289-92.

67   Mitchell, *Labour in Irish Politics*, pp 27-30.

68   Potter, *The Government and the People of Limerick*, p. 357.

69   I am grateful to Mr. Frank Prendergast, former city councillor, mayor and TD for this information.

70   See Brian Donnelly, 'Michael Joyce: Squarerigger, Shannon Pilot and M. P.' in *The Old Limerick Journal*, No. 27, (Autumn, 1990), pp 42-44 and Ciarán O'Gríofa, 'Michael Joyce-Maritime Mayor' in Lee, *Remembering Limerick*, pp 204-10.

71   For a good account of this episode see Dermot Keogh and Andrew McCarthy, *Limerick Boycott 1904: Anti-Semitism in Ireland*, (Cork, 2005). See also Jonathan McGee, 'The Mayoralty and the Jews of Limerick' in Lee, *Remembering Limerick*, pp 158-66 and Des Ryan, 'Jewish Immigrants in Limerick- A Divided Community' in the same work, pp 166-74.

72   CCM, 20 April 1904.

73   See Judith Crosbie, ' The Era of Radicalism: Limerick's Mayors During World War One' in Lee, *Remembering Limerick*, pp 213-23.

74   Liam Cahill, *Forgotten Revolution. Limerick Soviet 1919. A Threat to British Power in Ireland*, (Dublin, 1990), pp 32-34.

75   For the 1916 Rising and Limerick see Des Ryan, '1916 Rising-The Limerick Connection' in Lee, *Remembering Limerick*, pp 236-40.

76   Ibid., pp 239-40.

77   CCM, 1 June 1916.

78   Thomas J. Morrissey, *Bishop Edward Thomas O'Dwyer of Limerick*, 1842-1917, (Dublin, 2003), p. 376.

79   CCM, 1 June 1916.

80   Ibid.

81   Ibid., pp 221-23.

82   See Nora-Ann Toomey and David Lee, ' The General Strike as a Political Weapon-Limerick, 1918-20' in Lee, *Remembering Limerick*, pp 241-50.

83   Ibid., pp 241-42. See also Cahill, *Forgotten Revolution*, p. 42.

84 Cahill, *Forgotten Revolution*, pp 59-62.

85 Ibid., pp 59-78.

86 Ibid., pp 97-119. See also Toomey and Lee, 'General Strike', p. 245.

87 Cahill, *Forgotten Revolution*, pp 97-119.

88 O'Gríofa, 'Michael Joyce', p. 210.

89 9 & 10 Geo. V c. 19.

90 For the 1920 local elections see *Limerick Leader*, 20 January 1920.

91 CCM, 30 January 1920.

92 Ibid.

93 For Clancy see Jim Kemmy, ' George Clancy- Murdered Mayor' in Lee, *Remembering Limerick*, pp 250-52 and 'Portrait of the Martyr as a Young Man' in the same publication, pp 252-60.

94 For an account of the curfew murders based on eyewitness accounts see Mrs. O'Callaghan, Mrs. Clancy and others, 'The Limerick Curfew Murders of 7th March, 1921' in *Limerick's Fighting Story. Told by the Men who Made it*, (Tralee, no date of publication), pp 115-39. See also Des Ryan, 'Who Shot the Mayors?' in Lee, *Remembering Limerick*, pp 262-64.

95 See Jim Kemmy, 'James Casey-Soviet Treasurer' in Lee, *Remembering Limerick*, pp 264-66.

96 See Ciarán O'Gríofa, 'Stephen O'Mara and the Limerick Crisis, March 1922' in Lee, *Remembering Limerick*, pp 268-73.

97 CCM, 21 May 1921.

98 CCM, 30 January 1922.

99 O'Gríofa, 'Stephen O'Mara', pp 271-72.

100 See P. J. Ryan, 'Armed Conflict in Limerick' in Lee, *Remembering Limerick*, pp 274-76.

101 O'Gríofa, 'Stephen O'Mara', p. 273.

102 John W. de Courcy and Heather Cunningham, 'Bob de Courcy – The Republican Engineer' in Lee, *Remembering Limerick*, pp 277-79.

103 Act 4 of 1922 and Act 39 of 1924.

104 Act 5 of 1925.

105 CCM, 30 June 1925.

106 Act 42 of 1925.

107 Act 39 of 1927.

108 See Roche, *Local Government*, p. 100.

109 *Limerick Chronicle*, 27 June 1925.

110 *Limerick Chronicle*, 17 November 1934.

111 Act 35 of 1934.

112 Ibid.

113 Roche, *Local Government*, pp 103.

114 Ibid., pp 321-29.

115 Act 35 of 1934.

116 Ibid.

117 Department of the Environment and Local Government. Files relating to Limerick Corporation, 50905.

118 CCM, 8 November 1934.

119 CCM, 1945, 1975 and 2005 *passim*.

120 A modern and comprehensive description of the functions of Irish local authorities can be found in Callanan and Keogan, *Local Government*, Chapters 9-16, pp 165-298.

121 I am grateful to Mr. John Quinn, former mayor of Limerick (1992-93) for this information.

122 I am grateful to the distinguished Limerick artist and freeman of Limerick, Dr. Thomas Ryan, RHA and to Mr. Frank Prendergast for information concerning the mayoral wand.

123 Eileen McMahon, 'Robes of Office' in Lee, *Remembering Limerick*, p. 333.

124 Ibid., pp 332-34.

125 For Ted Russell, see Anne Yeoman, 'Throwing the Dart' in Lee, *Remembering Limerick*, pp 327-32 and Anne Yeoman, ' George E. (Ted) Russell, Mayor of Limerick, 1954-55, 1955-56, 1956-57, 1967-68, 1976-77, Freeman of Limerick' in Lee, *Remembering Limerick*, pp 324-27.

126 See Leonard, 'Provosts and Mayors of Limerick' pp 378-92.

127 For Mrs. Condell's mayoralty see Ciarán O'Gríofa, ' First Citizen Meets First Citizen. Frances Condell and the Visit of John F. Kennedy, June, 1963' in Lee, *Remembering Limerick*, pp 363-66.

128 Leonard, 'Provosts and Mayors of Limerick' p. 379.

129 Corporation of Limerick. *List of the Mayors and Sheriffs of the City from 1197 to the Present Day* (Limerick 2001).

130 Vincent Browne and Michael Farrell, *The Magill Book of Irish Politics*, (Dublin, 1981), pp 244-56.

131 The information is based on the Limerick chapters in successive editions of *Nealon's Guide to the Dáil and Seanad*, (Dublin, 1973-2002).

132 For the new City Hall see *Limerick Corporation City Hall. Limerick Celebrates* (June 2. 1990) a commemorative newspaper produced to mark its official opening.

133 Terry O'Sullivan, 'Local Areas and Structures' in Callanan and Keogan, *Local Government* p. 41.

134 Act 37 of 2001.

135 For a discussion of this issue see Liam Kenny, 'Local Government and Politics' in Callanan and Keogan, *Local Government*, p.116.

136 Act 17 of 2003.

137 *Irish Times*, 12 July 2007

The cradle given by Limerick Corporation to Mayor Michael Ryan
on the birth of a son during his term of office in 1859.
(Jim Kemmy Municipal Museum)

Chapter Six
Chronicle of the Mayors of Limerick
Part One 1842-1899

Introduction.

Since the establishment of Limerick Corporation/City Council, it is believed that approximately 580 different individuals have held the office of provost or mayor of Limerick. It would not be possible to produce an account, however brief, of the life of each of these incumbents, due to the paucity of primary source material for the medieval and early modern periods.[1] Such an exercise is only possible from the nineteenth century onwards, due to the existence of a complete set of Limerick Corporation minutes from the time of the coming into operation of the Municipal Corporations (Ireland) Act and to the increasing abundance and completeness of newspaper records. These considerations, plus the fact that the Act of 1840 resulted in the creation of the modern mayoralty of Limerick, have informed the decision to commence this chronicle of the mayors Limerick with the assumption of office by Mayor Martin Honan on 1 January 1842. It should be noted that while the term 'Limerick City Council' is used for the sake of convenience throughout the present and succeeding chapters, the usual designation from 1842 to 1899 was 'Town Council', from 1899 to 1934 it was known as 'County Borough Council' and it was officially named 'City Council' only in 1934. Councillors attached the initials TC after their names from 1842 to 1899 and BC in similar fashion from 1899 to 1934.

Martin Honan 1842 and 1843.

On 11 November 1841 the reformed Limerick City Council unanimously selected Martin Honan to be the first mayor of the city under the Municipal Corporations (Ireland Act) of 1840.[2] He took office on 1 January 1842 but did not become the undisputed mayor for another seven months, due to a legal technicality that resulted in two corporations co-existing in Limerick throughout the first half of 1842. At the beginning of 1842, the new corporation demanded possession of the Exchange, plus all the records, books and property of the corporation. The old corporation, headed by its mayor Charles Smyth Vereker refused to give way until amending legislation was enacted in July 1842, legalising the acts of the reformed corporation and declaring it to be the rightful local

Martin Honan
(Limerick City Gallery of Art)

authority. Mayor Vereker submitted at once, but the chamberlain, town clerk and common speaker of the old corporation refused to hand over the municipal records, until forced to do so by court order. In consequence, the first real meeting of the new corporation only took place on 3 August 1842.[3]

Martin Honan was a wealthy woollen merchant and draper who in the 1820s carried on his business at 8 Charlotte Quay, Limerick. This was also his residence until 1831 when he moved to a country house called Quinsboro which was situated in Parteen, outside the city. In 1826 Honan married Anna Maria Kane of Whitehall House, Parteen, whose brother Thomas was later to serve as mayor of Limerick in 1852 and 1857.[4] Honan was one of the original forty members elected to the new city council in 1841 and remained a member for seven years until his death. He was the first Catholic mayor since the Treaty of Limerick and was a supporter of Daniel O'Connell and of Repeal. In 1843 he served a second term as mayor.

The new corporation inherited a debt of over £12,000 from its predecessor and had also lost control of the liberties and of Scattery Island, and in consequence, its territory was reduced to one tenth of its previous size. A huge backlog of work had to be tackled, a sweeping programme of reform implemented, and a depleted financial base overhauled. The old city consisting of the Englishtown and Irishtown were in a state of dereliction and decay and were inhabited mainly by the poor, the unemployed and the marginalized. The prosperous area of Newtown Pery was still under the jurisdiction of the Commissioners of St. Michael's Parish, and thus outside the remit of the corporation (although remaining within the borough boundary). Consequently, the reformed corporation commenced its operations under the shadow of a financial crisis so bad that in 1842 Mayor Honan had to advance £1,500 of his own money to help the municipal finances.[5] Nevertheless Honan's two terms of office saw some progress in dealing with the city's problems and he seems to have been a vigorous and progressive mayor. Between 1842 and 1843, £4,300 was spent on repairing the streets and on reflagging the footpaths in the old city and in 1843, a new potato market was opened at Merchants' Quay.[6]

In his private life, Honan was a generous and charitable man, particularly in relation to his adopted parish of Parteen. He was a major benefactor to the new Catholic church erected there between 1831 and 1835 and in 1834 he built at his sole expense a primary school for the parish. He also contributed to a wide variety of charities and was very active in Famine relief.[7] He died on 19 March 1848 and was buried in a huge vault at Parteen Church.[8]

Pierse Shannon 1844.

The second mayor under the Act of 1840 took office on 1 January 1844. Pierse Shannon was born in the West of County Clare but was long established in Limerick city as a wealthy and successful merchant. He operated as a wholesale ironmonger and ships chandler in the Cornmarket in the city but in 1824 built a magnificent suburban residence which he named Corbally House after the district in which it was situated.[9] In 1833, Shannon purchased the greater part of the townland of Corbally at a cost of £22,000 from Colonel William Thomas Monsell, of Tervoe House, Clarina, County Limerick.[10] He subsequently developed the entire area, laying out the present Corbally Road and building several fine residences there, which he subsequently sold to other wealthy persons.[11] In effect, Pierse Shannon created Corbally as a residential area. He was a man of ability whose business interests 'stretched as far as the Baltic and Russia'.[12]

In 1841 Shannon was elected as one of the first members of the new Limerick city council and served for three years until his death. Like Martin Honan, he was a strong supporter of Repeal and of Daniel O'Connell of whom he was a close friend. Shannon died suddenly on 6 June 1844, almost halfway through his mayoralty, while he was about to chair a meeting in support of O'Connell who was then in prison.[13] In 1867, his son, also Pierse, sold Corbally House to Dr. George Butler, the Catholic bishop of Limerick, who renamed it 'The Palace, Corbally' and as such it served as the residence of successive bishops of Limerick until 1956. It was subsequently demolished and between 1960 and 1963, the present St. Munchin's College was built on its site.[14]

William J. Geary 1844 and 1845.

William John Geary was born in 1800, the son of Dr. John Geary, who was a very distinguished figure in the medical life of Limerick for many years. John Geary was the senior physician in St. John's Hospital for most of his life and was the author of *A Historical and Medical Report of the Limerick Fever and Lock Hospitals* (1819), which is of great interest to the student of both social and medical history as it covers the period 1779 to 1819. William Geary received his medical training in Edinburgh and worked as physician in St. John's Hospital from 1826 to 1832 and Barrington's Hospital from 1831 to 1851. Like his father, Geary combined a very busy professional life with a distinguished literary output on medical and social issues.[15]

William Geary was one of the original members of the new city council in 1841 and remained a member until 1851. On 10 June 1844 he was elected mayor in succession to Pierse Shannon and served out the remainder of the latter's term.[16] He subsequently served as mayor for the whole of 1845. Like his two immediate predecessors, he was a staunch Repealer. However, in the summer of 1845, a silly misunderstanding arose between the corporation and Daniel O'Connell.[17] Mayor Geary invited O'Connell (who had stopped in Limerick on his way to Derrynane, his Kerry residence), to a banquet in the Exchange, which was to be attended by the city council. Unfortunately, the judges of the court of assizes, who were also in town, were invited as well. One of these had sentenced O'Connell to a term of imprisonment the previous year, in the aftermath of the banning of the Repeal monster meeting at Clontarf. Consequently, O'Connell left Limerick rather than share a table with him at the banquet. The city council was furious at this perceived snub by O'Connell, and passed a resolution to the effect that the mayor had acted without the authority of the corporation, when he had invited O'Connell to the banquet. On 7 August 1845, O'Connell wrote a letter to the mayor in which he adopted a conciliatory tone, stating that 'I am now perfectly convinced that the mistake was mine', and expressing a desire that 'by-gones be by-gones.'[18]

Among the most significant events of Geary's period as mayor were the commencement of the rebuilding of Mathew Bridge in 1844 and the establishment of a night watch in the Irishtown and Englishtown in 1845.[19] More ominously, a cholera epidemic afflicted the city in 1845 and the potato blight arrived in Ireland, heralding the beginning of the Great Famine. Geary resigned from the city council in 1851 and in 1852, he was appointed as Medical Inspector under the Medical Charities Act (1851).[20] In this capacity he inspected the dispensary system in Counties Limerick, Cork, Clare and Kerry, a hugely difficult and onerous task, which he discharged until illness forced him to retire shortly before his death, which occurred on 1 February 1871. William J. Geary was buried in Mount St. Lawrence Cemetery, Limerick city.[21]

Edmond Fitzgerald Ryan 1846.

Born in Limerick city in 1819, Edmond Fitzgerald Ryan was the son of Michael Ryan, a leading merchant of the city, and as a young man he worked as a partner in the family business, Ryan Brothers, ship brokers and general commission agents. Edmond was a member of Limerick City Council from 1841 to 1847 and was a supporter of the Repeal movement. Daniel O'Connell once wrote to him: 'your grandfather was my friend, your father was my greatest friend and believe me, Edmund, I will always be your sincere friend'.[23] With such exalted connections, it was no surprise that Ryan became mayor of Limerick on I January 1846 at the early age of twenty-six. Indeed, he is the third most youthful person to have served as mayor of Limerick since 1842; only William O'Donnell (1890) and Thady Coughlan (1975-76) were younger than him.

One of the most important events of Ryan's mayoralty was the opening of Mathew Bridge in June 1846 and his name is immortalised on the commemorative plaque attached to the centre of the bridge.[24] However, this was one of the few positive developments of the year, as his term of office coincided with the beginning of the Great Famine. Ryan was very active in famine relief, although Limerick Corporation played a much smaller role than the Board of Poor Law Guardians in dealing with this crisis. In consequence of his good works, he was offered the choice of a knighthood or a resident magistracy when his term of office concluded. He chose the latter and in consequence resigned from the council in 1847. Ryan served as a resident magistrate in Counties Galway and Cork, before eventually settling in Wexford town in 1868. He lived there for the rest of his life and died there at his residence, 'Alma' on 15 August 1897.[25] His brother Michael also served as mayor of Limerick in 1859.

Thomas Wallnutt 1847.

Born in 1794, Thomas Wallnutt was a corn merchant whose business premises was in Thomondgate and who resided in Sunville, on the North Circular Road.[26] He was a member of the city council from 1841 to 1849 and in 1847 he became the first Protestant mayor of Limerick since 1842. His mayoralty was a turbulent one. The famine crisis reached its height in 1847 and thousands of starving people arrived in search of work and food.[27] The corporation petitioned the government to establish public works schemes in order to provide for the destitute poor. By January 1847, 506 people were employed in the city on such schemes but these were soon abandoned in favour of the distribution of free food.[28] Soup kitchens were set up throughout the country in the spring of 1847. The corporation gave the use of the new potato market on Merchants' Quay for the soup kitchen of St. Mary's Parish but in general had little or no role in famine relief.[29] At the end of 1847 the principal responsibility for managing this crisis was placed on the poor law system, and the soup kitchens were closed down. The result was disastrous, with huge numbers of destitute poor flooding the workhouses. In Limerick, the workhouse, built to house 1,600 paupers, had an average of 2,512 inmates in 1846, 2,204 in 1847, 2,830 in 1848 and an incredible 4,550 in 1849.[30] In the latter years, a second cholera epidemic swept Limerick city. It was believed that of the 4,000 people who died in Limerick workhouse during the famine, some 3,000 died of cholera.[31]

During Walnutt's mayoralty, the city council had its first meeting in the new Town Hall on 21 January 1847. However, the corporation was badly hit by the serious economic crisis brought on by the Famine and strict economies in the municipal finances were initiated. In September 1847, it was decided to reduce the mayor's salary from £500 to £400 per annum (although this decision was reversed a few months later). The treasurer's salary was fixed at £200 per year, instead of 5% of net annual receipts, as had previously been the case. No new appointments were to be made to fill vacancies caused by death, retirement or dismissal.[32]

Thomas Wallnutt died at his residence on 17 September 1849 and was buried in St. Munchin's Churchyard.[33]

Michael Quin 1848.

Michael Quin was born in 1777 and was a wealthy grocer and spirit merchant who conducted his business on 125 Georges Street.[34] A man of considerable wealth, he invested a lot of money in landed estates, which he had acquired from impecunious landowners. A Catholic, he was a supporter of Catholic Emancipation and of Daniel O'Connell.[35] He was active in public life for many years, serving as a member of St. Michael's Parish Commissioners from 1831 to 1853 and of Limerick City Council from 1841 to 1856.[36]

Quin served as mayor in 1848 and at seventy was one of the oldest persons ever to hold the office. He won praise for giving his entire mayoral salary to various charities in the city, although his considerable wealth meant that this may not have been a great sacrifice for him. However he was criticised for his role in a riot that occurred in Limerick on 29 April 1848 and became known derisively as the 'Battle of Limerick'. The Young Irelanders had split from O'Connell's Repeal movement in 1846 and tensions between the two groups remained high in the ensuing years. The Limerick riot occurred when a mob of O'Connell's supporters attacked a group of Young Irelanders who were attending a banquet in the city. Among the Young Irelanders present was William Smith O'Brien, one of Limerick city's two MPs who was injured during the melee. It was alleged that Mayor Quin, a supporter of O'Connell, did not discharge his duties as chief magistrate of the city in an impartial fashion on this occasion. Instead, it was believed by many that he had deliberately delayed his arrival at the scene of the riot in order to allow the attack on the Young Irelanders proceed unhindered, and that when he finally did appear, he took the part of the O'Connellite mob.[37]

Other prominent events of his mayoralty were the opening of railway communications between Limerick and Dublin and the acquisition by the corporation of the Island Bank, which was a path around the perimeter of the King's Island, used as an amenity by the public.[38] Quin's only son died in 1855, and the grief-stricken old gentleman retired both from his business and from public life. Michael Quin died on 7 March 1866 at the age of eighty-eight and was buried in Mount St. Lawrence Cemetery.[39]

John Boyse 1849.

John Boyse was a prominent solicitor who resided at 115 Georges Street.[40] He was a Catholic, a staunch Liberal and a firm opponent of the pre-1841 'Corrupt Corporation' who spent £1,400 out of his own pocket 'in sustaining the popular cause' against the Verekers.[41] He was a member of the city council from 1841 until 1849 and served as mayor for the year 1849.[42] When Queen Victoria made her first visit to Ireland in 1849, he attended a levee (a royal reception for men only) at Dublin Castle on the 8 August at which he presented the Queen with an address from Limerick Corporation in which they sent the Queen their 'warmest congratulations and welcome' on the occasion of her first visit to Ireland, and spoke of their 'devoted loyalty and attachment to your Majesty's throne and person'. Mayor Boyse also laid the foundation for the new floating docks, which were to be completed in 1853.[44] He died in office on 9 December and was buried in St. Munchin's Churchyard.[45] His son Thomas Boyse served as mayor of Limerick in 1869.

Laurence Quinlivan 1849 and 1850.

Born in 1800, Laurence Quinlivan was a successful businessman in Limerick for many years. In 1846 he is recorded as being the proprietor of Quinlivans Hotel in 10 William Street but by 1867 was described as a corn merchant in Upper William Street.[46] He was a member of Limerick City Council from 1842 until his death in 1876.[47] He was elected mayor in December 1849 to serve out the remainder of John Boyse's term of office and was also mayor for the whole of 1850. A Catholic, he was a Liberal in the 1850s and 1860s and a supporter of Home Rule in the 1870s, a common enough political evolution at this period. On 16 May 1850 Mayor Quinlivan hosted a public banquet for General Lord Gough who was a native of Castleconnell, County Limerick and had commanded the British forces during recent campaigns in India and China. Along with other mayors from the whole United Kingdom, Quinlivan attended the special banquet held by the Lord Mayor of London in honour of Prince Albert and 'in furtherance' of the Great Exhibition that was to be held in 1851 in the Crystal Palace, London.[48] Quinlivan died on 12 April 1876 and was buried in Mount St. Lawrence Cemetery.[49] One of his sisters, Anne was married to John Keatinge-O'Dwyer and their son was Edward Thomas O'Dwyer, the celebrated bishop of Limerick.[50]

Thaddeus McDonnell 1851 and 1860.

Born in 1807, Thaddeus McDonnell was described in 1846 as a corn merchant whose business premises was in Henry Street and whose residence was at 13 Upper Cecil Street.[51] He was a member of the city council from 1841 until his death in 1871.[52] McDonnell served as mayor of Limerick for the whole of 1851 and on 1 November 1860 was elected to succeed Mayor William Fitzgerald, who had died in office, to serve until the end of the year.[53] However he resigned on 6 December 1860 after serving for just a month and was replaced by John T. McSheehy.[54] In 1852, McDonnell stood for parliament as a Conservative in the Limerick city constituency, but came last out of four candidates, with a disastrous 94 votes out of a total of 1,524 votes cast.[55] He died on 14 December 1871 at the age of sixty-four and was buried in Mount St. Lawrence Cemetery.[56]

Thomas Kane 1852 and 1857.

Born in 1805, Thomas Kane lived in the North of Ireland, where his father was an officer with the County Limerick Militia, until 1817 and subsequently in Whitehall House in Parteen, County Clare, outside Limerick city.[57] He graduated from Trinity College, Dublin with a BA in 1826 and then trained as a medical doctor in the College of Surgeons in Dublin and in Glasgow. He had a general practice in Limerick for some sixty years until his death in 1890. He was also employed for many years as the medical officer for the Cratloe and Meelick district dispensary.[58]

It was virtually inevitable that Kane should become involved in local politics, due to the active part played by his family in the public life of Limerick city. His father Captain Richard Kane was a prominent advocate of municipal reform in Limerick in the late 1830s and early 1840s and served as a member of both Limerick City Council and the Board of Guardians of Limerick Poor Law Union, while his brother-in-law was Martin

Honan (mayor in 1842 and 1843). Thomas Kane himself was a member of Limerick City Council from 1848 to 1873. He served as mayor of Limerick in 1852 and again in 1857. The general election of 1852 occurred during his first mayoralty and was marked by the fierce rioting and disorder that was an inevitable feature of elections all over Ireland at this period. Kane was widely praised for the manner in which he intervened during an election riot in Limerick city and persuaded the mob to lay down their arms. During his second mayoralty, his first child was born on 23 June 1857 and in accordance with a custom of unknown antiquity, the corporation presented him with a silver cradle, to mark the happy event.[59] In July 1857, a foreign royal personage Prince Jerome Napoleon, nephew of the great Napoleon, and first cousin of the reigning French monarch, Napoleon III came to Limerick. The Prince was on a

Thomas Kane
(Limerick City Gallery of Art)

private visit to Ireland and was travelling incognito, but was welcomed to the city by Mayor Kane.[60]

However, Kane's main claim to fame is the role that he played in the erection of the O'Connell Monument in the Crescent. During his first mayoralty, Limerick Corporation took the decision to erect Ireland's first outdoor public statue of the Liberator and to finance it by public subscription. Kane was appointed treasurer of the fund and, along with Maurice Lenihan (the celebrated historian of Limerick and at that time a member of the city council), was responsible for raising an eventual total of £1,300. It was envisaged that the O'Connell Monument would be erected in the Crescent, perhaps the most prominent location in the city. In 1855, the unionist community in the city proposed that a statue of Viscount Fitzgibbon, (grandson of John Fitzgibbon, first Earl of Clare) who had recently been killed in the Battle of Balaclava should be erected there instead. A public row followed between the rival political factions. The result was that the O'Connell Monument was erected on the disputed site in the Crescent, while the Fitzgibbon Monument was relegated to the more peripheral location of Wellesley Bridge. On 15 August 1857, the O'Connell Monument was unveiled by Mayor Kane amidst scenes of considerable pomp and pageantry. The erection of this great monument, designed by the distinguished sculptor, John Hogan, was symbolic of the rise to power of the Catholic middle classes in Limerick that had resulted from the Municipal Corporations Act.[61]

After the high point of his 1857 Mayoralty, Kane's political career was relatively uneventful for the rest of his life. He remained a member of the city council until 1873 and as a former mayor was a magistrate until his death. He died on 5 March 1890 and was buried in St. Munchin's Churchyard.[62] His great-grandson is the distinguished writer and historian Fr. Mark Tierney OSB.

William H. Hall 1853.

William Henry Hall was born in Cork in 1798, but his work as a house, land and insurance agent brought him to Limerick in 1829, where he lived for the rest of his life.[63] He acted as agent for David Leahy Arthur, who owned a large amount of residential property in the city. Later Hall was appointed manager of the Union Bank. In his capacity as agent for the Arthur estate, he was described as a benevolent figure towards the tenants, and was reported to have been 'at all times willing and obliging, ever ready to attend to their household requirements in the way of decorations and repairs, which system led to most beneficial results, and afforded general satisfaction.'[64]

Hall was a member of the city council for only two years, from 1853 to 1855. He was a Protestant and a Conservative, and was elected Mayor by the narrow margin of 19 votes to 16, his opponent being Robert McMahon (later to be mayor in 1863).[65] Hall was a close ally of the prominent Alderman Henry Watson. The high point of his mayoralty was the opening of the new floating docks by the lord lieutenant, Earl St. Germains on 28 September 1853.[66] Hall was the last mayor to serve before the Limerick Corporation and Improvement Acts of 1853 were put into operation. He died on 3 December 1864, at the age of sixty-six.[67] One of his daughters was married to Ambrose Hall (mayor in 1875), to whom she was not otherwise related.[68]

Henry Watson 1854.

Born in 1789, Henry Watson had the unique distinction of being mayor of Limerick under both the old unreformed pre-1841 corporation and the new reformed post-1841 corporation. Son of Andrew Watson (Mayor in 1812-13), Henry succeeded his father as publisher of the *Limerick Chronicle* in 1810 and ran it, either alone or in partnership, for the next fifty years until shortly before his death.[69]

Henry Watson's role as publisher of Limerick's main newspaper for half a century would alone have made him one of the leading figures in the city but this only represented one aspect of his multi-faceted career. A loyal ally of the Verekers, he was a member of the old common council for some thirty years and of the new city council from 1841 until his death and was also an alderman under both regimes. He served as sheriff in 1811 and for three successive terms as mayor from 1823 to 1826. Later he became chamberlain (financial controller) in the 1830s. He served as a commissioner of St. Michael's Parish from 1827 to 1853, and was chairman of the Limerick Board of Poor Law Guardians for three years.[70]

The Limerick Corporation and Improvement Acts had both been enacted into law in 1853 and effected a transformation of the corporation almost as great as that brought about in 1840-42. It was all the more surprising, then that Henry Watson should have been elected as the first mayor under the new legislation, as he was both a Protestant and a Conservative like his predecessor and ally, William H. Hall. However, Watson's election occurred because of disputes in the ranks of the Liberals, while at the same time, he himself defected from the Tories and joined the Liberals.[71] Despite these crafty manoeuvres, and his previous associations with the hated pre-1841 corporation, Watson's mayoralty was a resounding success. He revived the ancient ceremony of riding the bounds of the city and in his capacity as Admiral of the Shannon travelled by steamer to Scattery Island with the entire city council, whom he entertained lavishly en voyage. The fact that Scattery Island was outside the jurisdiction of the corporation since 1841 did not in any way deter Watson from making such a visit, although the steamer ran aground in the vicinity of the island for a short time, thus introducing an element of farce into the proceedings.[72] Watson's popularity was such that, at the end of his term of office, he was chaired (carried ceremoniously on a chair) through the streets of Limerick by the 'congregated trades and the public, in testimony of his worth as chief magistrate'.[73] The most famous example of this curious practice, which represented the ultimate tribute from the populace, was the chairing of Thomas Spring-Rice on his election as MP for Limerick city in 1820, an event commemorated in the famous painting by William Turner de Lond, which is now kept in the Limerick Chamber of Commerce building, 96 O'Connell Street.[74] Henry Watson died on 10 March 1860 as a result of a surgical operation to remove a fishbone that had become lodged in his throat and was buried in St. Munchin's Churchyard.[75]

Henry O'Shea 1855.

Few if any mayors of Limerick have had such a colourful family as Henry O'Shea. Married to a Papal countess and father-in-law to one of the most famous women in Irish history, Henry O'Shea was himself a very prosaic though successful man. His father William was an impoverished landowner from Rich Hill near Limerick city and had three sons, Henry, John and Thaddeus. John emigrated to Spain and became a prosperous and successful banker. Thaddeus became a gambler and an unsuccessful horse-breeder. Henry was the eldest and inherited the broken-down and indebted family estate from his father. He became a very successful lawyer with offices at 88 Georges Street Limerick and also established a practice in Dublin. He specialised in the problems associated with indebted and bankrupt Irish estates, which was a widespread phenomenon in the aftermath of the Great Famine and in consequence became extremely wealthy.[76]

Henry O'Shea was a member of Limerick city council from 1853 to 1856 and served as mayor in 1855. During his term in office, he became involved in the controversy concerning the building of a monument to Daniel O'Connell in the Crescent. On 17 May 1855, Mayor O'Shea proposed that a statue of Viscount Fitzgibbbon should be erected there instead, as a sum of £1,040 had already been collected from the public for this purpose. After a great deal of controversy, the city council decided that the Crescent should become the site of the O'Connell Monument, a proposition supported by among others Michael Quin (mayor in 1848), Thomas Kane (mayor in 1852 and 1857) and Maurice Lenihan (mayor in 1884).[77]

O'Shea resigned from the council on 4 December 1856 and the following year was appointed clerk of the peace for County Limerick. The clerk of the peace was responsible for the routine functioning of the court of quarter sessions (equivalent to the modern district court) and the keeping of its records. Soon after Henry O'Shea and his family went to live in Dublin where he remained for the rest of his life.[78]

A staunch Catholic, Henry O'Shea was married to Catherine Quinlan who was a woman of stern religious views and was created a countess by the Pope. They had a son William and a daughter Mary who received the most expensive education that money could buy and spent long periods in France and Spain. William was a boarder at the exclusive St. Mary's College, Oscott in Warwickshire, England and then spent a period at the newly established Catholic University in Dublin where his wildness caused many problems for one of his lecturers, the celebrated philosopher and writer, John Henry, later Cardinal Newman. After a brief spell at Trinity College, William joined the British army in 1858, when his father bought him a commission in the 18th Hussars.[79] Henry O'Shea's son was to attain lasting fame (or infamy) as Captain William O'Shea, one of the central figures in the greatest scandal to rock Irish politics in the nineteenth century. He married Katherine Wood in 1867, and afterwards became Home Rule MP for Clare from 1880 to 1885 and for Galway from 1885 to 1886. His wife, satirically known as 'Kitty O'Shea', became the mistress (and later the wife) of Charles Stewart Parnell and this most famous love story in Irish history was eventually to bring about the downfall of the great Irish leader and to split the Home Rule Party for nearly a decade.[80]

In her memoirs, Katherine O'Shea portrayed her father-in-law Henry O'Shea as a kind, intelligent and successful man whose 'rich Irish brogue' contrasted sharply with the cut-glass English accent acquired by his son William at Oscott. She also recorded how the latter had accumulated debts amounting to £15,000 (equivalent in modern purchasing power to several million euro) and that Henry paid them all without complaining, thus demonstrating both how wealthy and how much of a doting father he was.[81] Henry O'Shea died in London on 18 June 1863 and was buried in Kensal Green Cemetery.[82]

Sir James Spaight 1856 and 1877.

Born in June 1818, James Spaight was the second son of Francis Spaight (1790-1861), one of Limerick's most prominent merchants. A native of County Clare, Francis Spaight had established a shipping company with his father-in-law in 1812 and introduced a paddle steamer to the Shannon in 1817.[83] Soon after he moved to Limerick city, where his business interests flourished. He founded a timber-importing business in Sarsfield Street while his shipping company went from strength to strength. Vast numbers of emigrants left Ireland on his ships between the 1820s and 1860s. In 1835, one of his ships, the *Francis Spaight*, was involved in one of the most celebrated tragedies in maritime history, when it was caught in a snow storm while returning from Canada with a cargo of timber. All of the food and drink aboard was washed overboard in the storm, and

James Spaight
(Limerick Chamber of Commerce. Photograph by Egleston Brothers Photographers).

the crew only survived on the long voyage to Limerick by killing and eating four of their shipmates, including the fifteen-year old cabin boy.[84] Francis Spaight became so wealthy that he was able to purchase Derry Castle, along with a 4,500 acre estate, near Killaloe in his native County Clare. He was a ruthless businessman, who gained infamy both for the manner in which he profited through emigration and the harshness with which he evicted insolvent tenants from the Derry Castle estate.[85]

Francis died in 1861 and his eldest son William succeeded him both as head of the business and as proprietor of the Derry Castle estate. This enabled his second son James to concentrate on public life. Both Francis and William Spaight were members of Limerick City Council for short periods, but James was a member from 1854 to 1882 and was one of the most prominent citizens in the city for nearly forty years.[86] He was a staunch Conservative and opponent of Home Rule, which resulted in his parliamentary career being singularly brief and unsuccessful, despite amazing persistence on his part, a situation that his obituary attempted to explain with the observation that 'he could have gone into parliament had he professed Home Rule principles'.[87] He was MP for the city for only a year (1858-59), but was defeated in the 1859 general election. He also stood unsuccessfully for parliament in 1865, 1874, 1879, 1880, 1883 and 1885.[88]

However, Spaight's career as a local political figure was a very successful one, lending credence to the explanation in his obituary for his brief parliamentary career. He served as a city councillor for twenty-eight years and was mayor on two occasions, separated by an unusually long interval of twenty years. On 1 December 1855, he was elected to serve as mayor in 1856 by the narrowest possible margin, twenty votes to nineteen.[89] The most important event of his first mayoralty was his attendance at the magnificent ceremony on 1 May, at which the foundation stone for the new Catholic St. John's Cathedral was laid. During the procession to the site of the proposed cathedral in St. John's Square, Mayor Spaight, a Protestant, rode with the Catholic bishop, Dr. John Ryan, in the latter's carriage, a notable gesture in a religiously polarised society.[90] On 1 December 1876, Spaight was elected mayor for 1877, by 17 votes to 11.[91] His second mayoralty was notable for the beginning of the modern system of conferring the freedom of the city on distinguished figures. The first two recipients, Isaac Butt and Richard O'Shaughnessy, the two MPs for Limerick city, received it on 1 January 1877. It was highly ironic that the leader of the Home Rule Party and one of his supporters should have received the freedom during the mayoralty of the staunchly unionist Spaight, who, however, did not sign the register of freemen on this occasion, as was customary.[92] One of Spaight's most notable achievements was the reform of the Limerick Night Watch. In 1877, he established a watch committee consisting of one member from each ward, and soon after a number of idle and drunken watchmen were dismissed. Consequently, their numbers were now reduced to twenty and two sub-inspectors appointed to 'watch the watchmen.'[93] Also in 1877, Mayor Spaight performed the opening ceremony of the People's Park.

Spaight was also involved in other local bodies. He was a long-serving and very active member of the Limerick Harbour Commissioners and served as chairman for a considerable period. In 1867, he was responsible for persuading the Government to cancel the enormous debt on Limerick Harbour, which had amounted to £175,000.[94] He was President of Limerick Chamber of Commerce from 1871 to 1892 and in that capacity and in the absence of any official welcome from the nationalist-dominated corporation, formally welcomed the Prince and Princess of Wales to Limerick in 1885, during their brief and inglorious visit to the city.[95] Spaight was involved with the Waterford and Limerick Railway (a private company that ran the railway system in much of Munster) as a director, vice-chairman and finally chairman. He was also active in the affairs of the Church of Ireland and of the Freemasons, was a member of Limerick Board of Poor Law Guardians and was a governor of both Barrington's Hospital and Limerick Lunatic Asylum. In 1887, he was among those knighted to mark Queen Victoria's Golden Jubilee and in 1888, he took over the running of the family business, on the death of his brother William and also inherited the Derry Castle estate.[96]

Sir James Spaight died on 21 January 1892 and was buried in the churchyard of St. Mary's Cathedral. He was the last ever Conservative and the last Protestant until 1962 to serve as mayor of Limerick. Despite his Conservative and unionist political views, he was a genuinely popular figure in Limerick city, due to his tactful and pleasant manner, staunch devotion to his native city and long and distinguished record of public service.[97] In terms of virtually universal popularity and multi-faceted public service, Spaight's nearest equivalent in twentieth-century Limerick was probably Ted Russell.

Thomas Kane 1857.
See above under 1852.

Edmund Gabbett 1858.
A member of a long established family in Limerick city and county, Edmund Gabbett was born in 1816 and was secretary to the grand jury of county Limerick for many years.[98] A Protestant and a Conservative, he was a member of Limerick City Council from 1846 to 1858 and again from 1859 to 1865.[99] He was elected mayor for the year 1858 by a vote of twenty votes to nineteen.[100] The high point of his mayoralty was the brief visit of Prince Alfred (1844-1900), the second son of Queen Victoria, to Limerick city on 26 June. Although he was only thirteen years of age, the prince made history on his visit as he was the first British royal person to visit the city since Lionel, Duke of Clarence (second son of King Edward III) in 1365. Prince Alfred arrived in Limerick by train and was met by Mayor Gabbett, who took him on a walking tour of the city along Queen Street (now Davis) Street, Glentworth Street, Georges Street and the Crescent, where the mayor showed Alfred the new O'Connell Monument. Then, they entered the mayor's carriage and drove through the city. After a brief visit to Castleconnell, the prince left Limerick. The teenage Prince Alfred was described as being an 'intelligent sprightly boy' with an 'animated, intellectual expression'.[101] Sadly, the adult Prince Alfred, while continuing to be 'intelligent' and 'intellectual', turned out to be a gruff, surly, bearded alcoholic, who was created Duke of Edinburgh in 1866, married the fabulously wealthy daughter of the Russian Emperor Alexander II in 1874 and lived for much of his life in Clarence House, which is more famous for having later served as the official residence of Queen Elizabeth, the Queen Mother, and at the time of writing is the principal home of the Prince of Wales.[102]

Edmund Gabbett continued to be active in public life for the rest of his life. Unfortunately, he did not live to a great age and died at forty-nine on 25 February 1865.[103]

Michael R. Ryan 1859.
A brother of Edmond Fitzgerald Ryan (mayor of Limerick in 1846), Michael Robert Ryan was born in 1822, the son of a well-to-do family and as a youth went to sea as a member of the merchant navy.[104] After the accidental drowning of his brother William on Lough Derg in 1845, he left the navy and worked for a time in the family business, Ryan Brothers, ship brokers and general commission agents.[105] Later he worked as agent to a number of landowners, including William Monsell, of Tervoe House in Clarina, County Limerick, the prominent statesman and MP. Ryan was a conscientious land agent who worked assiduously for his clients while at the same time treating the tenants with

kindness and consideration. Following his marriage in 1850, Ryan lived for a time in Mallow Street, but in the latter half of the 1850s, he built Templemungret House, just outside the city, as a large country house for his rapidly growing family. Michael and his brother Edmond were married to two sisters named Kiernan from County Louth.[106]

Michael Ryan was elected to Limerick City Council on 26 November 1856 and served until his death in 1874.[107] He was mayor in 1859. On 30 January of that year, a son and heir was born to Ryan and his wife Julia and the corporation presented the happy couple with the customary silver cradle, which is now kept in the Jim Kemmy Municipal Museum. In 1873 Ryan became High Sheriff of County Limerick.[108] He died of heart disease in Dublin on 15 December 1874 at the age of fifty-two and was buried in Mount St. Lawrence Cemetery.[109] In 1946, a book was published based on the memoirs of his daughters Eugenie (1853-1923) and Bertha (1862-1941) who became nuns in the Society of the Holy Child of Jesus under the names of Mother Aloysius and Mother Mary Magdalen respectively.[110]

William Fitzgerald 1860.

Born in 1826, William Fitzgerald was the son of David Fitzgerald, who was a land and insurance agent and a stock broker based at 109 Georges Street.[111] William became a member of Limerick City Council on 23 May 1856 at the age of thirty and was elected mayor on 1 December 1859.[112] His term of office was cut short prematurely, for he died of apoplexy on 26 October while preparing to attend the funeral of his colleague Alderman Sheehy, and was buried in St. Munchin's Churchyard.[113]

Thaddeus McDonnell 1860.

See above under 1851.

John T. McSheehy 1860 and 1861.

John Thomas McSheehy, sometimes known as Sheehy was a grocer and spirit merchant whose business premises was at 30 William Street and who resided at Shannon Lawn, near the city.[114] He was a member of the city council from 1853 to 1866.[115] 1860 was unusual in the annals of the mayoralty of Limerick as the city had three mayors in the course of the year. McSheedy was elected on 1 December 1860 to be mayor for 1861, but on 6 December, Thaddeus McDonnell resigned after serving for only a month and McSheehy was then elected on 11 December to serve out the rest of the year.[116] In 1861, he served as mayor of Limerick for the entire year and was presented with a valuable silver testimonial on leaving office. On 4 January 1866 he resigned from the council to take up the post of city treasurer, which he held until 2 January 1870, when he was appointed a resident magistrate.[117] In the latter capacity, he adjudicated in a number of very controversial court cases, to the intense annoyance of his former colleagues in Limerick Corporation, who eventually 'erased his name from the honour scroll of past mayors that stands in their council chamber.'[118] He lived in Parsonstown, Kings County (now known as Birr, County Offaly) at the end of his life. McSheedy died suddenly from heart disease while on holiday in Belgium on 1 September 1892.[119]

William Lane Joynt
(Dublin City Council)

William Lane Joynt 1862.

William Lane Joynt is the only person to have been both mayor of Limerick and lord mayor of Dublin. Born in Limerick in 1824, he became an apprentice solicitor to Sir Matthew Barrington in Dublin, but later returned to his native city and set up what soon became a thriving practice there. He also became land agent to the White family who held the title of Lord Annaly, and who owned land in Counties Limerick, Clare, Tipperary and Meath. In the latter capacity, Lane Joynt was a benevolent figure and was well liked by the tenants; for example it was at his suggestion that Colonel Charles White provided a free water supply for the tenants on his estate in Ballyvaughan, County Clare.[120]

Throughout his life, Lane Joynt was a major figure in public life. He was a life-long and very prominent Liberal until his opposition to Home Rule caused him to leave the party at the time of the crisis caused by the first Home Rule Bill of 1886. He was a member of Limerick City Council from 1848 to 1864 and served as mayor in 1862. When the lord lieutenant, the Earl of Carlisle visited Limerick, he offered Mayor Lane Joynt a knighthood, which he declined. Along with other Irish mayors, Lane Joynt became a trustee of the fund established to build the O'Connell Monument in Dublin and had the satisfaction of seeing this great edifice completed in 1875. Lane Joynt was also an active member of the Limerick Harbour Commissioners and was clerk of the crown from 1857 to 1869 and as such was responsible for the routine administration of the assize court (equivalent to the modern circuit court).[121] He resigned from the council on 21 January 1864, and his colleagues passed a resolution stating that 'his abilities were of the first order, his kindness, courtesy and public utility will long occupy a prominent place in the recollection of his friends in Limerick'.[122]

In 1863, Lane Joynt moved to Dublin and resided there for the rest of his life. He was elected a member of the city council there and in 1867 he became lord mayor of Dublin. In this capacity he attended the Great International Exhibition in Paris and was offered the Legion of Honour by the French Emperor, Napoleon III. In 1869 he became Crown and Treasury Solicitor, the highest position that a solicitor in Ireland could attain, and in this capacity acted as the legal advisor for various government departments. He held this position until it was abolished in 1887.[123]

Lane Joynt was very interested in education and learning and one of his greatest achievements was the founding of the Limerick Athenaeum.[124] An athenaeum is an institution for literary or scientific study, and is called after Athene, the Greek goddess of wisdom. In the nineteenth century, the athenaeum movement was associated with adult education and several such institutions were established in Britain and Ireland. In 1852, Lane Joynt proposed that a Limerick Athenaeum be established, consisting of a lecture theatre, library and museum, and which he hoped would also act as a forum where various learned societies could meet and carry on their business. In 1854, he purchased the lease of the former headquarters of St. Michael's Parish Commissioners on Cecil Street and a lecture theatre seating 600 was constructed in the building. On 11 July 1856, the Earl of

Carlisle, lord lieutenant of Ireland, performed the formal inauguration of the Limerick Athenaeum. For the next forty years, the lecture theatre was used for a variety of purposes, including public lectures, concerts, operas, public meetings, and political meetings. In the twentieth century, the Athenauem was chiefly used as a cinema.[125] The Limerick School of Art, which was founded in 1852, was housed in the Athenaeum from 1855 to 1912.[126]

Lane Joynt was Vice-President of the Association of Librarians and presented valuable books to the public libraries in Limerick. He was very committed to the development of the fishing industry on the West coast and in the 1880s and 1890s obtained funding for the building of piers and landing slips there. He was also a pioneer in the development of the Irish tourism industry.[127] Lane Joynt was a staunch member of the Church of Ireland, but like many Irish Liberal political figures, enjoyed warm relations with the Catholic Church. Although he spent the last thirty years of his life in Dublin, he always remained a proud Limerickman, devoted to the welfare of his native city. He died on 3 January 1895 and was buried in St John's Churchyard in Limerick city.[128]

Robert McMahon 1863.

Born in 1789, Robert McMahon was a woollen and drapery merchant who was based in Charlotte Quay in 1823 and in 19 George Street in 1846. In later years he resided at Prospect House near the city. He was a member of the Commissioners of St. Michael's Parish from 1841 to 1853 and of the chamber of commerce from 1846 until his death. He was also prominent in the corporation and was a member of the city council from 1842 until his death in 1871.[129] He served as mayor in 1863, the year in which the Prince of Wales, later King Edward VII was married to Princess Alexandra of Denmark. Mayor McMahon travelled to London and on behalf of the corporation, presented an address of congratulation to the Prince and Princess of Wales in their palace of Marlborough House. On 8 June, he was back in London and attended a levee in St. James Palace.[130]

In the 1840s, McMahon had been a Repealer, and at the time of his death was reputed to be sympathetic to the newly formed Home Rule movement. He died on 2 April 1871 and was buried in Mount St. Lawrence Cemetery.[131]

Eugene O'Callaghan 1864.

Born in 1800, Eugene O'Callaghan operated a successful business as a leather merchant at Bank Place in 1846 and Cornwallis Street (now Gerald Griffin Street) in 1867.[132] At the time of his death, he resided at a house called Lota on the North Circular Road in Limerick. He was a member of the city council from 1841 to 1868 and again from 1869 until his death in 1881.[133] O'Callaghan was a supporter of Daniel O'Connell and on 1 May 1843 successfully proposed the motion calling for the repeal of the Act of Union, the first time that the corporation ever adopted an overtly nationalist political position.[134] He served as mayor of Limerick in 1864 and was later high sheriff during the first two mayoralties of Sir Peter Tait. O'Callaghan was also a governor of the lunatic asylum and Vice-Chairman of Limerick Board of Guardians. His grandson, Michael O'Callaghan was to serve as mayor between 1920 and 1921 and was one of the two 'martyred mayors' murdered by the Black and Tans on 7 March 1921.[135] Eugene O'Callaghan died on 31 May 1881 and was buried in Mount St. Lawrence Cemetery.[136]

John Rickard Tinsley 1865.

Born in 1815, John Rickard Tinsley was a very wealthy salt, fish and oil merchant whose business premises was on William Street and Cornwallis (now Gerald Griffin Street) and who resided at Castleville, in Castletroy, outside the city.[137] He was a Catholic and a Liberal and did not support Home Rule.[138] He was active in public life for much of his adult life, serving as a member of the chamber of commerce for forty years and of the Harbour Commissioners from 1864 to 1888. He was a member of the city council from 1853 to 1880 and served as mayor in 1865.[139] His mayoralty was a time of economic recession and Tinsley worked hard to alleviate the distress of the poor. At his instigation, the corporation spent £3,000 on extending the sewerage system in Newtown Pery and the Irishtown, thus creating much needed employment.[140] A number of significant additions to the streetscape of Limerick were also made or instigated during Tinsley's mayoralty. The Treaty Stone was placed on a splendid pedestal and thus took on the iconic appearance that it possesses to the present. A splendid fountain was erected in St John's Square and the decision was made to erect the Tait Clock in Baker Place.[141] Tinsley was later to be a central figure in the disputed mayoral elections of 1874 and 1879. He died on 19 April 1892 and was buried in St. John's Churchyard.[142]

Sir Peter Tait 1866, 1867 and 1868.

Arguably the most flamboyant and unusual person ever to be mayor of Limerick, Peter Tait is, perhaps unsurprisingly, the only holder of the office to date to be the subject of a full biography.[143] The son of a shopkeeper, he was born 8 August 1828 in Lerwick, the capital of the Shetland Islands and came to Limerick in 1844 at the age of sixteen. He became an apprentice in the drapery firm of Cumine and Mitchell, on George's Street, but the work was seasonal and he was laid off during the winter months. Tait worked as a pedlar during these lean months and in particular, sold shirts to sailors from ships newly arriving in Limerick port.[144]

Peter Tait
(Limerick City Archives)

125

In 1850 he rented premises in Bedford Row and set up his first shirt factory there. Later he built a large shirt factory on Edward Street. He obtained contracts to provide uniforms for the British army, the Canadian Volunteer Militia, the Irish Constabulary (later to be known as the RIC) and the Confederate forces during the American Civil War. At its height his clothing factory in Limerick was reputed to have employed around 1,000 to 1,100 persons, nearly all of them female.[145] He was a pioneer of the production line system under which each worker manufactured a single component rather than the entire product.[146] Tait also became involved in a number of other business ventures. In 1850, Cumine and Mitchell, Tait's first employers in Limerick, were taken over by John Arnott and George Cannock, who had established the iconic Arnotts drapery shop in Henry Street, Dublin, some years previously. In 1858, Tait bought Arnott's share of the Limerick shop and in 1859, he rebuilt it at a cost of £9,000. As Cannock took no part in the day-to-day running of the business, Tait was effectively in charge for the next ten years.[147] (Subsequently, Cannock's department store continued in business until the late twentieth century, when it was taken over by Penneys). In 1864, Tait established a flax spinning industry in the city which operated until 1869 and in 1867 he set up a steamship company with ships travelling between London, Ostend and Antwerp on the one hand and Rio de Janeiro, Buenos Aires and Montevideo on the other. Unfortunately this venture ended in 1870, when the company went bankrupt.[148]

In the 1860s, Tait was at the height of his success and power and was probably the leading figure in Limerick's business community. In 1853, he had married Rose Abraham, daughter of a wealthy businessman and in 1859 he took up residence in the magnificent Southill House, on the Roxboro Road. His wife's brother, William Abraham (1840-1915) was later to have a successful political career and was Home Rule MP for various Irish constituencies between 1885 and 1915.[149] Peter Tait became known as a generous philanthropist and was a patron of the celebrated, though acerbic local poet, Michael Hogan (1832-99), known as the Bard of Thomond.[150] Although a Protestant, Tait was on friendly terms with the Catholic clergy in Limerick.

It was inevitable that Tait should be drawn into public life for he was a close friend of William Monsell, MP for County Limerick and he himself harboured ambitions to enter Parliament. He began well by getting himself elected to the city council as alderman for the Castle ward in March 1865. His career as a local representative was to be an extraordinary one, for he only remained a member of the council until 1 December 1868, and was mayor for virtually all of this period, except for the initial nine months. On 2 December 1865, he was unanimously elected mayor for 1866. He filled the office with panache, for he loved pomp and splendour. On 18 January, he gave a magnificent banquet for 400 dignitaries and the following night he entertained 1,300 guests at a great ball, both held in the New Hall, which he had recently constructed as an extension to his factory on Edward Street. In 1866 and 1867, Tait was again elected unanimously to be mayor for the years 1867 and 1868 respectively. No other mayor of Limerick since 1842 has ever equalled his achievement of being unanimously elected to three successive terms.[151] Also unique was the erection of a monument to a still-living and indeed still-serving mayor. The Tait Clock was constructed between 1866 and 1867 and officially handed over to the corporation at a ceremony held on 21 February 1867, during Tait's second mayoralty. The occasion was rendered even more memorable by the attendance of the lord mayor of Dublin and former mayor of Limerick, William Lane Joynt.[152]

On 10 July 1867, Tait displayed his usual talent for pomp by performing the ceremony of throwing the dart, the first such enactment since Henry Watson's in 1854. As Admiral of the Shannon, he sailed to Scattery Island with a large party, accompanied by the band of the Limerick Militia, and using a 'large and handsome bow' fired three silver arrows in succession into the Shannon, while 'in accordance with tradition, the shooting of each arrow was accompanied by the discharge of a cannon'.[153] Nevertheless, Tait took little part in the day-to-day business of the corporation, as from 1865 onwards, he was spending a lot of time in London, attending to his growing business interests there. In 1866, he attended nearly all of the meetings of the city council, but in 1867 he was present at only eight out of eighteen meetings and in 1868 at a mere three meetings.[154]

The career of Tait culminated in 1868 at the time of his third and final mayoralty. At the general election held in November of that year, he stood for parliament in the Limerick city constituency in opposition to the two sitting Liberal MPs and in alliance with Richard Piggott, later to be the notorious forger of letters designed to destroy the career of Charles Stewart Parnell. Although Tait was not a Conservative, and was running as a sort of Independent, he did not make this clear during the election campaign, and in consequence was assumed by many to be a Conservative, a damaging association in an overwhelmingly Catholic city, at a time when the Tories were considered to be natural allies of the Orange Order. In consequence he was defeated and his prestige suffered heavily as a result. He resigned both his mayoralty and his seat on the council on 1 December 1868, ostensibly due to his pressing business commitments. His connection with the corporation ended in bathos as he became involved in a ridiculous squabble over the mayoral chain. Before leaving office, Tait had removed two of the roundels (medallions) on the chain and replaced them with one commemorating his three mayoralties. Unfortunately, he had not informed the council of his action, and to add insult to injury, his roundel was much bigger than was usual. The council asked him to replace the two missing roundels and to substitute a normal sized one for his own large medallion. He agreed to replace the missing roundels but indignantly insisted that his large one be retained. Eventually it was removed and returned to him and Tait was never to attach a commemorative roundel to the chain, a regrettable and ironic commentary on his three extraordinary mayoralties.[155]

On 5 December 1868 he was knighted 'in recognition of the services that he had rendered to the people of Limerick'.[156] Thereafter his fortunes declined rapidly. After 1868, he seldom lived in Limerick and he disposed of Southill House in 1873. In 1869 he went bankrupt, largely due to the fraudulent practices of a business associate,

Alexander Collie, and his shipping company collapsed soon after. The clothing factory was sold in the early 1880s but continued to operate until it was closed in 1975. Tait stood unsuccessfully for parliament in his native Orkney and Shetland constituency in 1873 and for Limerick city in 1874 and was defeated on both occasions. He spent his last years far from both Shetland and Limerick. He became involved in disastrous business ventures in the challenging environment of the Ottoman Empire and lived almost continuously in Constantinople (now Istanbul) from 1876 to 1885. He lived in London from 1885 onwards, but made three visits to Batoum (now known as Batumi), a port on the Eastern shore of the Black Sea in Georgia, now an independent republic, but then part of the Russian Empire. He became involved in the oil business there and in May 1890 paid his third and final visit to Batoum. There he died on 15 December 1890 aged sixty-two and was buried in the English cemetery in Batoum. At the time of his death the total value of his estate was a mere £50. Thus ended the life of Limerick's only Scottish mayor, whose incredible career is unique in the annals of the city's mayoralty, and who may be compared, without exaggeration to Dick Whittington.[157]

Thomas Elliot Carte 1868.

Thomas Elliott Carte has the shortest term of office of any mayor of Limerick since 1842 and indeed one of the shortest terms in the entire history of the mayoralty of Limerick. Born in 1808, he became a successful attorney who lived and worked at 7 Upper Glentworth Street, Limerick.[158] In view of his remarkably short term as mayor, it is ironic that he was one of the longest serving members of Limerick City Council in the nineteenth century. He was a member from 1842 to 1875 and was an alderman from 1860 to 1875.[159] A Protestant, Carte was acting mayor for virtually all of 1868 as Mayor Peter Tait seldom attended council meetings and was nearly always in London. Consequently, it was considered a fitting tribute to Carte that he was elected mayor of Limerick on 1 December 1868 to serve out the last month of Mayor Tait's term.[160]

Carte served as mayor for only one month and while he was a candidate for the mayoralty in 1875, he only secured nine votes in the first round of voting in the election held on 1 December 1874 and in consequence, was eliminated.[161] Sadly for him, he was never to serve a full term as mayor of Limerick. On 16 September, 1875, he resigned from the city council and soon after, he went to live in Dublin.[162] He died at his residence at 4 Ranelagh Road, Dublin on 7 March 1883, at the age of seventy-four.

Thomas Boyse 1869.

Born in 1812, Thomas Boyse was a son of John Boyse (mayor in 1849) and was a member of Limerick City Council from 1849 to 1870. Thomas Boyse was a landowner who resided at Springfort House in Patrickswell, County Limerick.[163] He was elected mayor of Limerick on 1 December 1868 to serve in 1869.[164] Religious issues were a significant feature of his mayoralty. The legislation providing for the disestablishment of the Church of Ireland was enacted into law and Mayor Boyse and the city council in their robes of office attended Mass in state for the first time since the Treaty of Limerick.[165] Towards the end of Boyse's mayoralty, Councillor Ambrose Hall (later to be mayor in 1875) took court proceedings in the Court of Queen's Bench seeking an order that Boyse was not entitled to be a burgess (that is to say, on the electorate) of Limerick city on the grounds that he did not fulfil the residency requirements set out in the Municipal Corporations (Ireland) Act of 1840. The Court of Queen's Bench duly removed Boyse's name from the burgess roll and he was forced to resign as a member of the city council on 3 January 1870.[166] However, he remained a magistrate for the rest of his life. Later he moved to Limerick city and died at his residence, 1 Wellington Terrace on 9 January 1881 aged sixty-eight.[167]

William Spillane 1870.

Born in 1839, William Spillane was a member of a wealthy family of tobacco manufacturers. He was elected to the city council on 4 January 1867 and served as mayor in 1870.[168] The high point of his mayoralty was the opening of the Corcanree Embankment on 14 October. Between 1865 and 1870, a promenade for the recreation of the public had been constructed in the vicinity of the Ballinacurra Creek, and was financed by means of a loan. Spillane also worked to abolish the tolls on Wellesley Bridge and advocated the erection of a statue of Patrick Sarsfield.[169] He also gave his name to the Spillane Tower, erected in the Shannon during his mayoralty as an aid to navigation.

Spillane was president of the Limerick Athenauem and of the School of Art, and was the driving force behind the setting up of the Limerick City Library.[170] The Public Libraries (Ireland) Act of 1855 had allowed the council of urban areas to levy a rate not exceeding one penny in the pound for the purposes of establishing and running a library. This was a permissive act, which meant that a city or town council had the option of using its provisions, or not as they pleased.[171] In 1866, a wealthy Limerick merchant, journalist and publisher named George Geary Bennis bequeathed his private library to the city, 'for the free use of the citizens.'[172] The corporation duly took possession of the books, but stored them in the Town Hall for four years. The corporation's failure to establish a library at this juncture attracted a great deal of derision. In 1870, Mayor Spillane moved the books to the Athenaeum at his own expense and a library was opened there, which remained in existence for twenty-three years. However, the public never had free access to the books, and on 6 March 1889, at the instigation of Spillane the city council formally adopted the Library Act of 1855 and its amending acts. On 11 December 1893, the first free public library in Limerick, financed and administered by the corporation was opened in Lower Glentworth Street.[173]

In 1871, Spillane funded the installation of an organ in the Athenaeum at his own expense.[174] He resigned from the council on 7 October 1875 and soon after was appointed manager of the corporation gas undertaking, a post he held until his death in 1897.[175] Under his management, the corporation bought the United General Gaslight Company in 1880 and the gas undertaking moved from Watergate to the Dock Road in 1884. Spillane's position as gas manager was one of the most senior in the corporation as the gas undertaking was the largest single department and the second largest source of income after rates.[176] He died at his residence at 67 Georges Street on 24 July 1897 and was buried in Mount St. Lawrence Cemetery.[177] At the time of writing, his great-grandson, Michael Spillane, is a director of Argosea Services Ltd, of 25 William Street, Limerick.[178]

Robert McDonnell 1871.

Born in 1831, Robert McDonnell was the son of John McDonnell, a very wealthy timber and slate merchant who also owned saw mills and was the proprietor of a fleet of trading ships. The McDonnells had their business premises at Mount Kennett and Bedford Row, but they resided at a town house in Hartstonge Street, Limerick and a country house at Fairy Hill Parteen.[179]

Robert McDonnell was elected to the city council on 28 November 1864 and remained a member until 1891.[180] He was mayor of Limerick in 1871 and had a crowded and memorable mayoralty. In 1870, Isaac Butt had launched the Home Rule movement and in 1871, he was returned as one of Limerick city's two MPs. On 11 May 1871, the city council carried a resolution stating they approved 'the principle of Home Rule.'[181] Limerick Corporation remained committed to this position until 1920. An address was presented by Limerick Corporation to William Monsell, MP, on the occasion of his appointment as Postmaster-General, a ministerial position, but one that was outside the cabinet.[182] This was the most senior position attained by a Catholic in a British administration since 1688, and in consequence was regarded as being a significant step in the progress of the Catholic community in both Britain and Ireland.[183]

Also in 1871, Mayor McDonnell entered into what was described as 'a lengthened and heated controversy' with the mayor of Cork over 'whether Limerick or Cork should have precedence as a municipal body'.[184] The row had started when the lord mayor of Dublin had given precedence to the mayor of Limerick at a banquet. Cork Corporation furiously repudiated this action, but Limerick City Council passed a vote of thanks to the lord mayor of Dublin, for 'having sustained the recognised right of Limerick and its mayor and corporation to precedence on all public occasions, under its charter, which bears date prior to that of Cork'.[185] The issue remained unresolved at the end of McDonnell's mayoralty.

During McDonnell's term of office, his father John served with him as high sheriff of Limerick city, a rare combination of offices in one family. Like many of the city's merchant elite, McDonald was active in the Harbour Commissioners. In 1892, he became the first ex-mayor since 1842 to be appointed town clerk of Limerick city and filled that position until his death four years later. McDonnell died on 13 May 1896 and was buried in Mount St. Lawrence Cemetery.[186]

John Watson Mahony 1872.

Born in 1811, John Watson Mahony was a stockbroker who conducted his business and resided at 66 Georges Street. He was elected to the city council on 1 November 1860 and remained a member until his death.[188] He was a Protestant and a member of the Conservative party, and as such was representative of a large and influential minority on Limerick City Council. He was also on the governing body of the lunatic asylum and a member of the Limerick Board of Poor Law Guardians. On 1 December 1871, he was elected mayor for 1872.[189] He served for only four months, as he died in office on 27 April 1872 and was buried in St. Munchin's Cemetery.[190]

John J. Cleary 1872, 1873 and 1874.

Born in Kildare in 1833, John Joseph Cleary spent most of his life in Limerick city. He became a very significant figure in the commercial life of the city by virtue of his being the proprietor of Cruises Royal Hotel at 5 Georges Street for many years.[191] He was elected to the city council on 25 November 1869 and remained a member until 1899.[192]

John J. Cleary using a bow to shoot the ceremonial dart into the River Shannon in 1873. (Jim Kemmy Municipal Museum)

Following the death of Mayor Mahony, Cleary was elected mayor on 2 May 1872 to serve out the remainder of the term.[193] Subsequently he served as mayor for the whole of 1873 and 1874. During his first mayoralty, Cleary officially welcomed to Limerick the lord lieutenant, Earl Spencer and his wife Countess Spencer (one of their descendants was Diana, Princess of Wales) and presented them with a formal address of welcome on behalf of the corporation. Having been re-elected unanimously as mayor for 1873, Cleary again welcomed the Spencers to Limerick for the opening of a major new extension to Limerick docks on 14 May. On that occasion, Cleary performed the ceremony of 'throwing the dart' with considerable panache. A party of 300, including Lord and Lady Spencer, accompanied him by steamer to Scattery Island, where he used a bow to fire the darts in the same manner as Sir Peter Tait had done in 1867. In his third and final mayoralty, Cleary attended the annual banquet of the lord mayor of London on 3 June 1874, and he led a delegation of the corporation to the Viceregal Lodge (now Áras an Úachtaran) in Phoenix Park, to present an address of congratulations to the Duke of Abercorn, who had just been appointed as lord lieutenant. Cleary turned the first sod of the new People's Park in Pery Square on 26 October 1874, on which occasion he was presented with a silver spade and trowel. His wife was presented with a silver cradle worth 250 guineas on the occasion of the birth of a child during her husband's mayoralty. Cleary attached three roundels to the mayoral chain to commemorate each of his terms of office, which is the largest number of additional medallions ever added by a single individual to the Limerick mayoral chain.[194]

Cleary remained a member of the council for a quarter of a century after his last term as mayor. He sold Cruises Royal Hotel and purchased the Eagle Hotel in Lisdoonvarna.[195] In 1899, he was one of the sixteen sitting members of the council defeated in the first local elections held under the terms of the 1898 Local Government Act and he retired from public life soon after.[196] He died in the Eagle Hotel, Lisdoonvarna, on 1 June 1902 and was buried in the family burial place in Kildare.[197]

Ambrose Hall 1875.

Born in 1824, Ambrose (often known either affectionately or derisively as Amby) Hall was one of the most prominent figures in the public life of Limerick city for some fifty years.[198] In his early life, he was a wholesale ironmonger in William Street but later became a house and land agent. He also owned a lot of house property in the city and was a landed proprietor in County Clare. He constructed a scheme of houses called Hall's Range off Edward Street, which was demolished in the late twentieth century.[199] Hall resided at 'Mignon' on the North Strand. He was first elected to the city council on 2 December 1861 and remained a member until 1899, except for two intervals in 1876-80 and 1888-92.[200] He was a Liberal and was a close friend and ally of Sir Peter Tait, but had little interest in, or involvement with, the Home Rule movement.[201]

The election held on 1 December 1874 to choose a mayor for 1875 was one of the most controversial ever held in Limerick. Ambrose Hall and John Francis Walker secured eighteen votes each and Mayor Cleary then gave his casting vote to the latter and declared him elected. However, Alderman John R. Tinsley (who had himself been mayor in 1865) claimed that, as senior alderman, he had the casting vote and cast it in favour of Hall. Mayor Cleary then vacated the chair and thus ended the meeting.[202] On 3 December, three former mayors, James Spaight (1856), John R. Tinsley (1865) and William Spillane (1870) objected to the minutes of the meeting of 1 December being signed due to this dispute, but Mayor Cleary refused to receive any resolution concerning them and several councillors then walked out.[203] On 1 January 1875, Walker was installed as mayor but all but four of the councillors who had voted for Hall boycotted the ceremony. Hall then took proceedings before the Court of Queen's Bench, where Judge William Keogh (notorious for his role in the Tenant Right League and Independent Irish Party in the early 1850s) ruled that the senior alderman and not the mayor was entitled to the casting vote. In consequence, the judge duly declared Hall the rightful mayor of Limerick for 1875.[204]

Hall was installed as mayor on 1 February 1875 and proved to be a very active first citizen. He held a great fancy dress ball in the Theatre Royal on Henry Street and by this means raised £120 for charity. He led a delegation that included Maurice Lenihan to Dublin for the celebrations of the centenary of the birth of Daniel O'Connell, which culminated with unveiling of the O'Connell Monument on Sackville (later O'Connell) Street.[205] The statue of Patrick Sarsfield at Cathedral Place, Limerick was erected largely as a result of the efforts of Hall and during his mayoralty the subscription list to pay for it was opened. Hall had established a committee to erect a Sarsfield monument and originally envisaged it taking the form of a triumphal arch adjoining King John's Castle on Thomond Bridge. The arch would be decorated with relief sculptures and topped by a suitably martial statue of Sarsfield. However, the actual monument, designed by John Lawlor, was much less imposing, and merely depicted Sarsfield standing on a pedestal holding a drawn sword. Hall later suggested that the monument should be erected on the corner of Mallow Street and Georges Street, but to his intense anger, the corporation refused to allow this. Instead it was erected in the grounds of St. John's Cathedral in 1881, after Hall and his committee had declined the offer by the city council of a site in Bank Place. [206]

Hall was a very determined and controversial figure as was evidenced by his dogged pursuit of his right to the mayoralty though the courts in 1875 and his tireless campaign to have the Sarsfield Monument erected, but was also widely respected for his sincerity, integrity and deep concern for Limerick city.[207] His long political career came to an unhappy conclusion in 1899 when, at the age of seventy-four, he lost his seat on the council in the Labour landslide. Indeed he was one of three mayors to lose their seats in that election, the other two being John J. Cleary and Michael Cusack.[208] Nevertheless, Hall came to be regarded as the grand old man of Limerick public life and was considered to be an authority on the history of the city, having lived through so much of it and even helped to shape it himself. Hall was married twice, his second wife being a daughter of William H. Hall who had been mayor in 1853 and to whom he was not otherwise related. Ambrose Hall died at his residence on 17 January 1908 and was buried in Mount St. Lawrence Cemetery.[209]

John Francis Walker 1876.

John Francis Walker was born in 1809 and was the owner of a bonded warehouse and a tobacco business in the Mardyke area near Charlotte Quay in Limerick city.[210] He was a member of Limerick City Council from 1871 to 1892. He was elected mayor of Limerick for 1875 on 1 December 1874 but served for only one month as Judge William Keogh ruled in the Court of Queen's Bench that Ambrose Hall was the rightful mayor of Limerick.[211] In consequence of the very disappointing fashion in which he was thus deprived of the mayoralty and the good-humoured manner in which he had born his defeat, Walker was unanimously elected mayor on 1 December 1875 to serve in 1876.[212] At sixty-six years of age, he was one of the oldest persons ever to be mayor of Limerick but went on to have a very successful year in office. One of the most significant events of his mayoralty was the laying of the foundation stone of the tower and spire of the Redemptorist Church at Mount St. Alphonsus. The cost of this great undertaking was borne entirely by Walker's extremely wealthy colleague Alderman John Quin.[213] Walker resided for many years at Rose Cottage on the North Strand in Limerick city but following his retirement both from the city council and from business, he went to live in Askeaton in county Limerick and there he died on 6 February 1900, at the age of ninety.[214]

Sir James Spaight 1877.

See above under 1856. On leaving office at the end of 1877, he became the last ever Mayor of Limerick to belong to the Conservative Party or to openly support the unionist cause and the last non-Catholic mayor before the election of Frances Condell in 1962.

Stephen Hastings 1878.

Stephen Hastings was born in Limerick in 1813 and for many years carried on an extensive brush-manufacturing business at 4 Charlotte Quay and 1 Georges Street, but later re-located to 36 Georges Street.[215] Consequently, a frequent catcall from the public gallery at council meetings attended by Hastings was 'where's your brush?' At the time of his death, his residence was in Glentworth Street. Hastings was a member of the city council from 1847 to 1885 and was for many years alderman of the Irishtown ward.[216] He was unanimously elected mayor on 1 December 1877 for the year 1878.[217] The most significant event of his mayoralty was the purchase of the private gasworks belonging to the Limerick Gas Company and its subsequent amalgamation with the gasworks under the control of the corporation. Henceforth, until 1987, the sale and manufacture of gas in Limerick city was to be a monopoly of the corporation.[218]

In the 1840s Hasting was an ardent supporter of Repeal and took an active part in parliamentary election campaigns in the 1840s and 1850s. He was a zealous Catholic and during his mayoralty forwarded a congratulatory address to the newly elected Pope Leo XIII. He was active in charitable work and for some fifty years was president of the St. Mary's Conference (or branch) of the St. Vincent de Paul Society. Hastings' son, also Stephen, was a solicitor and was a member of the city council in the 1890s. Ex-mayor Stephen Hasting died on 19 September 1895 at the age of eight-two and was buried in Mount St. Lawrence Cemetery.[219]

Michael O'Gorman 1879 and 1880.

Michael O'Gorman was born in 1827 and was employed by the Grand Canal Company as their chief agent in Limerick city and the surrounding district. Later he established his own business as a house, land and insurance agent.[220] He was elected to the city council on 1 December 1870.[221] He was elected mayor for 1879 and in the course of the year, along with other members of the council attended the official opening of the tower and bells of the Redemptorist Church at Mount St. Alphonsus.[222] Both the tower and bells had been financed by one of Mayor O'Gorman's colleagues on the council, Alderman John Quin.[223]

On 1 December 1879, O'Gorman was re-elected mayor in controversial circumstances. Both he and Thomas George O'Sullivan secured seventeen votes each, but the senior alderman John R. Tinsley, who had been at the centre of the last disputed mayoral election in 1874, gave his casting vote in favour of O'Gorman.[224] O'Sullivan, attempting to emulate Ambrose Hall in 1875, disputed the election result on the grounds that Tinsley should be unseated as an alderman on various technical grounds.[225] However, the law agent of the corporation presented a report to the council on 23 December 1879, in which he stated that Tinsley was a properly elected and qualified alderman.[226] O'Sullivan accepted the findings of the report and O'Gorman was duly installed as mayor for the second time on 1 January 1880. In the course of his second mayoralty, O'Gorman, along with his fellow councillors, presented an address of welcome to the new lord lieutenant, Earl Cowper. In the same year, the foundation stone of the clock tower in Limerick docks was laid by the mayor's daughter.[227] On 14 July1880. the freedom of Limerick was conferred on Charles Stewart Parnell. O'Gorman died on 16 November 1908 at his residence at 77 Georges Street and was buried in Mount St. Lawrence Cemetery.[228]

Thomas George O'Sullivan 1881.

Born in Cork in 1833, Thomas George O'Sullivan was a medical doctor and came to Limerick in 1861 to take up the position of medical officer at the Limerick Union Workhouse on Shelbourne Road. Later he established his own very successful medical practice at his residence, 16 William Street [230] O'Sullivan was elected to the city council on 3 July 1873.[231] Following his unsuccessful attempt to become mayor in the disputed election of 1879, O'Sullivan was unanimously elected on 1 December 1880, in the same manner as John F. Walker, the unsuccessful candidate in the last disputed election, that of 1874, had been unanimously elected the following year.[232] Mayor O'Sullivan was a popular figure, due to his charitable work and in particular his interest in improving the city's water supply.[233] He continued to practice medicine in Limerick for some forty years until shortly before his death on 31 December 1906, after a long illness. He was buried in Mount St. Lawrence Cemetery.[234] One of his daughters was married to John J. Peacocke, who was city surveyor (equivalent to city engineer) from 1899 to 1932.[235]

Jerome Counihan 1882 and 1883.

Jerome Counihan was born in 1840 and was the son of Francis Counihan, who ran a thriving printing business and was the proprietor of the *Munster News* (which from 1887 onwards was known as the *Munster News and Limerick and Clare Advocate*), one of the most important newspapers in the city throughout its existence from 1851 to 1935. He worked in the family business both as a journalist and in administration, and later, when his father retired, became the proprietor and editor of the *Munster News*. Like Henry Watson (mayor in 1854), his career in journalism greatly facilitated his career in public life.[236]

Counihan was first elected to the council on 20 January 1870 and remained a member until his death in 1894.[237] He served two terms as mayor in 1882 and 1883. The most important event of his period in office was the enactment of the Limerick Waterworks Act of 1883, which provided for the purchase of the Limerick Waterworks Company by the corporation. Under this legislation, the corporation duly purchased the complete network for providing a water supply to the city. Also in 1883, both Athlunkard and Wellesley Bridges ceased to be toll bridges and the latter was renamed Sarsfield Bridge to mark the occasion. In June 1883, Counihan welcomed Lord Spencer (who had been appointed lord lieutenant again) and his wife to Limerick for the magnificent Royal Agricultural Show and Art Exhibition and a grand ball was held in the Theatre Royal to mark the occasion.[238]

Counihan was active in other public bodies, including the Harbour Commissioners, Market Trustees and Board of Guardians, and was on the governing bodies of both Barringtons and St. John's Hospitals. He was also a member of the Shannon Fisheries Board. He died after a short illness at his residence on Glentworth Street on 5 October 1894 and was buried in Mount St. Lawrence Cemetery.[239]

Maurice Lenihan 1884.

One of the most celebrated and distinguished figures ever to be mayor of Limerick, Maurice Lenihan was not a Limerickman and did not even come to live in the city permanently until he was thirty-eight years old.[240] The son of a woollen merchant, he was born on 5 February 1811 in Waterford city and was educated in St John's College, Waterford and St. Patrick's College, Carlow. The latter was a seminary for most of its history but Lenihan was one of the lay-students that were then permitted to attend. In 1831, he started work as a journalist with the *Tipperary Free Press* in Clonmel and from there he moved to the *Waterford Chronicle* in his native city in 1833. Lenihan was an ardent supporter of Daniel O'Connell (who became a close friend of his) and of the Repeal movement and was to remain a life-long constitutional nationalist.[241]

In June 1841, Lenihan was appointed editor of the *Limerick Reporter*, a newspaper of nationalist sympathies that had been founded in 1829 and he moved to Limerick to take up his new post. However, he only remained until March 1843, when he moved to Cork to work for the *Cork Examiner*, which had been established two years previously. In the autumn of 1843, at the instigation of Daniel O'Connell and the Catholic Bishop of Killaloe, Lenihan founded the *Tipperary Vindicator*, which was published in Nenagh as a Repeal newspaper and he continued to publish it throughout the 1840s. During this period, Lenihan became very friendly with many of the leaders of the Young Ireland movement, including his fellow Waterford man Thomas Francis Meagher and Michael Doheny.[242]

At the end of 1849, Lenihan bought the *Limerick Reporter* and amalgamated it with the *Tipperary Vindicator*. This necessitated him moving to Limerick city and he lived there for forty-six years until his death in 1895. Initially, he lived and conducted his business in Denmark Street, but then moved to 2 Patrick Street, where he wrote his famed History of Limerick. Later he lived and worked at 104 Georges Street, but in 1887, his declining fortunes obliged him to re-locate to 17 Catherine Street.[243] In 1843, Lenihan had married Elizabeth Spain from Nenagh and they had nine children of whom five predeceased him. In 1866, at great expense, he published his monumental History of Limerick, described by Liam Irwin, as 'the most comprehensive and authoritative work on the history of the city and county.'[244] It received critical acclaim but sales were small and ironically this huge book, which became Lenihan's greatest claim to fame also played a significant role in the decline of his finances in later life.

Lenihan was a member of Limerick City Council from 1853 to 1864 and again from 1868 to 1888.[245] He resigned from the council in 1864 in order to complete his History of Limerick and returned when it was safely launched. His political views remained unchanged throughout his life. He was a constitutional nationalist who supported Repeal in the 1840s and Home Rule in the 1870s, 1880s and 1890s and like his idol O'Connell, he was always opposed to the use of force. In the 1850s he played a major role in the erection of the O'Connell Monument in Limerick. The culmination of his political career was his unanimous election as mayor on 1 December 1883 and his year in office in 1884.[246] Ironically, his predecessor as mayor had been another journalist and newspaper proprietor, Jerome Counihan. One of the high points of Lenihan's year in office occurred when Michael Davitt, the founder of the Land League received the freedom of the city on 14 April 1884. However, the most significant development of his mayoralty was the struggle over the extra police tax. In 1882 the lord lieutenant of Ireland had proclaimed that Limerick was in a 'state of disturbance' in the aftermath of the Phoenix Park murders and extra police were drafted into the city to deal with what was in fact a non-existent crisis. Limerick Corporation refused to pay for the cost of this extra policing and the Dublin government attempted to collect it by initiating proceedings in the law courts. Mayor Lenihan and three members of the council travelled to London and met Charles Stewart Parnell and other members of the Irish Party at Westminster to discuss the issue. Subsequently it was discussed in parliament, and Limerick Corporation received great publicity and messages of support from all over the country.[247]

From the early 1880s onwards, Lenihan found himself falling into poverty, due to family illnesses, poor sales of his History of Limerick and the decline of his newspaper. Consequently, he was obliged to continue working until the end of his life. He died a forgotten and impoverished figure at his residence, 17 Catherine Street, on Christmas

Day, 1895 and was buried in Mount St. Lawrence Cemetery.[248] Some fifty years after his death, Lenihan Avenue, in Prospect was named in his honour.[249] His combination of historical scholarship and an active political career was unique in the ranks of nineteenth-century mayors of Limerick and only matched by a few of his successors in the twentieth century.

Stephen O'Mara 1885 and 1886.

On one of the medallions that he attached to the mayoral chain, Stephen O'Mara described himself as the first nationalist to be elected mayor of Limerick.[250] While many would dispute that claim, considering the many mayors who had supported Repeal in the 1840s and Home Rule in the 1870s and early 1880s, there is no doubt that O'Mara's period in office saw the espousal of a more resolute form of nationalism than had hitherto been the case. In addition, he became the founder of a political dynasty that would provide Limerick with a total of three mayors between 1885 and 1923.[251]

Stephen O'Mara
(Limerick City Archives)

He was born on 26 December 1844, the son of James O'Mara (1817-99), a wealthy businessman. James was a native of Toomevara, County Tipperary, who had arrived in Limerick in his youth and for a time worked in Mattersons Bacon Factory. In 1839, he founded O'Mara's Bacon Company and over the next sixty years built it into one of the largest in the city. James O'Mara lived at 17 Thomas Street near his bacon factory which was situated on Roches Street and was high sheriff of Limerick city in 1887. He was married to Hanora (or Honor) Foley and had a family of thirteen children, including Stephen, the future mayor, and Joseph (1866-1927), the famous operatic tenor, who was to receive the freedom of Limerick in 1908.[252]

This was not the only musical connection that the family had. Connie O'Mara, a granddaughter of James and niece of Stephen was married to Baron Werner von Trapp, an Austrian nobleman whose brother Baron George von Trapp was married firstly to Agatha Whitehead (whose grandfather was one of the inventors of the torpedo) and secondly to Maria Kutschera, who was portrayed by Julie Andrews in the classic film *The Sound of Music*. The celebrated musical von Trapps came to Limerick on a number of occasions in the 1920s and 1930s to visit their relatives the O'Maras and the O'Sullivans (a sister of Connie von Trapp was married to Dr. William O'Sullivan, son of Mayor Thomas George O'Sullivan).[253]

Stephen O'Mara was the eldest son of James and worked in the family business which he eventually took over on his father's death. In 1906 he also took over Donnellys bacon factory in Dublin. He married Ellen Pigott in 1867, by whom he had thirteen children, and lived first in Chapel Lane and later in Roches Street before moving into Hartstonge House (now Ozanam) House in Hartstonge Street in the 1880s. In 1908, he moved to

Strand House, at the junction of Ennis Road and O'Callaghan Strand, which stood on the site of the present-day Hilton Hotel.[254]

Stephen O'Mara was elected to the city council on 27 November 1879 and remained a member until 1908.[255] In politics he was a Home Ruler of the more advanced Parnellite type. He was mayor for two successive years. His first mayoralty saw the government finally abandon the campaign to collect the extra police tax, but was most famous for the only visit to Limerick city ever made by a future British king and queen. Before the 1880s, the British monarchy had been respected by all political parties in Ireland and had not been regarded as a Protestant or Conservative institution.[256] The turning point came when the rise of Parnellism resulted in the British government foolishly attempting to use the monarchy as a political weapon. Not surprisingly, it soon came to be seen as a partisan institution, and its prestige in Ireland declined considerably.[257] As part of this policy, the Prince and Princess of Wales (later King Edward VII and Queen Alexandra) made a disastrous tour of Ireland in 1885, meeting hostile demonstrations wherever they went. On 20 April 1885 they arrived in Limerick city by train from Killarney, but only stayed for a few hours and did not leave the railway station. It was reported that 5,000 people were at the station to give the royal couple a warm welcome. In a sharp break with the past, O'Mara and the corporation refused to receive the royal visitors, in contrast to the actions of previous mayors, who had shown marked deference to successive lords lieutenant, and had accorded them official welcomes on their visits to Limerick. Because the corporation, headed by Mayor O'Mara, refused to be associated with any official welcome for the Prince and Princess, it was left to the unionist-dominated chamber of commerce and its president, ex-mayor James Spaight, to do the honours. The royal couple and their entourage were entertained to a luncheon in the boardroom of the station before leaving for Dublin.[258]

During his second mayoralty, O'Mara was elected MP for the Ossory Division of Queen's County (now Laois), but retained his seat for only five months. Nevertheless, he was the first serving mayor of Limerick to sit in parliament since Thomas Smyth (mayor 1776-77) and the first ever to sit in the British parliament (Smyth had been a member of the Irish parliament).[259] On 4 October, 1886, O'Mara travelled to Hawarden Castle, in North Wales, the residence of William Ewart Gladstone, accompanied by representatives from the corporations of Cork, Waterford and Clonmel, where the once and future prime minister received the freedom of the four cities at a unique joint ceremony.[260]

In 1888, Stephen O'Mara succeeded his father as High Sheriff of Limerick and in 1889, he was imprisoned for a week in Limerick prison for refusing to give evidence as a crown witness in a significant court case. On this occasion, Edward Carson, the future unionist leader, was crown prosecutor.[261] O'Mara was greatly saddened by the Parnell split and was a Parnellite throughout the 1890s. His continued popularity is evidenced by his performance in the 1899 local elections, when he topped the poll in the Shannon ward, and thus became the only one of the four ex-mayors who had contested the election to be returned to the council.[262] He remained a member until 1908. In 1918, he broke with the Home Rule party after some forty years of loyal service and embraced the new Sinn Féin Party. He lived to see two of his sons serve as mayors of Limerick: Alphonsus (1918-20) and Stephen (1921-23). Another son James (1873-1948) enjoyed a long and varied political career as Home Rule MP for South Kilkenny (1900-07), Sinn Féin TD for Kilkenny South (1918-21) and Cumann na nGaedhal TD for Dublin South (1924-27).[263]

Stephen O'Mara was a staunch supporter of the Treaty and in 1925 was elected to the Senate of the newly established Free State, thus becoming the first ex-mayor of Limerick to be a senator. He died at Strand House on 26 July 1926, having collapsed while crossing Sarsfield Bridge on his way home from his office, and was buried in Mount St. Lawrence Cemetery.[264]

Francis A. O'Keeffe 1887, 1888 and 1889.

Born on 4 October 1856, Francis Arthur O'Keeffe was the son of Lawrence O'Keeffe, a wealthy cigar importer and tobacconist who conducted his business on 126 Georges Street, Limerick and also operated from premises in Waterford and Kilkenny cities.[265] The elder O'Keeffe was also a member of Limerick City Council and served as high sheriff of the city in 1886. Francis was educated by the Jesuits at the Crescent College, Limerick and at Clongowes Wood, County Kildare and later attended Trinity College, Dublin. He became a solicitor and established a practice in Limerick city, firstly on his own and later in partnership with Stephen Hastings, son of the former mayor of the same name.[266]

Francis A. O'Keeffe
(Limerick City Archives)

O'Keeffe was a member of the city council from 1885 to 1893. He served as mayor of Limerick in 1887, 1888 and 1889, the only person to serve three entire terms between Henry Watson (1823-26) and John Daly (1899-1902). (Sir Peter Tait and John J. Cleary also served three terms each, but neither served for the full three years). O'Keeffe's mayoralties were eventful and coincided with the climax and impending collapse of Parnell's political career. O'Keeffe himself was a supporter of Home Rule and after the Parnell split became an anti-Parnellite. As mayor he hosted various events attended by prominent figures in the Home Rule Party, including a mass meeting held in the Markets Field on 2 November 1887, attended by 30,000 people, and at which two English and eleven Irish MPs were present. That same evening, a public banquet for 300 guests was held in the city. The culmination of O'Keeffe's political career came on 17 April 1888, when he was elected MP for Limerick city, the first person to be mayor and MP for the city simultaneously since Thomas Smyth in 1776-77 and only the fourth mayor of Limerick to have done so since 1691. When he took his seat in the House of Commons, O'Keeffe was formally introduced to his new colleagues by Joseph Biggar, a notable Parnellite MP and William Abraham, MP for Limerick West, brother-in-law of Sir Peter Tait.[267]

The first ever social houses were constructed in Limerick during O'Keeffe's mayoralties. In 1887, Limerick Corporation built its first social housing scheme, when it constructed eighteen houses in Sir Harry's Mall and lanes adjoining it. In the same year, six more dwellings were constructed on Athlunkard Street and an adjoining lane. A total of £2,400, repayable over forty years was borrowed from the Board of Works to pay for these schemes.[268] Mayor O'Keeffe also turned the first sod on the new waterworks at Clareville, on 18 April 1888.[269]

O'Keeffe resigned from the city council on 25 November 1893.[270] He remained MP for Limerick city until 1900, having been successfully returned to parliament in the general elections of 1892 and 1895, standing as an anti-Parnellite on both occasions. Both of these election campaigns were marked by much violence in Limerick city and throughout Ireland. However, O'Keeffe's victory in 1895 was a somewhat tarnished one. On that occasion, John Daly, the celebrated Limerick Fenian who was serving a prison sentence in England for alleged involvement in the IRB bombing campaign of the 1880s, was selected as the Parnellite candidate and O'Keeffe withdrew, allowing Daly to be returned unopposed as MP for the city. However, the election was declared null and void and O'Keeffe was victorious at the subsequent by-election.[271] Ironically, Daly was later to emulate O'Keeffe's feat of serving as mayor of Limerick for three full consecutive years. O'Keeffe retired early from the legal profession and moved to Dublin where he lived for several years before his death, although he continued to make frequent visits to both Limerick and Kilkee. He died on 21 September 1909 and was buried in Mount St. Lawrence Cemetery.[272]

William J. O'Donnell 1890.

William O'Donnell is the second youngest person ever to have served as mayor of Limerick since 1842 (Thady Coughlan who served in 1975-76 was the youngest mayor). He was born on 7 September 1864, the son of William O'Donnell, who in 1839 had founded the St. Francis Abbey Tannery, situated at 2-3 Cornwallis (now Gerald Griffin Street).[273] The younger William was educated at the Crescent College and on his father's death became proprietor of the extensive and successful tannery business. He was elected to the city council at the age of twenty-two in 1886 and remained a member until his death in 1893. He was high sheriff in 1889 and became mayor of

William J. O'Donnell
(Limerick City Archives)

Limerick at the age of twenty-five on the 1 January 1890. He was also a member of the chamber of commerce and of the Harbour Commissioners. He was believed to be the youngest mayor in the United Kingdom at the time and was thought to be at the beginning of a glittering political career. However it was not to be and in fact he only lived three years after completing his term as mayor. He was taken ill, while on holidays with his wife in Paris and died there on 19 August 1893, aged only twenty-eight. He was buried in Mount St. Lawrence Cemetery.[274]

Patrick Riordan 1891.

Born in 1832, Patrick Riordan was a prosperous chandler (maker of candles) and oil and colour merchant (selling oil, paint and related products) who, as was the practice at the time, lived over his business premises at 27 William Street.[275] He was elected to the city council on 9 November 1875 and remained a member until 1897.[276] He was a supporter of Home Rule and was a personal friend of Parnell, whom he greatly revered. Riordan's mayoralty in 1891 coincided with the Parnell split, which caused great bitterness and dissension on Limerick City Council as it did throughout Ireland. Riordan was an ardent Parnellite and presided at Parnell's last meeting in Limerick, which the fallen leader addressed from an upstairs window in Cruises Hotel.

Patrick Riordan
(Jim Kemmy Municipal Museum)

Riordan later attached a roundel to the mayoral chain depicting the head of Parnell on one side, accompanied by the inscription 'The leader of the Irish Party, Charles S. Parnell died October 6th 1891.' Interestingly, when John Daly was released from prison in 1896, he set up a bakery and lived at 26 William Street, next door to Riordan and despite their political differences the two men and their respective families became very friendly.[277]

On the death of former Mayor William Spillane on 24 July 1897, Riordan was appointed to succeed him as manager of the Limerick Corporation gas undertaking, a position that he held until his death ten years later. It was an important and lucrative post, with an annual salary in 1902 of £300, and a staff complement of 133, the largest of any department in the corporation.[278] Riordan died on 3 October 1907 and was buried in Mount St. Lawrence Cemetery.[279]

Denis F. McNamara 1892.

Denis F. McNamara was born in 1840 and was an extensive farmer who resided at Shanakyle House in Parteen, County Clare, near Limerick city. He was elected to the city council for the Abbey Ward on 1 July 1880 to succeed his late father who had been a member for a number of years.[280] On 1 December 1891, Denis McNamara, an anti-Parnellite was elected mayor, defeating Patrick Riordan, who was again a candidate for the post, by twenty votes to eighteen.[281] McNamara was also a member of the Limerick Board of Guardians. He died on 8 January 1911 and was buried in Mount St. Lawrence Cemetery.[282]

Bryan O'Donnell 1893, 1894 and 1895.

Brian O'Donnell was born in September 1848 in Kildimo, County Limerick and came to live in Limerick city at an early age. By 1880, he was established as a very successful flour merchant and as was the practice at the time lived over his business premises at 58 William Street.[283] A man of great wealth he also had a country residence, Ballyclough House, near the city, where he had an extensive stud farm.[284] In his youth he was a champion oarsman with Shannon Rowing Club, and in later life he took a great interest in horse racing. His obituary in the *Limerick Chronicle* noted that 'for years, his racing colours were seen and carried to victory in every racecourse in Ireland.'[285] Indeed, he was Chairman of Limerick Race Company from 1922 to 1940.[286]

Bryan O'Donnell
(Jim Kemmy Municipal Museum)

Bryan O'Donnell was a member of Limerick City Council from 1880 to 1895. He was an ardent Parnellite and attended Parnell's last meeting in Limerick in 1891, at which Mayor Patrick Riordan presided. O'Donnell later recalled how shocked he was on this occasion at the dishevelled appearance of the once elegant Parnell, whose career lay in ruins and whose broken health was a harbinger of his approaching death. O'Donnell later marched in Parnell's funeral procession and continued to revere him for the rest of his life.[287]

It was as a Parnellite that O'Donnell was elected mayor on 1 December 1892 to serve for 1893. Both he and the anti-Parnellite candidate, Thomas McMahon Cregan polled eighteen votes each, so the senior alderman, the ex-mayor and fellow Parnellite Patrick Riordan gave his casting vote in favour of O'Donnell.[288] O'Donnell's first mayoralty was so successful that he was re-elected unanimously on 1 December 1893 for the year 1894 and again on 1 December 1894 for 1895.[289] This was a remarkable achievement considering the bitter rivalry between the Parnellites and anti-Parnellites on the city council. However, even the latter paid tribute to O'Donnell for his excellence as mayor.[290] On 8 June 1894, Ishbel, Countess of Aberdeen (1857-1939), wife of the seventh Earl of Aberdeen was given the freedom of Limerick, the first woman ever to receive this honour. Her husband had been appointed lord lieutenant of Ireland by Gladstone at the time of the first Home Rule Bill and was to serve in that position again between 1905 and 1915. He was also governor-general of Canada from 1893 to 1898, the position that he held at the time of the conferring of the freedom. Lord Aberdeen, who accompanied his wife to Limerick for the ceremony offered to obtain a knighthood for O'Donnell, but the latter declined the honour, in accordance with the usual practice of Irish nationalist politicians.[291] Six days later, on 14 June, the freedom of Limerick was conferred on William, Cardinal Logue, archbishop of Armagh, who was the first cardinal to receive this honour.

O'Donnell did not serve a full third term in office as he was appointed to the post of city rate collector on 12 February 1895. The holder of this position was a very senior official, who received $2^1/2\%$ of all the money that he collected and lodged. In 1894, this would have given him an annual income of £512, making him the highest paid official in the corporation. By contrast, the mayor only received £250 per year.[292] O'Donnell served with distinction in this position for an incredible forty years, before he finally retired at the age of eighty-seven in 1935. His nephew Laurence O'Donnell (1879-1959) was also a member of the city council but followed his uncle's path into administration, though in his case with Limerick County Council, where he was county secretary from 1927 to 1945. Laurence's brother John was a member of Limerick County Council from 1925 to 1928 and from 1941 to 1942.[293] Bryan O'Donnell died on 31 December 1940 at the age of ninety-two and was buried in Mount St. Lawrence Cemetery.[294] His grandson Bryan McHugh is a well-known accountant whose business premises are at 58 William Street, Limerick.

William Nolan 1895 and 1896.

William Michael Nolan was born on 29 September 1855, the son of James Nolan, a corn and flour merchant, originally from Greenville, Gurtcurreen, just outside Listowel, County Kerry, who lived and worked at 43 William Street, Limerick. James Nolan had prospered in his native city, building up a thriving business and becoming a member of the city council and

Mayor William Nolan and members of Limerick City Council at the Garryowen Fete, 1895. (Jim Kemmy Municipal Museum)

of the board of guardians. William Nolan, the eldest of four sons, was educated by the Christian Brothers, at Weirs Academy and as a lay boy at the Limerick diocesan seminary and in 1888 succeeded his father as proprietor of the family business.[295]

William Nolan was a member of the city council from 1888 to 1896 and served as high sheriff in 1890. He has the rare distinction of having served as mayor of Limerick on two occasions, while never completing a full term. His first mayoralty was brought about by the resignation of Bryan O'Donnell, who had been appointed rate collector. Nolan, a Parnellite was elected unanimously to replace O'Donnell and had a distinguished mayoralty. He was president of the organising committee of the Garryowen Fete which raised £3,000 for Barrington's Hospital.[296] Also in 1895, a social housing scheme consisting of thirteen houses was constructed and named Nolan's Cottages after the serving mayor. A forty-year loan amounting to £2,000 respectively were obtained from the Board of Works to build these houses, the first corporation scheme to be called after a mayor. Some ninety years later, Nolan's Cottages were demolished in 1987 to facilitate the building of the new City Hall.[297] In the general election of 1895, the Parnellite mayor Nolan supported the candidacy of the Fenian prisoner and future mayor John Daly against the sitting MP and former mayor, Francis A. O'Keeffe, an anti-Parnellite.[298]

On 2 December 1895, Nolan was unanimously elected mayor for 1896. However, the death of Robert McDonnell, former mayor and sitting town clerk, on 13 May 1896 created a vacancy for that position. Nolan's last official function as mayor was the official opening of the bandstand in the People's Park.[299] He resigned both as mayor and as councillor and on 28 May was appointed as town clerk, whose role as day-to-day chief executive was similar to that of the modern city manager. In 1902, his salary was £400 per year.[300] Nolan filled that position for a record thirty-six years, working with twenty mayors. He was an able and conscientious public servant who guided the corporation through wars, revolution, and financial crises, until he retired in 1932, at the age of seventy-six. In his private life Nolan was a cultivated man, fond of literature, music, drama, and painting. He lived at 8 Upper Mallow Street in his early years and later at 'Mentana' Laurel Hill Avenue, off the South Circular Road. He died at the latter residence on 22 March 1941 and was buried in Mount St. Lawrence Cemetery.[301]

Michael Cusack 1896, 1897 and 1898-99.

Michael Cusack was born in 1834 and had a large business as a painter and decorator at 49 Georges Street, where he also lived.[302] He was elected to the city council and after the Parnell split became an anti-Parnellite. He was elected mayor to succeed William Nolan on 28 May 1896, defeating Alderman Kenna by sixteen votes to thirteen. On 1 December 1896, he was unanimously returned as mayor for 1897 and on 1 December 1897, he defeated Michael Donnelly, the Parnellite candidate by twenty-eight votes to eight to become mayor for 1898.[303] Michael Cusack spent much of his period in office attempting to square various political circles. When the Fenian John Daly was released from prison, Mayor Cusack headed the welcoming party that greeted him on

Mayor Michael Cusack with a female relative in Belgium in the 1890s.
(Jim Kemmy Municipal Museum)

his return to Limerick in August 1896 and entertained him at a banquet in the Town Hall in October of the same year.[304] By contrast, on 19 June 1897, Cusack proposed that the Diamond Jubilee of Queen Victoria's accession to the throne should be a holiday. He stated that businesses should be encouraged to close for the day, though they should not be compelled to do so.[305]

Indeed the Diamond Jubilee made more headlines in Limerick that year than the septcentenary of the corporation. In 1897 Limerick Corporation was 700 years old and at a meeting of the city council held on 27 April, a committee consisting of all members of the council was set up to decide on the best way of celebrating the occasion.[306] However nothing was done to advance the matter until 25 November when a public meeting was convened in the Town Hall by Mayor Cusack and all those present formed a committee to organise a commemoration. Various proposals were put forward at this meeting and at another held on 29 November, including the establishment of a factory, the erection of social houses and even the setting up of Limerick's first crèche.[307] None of these were put into action and instead a magnificent fancy dress ball was held in the Theatre Royal, Henry Street on 28 December attended by 300 guests including Mayor Cusack and a great many of the elite of the city and county.[308] The most permanent legacy of the septcentenary was the commissioning of the mayoral chair, which was made by a Limerick city cabinetmaker named Joseph P. Lynch to mark the occasion. It is a magnificent example of the Neo-Celtic style that was very fashionable at the time. The chair, which is the most recent items of Limerick's civic insignia, has not been used for many years and is now kept in the Jim Kemmy Municipal Museum.[309]

Cusack was the last mayor to serve under the restricted franchise that had been established under the Municipal Corporations (Ireland) Act of 1840. The Local Government Act of 1898 ushered in the period of democracy in Limerick Corporation and ended the oligarchic rule that had been the norm since 1197. The first local elections under the new Act were held on 15 January 1899 and resulted in an apparent revolution. Twenty-seven of the old council had stood again for election but only eleven were returned. Michael Cusack, whose mayoralty had been extended into January 1899, in accordance with the Act of 1898, suffered a humiliating defeat in the Glentworth ward, which he had long represented. He came ninth out of thirteen candidates, polling only 126 votes, compared to the five successful candidates in that ward, who received 293, 292, 277, 277 and 250 votes respectively. He ceased to be mayor on 23 January 1899, on the election of his successor, John Daly.[310] After losing his seat, Michael Cusack went to live in Dublin and a few years later, he died there on 11 July 1907.[311] In 1910, a cousin of his, also named Michael Cusack, founded the well known firm of Limerick fishmongers now known as Rene Cusack Ltd.

Endnotes

1   For the number of individuals who have held office as provost or mayor, see Leonard, 'Provosts and Mayors of Limerick,' p. 379.

2   The best account of Martin Honan can be found in Sarah McNamara, *Development of Limerick by Honan Merchants. The Unfolding of a Hidden History*, (Limerick, 2003), pp 30-93. See also Lenihan, *History of Limerick*, pp 497-98.

3   CCM, 3 August 1842.

4   McNamara, *Honan Merchants*, pp 31-33; 35-38.

5   Ibid., p. 60.

6   CCM, 5 August 1848.

7   McNamara, *Honan Merchants*, pp 67-77.

8   *Limerick Chronicle*, 22 March 1848.

9   John Fleming and Sean O'Grady, *St. Munchin's College Limerick 1796-1996*, (Limerick, 1996), p. 110.

10   Lenihan, *History of Limerick*, p. 473.

11   Kevin Hannan, *Limerick. Historical Reflections*, (Limerick, 1996), p. 52.

12   Fleming and O'Grady, *St Munchin's College*, p. 110.

13   Lenihan, *History of Limerick*, p. 503.

14   Fleming and O'Grady, *St Munchin's College*, p. 110-11.

15   See M.E. Gleeson, 'Dr. John Geary and Dr. Wm. John Geary: 1779-1853' in *The Old Limerick Journal, Barringtons' Edition*, No. 24 (Winter, 1988), pp 25-28.

16   CCM, 10 June 1844.

17   Lenihan, *History of Limerick*, pp 503-05.

18   Ibid., p. 504.

19   For Mathew Bridge, see Lenihan, *History of Limerick*, p. 346. For the night watch see Chris O'Mahony, 'Limerick Night Watch 1807-1853' in *The Old Limerick Journal*, No. 21, (Autumn, 1987), pp 9-12.

20   Gleeson, 'Dr. John Geary and Dr. Wm. John Geary', pp 26-27.

21   *Limerick Chronicle*, 2 February 1871.

22   *Limerick Chronicle*, 17 August 1897.

23   Ibid.

24   Lenihan, *History of Limerick*, p. 346.

25   *Limerick Chronicle*, 17 August 1897.

26   See *Slaters Directory of Munster* (1846), p. 270 and *Limerick Chronicle*, 19 September 1849.

27   For the Famine in Limerick see Anonymous, *Limerick City and the Great Hunger*, (Limerick, 1997) and *The Old Limerick Journal. Famine Edition*, No. 32, (Winter, 1995).

28   Ibid., p. 28.

29   CCM, 21 January 1847.

30   Anon, *Limerick City and the Great Hunger*, p. 51.

31   Ibid., p. 41.

32   CCM, 16 September 1847.

33   *Limerick Chronicle*, 19 September 1849.

34   *Slaters Directory*, p. 269. See also *Limerick Chronicle*, 7 March 1866.

35   Robert Cussen, 'Caleb Powell, High Sheriff of County Limerick, 1858, sums up his Grand Jury' in Etienne Rynne, (ed.), *North Munster Studies. Essays in Commemoration of Monsignor Michael Moloney*, (Limerick, 1967), pp 422-23.

36   Mulligan, 'The Enemy Within: The Enemy Without', pp 162 and 173.

37   For the 'Battle of Limerick' see Laurence Fenton, 'A Riot in Limerick, 1848' in *The Old Limerick Journal*, No. 40, (Winter 2004), pp 10-13.

38   Lenihan, *History of Limerick*, p. 508.

39   *Limerick Chronicle*, 7 March 1866.

40   *Slaters Directory*, p. 271.

41   *Limerick Chronicle*, 4 December 1858.

42   Mulligan, 'The Enemy Within: The Enemy Without', p. 167.

43   CCM, 23 July 1849.

44 Lenihan, *History of Limerick*, p. 509.

45 *Limerick Chronicle*, 12 December 1849.

46 *Slaters Directory*, p. 269 and *General Directory of Cork for 1867 with which is Incorporated Wynne and Co's Business Directory of the Principal Towns in the Province of Munster*, (London, 1867), p. 380.

47 Mulligan, 'The Enemy Within: The Enemy Without', p. 172.

48 Lenihan, *History of Limerick*, pp 509-10.

49 *Limerick Chronicle*, 13 April 1876.

50 Morrissey, *Bishop O'Dwyer*, p. 4.

51 *Slaters Directory*, p. 266.

52 Mulligan, 'The Enemy Within: The Enemy Without', p. 172.

53 Lenihan, *History of Limerick*, pp 510 and 708.

54 6 December, 1860.

55 For the 1852 election, see Brian M. Walker (ed.), *Parliamentary Election Results in Ireland, 1801-1922*, (Dublin, 1978), p. 292.

56 *Limerick Chronicle*, 14 December 1871.

57 For a good account of Kane, see Fr. Mark Tierney, 'Citizen Kane, Mayor of Limerick' in Lee, *Remembering Limerick*, pp 136-39.

58 Ibid. p. 136.

59 Ibid. pp 137-39.

60 *Limerick Chronicle*, 24 July 1857.

61 For the building of the O'Connell Monument see Lenihan, *History of Limerick*, pp 511-18 and Hill, *Irish Public Sculpture*, pp 90-91.

62 Tierney, 'Citizen Kane', p. 139.

63 *Limerick Chronicle*, 3 December 1864.

64 Ibid.

65 For Hall's election as Mayor, see *Limerick Chronicle*, 4 December 1852.

66 Lenihan, *History of Limerick*, p. 512.

67 *Limerick Chronicle*, 3 December 1864.

68 *Limerick Chronicle*, 18 January 1908.

69 Mulligan, 'The Enemy Within: The Enemy Without', pp 153-54.

70 Ibid.

71 Lenihan, *History of Limerick*, p. 512-13.

72 Ibid.

73 *Limerick Chronicle*, 14 March 1860.

74 See Robert Herbert, 'The Chairing of Thomas Spring Rice' in *North Munster Antiquarian Journal*, Vol. 4, No. 4, (Autumn, 1945) pp 133-42.

75 *Limerick Chronicle*, 14 March 1860.

76 For the family background of Henry O'Shea, see Katherine O'Shea, *Charles Stewart Parnell: His Love Story and Political Life*, 2 Vols., (London, 1914), Vol. 1, pp 22-25 and Mary Rose Callaghan, '*Kitty O'Shea*', *The Story of Katherine Parnell*, (London, 1989), pp 28-34.

77 Lenihan, *History of Limerick*, p. 513.

78 *Munster News*, 20 June 1863.

79 O'Shea, *Charles Stewart Parnell*, Vol. 1, pp 22-25.

80 I am very grateful to Mr. Bryan McHugh for drawing to my attention the relationship between Henry O'Shea and Captain William O'Shea.

81 O'Shea, *Charles Stewart Parnell*, Vol. 1, pp 22-25 and Callaghan, '*Kitty O'Shea*', pp 28-34.

82 For Henry O'Shea's death see Munster News, 20 June 1863.

83 James McMahon, *Limerick Athenaeum. If Walls Could Talk. The Story of an Irish Theatre*, (Limerick, 1996), p. 13.

84 For an account of this episode see Jim Kemmy, 'The Death of a Cabin-Boy' in Jim Kemmy (ed.), *The Limerick Anthology*, (Limerick 1996), pp 114-15.

85 McMahon, *If Walls Could Talk*, p. 13.

86 *Limerick Chronicle*, 29 November 1854 and 21 January, 1892.

87 *Limerick Chronicle*, 21 January, 1892.

88   For Spaight's electoral contests, see Walker, *Parliamentary Election Results*, pp 292-93 and 360.

89   CCM, 1 December 1855.

90   Lenihan, *History of Limerick*, p. 514-17.

91   CCM, 1 December 1876.

92   I am very grateful to Mr. Tadhg Moloney for pointing out to me that Mayor Spaight did not sign the register on this occasion.

93   *Report of the Committee of 1877*, p. 23.

94   Hannan, *Limerick. Historical Reflections*, p. 107.

95   Denis O'Shaughnessy, *How's your Father? Stories of Limerick*, (Limerick, 2002), pp 51-55.

96   *Limerick Chronicle*, 21 January, 1892.

97   Ibid.

98   *Limerick Chronicle*, 25 February, 1865.

99   Mulligan, 'The Enemy Within: The Enemy Without', p. 172.

100 CCM, 1 December 1857.

101 *Limerick Chronicle*, 26 June 1858.

102 For the Prince, see John Van Der Kiste and Bee Jordaan, *Dearest Affie- Alfred, Duke of Edinburgh, Queen Victoria's Second Son*, (London, 1995).

103 *Limerick Chronicle*, 25 February, 1865.

104 I am very grateful to Mr. Bryan McHugh for drawing my attention to the relationship between Edmond Fitzgerald Ryan and Michael Robert Ryan.

105 *Slaters Directory*, p. 269.

106 A good account of Ryan can be found in John O'Connor, *On Shannon's Shore. A History of Mungret Parish*, (Mungret, 2003), pp 26-27.

107 *Limerick Chronicle*, 27 November 1856 and 15 December 1874.

108 O'Connor, *On Shannon's Shore*, pp 26-27.

109 *Limerick Chronicle*, 15 December 1874.

110 M.M. Xavier Gwynn, SHCJ, *From Hunting Field to Cloister*, (Dublin, 1946).

111 *Slaters Directory*, p. 264.

112 CCM, 23 May 1856 and 1 December 1859.

113 *Limerick Chronicle*, 27 October 1860.

114 *Slaters Directory*, p. 269.

115 Mulligan, 'The Enemy Within: The Enemy Without', p. 173.

116 CCM, 1, 6 and 11 December 1860.

117 CCM, 4 January 1866 and 2 January 1870.

118 *Limerick Chronicle*, 8 September 1892.

119 Ibid.

120 See obituaries of Lane Joynt in *Limerick Leader*, 4 January 1895 and *Limerick Chronicle*, 5 January 1895.

121 Ibid.

122 CCM, 21 January 1864.

123 *Limerick Leader*, 4 January 1895.

124 For the history of this institution see McMahon, *If Walls Could Talk*,

125 Ibid.

126 See J.J. Hogan, *From Small Beginnings. The Story of the Limerick School of Art and Design 1852-2002*, (Limerick, 2004), pp 51-85.

127 *Limerick Chronicle*, 5 January 1895.

128 Ibid.

129 Details of McMahon's career may be found in Mulligan, 'The Enemy Within: The Enemy Without', pp 161 and 172.

130 Herbert, 'Antiquities of the Corporation', p.100.

131 *Limerick Chronicle*, 4 April 1871.

132 See *Slaters Directory*, p. 268 and *Wynn's Directory*, p. 391.

133 Information from his descendant Mr. Eugene O'Callaghan, for which I am most grateful.

134 CCM, 1 May 1843.

135 Information from Mr. Eugene O'Callaghan.

136 *Limerick Chronicle*, 1 June 1881.

137 *Limerick Chronicle*, 19 April 1892.

138 Ibid.

139 Mulligan, 'The Enemy Within: The Enemy Without', p. 172.

140 Lenihan, *History of Limerick*, p. 526.

141 Herbert, 'Antiquities of the Corporation', p.100.

142 *Limerick Chronicle*, 19 April 1892.

143 For the biography of Tait, see Waite, *Peter Tait*. See also Kevin Hannan, 'Sir Peter Tait' in The Old Limerick Journal, No. 31, (Winter, 1994), pp 26-30. In 2006, Tony Bromell, mayor of Limerick in 1982-83 became the first mayor of Limerick to publish his autobiography.

144 Hannan, 'Sir Peter Tait', p. 26.

145 Waite, *Peter Tait*, pp 23, 39.

146 Hannan, ' Sir Peter Tait', p. 26.

147 Waite, *Peter Tait*, pp 31-32.

148 Ibid, pp 42-44 and 154-67.

149 Ibid., pp 9-11 and 288-89.

150 Hannan, ' Sir Peter Tait', p. 27.

151 For Tait's mayoralties, see Waite, *Peter Tait*, pp 115-46.

152 Ibid, p. 122. See also Hannan, ' Sir Peter Tait', p. 28.

153 Waite, *Peter Tait*, pp 131-32.

154 Ibid., p. 116.

155 Ibid, pp 137-46.

156 Ibid., p. 144.

157 For Tait's career after 1868, see Waite, *Peter Tait*, pp 168-284.

158 *Slaters Directory*, p. 263.

159 Mulligan, 'The Enemy Within: The Enemy Without', p. 172.

160 CCM, 1 December 1868.

161 CCM, 1 December 1874.

162 CCM, 16 September 1875.

163 CCM, 17 February 1870.

164 CCM, 1 December 1868.

165 Herbert, 'Antiquities of the Corporation', p.97.

166 CCM, 1 December 1869 and 3 January 1870. See also *Limerick Chronicle*, 17 February 1870.

167 *Limerick Chronicle*, 10 January 1881.

168 CCM, 4 January 1867.

169 *Limerick Chronicle*, 27 July 1897.

170 See Jim Kemmy, A History of the Limerick City Library and Granary, (Unpublished manuscript, 1985), p. 1.

171 18 & 19 Vict. c. 40.

172 Kemmy, A History of the Limerick City Library, p. 2.

173 Ibid., pp 2-3.

174 McMahon, *If Walls Could Talk!*, p. 52.

175 Ibid. See also CCM, 7 October 1875.

176 Potter, *The Government and the People of Limerick*, pp 331-33.

177 *Limerick Chronicle*, 27 July 1897.

178 Information from Mr. Bryan McHugh.

179 William Bassett, *Limerick City and County and the Principal Towns in the Counties of Clare, Tipperary and Kerry, Directory, 1880-1*, (Limerick, 1880), p. 56.

180 CCM, 28 November 1864.

181 CCM, 11 May 1871.

182 *Limerick Chronicle*, 14 May 1896.

183 Potter, 'A Catholic Unionist', p. 214.

184 *Limerick Chronicle*, 14 May 1896.

185 Ibid.

186 Ibid.

187 *Wynns Directory*, p. 391.

188 CCM, 1 November 1860.

189 CCM, 1 December 1871.

190 *Limerick Chronicle*, 27 April 1872.

191 *Limerick Chronicle*, 3 June 1902.

192 CCM, 25 November 1869.

193 CCM, 2 May 1872.

194 For the events of his mayoralties see Herbert, 'Antiquities of the Corporation', pp 98-100.

195 *Limerick Chronicle*, 3 June 1902.

196 McKay, 'The Limerick Municipal Elections,' pp 6-7.

197 *Limerick Chronicle*, 3 June 1902.

198 *Limerick Chronicle*, 18 January 1908.

199 Information from Mr. Tony Browne, for which I am most grateful.

200 CCM, 2 December 1861, 8 February 1876, and 5 February 1880.

201 *Limerick Chronicle*, 18 January 1908.

202 CCM, 1 December 1874.

203 CCM, 3 December 1874.

204 CCM, 1 January and 1 February 1875.

205 Herbert, 'Antiquities of the Corporation', p. 98.

206 Hill, *Irish Public Sculpture*, pp 111-13. For a general survey of Limerick's monuments in this period see Judith Hill, 'Reputations: Nineteenth-Century Monuments in Limerick' in *The Old Limerick Journal*, No. 33, (Winter, 1996), pp 19-24.

207 *Limerick Chronicle*, 18 January 1908.

208 McKay, 'The Limerick Municipal Elections,' p. 7.

209 *Limerick Chronicle*, 18 January 1908.

210 *Bassetts Directory*, p. 87.

211 CCM, 1 January and 1 February 1875.

212 CCM, 1 December 1875.

213 Herbert, 'Antiquities of the Corporation', p. 98.

214 *Limerick Chronicle*, 8 February 1900.

215 *Slaters Directory*, p. 272 and *Bassetts Directory*, p. 34.

216 Mulligan, 'The Enemy Within: The Enemy Without', p. 172.

217 CCM, 1 December 1877.

218 Potter, *The Government and the People of Limerick*, pp 326-27.

219 *Limerick Chronicle*, 19 September, 1895.

220 *Limerick Chronicle*, 17 November 1908.

221 CCM, 1 December 1870.

222 Herbert, 'Antiquities of the Corporation', p. 100.

223 See Quin's obituary in *Limerick Chronicle*, 13 February 1883.

224 CCM, 1 December 1879.

225 CCM, 4 December 1879.

226 CCM, 23 December 1879.

227 Herbert, 'Antiquities of the Corporation', p. 100.

228 *Limerick Chronicle*, 17 November 1908.

229 *Limerick Chronicle*, 1 January 1907.

230 Information from Mr. Bryan McHugh.

231 CCM, 3 July 1873.

232 CCM, 1 December 1880.

233 *Limerick Chronicle*, 2 December 1880.

234 *Limerick Chronicle*, 1 January 1907.

235 Ibid.

236 *Limerick Chronicle*, 6 October 1894.

237 CCM, 20 January 1870.

238 *Limerick Chronicle*, 6 October 1894.

239 Ibid.

240 For Lenihan's biography see Fr. Francis Finegan's four articles which originally appeared in *Studies* between September 1946 and March 1948 and were reprinted in *The Old Limerick Journal*. These are 'Maurice Lenihan- Historian of Limerick, Part One', in *The Old Limerick Journal*, No 17, (Winter, 1984), pp 11-14; 'Maurice Lenihan- Historian of Limerick, Part Two', in *The Old Limerick Journal*, No 18, (Winter, 1985), pp 27-30; 'Maurice Lenihan- Historian of Limerick, Part Two', (in reality Part Three) in *The Old Limerick Journal*, No 19, (Summer, 1986), pp 5-9 and 'Maurice Lenihan- Historian of Limerick, Part Four', in *The Old Limerick Journal*, No 20, (Winter, 1986), pp 7-10. See also Liam Irwin, 'Introduction to the 1991 Edition' in Lenihan, *History of Limerick*, pp ix-xiii.

241 Finegan, 'Maurice Lenihan, Part One' pp 11-14.

242 Finegan, 'Maurice Lenihan, Part Two' pp 27-30.

243 Irwin, 'Introduction to the 1991 Edition', pp x-xi.

244 Ibid., p. ix.

245 Mulligan, 'The Enemy Within: The Enemy Without', p. 172.

246 CCM, 1 December 1883.

247 Finegan, 'Maurice Lenihan, Part Four' pp 9-10.

248 Ibid, pp 8-10.

249 Joyce, *Limerick City Street Names*, p. 36.

250 Herbert, 'Antiquities of the Corporation', p. 98.

251 See Patricia Lavelle, *James O'Mara a Staunch Sinn Féiner 1873-1948*, (Dublin, 1948).

252 See website on O'Mara family history at http://humphrysfamilytree.com/OMeara/contents.html.

253 Ibid.

254 Ibid.

255 CCM, 27 November 1879 and 15 January 1908.

256 For the British monarchy and nineteenth century Ireland see James H. Murphy, *Abject Loyalty. Nationalism and Monarchy in Ireland During the Reign of Queen Victoria*, (Cork, 2001).

257 Ibid., pp 198-242.

258 For an account of the royal visit and the local response see Denis O'Shaughnessy, *How's your Father? Stories of Limerick*, (Limerick, 2002), pp 51-55.

259 For the principal events of O'Mara's Mayoralties, see Herbert, 'Antiquities of the Corporation', p. 98.

260 Potter, *The Government and the People of Limerick*, p. 340.

261 http://humphrysfamilytree.com/OMeara/contents.html.

262 McKay, 'The Limerick Municipal Elections,' p. 9.

263 *Limerick Chronicle*, 27 July 1926.

264 Ibid.

265 *Bassetts Directory*, p. 67.

266 *The Crescent College Review*, No. 1, (Midsummer, 1897), pp 36-37.

267 Ibid.

268 Potter, *The Government and the People of Limerick*, pp 328-30.

269 Herbert, 'Antiquities of the Corporation', p. 99.

270 CCM, 25 November 1893.

271 For O'Keeffe's electoral contests see Walker, *Parliamentary Election Results*, p. 360.

272 *Limerick Chronicle*, 22 September 1909.

273 *Bassetts Directory*, p. 130.

274 *Limerick Chronicle*, 19 August 1893 and *The Crescent College Review*, No. 1, pp 45-47.

275 For a biography of Riordan see Anthony Riordan, 'A nineteenth-Century Citizen' in *The Old Limerick Journal*, No. 18, (Winter 1985), pp 12-14.

276 CCM, 9 November 1875.

277 Riordan, 'A nineteenth-Century Citizen', pp 12-14.

278 Potter, *The Government and the People of Limerick*, pp 331-33.

279 Riordan, 'A nineteenth-Century Citizen', p. 14.

280 CCM, 1 July 1880.

281 CCM, 1 December 1891.

282 *Limerick Chronicle*, 9 January 1911.

283 *Bassetts Directory*, p. 64.

284 Information from Mr. Bryan McHugh.

285 *Limerick Chronicle*, 31 December 1940.

286 Information from Mr. Bryan McHugh.

287 Information from Mr. Bryan McHugh.

288 CCM, 1 December 1892.

289 CCM, 1 December 1893 and 1 December 1894.

290 Ibid.

291 Information from Mr. Bryan McHugh.

292 Potter, *The Government and the People of Limerick*, p. 332.

293 Information from Mr. Bryan McHugh.

294 *Limerick Chronicle*, 2 January 1940.

295 De Bhaldraithe and de Bhaldraithe, 'The Nolans and the Costellocs', pp 13-15.

296 Herbert, 'Antiquities of the Corporation', p. 98.

297 Potter, *The Government and the People of Limerick*, p. 330.

298 Information from Mr. Tadhg Moloney.

299 Information from Mr. Tadhg Moloney.

300 Potter, *The Government and the People of Limerick*, pp 331-32.

301 *Limerick Chronicle*, 22 and 25 March, 1941.

302 Information from Mr. Tadhg Moloney.

303 CCM, 1 December 1896 and 1 December 1897.

304 *Limerick Chronicle*, 14 August and 6 October, 1896.

305 *Limerick Chronicle*, 19 June1897.

306 *Limerick Chronicle*, 27 April 1897.

307 *Limerick Chronicle*, 25 and 30 November 1897.

308 *Limerick Chronicle*, 30 December 1897.

309 Walsh, *Historic Limerick*, pp 13-14.

310 McKay, 'The Limerick Municipal Elections,' pp 8-10.

311 *Limerick Chronicle*, 11 July 1907.

312 *Irish Times*, 23 November 2005.

John Daly with Thomas Clarke and Sean MacDiarmada
(Jim Kemmy Municipal Museum)

Chapter Seven
Chronicle of the Mayors of Limerick. Part Two 1899–2007

Introduction.

The Local Government (Ireland) Act of 1898 provided the legislative framework for the constitutional revolution wrought at the local elections held on 15 January 1899, the most dramatic in the history of Limerick Corporation as they marked both the end of the oligarchic rule that had been the norm since 1197 and the beginning of democracy in the city. From 1899 onwards, the mayor no longer served for a calendar year but instead took office in the middle of January. In 1925 the time of the mayoral election was changed to June, where it remains to the present.

John Daly 1899–1900, 1900–01 and 1901–02.

One of the most significant figures in the history of Limerick's mayoralty, John Daly was born in Limerick city in 1845 and having left school at the age of sixteen worked as a lathe splitter in a timber yard.[1] In 1863 he was sworn in as a member of the Irish Republican Brotherhood (IRB) or the Fenians as they are better known and was an active member throughout the 1860s. He was imprisoned in Limerick Jail for three months between November 1866 and February 1867 and a month later took part in the abortive attack mounted on Kilmallock RIC Barracks by the Limerick city IRB, as part of the Fenian Rising. After the failure of the Rising, he lived in exile in the USA for two years, but returned to Limerick and throughout the 1870s and early 1880s, was actively involved in IRB activities in the city.[2]

In the 1880s, the IRB commenced a dynamiting campaign in mainland Britain, similar to the IRA bombing campaign a century later. Daly became involved and lived in England for a time, in order to assist his Fenian colleagues there. However, he was arrested on 9 April 1884, put on trial and sentenced to penal servitude for life, although it has been alleged that he had committed no crime and that his conviction was based on perjured evidence.[3] Daly served twelve years of his sentence in the typically harsh conditions of a nineteenth century English prison and during this period became very friendly with a fellow Fenian convict, Thomas Clarke, who was to marry his niece Kathleen Daly in 1901. Eventually, Daly was released on 21 August 1896, and following lecture tours in England and the USA, settled permanently in Limerick in the summer of 1898. Despite having no previous experience in or knowledge of the business, he established a bakery at 26 William Street, next door to where ex-mayor Patrick Riordan lived. Daly's bakery attracted much attention, not only because of its celebrated proprietor, but also due to the name over the shop and on the vans being in the Irish language.[4]

Even while he was still in prison, Daly's long involvement with the IRB and his status as a political prisoner had made him one of the most celebrated figures in the city, so it is not surprising that he should have become involved in the public life of Limerick. His return to Limerick coincided with the enactment of the Local Government (Ireland) Act, which became law on 12 August 1898 and brought about the democratisation of Limerick Corporation. The ensuing local elections of 15 January 1899 created a sensation with the so-called Labour Party winning twenty-four out of the forty seats and Daly himself heading the poll in the Irishtown ward, with the highest number of votes polled by any candidate in Limerick city. He thus became the senior alderman of the corporation and at the first meeting of the new council on 23 January 1899, was unanimously elected mayor of Limerick.[5]

In total, Daly served as mayor for three consecutive years. His mayoralties were often controversial. Within two months of his election, he presided over the granting of the freedom of Limerick to Thomas Clarke, who was soon to marry Daly's niece Kathleen. Incidentally, Clarke was the only signatory of the 1916 Proclamation who was also a freeman of Limerick. His widow Kathleen was later to receive the freedom of Limerick and became the first female Lord Mayor of Dublin. In 1900, the freedom of Limerick was granted to James Egan, the sword bearer of Dublin Corporation who had refused to meet Queen Victoria, and on Maud Gonne who had orchestrated the nationalist campaign against this royal visit to Ireland. The Labour Corporation even wanted to go further, and grant the freedom to President Kruger of the Transvaal, who had led the Boers in the early stages of their conflict with the British Empire, but nothing came of this. In the second half of 1902, after he had ceased to be mayor, Daly tried and failed to have the freedom given to three prominent Boer generals, including Louis Botha, later to be the first prime minister of South Africa.

Daly removed the royal coat of arms from the doors of the Town Hall, thus breaking a tradition going back to Mayor Yorke in 1673. He also added a link to the mayoral chain which had an inscription in the Irish language for the first time ever and depicted a rising sun (symbolising the dawn of Irish freedom), a pair of handcuffs (a reminder of his long imprisonment) and a rifle and pike crossed, all surrounded by a circle of shamrocks.[6] This inflammatory addition to the chain was not universally welcomed. In addition Daly was not allowed to take up the customary mayoral position of *ex officio* magistrate, due to his status as an ex-convict. Rumours circulated both at the time and since that Queen Victoria had intended to promote Limerick's mayor to Lord Mayor as happened in Cork on the occasion of her final visit to Ireland in April 1900, but nothing came of it. Again, it was believed by some that having a Fenian as mayor had caused Limerick to be denied an important civic honour, which the ancient rival Cork had successfully secured.[7]

On the other hand, Mayor Daly was by present day standards, a social and administrative conservative. As a businessman, he did not want to see social as distinct from political revolution in Limerick and as head of the corporation conducted routine civic business in a sensible and competent fashion. He stepped down as mayor in January 1902, and thereafter it was clear that his best years were behind him. Indeed, his career on Limerick City Council was comparatively short as he resigned as alderman of the Irishtown ward on 2 August 1906, having served for just seven years. He continued to take an active interest in the bakery and in IRB activities, but the end of his life was marked by tragedy. Following the 1916 Rising, both his nephew Edward Daly and his beloved friend Thomas Clarke were executed. A few weeks later, on 30 June 1916, John Daly died at his residence on Barrington Street, Limerick and was buried in Mount St. Lawrence Cemetery.[8]

James F. Barry 1902–03.

James Francis Barry was born in 1872 and was a horse dealer by profession. He was elected to the city council at the age of twenty-six on 15 January 1899 and was a member of the 'Labour' Party, though not of the IRB.[9] He was high sheriff for the year February 1901 to February 1902 and at the age of twenty-nine, he succeeded Daly in January 1902, becoming the youngest mayor of Limerick since William O'Donnell in 1890. He thus achieved the rare distinction of being high sheriff and mayor simultaneously as his terms of office in both offices overlapped in February 1902. Barry

James F. Barry.
(Jim Kemmy Municipal Museum)

served one term as mayor and continued as a member of the council until 1906 when he resigned, and in 1911 was appointed as city coroner, a post that he held until 1920.[10]

Barry was an avid sportsman, and was involved in horseracing, rugby and rowing. He was a sociable person, with a good singing voice, and often took part in charity concerts. While his political views were sometimes regarded as being comparatively radical, he was a pious Catholic and was a member of the Arch-Confraternity of the Holy Family, the Redemptorist association for laymen. He resided in Janesboro for much of his life. Barry died in Barrington's Hospital at the early age of forty-nine on 30 July 1921 and was buried in Mount St. Lawrence Cemetery.[11]

Michael Donnelly 1903–04 and 1904–05.

Born in 1848, Michael Donnelly was a grocer and publican, who carried on his business at 28 Mungret Street and was first elected to the city council in the 1880s. In the 1890s he was a Parnellite and was that party's candidate at the mayoral election of

1 December 1897. However he was defeated by the sitting mayor, Michael Cusack by twenty-eight votes to eight.[12] At the time of the 1899 local elections, he was believed by the RIC to be a member of the Fenians and although not classified as one of John Daly's 'Labour' Party, was popularly believed to be closely aligned with them. No doubt, it was these connections that enabled him to be re-elected to the council for the Irishtown ward in 1899. He polled an excellent 503 votes, second only to Daly himself, which is even more remarkable, considering that the latter was also returned for the Irishtown ward.[13]

Donnelly served two terms as mayor between January 1903 and January 1905. During his first mayoralty, Andrew Carnegie came to Limerick on 20 October 1903, and laid the foundation stone for the new city library in Pery Square. On the same day, he was also accorded the honour of a civic reception by Mayor Donnelly, and made a Freeman of the city at a special meeting of the corporation.[14] Donnelly's second mayoralty was marked by the crisis caused by the Jewish Boycott. On 20 April 1904, he called a special meeting of the city council in aid of John Raleigh, the fifteen-year old imprisoned for throwing a stone at the rabbi of the Limerick Jewish community, and also to counter the bad publicity that Limerick was receiving owing to the boycott.[15] A resolution was passed unanimously calling on the lord lieutenant to have the boy released. The mayor himself stated that there was no boycott or violence being carried on in Limerick against the Jews. He stated that the problem had nothing to do with the religion of the Jewish community in Limerick but rather their 'usurious methods of dealing.'[16] While Donnelly's role in the whole affair was not a heroic one, he was merely reflecting the opinion of the majority of the city council and no doubt the attitudes of the general public as well.

Donnelly remained a member of the council until 1911, when he lost his seat in the local elections of that year. He died at his residence, 54 Parnell Street, on 24 September 1917 and was buried in Mount St. Lawrence Cemetery.[17]

Michael Joyce 1905–06 and 1906–07.

Michael Joyce, who claimed, with some justification, to be the first working class mayor of Limerick, dominated the political scene in Limerick from 1900 to 1918.[18] He was born on 4 September 1851 in Merchants' Quay, Limerick and was educated at the Christian Brothers' schools at Bridge Street and Sexton Street. He came from a family with a strong maritime tradition, and at the age of fourteen he left school and became a sailor. Over the next five years, he undertook voyages all over the world and was shipwrecked four times. Eventually, he returned to Limerick and served his apprenticeship as a river pilot, his father's profession. In 1878, he was granted a licence to practice as a river pilot and spent the next two decades guiding ships up and down the Shannon Estuary and into Limerick port.[19]

From an early age, Joyce took an active part in the public life of his native city. He was a staunch supporter of Home Rule and in 1882, he and a local priest founded the Limerick branch of the Irish National League, which was the constituency organisation of Parnell's Irish Party at Westminster. In 1884, he was a founder member of a new rugby club in Limerick that, at his suggestion, was called Garryowen. He played for the new club himself as well as acting as its first treasurer. He also played hurling and was a member of St. Michael's Temperance Society.[20]

At the local elections of 1899, Joyce was elected alderman for the Custom House ward and remained a member of the council until 1920. The general election of 1900 saw Joyce

Michael Joyce
(Limerick City Archives)

returned as MP for Limerick city, in place of former mayor, Francis A. O'Keeffe, who had retired from politics. On this occasion Joyce won a crushing victory, polling 2,521 votes, while his opponent, the unionist Francis Kearney, received a mere 474 votes. Joyce was returned by overwhelming majorities at the subsequent general elections of 1906 and 1910, and remained in parliament until 1918.[21] Joyce was mayor for two successive terms from January 1905 to January 1907 and the first holder of the office to be simultaneously an MP since Francis A. O'Keeffe in 1888–89. Joyce's mayoralties were free of controversy, unlike those of John Daly and Michael Donnelly, but his parliamentary duties meant that he often missed council meetings. In 1906, during his second mayoralty, the name of Limerick's main street was changed from George's Street to O'Connell Street. Like his predecessor, Bryan O'Donnell, he refused a knighthood from Lord Aberdeen, who was again lord lieutenant of Ireland and who visited Limerick to attend the Munster and Connaught Exhibition in 1906.[22]

Joyce was very interested in the provision of social housing in Limerick, an issue that had been neglected by Limerick Corporation since the building of Nolan's Cottages in 1895. In 1904, a national organisation named the Town Tenants' League was founded which provided a strong pressure group in favour of social housing. Its initial aims were to obtain the same legal protection for urban tenants as had been already won by rural tenants (the three Fs of fair rent, fixity of tenure and free sale, plus the ultimate right to buy out the landlords). In Limerick, an active branch of the League soon came into existence, which threw its weight behind the demand for the corporation to build social housing. The role of Michael Joyce became a crucial one. He became president of the Limerick branch of the Tenants' League, and put his formidable energies and prestige into the campaign for social housing in the city.[37] Joyce was proud of his claim to be the 'first working man' to be mayor of Limerick and in 1914 spoke of how, as a member of that class, he had not 'even the privilege of voting for a member of the corporation' before 1899, let alone becoming a councillor himself.[38] He saw the provision of decent and affordable housing for his fellow working men as being among the most important of his policy aims. The efforts of Joyce and the Town Tenants' League eventually bore fruit and Limerick Corporation borrowed £19,000 between 1911 and 1912 to build eighty-nine houses, at John Street, Prospect and Garryowen.[23]

Besides Home Rule and social housing, Joyce's other main policy interest lay in river pilotage. He was president of the United Kingdom Pilots' Association from 1910 to 1923 and played an important role in the drawing up and enactment of the Pilotage Act of 1913. Indeed Joyce was known at Westminster as 'the Admiral' or 'the Pilot' and was well liked by his colleagues from all parties. He was an active member of the Limerick Harbour Commissioners and of the Ancient Order of Hibernians, a Catholic organisation similar to the Orange Order (with sashes, banners and marches) that flourished chiefly before 1918 and mainly in Ulster.[24]

Joyce's political career came to an end as a result of the 1916 Rising and the rise of Sinn Féin. In 1918, he had intended to stand again for parliament, but when his election meeting, held in the council chamber of Limerick Town Hall on 25 November 1918, was disrupted by Sinn Féin hecklers, he reconsidered and withdrew his candidature. Subsequently, the Sinn Féin candidate, Michael P. Colivet, was returned unopposed. Joyce also retired from the city council in January 1920. Nevertheless, he continued to be active in the public life of Limerick for the last two decades of his life. Michael Joyce died at his residence, 'The Moorings', O'Connell Avenue, on 9 January, 1941, aged eighty-nine, and was buried in Mount St. Lawrence Cemetery.[25]

John Kerr 1907–08.

Born in 1856, John Kerr was employed as mill manager of Bannatynes on Roches Street for many years.[26] He was a member of the city council from 1905 to 1911 and served as mayor from January 1907 to January 1908. During his mayoralty, Kerr opened the All-Ireland Industrial Conference in the Town Hall on 28 November 1907 and the Tuberculosis Exhibition at the Athenaeum two days later.[27] He died on 5 December 1932 at his residence, 56 Clare Street, and was buried in Mount St. Lawrence Cemetery.[28]

John Kerr
(Limerick City Archives)

Thomas Donnellan 1908–09 and 1909–10.

Thomas Donnellan was one of the great survivors of Limerick politics. He was a member of the city council from 1891 to 1924, except for a brief interval from 1911 to 1914, and was the only pre-1899 councillor to be successfully re-elected in both of the pivotal local elections of 1899 and 1920, in contrast to so many of his colleagues, who either lost their seats or did not choose to run. Born in 1854, he was descended from a tenant farmer who had been evicted from his holding in County Clare as a punishment for voting in favour of Daniel O'Connell in the famous 1828 election. Subsequently, the family moved to the Thomondgate

Thomas Donnellan
(Limerick City Archives)

area, north of Limerick city and prospered there. Some of the family are believed to have had Fenian sympathies in the 1860s, which would not be surprising considering their harsh experiences in County Clare. Thomas Donnellan was an extensive farmer in Thomondgate and was first elected to the city council for the Castle ward on 26 November 1891.[29] Initially he was an anti-Parnellite, but was later aligned with the Parnellites. In the 1899 local elections, he was one of only eleven out of twenty-seven outgoing members who stood for re-election. According to the RIC, Donnellan was a member of the Fenians at this time.[30]

Thomas Donnellan served as mayor of Limerick for two successive terms, between January 1908 and January 1910. During his first mayoralty, the freedom of Limerick was conferred on Joseph O'Mara, the famous opera singer, on 2 October 1908. Interestingly, O'Mara's brother had been mayor of Limerick in 1885 and 1886. On 7 December 1908, the fourth Earl of Dunraven was also given the freedom of Limerick. On 5 June 1909, during Donnellan's second mayoralty, the freedom of the city was bestowed on Dr. Douglas Hyde, at the time the president of the Gaelic League, and later to be the first president of Ireland.[31]

After nineteen years of unbroken service, Donnellan lost his seat in the 1911 local elections but was returned at the 1914 local elections. The 1920 elections resulted in Sinn Féin winning twenty-six seats, the Ratepayers four, Independents four and Labour six. Many of the councillors elected under the labels of Ratepayers or Independents were former Home Rulers and Donnellan belonged to the latter group.[32] He had the distinction of being the only pre-1899 councillor in Limerick city to be returned in the 1920 local elections. He remained on the council until his death, which occurred on 1 March 1924. Donnellan was buried in Mount St. Lawrence Cemetery.[33] One of his sons, Patrick was a member of the city council from 1925 to 1960 and was mayor from 1930 to 1933. Another son, Michael was a senior official of Limerick Corporation for many years and served as acting city manager on two occasions (1938-39 and 1944-46).[34]

Timothy Ryan 1910–11, 1911–12 and 1912–13.

Timothy Ryan was born in County Tipperary in 1856 but lived and worked for most of his life in Limerick city. For many years, he was manager of J. P. Evans and Company of 131 O'Connell Street, who were oil and colour merchants, druggists (or pharmacists) and vendors of agricultural machinery. He was also consulting engineer with the Condensed Milk Company of Ireland, which was based in Lansdowne, off the North Circular Road, Limerick and owned by the Cleeve family. In this capacity, he was responsible for establishing branch creameries all over the South of Ireland and in the company of Sir Thomas Cleeve, the proprietor of the firm, travelled all over Europe on business.[35]

Mayor Timothy Ryan with Garryowen Rugby Football Club, Winners Munster Cup 1910-11
(Jim Kemmy Municipal Museum)

Timothy Ryan was elected to the city council on 17 January 1905.[36] He was mayor for three successive years, from January 1910 to January 1913. Although a supporter of Home Rule, Ryan became a controversial figure for displaying what was considered to be excessive loyalty to the British crown. In May 1910, in conjunction with the unionist high sheriff, he officially proclaimed the accession of King George V to the throne.[37] The following year, he created an even greater sensation by actually attending the King's coronation in Westminster Abbey on 22 June 1911, although the Home Rule Party were still continuing their long-standing policy of boycotting royal ceremonies.[38]

Ryan retired from the city council on 17 January 1914. He was also a member of the chamber of commerce and of the Harbour Commissioners. He died at his residence, 'Indiaville,' Corbally on 5 July 1930 and was buried in Mount St. Lawrence Cemetery.[39]

Philip O'Donovan 1913–14, 1914–15 and 1915–16.

The son of a farmer, Philip O'Donovan was born in Murroe, County Limerick in 1876 and came to Limerick city at a young age. He established a business in Cathedral Place where he sold groceries, wines and spirits, and he also manufactured mineral waters there. Later he opened a coal yard in Honan's Quay, which soon became one of the largest in the city.[40]

O'Donovan became very prosperous and successful and, in the manner of many of the pre-1899 mercantile elite, became involved in local politics. He stood in the local elections of 1911 and was elected alderman of the Irishtown ward, in the

Philip O'Donovan
(Limerick City Archives)

process defeating the sitting alderman and former mayor, Michael Donnelly.[41] Like his immediate predecessor Timothy Ryan, O'Donovan was mayor of Limerick for three successive years (January 1913 to January 1916). He was a moderate and conciliatory figure and his first year in office was notable for the manner in which he mediated in various industrial disputes. However, he was also considered by some to be politically naïve and out of touch with current political developments, while his studied neutrality when chairing council meetings tended to make him seem aloof and ineffectual.[42]

O'Donovan's mayoralties were dominated by the First World War which broke out in the late summer of 1914. He was a supporter of Home Rule and of John Redmond and on the outbreak of the war, he also approved of Redmond's call for Ireland to support the war effort and for Irishmen to enlist in the British army. When the lord lieutenant, Lord Wimbourne paid an official visit to Limerick on 17 August 1915, Limerick Corporation presented him with an official address of welcome. However, this was only done after a heated debate, which ended with the council voting by thirteen votes to ten in favour of presenting the address. In his anxiety to be seen to be neutral on the issue, the mayor abstained in the vote and did not present the address to Lord Wimbourne, leaving this task to Michael Joyce to perform instead.[43]

O'Donovan was more forceful on local issues and led the corporation into battle with the Harbour Commissioners over the question of Sarsfield Bridge. The latter wanted to convert the swivel element of the bridge into a fixed crossing, which would have cut off Arthur's Quay from the rest of the harbour. The corporation opposed this plan and the issue went to the law courts and was only resolved when the House of Lords decided in favour of the corporation.[44]

O'Donovan remained a member of the council until 1920.[45] He died on 8 September 1953 at his residence, 'Avoca' Dooradoyle, near Limerick city and was buried in Mount St. Lawrence Cemetery.[46]

Sir Stephen Quin 1916–17 and 1917–18.

Stephen Byrne Quin was born on 26 December 1860, the son of John Quin (1812-83) one of the richest men in Limerick.[47] John Quin resided at 70 Georges Street and was the owner of a flourishing wholesale and retail wine business, John Quin and Company, of Patrick Street and Ellen Street, which had been founded in 1822. (Incidentally, Michael Quin, who had served as mayor of Limerick in 1848 was not related to the family at all). John Quin was a member of the city council for a number of years, but he made his biggest contribution to the life of Limerick city in the field of philanthropy. He contributed £7,000 to pay for the erection of the tower of the

Stephen Quin
(Limerick City Archives)

Redemptorist Church at Mount St. Alphonsus and a further £2,000 for the installation of a carillon of bells and other fittings. He also contributed large sums towards the building of the spire of St. John's Cathedral and to the erection of the new St. Michael's Church in Denmark Street. In addition, he was believed to have donated a large sum of money annually to the St. Vincent de Paul Society.[48]

Stephen Quin was educated at Ushaw College, Durham, one of the most elite Catholic public schools in Britain. Later he worked in the family business with his elder brother James. In 1886 he married Emma Crean, the daughter of a wealthy barrister, and they had two sons.[49] Quin resided at Shannon Lawn and later at Ballinacourty House, Castleconnell in County Limerick. He was high sheriff of Limerick city in 1897 and in the same year received Queen Victoria's Jubilee Medal for helping organise the celebrations in Limerick to mark the sixtieth anniversary of the Queen's accession to the throne.[50] Although this episode resulted in Quin being roundly criticised by nationalists in the city, he still managed to get himself elected to the city council on 15 January 1899 as one of the Mercantile group.[51] He resigned from the council soon after but was re-elected on 17 January 1914.[52]

Quin was elected mayor on 25 January 1916, by twenty-two votes to thirteen, having been proposed for the position by former mayor, Councillor Thomas Donnellan. Quin was a controversial choice, for though he professed himself to be a supporter of Home Rule, he was perceived by some to be sympathetic to unionism, and was widely distrusted by many nationalists. However, Donnellan and his supporters hoped that Mayor Quin, a wealthy businessman who was reputed to be a friend of Lord Wimbourne, the lord lieutenant might be able to attract munitions factories to Limerick and thus bring much needed employment to the city. Unlike the studiously neutral O'Donovan, Quin was an active supporter of the British war effort in Ireland. Both of his sons were serving in the British army and he presided at a large recruiting rally in Doon, County Limerick. However, his stance enjoyed the support of the majority in the city council and of the general public at this time.[53]

The 1916 Rising was to change everything and was eventually to terminate Quin's political career. Following the Easter Rising, the mayor won widespread praise for his role in its aftermath. He issued an appeal for calm, and then orchestrated the disarmament of the Irish Volunteers in Limerick, by agreeing to accept their arms, and in turn, pass them onto the garrison in Limerick, headed by Sir Anthony Weldon. Most of the arms were handed into the Town Hall on 5 and 6 May 1916. The mayor was regarded by both sides as an honest broker, and a resolution was passed unanimously by the council on 1 June, 1916, expressing the 'fullest and most grateful appreciation' of all of the aldermen and city councillors for the efforts of the first citizen in successfully preserving 'the peace, good order and safety of the city during the recent crisis'.[54] Quin's vigorous and successful leadership of the city had temporarily muted the opposition to his pro-government stance at a moment of national crisis.[55]

However, public opinion had already begun to move in favour of the rebels, following the execution of their leaders in May 1916. Bishop O'Dwyer played a major role in this transformation of the public mood and some months later was honoured by the corporation with the freedom of the city. Mayor Quin had been the only member of the council to vote against the resolution in favour of the bishop being so honoured and was very uneasy at having to preside over the actual conferring ceremony, which was held in the Town Hall on 14 September 1916. Although Quin was re-elected mayor in January 1917, the tide of public opinion was now running against both the Home Rule party, and Quin's policy of accommodation with the British administration in Ireland. The main plank of his political platform, the obtaining of munitions factories for Limerick did not happen. In 1917, the British government established an all-party Irish Convention in order to attempt to solve the Irish question, by bringing together all Irish political parties, both unionist and nationalist. Mayor Quin attended as a representative of the corporation, but was widely suspected of being a unionist, atlthough he was registered at the Convention as a nationalist. Many of his fellow-councillors feared that he was unsound on the question of the partition of the country, which was now a live issue in the aftermath of the Rising. His vague comments on this and on his general political philosophy did not re-assure them.[56]

On 1 January 1918, Stephen Quin was knighted by King George V, the first serving mayor of Limerick to be so honoured since Richard Franklin in 1839 (James Spaight had been the last mayor to be knighted but had received the honour ten years after his final mayoralty). To many nationalists, this confirmed their worst fears.[57] On 18 January the newly knighted Quin put himself forward as a candidate for mayor for the third time and thus hoped to emulate his two immediate predecessors, who had each served for three years in a row. It was not to be. At the council meeting Councillor Matthew Griffin described Quin as a 'garrison mayor' and a protégé of Lord Wimbourne, 'Ireland's chief jailor' and claimed that he was a friend of the British government. The other candidate for the mayoralty was Alphonsus O'Mara, a strong supporter of Sinn Féin. Not surprisingly, Quin was defeated by twenty-three votes to thirteen.[58]

This defeat effectively ended Quin's career in Limerick's public life. He ceased to be a member of the city council in 1920 and after the Anglo-Irish Treaty of 1921, went to reside in England. Somewhat ironically, his final residence was at Ascot near Windsor Castle, and it was in this house that he died on 11 May 1944. However the family name has not vanished from the city. The family business continued to operate in Ellen Street, Limerick until the early years of the twenty-first century. Quin Street, across from the Redemptorist Church is named in honour of Alderman John Quin and Quin's Cottages, a social housing scheme built during his mayoralty is named after Sir Stephen Quin.[59] Indeed, the latter's place in the history of Limerick's mayoralty is secure, for he was the last mayor of the city ever to be knighted, a circumstance that is unlikely to occur again.

Alphonsus O'Mara 1918–19 and 1919–20.

Alphonsus O'Mara was born on 13 October 1887, the eleventh of the thirteen children born to Stephen O'Mara (mayor in 1885 and 1886) and his wife Ellen Pigott.[60] He worked in the family business all his life. He was elected to the city council on 17 January 1914 and was associated with the more advanced nationalist position throughout the mayoralties of O'Donovan and Quin. O'Mara voted against the presenting of an address to Lord Wimbourne in August 1915, and was a consistent opponent of Mayor Quin.[61] Following the re-organisation of the Sinn Féin Party in 1917, Alphonsus O'Mara, along with his father and brothers James and Stephen became involved in the new political movement and played a very significant role in the events of the next six years.

Alphonsus O'Mara
(Limerick City Archives)

Alphonsus O'Mara defeated Sir Stephen Quin by twenty-three votes to thirteen in the mayoral election, held on 18 January 1918.[62] He was to serve for two consecutive terms until 30 January 1920. He was the first Sinn Féin mayor of Limerick and represented a complete contrast to his immediate predecessor. He refused to take the Oath of Allegiance to the King required of him in his capacity as a magistrate, and ridiculed the Irish Convention as 'simply a talking shop'.[63] O'Mara's mayoralty was the most eventful and turbulent since 1691. He was involved in the anti-conscription campaign in April 1918, culminating in a twenty-four hour general strike on the 23 of the month. Later he worked with Dr. Hallinan, the Catholic bishop of Limerick, to bring about a peaceful solution to the Limerick Soviet crisis. He was also heavily involved in the general election of 1918, which saw the return of Sinn Féin's Michael Colivet as MP for the city.[64]

More people (a total of six) received the freedom of Limerick during the mayoralties of O'Mara than received it under any other mayor, before or since. On 7 November 1918, Mrs. Kathleen Clarke, Eoin MacNeill and Eamon de Valera the respective standard bearers of the three banned nationalist organisations, Cumann na nBan, the Gaelic League and Sinn Féin, were given the freedom, although only MacNeill could attend the conferring ceremony, for the other two were in prison. Mrs. Clarke was the widow of the executed 1916 leader Thomas Clarke, who had been made a freeman of Limerick in 1900, making them the only husband and wife to be so honoured. She was a Limerick woman, a niece of the Fenian Mayor John Daly and in 1939 she was to become the first female Lord Mayor of Dublin. On May 8, 1919, three Irish-Americans, named Michael P. Ryan, Edward S. Dunne, and Frank P. Walsh, were also given the freedom of the city. They had stopped in Ireland on their way to the peace conference then meeting in Versailles to mark the end of the war with Germany, where they hoped to put the case for Irish independence, in accordance with the official Sinn Féin policy. The only instance of someone being deprived of the freedom of the city also occurred during O'Mara's time in office when, on 2 May 1918, the fourth Earl of Dunraven was divested of the city's highest honour, due to his support for conscription.[65]

The local elections held on 15 January 1920 resulted in Sinn Féin taking control of Limerick City Council, winning twenty-six out of forty seats. O'Mara was succeeded as mayor by Michael O'Callaghan on 30 January 1920. He remained a member of the council until 1925. Following the signing of the Anglo-Irish Treaty, Alphonsus O'Mara, along with his father and brother James took the pro-Treaty side, while his brother Stephen was anti-Treaty. Soon after Alphonsus retired from politics and devoted the rest of his life to his business concerns. He moved to Dublin to run Donnelly's Bacon factory, which flourished and expanded under his direction. He also established a chain of retail stores, known as Bacon Shops Limited. Alphonsus O'Mara died in Monte Carlo on 16 February 1958 and was buried in Glasnevin Cemetery, Dublin, near his brother James.[66]

Michael O'Callaghan 1920–21.

Born in Eden Terrace, North Circular Road, Limerick on 6 September 1879, Michael O'Callaghan was the grandson of Eugene O'Callaghan (mayor in 1864), while his mother was a member of the wealthy Smithwick brewing family of Kilkenny. As a child he suffered from asthma and was educated largely at home. Later he attended the Leather-Sellers College in London for four years before graduating as an industrial chemist. His family owned the City Tannery at Lower Gerald Griffin Street and he worked in the family business all his life, eventually becoming managing director.[67] On 30 July 1914, O'Callaghan married Kate Murphy (1885–1961), from County Cork, one of three sisters who successively lectured in Mary Immaculate College, Limerick in the first half of the twentieth century. Kate's sister Maire was later to be the first female to act as mayor of Limerick. [68]

Michael O'Callaghan
(Limerick City Archives)

Both Michael and Kate O'Callaghan were deeply involved in the public life of the city. In 1905 he joined the first Sinn Féin club in Limerick and was also a member of the Gaelic League. However as late as 1914 he appears to have continued to be a supporter of Home Rule and of the Irish Party at Westminster, although he seems to have become more radicalised around this time. He became a member of the Irish Volunteers and served on the Executive Committee from 1914 to 1919. Kate O'Callaghan was also a member of the Gaelic League and was a founder member of Cumann na mBan. Following the 1916 Rising, they both campaigned for the release of prisoners and were active in the revived Sinn Féin movement.[69]

O'Callaghan was elected to the city council on 17 January 1911 and remained a member until his death in 1921.[70] The 1920 local elections had resulted in Sinn Féin taking control of Limerick Corporation for the first time and when the new council held its first meeting on 30 January 1920 O'Callaghan was elected mayor. At the same meeting, the council voted to 'hereby acknowledge Dáil Eireann as the lawful government of Ireland', and to tender 'its full allegiance.'[71] This represented the first time in its entire history that Limerick Corporation voted in favour of a complete severance with the British connection. It was also decided not to put forward the names of three persons, one of whom would be appointed high sheriff by the lord lieutenant, as provided for by the 1876 Act. This effectively brought an end to the office of sheriff, although it was not to be formally abolished until 1926. The War of Independence raged throughout O'Callaghan's mayoralty. It is believed that Mayor O'Callaghan coined the term 'Black and Tans' to describe the notorious new recruits to the police, who wore uniforms that were partially RIC dark green (almost black) and army khaki (tan) and that he took the name from a local pack of foxhounds. On 18 November 1920, the RIC raided the Town Hall and took away large amounts of documentation, including the minute book of the council meetings, which were not returned until after the Truce.[72]

O'Callaghan's term of office ended on 31 January 1921. As a prominent member of Sinn Féin, he knew that his life was under threat and he often slept away from home, either in the Royal George Hotel or in the homes of friends. Sadly he was destined to meet a terrible end. At 1:00 a.m., on Monday morning the 7 March 1921, he was shot dead by two men in the presence of his wife in his own house, 'St. Margaret's Villa' on the North Strand. Kate was shot in the arm during the struggle. Half an hour later, his successor as mayor, George Clancy was also murdered, as his wife looked on, in his residence in Castleview Gardens. It is believed that these savage murders were the work of the Black and Tans. O'Callaghan was buried, along with the other two victims of the 'curfew murders' in Mount St. Lawrence Cemetery.[73] Both O'Callaghan Strand, where he had lived, and O'Callaghan Avenue, Kileely were later named in his honour.[74] His widow Kate was later a member of the Dáil from 1922 to 1923. She lived in Limerick for the rest of her life, and remained active in the cultural life of the city until her death in 1961.[75]

George Clancy 1921.

Born in Grange, County Limerick in 1879, into a staunchly nationalist family, George Clancy was educated in the local primary school and at St. Patrick's Seminary, Bruff. Later he attended university in Dublin from 1899 to 1904, where he befriended James Joyce, Arthur Griffith and Padraig Pearse. Indeed Joyce wrote fondly of Clancy in *Portrait of the Artist as a Young Man*, basing his character Davin, the 'peasant scholar' and ardent nationalist on his Limerick friend. Later Clancy taught in Clongowes Wood College and came to Limerick city

George Clancy
(Limerick City Archives)

in 1908 as an Irish teacher. Ill health forced him to leave teaching and he then worked with the National Assurance Company. Clancy was steeped in the nationalist movement, and was a member of the Gaelic League, GAA, Irish Volunteers and Sinn Féin. After the 1916 Rising, he was briefly imprisoned.[76]

He was first elected to the city council in January 1920, and his election as mayor the following year, on 31 January 1921, indicated a meteoric rise to political prominence. However, his mayoralty was to be the shortest since that of Thomas Elliot Carte in 1868. Five weeks after his election, at 1:30 a.m., on Monday morning the 7 March 1921, Mayor Clancy was brutally murdered, as his wife looked on, in his residence in Castleview Gardens. As with O'Callaghan's killing, Clancy's wife was also wounded in the struggle. Ex-mayor O'Callaghan had been killed half an hour before and a third man named Joseph O'Donoghue had been murdered in Janesboro a few hours earlier. It would appear that British security forces killed the 'murdered mayors of Limerick' in order to decapitate the Sinn Féin leadership in Limerick.[77] Clancy was buried in Mount St. Lawrence Cemetery. Clancy Strand is named after him.[78]

James M. Casey, Deputy Mayor 1921.

After the killing of Mayor Clancy, James Casey, a Labour borough councillor who had been one of the leaders of the Limerick Soviet, served as acting first citizen of Limerick from 7 to 22 March 1921.[79] His official title was deputy mayor. As such, he was the first member of the Labour Party (which had been founded in 1912) to head the municipal authority. During his brief tenure in office, he organised the funerals of the three victims of the curfew murders, which were attended by very large crowds. For a full account of Mayor Casey, see below under 1934–35 and 1935–36.

Stephen O'Mara 1921–22, 1922–23, 1923.

The tenth child in a family of thirteen, Stephen O'Mara was born on 5 January 1884, the son of Stephen O'Mara (mayor 1885 and 1886) and his wife Ellen. He was educated by the Christian Brothers and later by the Jesuits at Clongowes Wood College. His entire life was spent working in the family business. He was married to Nancy O'Brien, a sister of the celebrated Limerick writer Kate O'Brien (1897–1974).[80] Like his father and brothers James and Alphonsus, Stephen became involved with the re-organised Sinn Féin movement in the aftermath of the 1916 Rising. He was elected to the city council on the Sinn Féin ticket in the 1920 elections and remained a member until 1925.

Stephen O'Mara
(Limerick City Archives)

On 22 March 1921, Stephen O'Mara was elected mayor of Limerick to serve out the remainder of George Clancy's term.[81] In the early months of his mayoralty, he was in danger of suffering the fate of his two immediate predecessors, and in consequence he often slept away from his own home and was protected by bodyguards. His brother James was Sinn Féin TD for Kilkenny South and spent most of 1919–21 in the USA as Dáil Eireann's principal fundraiser. When he resigned due to a disagreement with de Valera, he was succeeded by his brother Stephen. This necessitated the latter spending a lot of time in the USA, and he was absent from Limerick for much of his mayoralty.[82] During his period in the USA, he raised thousands of dollars for the Dáil. It was this circumstance that resulted in Alderman Mrs. Máire O'Donovan acting as deputy mayor from 21 May 1921 to 30 January 1922.[83] On 6 December 1921, Eamon de Valera was in Limerick to be conferred with the freedom of the city which he had received in 1918 while he was in prison. That night, he stayed in Strand House with his friends the O'Maras, and it was there that he heard news of the signing of the Treaty for the first time.[84] However, Mayor Stephen O'Mara was still in the USA at this time.

Stephen O'Mara was re-elected mayor by a unanimous vote of the city council on 30 January 1922.[85] He had been absent from Limerick for most of 1921, but was now to preside in person over the city during the Civil War and the fourth siege of Limerick. In March 1922, Mayor O'Mara prevented fighting from breaking out by bringing about an agreement between the pro- and anti-Treaty forces in the city. He also established a municipal police force to replace both the RIC, which had withdrawn from Limerick city, and the Night Watch, which had been abolished, but it was soon replaced by the Garda Síochána, which was founded on 8 February 1922, and deployed all over the country over the next few months.[86] In June 1922, O'Mara again brokered a peace deal, but it was repudiated by army headquarters in Dublin, acting on behalf of the Pro-Treaty side. On 11 July 1922, the fourth siege of Limerick commenced and fighting lasted until 21 July, resulting in the capture of the city by the pro-Treaty forces.[87] Also in 1922, the mayor ceased to be an ex officio magistrate and both the mayor's court of conscience and the Limerick Night Watch were abolished. Thus the corporation's involvement in both policing and the judicial system ended at the same time.

The city saw no further fighting, but continued to be affected by the civil war, which continued until the summer of 1923. Mayor O'Mara took the anti-Treaty side, in contrast to his father and brothers James and Alphonsus and was imprisoned for four months, from December 1922 until March 1923. It was the first time that a serving mayor had been jailed for many centuries. Councillor Paul A. O'Brien (later to be mayor from 1925 to 1927) acted as deputy mayor in the absence of O'Mara. Local elections were due to be held in the urban areas in January 1923. However, the Local Elections Postponement Acts of 1922, 1923 and 1924 allowed the Minister for Local Government to put them off to a more convenient time, and they were not held until 1925. In consequence, Stephen O'Mara's term of office, due to expire in January 1923, was extended indefinitely and he entered a third term as mayor in January 1923, while still in prison. Following his release, O'Mara continued in office until 17 October 1923, when he resigned prematurely, worn out and disillusioned by his unhappy experiences as mayor.[88]

Like his brother Alphonsus, Stephen O'Mara did not stand for re-election to the city council in 1925. He was a close friend of de Valera and in 1926 he became a founder member of Fianna Fáil. He was actively involved in the family business until shortly before his death and under his guidance, the firm opened bacon factories in Counties Mayo and Donegal. O'Mara demolished the old Strand House and erected New Strand House on the site. In October 1959, de Valera, newly elected as president, appointed O'Mara to the Council of State, the first Limerickman to be so honoured. One month later, Stephen O'Mara died on 11 November 1959.[89]

Maire O'Donovan, Deputy Mayor 1921–22.

The first woman ever to act as mayor of Limerick, Maire O'Donovan was born at Lassarda, Crossmahon, near Macroom in County Cork in 1 February 1876, the daughter of Cornelius Murphy, a Fenian activist, and his wife Julia.[90] She was one of a family of fourteen children and grew up in a house steeped in nationalism and Catholicism. Indeed, her birthplace was situated in the area later to be most associated with the War of Independence and its aftermath, as Crossbarry, Kilmichael and Beal-na-Blath are all situated nearby. Along with her sisters, she attended St. Angela's High School run by the Ursuline nuns in Cork city. Later she obtained an Honours BA in Classics and an MA from the Royal University and in 1901 received a teacher's diploma from a teacher training college in Cambridge. She taught in a convent school in Cambridge before securing the position of principal lecturer in education at Mary Immaculate College in Limerick, which had been founded by Bishop O'Dwyer in 1898.[91] Maire's official title was Professor of the Methods of Teaching and she held this position from 1905 to 1912. In 1905, she married Dairmuid O'Donovan, a native of Skibbereen, County Cork, and in 1912, her sister Kate succeeded to her position in Mary Immaculate College. When the latter married the future Mayor Michael O'Callaghan in 1914, she also resigned from her lectureship and was in turn succeeded by a third sister, Eilis, who never married and held the position until her retirement in 1949.[92]

Along with her husband and sisters, Maire O'Donovan took a prominent part in the public life of their adopted city. She was involved in the Gaelic League, Cumann na mBan and the suffragettes, while her husband was active in the Co-operative Movement.[93] Her involvement in local politics was brief but very dramatic. Her brother-in-law Michael O'Callaghan was murdered on 7 March 1921. On 7 April 1921, two new members were elected to the city council to replace the martyred mayors.[94] Clancy was replaced by Maire O'Donovan, who thus became the second female member of Limerick's city council, after Mrs. Emily Crowe, who had been elected in January 1920. O'Callaghan was replaced by Robert de Courcy, later mayor from 1923 to 1925.

When Stephen O'Mara went to the USA as principal fund-raiser for Dáil Éireann, it was necessary for a replacement to be appointed as he was absent for most of his first mayoralty. On 21 May, Mayor O'Mara appointed 'Alderman Mrs. O'Donovan as his locum tenens during his absence from the borough on and after that date'.[95] She thus made history by becoming the first female to be Limerick's first citizen and remained in office until 30 January 1922.[96] Her title was variously described as being deputy mayor (which had been the title used by James Casey) and locum tenens mayor. Mrs. O'Donovan presided over the memorable ceremony at which Eamon de Valera and Mrs. Thomas Clarke received the freedom of the city in the Theatre Royal, Henry Street, Limerick, on 5 December 1921.[97] They had been unable to accept the honour in person when it had been conferred on them in 1918, due to their having been in prison at the time. On the night of the conferral ceremony, de Valera stayed in Strand House with his friends the O'Maras, and it was there that he heard news of the signing of the Treaty for the first time.[98]

After she stepped down as deputy mayor, Maire O'Donovan, her sister Kate O'Callaghan and other members of her family all took the anti-Treaty in the Civil War. She provided a safe house for men on the run, and support for the dependants of anti-Treaty activists and while she was not imprisoned herself, her sisters Kate O'Callaghan and Eilis Murphy and brother Matt Murphy were jailed. In 1925, she did not seek re-election to the city council but remained active in the life of Limerick city for many years afterwards. She and her husband were involved in the Thomond Archaeological Society and she was vice-president for a time. She was also an examiner in the Classics for secondary schools and was involved in the running of the O'Curry College in Carrigaholt, County Clare. She died at her residence at Eden Terrace, Limerick on 20 January 1961 and was buried in Mount St. Lawrence Cemetery.[99]

Robert W. de Courcy 1923–24, 1924–25, 1925.

Born on 2 January 1880, Robert Wyndham de Courcy (always known as Bob) was the son of a prominent solicitor, Matthew John de Courcy who was coroner of Limerick city and was related to Robert McDonnell (mayor in 1871) and to the three O'Mara mayors. Bob de Courcy was educated at the Crescent College, Limerick and in 1902 graduated from the Royal University with the degree of Bachelor of Engineering. He was involved in various nationalist movements and in the 1918 general election campaign, he played a major part in securing a Sinn Féin victory in Limerick city.[100] Later he joined the IRA and used his engineering training to good effect in the War of Independence. He took the anti-Treaty side in the Civil War and served as divisional engineer with the Second Southern Division of the anti-Treaty forces, in which capacity he designed an artillery piece. He was captured in the Glen of Aherlow and imprisoned for the whole of 1923 and into 1924, in Limerick, Mountjoy and Kilmainham Jails.[101]

On 7 April 1921, two new members had been elected to the city council to replace the murdered mayors. Clancy was replaced by Maire O'Donovan while O'Callaghan was replaced by Bob de Courcy.[102] When Stephen O'Mara resigned on 17 October 1923, Bob de Courcy was unanimously elected as the new mayor and served from 17 October 1923 until 30 June 1925. What was so strange about his election was that he was on hunger strike in prison in Dublin at the time and was only to be released on 26 June 1924. His friend and fellow-prisoner, the celebrated republican activist and writer Ernie O'Malley was on hunger strike with him. After forty-four days, the hunger strike was called off, and following a period in a military hospital, de Courcy was sentenced to a term of ten years imprisonment. His subsequent release on 26 June 1924 was part of an amnesty for anti-Treaty prisoners introduced at the time.[103] As de Courcy had not been able to perform his mayoral duties for the first eight months of his term of office, Alderman Patrick Walshe of the Labour Party acted as deputy mayor in his place.[104]

Like his immediate predecessor, Stephen O'Mara, Bob de Courcy's mayoralty was prolonged indefinitely under the terms of the Local Elections Postponement Acts of 1922, 1923 and 1924. The situation was somewhat regularised by the Local Government Act of 1925, which provided for local elections to be held not later than 26 June 1925. On 23 June 1925, local elections were finally held and on 30 June the new city council elected Councillor Paul A. O'Brien in place of de Courcy who did not stand for mayor again.[105] De Courcy remained a member of the city council until 9 November 1934.[106] He never married and continued in practice as a consulting engineer and architect for many years from offices at 11 Alphonsus Place, South Circular Road, where he resided with his sister Kathleen. He died on 2 May 1951 at the age of seventy-one and was buried in Mount St. Lawrence Cemetery.[107] Bob de Courcy was related to the owners of the well-known auctioneering firm de Courcy Estate Agents, 7-8 Glentworth Street Limerick.

Paul A. O'Brien 1925–26 and 1926–27.

The first mayor of Limerick to be elected in June, Paul A. O'Brien was born in Limerick city in 1878. He worked as district manager of the Texaco Oil Company, and built up a large business in Limerick and throughout Munster. He was first elected to the city council on the Sinn Féin ticket on 15 January 1920 and remained a member until his death in 1931. At the time of the Civil War, O'Brien took the pro-Treaty side and was later chairman of the local branch of the Cumann na nGaedheal Party. Between December 1922 and March 1923, he acted as deputy mayor when Mayor Stephen O'Mara was in prison.[108]

Paul A. O'Brien
(Jim Kemmy Municipal Museum)

The Local Government Act of 1925 provided for local elections being held not later than 26 June 1925 and in fact they were held on 23 June. The Progressive Party secured twelve seats but many of its members, including Paul A. O'Brien, were aligned with Cumann na nGaedheal.[109] The new council met on 30 June, and elected O'Brien as mayor, to hold office until the next mayoral election which under the Local Government Act of 1898 was due to be held in January, 1926.[110] Later the Local Elections Postponement Act of 1925 provided for mayors of boroughs to remain in office until 30 June 1926. However, this was yet another temporary provision until the Local Elections Act of 1927 finally clarified the issue and provided that the election of the mayor would always place in June. Thus, after five years of repeated postponements, the statutory date for the mayoral elections was finally determined and since 1925, Mayors of Limerick have always been elected in June.[111]

Paul O'Brien served two consecutive terms as mayor from June 1925 to June 1927 and was the first of four mayors of Limerick who belonged to the Progressive Party. On 5 August 1925, Dr. Daniel Mannix, archbishop of Melbourne, a native of Charleville, County Cork and a well-known nationalist at the time of the War of Independence was made a freeman of Limerick. Mannix has been described as the most influential clergyman in the entire history of Australia. O'Brien later donated a roundel to the mayoral chain and it is interesting to see what he had inscribed on it. He noted that during his mayoralty, the Shannon Hydro-Electric Scheme was started in August 1926 and that the Dominicans celebrated 700 years in Limerick. He also included a number of sporting references, including the completion of the Athlunkard Boat Club boathouse in December 1925, Bohemians Rugby Club winning the first Munster Cup in January 1926 and the acquisition of the Gaelic Grounds on the Ennis Road by the GAA in April 1926.[112] O'Brien died at his residence on Newenham Street, Limerick, on 4 April 1931 aged fifty-three and was buried in Mount St. Lawrence Cemetery.[113] At the time of writing, two of his grandsons are the proprietors of P. and W. O'Brien, Auctioneers and Valuers, 41 Cecil Street, Limerick.[114]

John George O'Brien 1927–28.

John George O'Brien was born in Limerick in 1864, and despite a permanent injury to his right leg, participated actively in the sporting life of his native city in his youth. Like his predecessor in the mayoralty, Michael Joyce, he was a founder member of Garryowen Rugby Club, and in addition was an expert yachtsman. He was also a member of the Catholic Institute and of Shannon Rowing Club. O'Brien was largely responsible for the foundation of Limerick Cycling Club and according to his obituary in the *Limerick Leader*, he 'manipulated the 'penny-farthing' expertly!'[115]

O'Brien was a well-known figure in the business community of Limerick city for many years. He was the proprietor of the Limerick Hotel and Bar at 2 Sarsfield Street and had interests in other business concerns in the city. He was a member of the city council from 1906 to 1911 and again from 1925 to 1934. During his second period as a councillor,

O'Brien was associated with the Progressives and succeeded a fellow-Progressive as mayor in June 1927.[116] The high point of his mayoralty occurred in 1928 when he entertained the Irish aviator Captain James Fitzmaurice and his two German co-aviators, following their completion of the first flight across the Atlantic from East to West.[117]

O'Brien did not stand for the city council at the 1934 local elections as he was then a man of seventy years old.[118] He died ten years later, on 18 November 1944 and was buried in Mount St. Lawrence Cemetery.[119]

Michael J. Keyes 1928–29 and 1929–30.

One of the most influential political figures in the political history of twentieth- century Limerick, Michael Keyes (generally known as Mick) was born on 2 April 1886, in the Blackboy Pike area of Limerick city. He was educated by the Christian Brothers and while still a boy he secured a position as a clerk with the Waterford-Limerick Railway. When this company was absorbed by the Great Southern Railways, Keyes switched to the wagon-building yard, where he became an apprentice carpenter.[120]

Michael J. Keyes
(Limerick City Archives)

In his youth, Keyes was heavily involved in the sporting life of his native city. He was a founder member of Young Munster RFC and captained the team in the 1901–02 and 1902–03 seasons. Later, he served as president of the club in 1947–49 and 1954–55. Keyes also played with Garryowen RFC, with whom he won seven medals, including three senior Munster Cup medals. He played hurling with Claughaun GAA Club and in later life he was involved with Pike Rovers Soccer Club, of which he was president at the time of his death. He was also very interested in amateur boxing, for which he donated various prizes.[121]

At a young age, he joined the National Union of Railwaymen (NUR) and thus began a life-long involvement with the trade union movement. He held every office of honour with the NUR and had a long association with the Limerick Trades and Labour Council, which was the supreme administrative body of the trade union movement in the city and thus the forerunner of the Limerick Council of Trade Unions. On a national level he was a member of the National Executive of the Irish Trade Union Congress (a forerunner of the ICTU) from 1938 to 1949 and became president of that body in 1943. In the trade union movement, he was regarded as being pragmatic and moderate, rather than as a 'stormy figure.'[122]

As a committed trade unionist, Keyes soon became involved in the Labour Party, which had been founded in 1912. He was first elected to the city council in 1920 as one of six Labour councillors and remained a member until he was promoted to the cabinet in 1949. In 1927 there were two general elections in the Irish Free State, one in June and the other in September. Keyes was elected to the Dáil for Limerick in the first of these but lost his seat in the second. However he was again returned in 1933 and remained a member of the Dáil until 1957. He thus inaugurated the tradition of the Left holding a seat in Limerick, which has continued to the present day, except for one period (1957–61).[123]

During the interval between his two periods in the Dáil, Keyes served as mayor of Limerick for two successive terms (June 1928 to June 1930), thus becoming the first member of the Labour Party to hold the position (James Casey had been deputy mayor for a month in 1921). Like most members of the Irish Labour Party, though unlike many socialists in other countries, Keyes was a very devout Catholic. Within a few weeks of his election, he participated in the celebrations of the sixtieth anniversary of the founding of the Arch-Confraternity of the Holy Family by the Limerick Redemptorist community. In connection with this event, he welcomed three senior Catholic churchmen to Limerick: Monsignor Paschal Robinson, who had been recently appointed the first Papal Nuncio to Ireland; Cardinal van Rossum, the Prefect of Propaganda, and thus one of the most powerful figures in the Vatican, and Dr. Patrick Murray, the Superior-General (supreme head) of the Redemptorist Order. All three of them received the freedom of Limerick on 21 July 1928.[124] Some twenty years later, Keyes who was then a cabinet minister, and his wife went to Rome for the Holy Year of 1950 and were received by Pope Pius XII.[125]

When the first Inter-Party or Coalition government was established in 1948, Michael Keyes was not initially appointed to the cabinet. However, the death of Timothy J. Murphy who had been Minister for Local Government, on 29 April 1949 created a vacancy. His successor, who served from 11 May 1949 to 14 June 1951, was Michael Keyes who thus became the first Limerick person to serve in the cabinet. Shortly afterwards, the honour of granting Limerick city its only major boundary extension since 1841 fell to Keyes, the only Limerick man to ever hold the office of Minister for Local Government. On 11 January 1950 he signed the City of Limerick (Extension of Boundary) Provisional Order and brought it into effect in the Local Government Provisional Orders Confirmation Act, which became law on 30 March 1950. However, it is only fair to point out that the decision to grant the boundary extension had already been made by his predecessor T. J. Murphy. As minister, Michael Keyes also continued the major housing and slum clearance programme begun by Murphy.[126]

In the second Coalition Government of 1954 to 1957, Keyes held the position of Minister for Posts and Telegraphs. Throughout his long political career, Keyes was famous for being a very fluent and rapid speaker. He resigned from the Dáil at the time of the general election of 1957, due to failing health. He died on 8 September 1959 and was buried in Mount St. Lawrence Cemetery. Keyes Park in Southill is named in his honour.[127]

Keyes was the founder of the most durable political dynasty to sit in Limerick City Council since Independence. His son Christy Keyes was a member of the council from 1949 to 1960 and was mayor in 1957–58. Two of his nephews, the brothers Frank and Tim Leddin were also long serving members of the council. Frank sat on the council from

1960 to 1985 and from 1991 to 1999, and was mayor in 1965–66 and 1997–98. Tim was on the council from 1985 to 1999 and was mayor in 1987–88. At the time of writing, two members of Limerick City Council, who are both members since 1999, are members of the Leddin family: Joe who served as mayor of Limerick in 2006–07 and is a nephew of Tim and Frank; and Kathleen, who is the widow of Tim.

Patrick Donnellan 1930–31, 1931–32 and 1932–33.

A member of another durable political dynasty in the history of Limerick Corporation, Patrick Donnellan (usually known as Paddy) was born in 1898, a son of Thomas Donnellan who had been mayor between 1908 and 1910. He was manager of the Condensed Milk Company in Lansdowne for virtually all of his working life (1916–68) and during the Civil War brought in troops to prevent its seizure by a workers 'Soviet.' For a short time, he served in the Free State army with the rank of captain and was quartermaster with the Seventh infantry Battalion and the Twelfth Battalion in Sarsfield Barracks, before he returned to civilian life in 1924.[128]

Patrick Donnellan
(Limerick City Archives)

Patrick Donnellan was elected to the city council in 1925, shortly after the death of his father and was successfully returned in seven subsequent local elections, remaining a member until 1960. Like his father, he represented Thomondgate in the city council and was well respected in that area. In the 1920s and early 1930s he was a member of Cumann na nGaedhal and was also involved in the Progressive movement. When Fine Gael was founded in 1933, Donnellan became an Independent member of the city council, though privately he was sympathetic to the new party that had so much in common with Cumann na nGaedheal.[129]

He served three successive terms as mayor from June 1930 to June 1933, and was the third Progressive to hold the position. As such he was a strong supporter of the introduction of the management system to Limerick. At the Eucharistic Congress of 1932, he was, with the other mayors in Ireland, a canopy-bearer for the Papal Nuncio at the solemn Mass in Phoenix Park, Dublin, which was attended by a million people and was as great an occasion as the Papal Mass there in 1979. The most important event of his period in office was the MacLysaght Enquiry. Acting on the instructions of the Minister for Local Government, a local government inspector named James MacLysaght conducted a sworn enquiry 'into the powers, duties and obligations of the Limerick Corporation and the Limerick County Borough Board of Health' between 20 to 29 September 1932. His magisterial and informative report was published soon after and recommended the introduction of the management system, a proposal that Mayor Donnellan enthusiastically endorsed, but which was not implemented during his mayoralty.[130]

Other important events that occurred during Donnellan's period in office were the building of O'Dwyer Bridge (which connects the Corbally area with the city centre) between 1930 and 1931 and the construction of the Castle Barracks social housing scheme in the courtyard of King John's Castle in 1932. The Castle Barracks scheme thus made history on two counts: it was the first social housing to be built in the city as part of the great social housing revolution of 1932–1987 and it was situated in the most bizarre location of any housing estate, public or private, in the history of the State.[131] A social housing scheme of thirty-two houses built in Rosbrien between 1931 and 1932 were called Donnellan's Buildings in honour of the mayor. The establishment of Limerick City Vocational Educational Committee under the Vocational Education Act of 1930 was another development of Donnellan's period in office that had particular resonances for him as he became the first chairman and held office until 1967, a record thirty-seven years.[132] Donnellan was also a member of the Harbour Commissioners for many years and was chairman from 1964 to 1966.

Donnellan, who resided at 18 Belfield Park, Ennis Road, Limerick, retired from the Council in 1960, thus ending a family tradition that dated back to 1891, albeit with brief intervals between 1911–14 and 1924–25. He died on 11 January 1977 and was buried in Mount St. Lawrence Cemetery.[133] His son Michael continued the family connection with local government as he was an engineer with Limerick County Council from 1970 to 1972, with Clare County Council from 1972 to 1974 and with Limerick Corporation from 1974 to 1999.[134]

Mayor Patrick F. Quinlan with Judge Edward J. McElligott, KC
(Limerick City Archives)

Patrick F. Quinlan 1933–34, 1934.

Born in 1883, Patrick Francis Quinlan was one of five partners in the car firm Messrs. Irwin Brothers, later known as the Limerick Motor Works, one of the largest companies of its type in Limerick city. He was founder member of Castletroy Golf Club in 1936 and was a trustee of Garryowen RFC.[135]

He was a member of Limerick City Council from 1931 to 1942 and was aligned with the Progressive movement. He served a full term as mayor from June 1933 to June 1934. He turned the first sod on the Island Field Housing Scheme on 7 June 1934, thus commencing work on the first large-scale social housing estate in Limerick city. Quinlan was unanimously elected to a second term as mayor on 9 July 1934.[136] However the Limerick City Management Act became law on 6 September 1934 and under its provisions, elections were held for the new fifteen-member city council on 8 November. On 22 November, the new council met and in accordance with the terms of the Management Act, Mayor Quinlan's term of office was terminated prematurely.[137]

Patrick F. Quinlan, the last mayor of Limerick to serve before the Management Act and the last to belong to the Progressive movement died on 27 June 1967 at the age of eighty-four and was buried in Mount St. Lawrence Cemetery.[138]

James M. Casey 1934–35 and 1935–36.

Born in 1881, James Casey became a printer, a profession often associated with political activism. At an early age he became involved in the trade union movement and eventually became a delegate to the Limerick Trades and Labour Council, which was the supreme administrative body of the trade union movement in the city. Casey played a central role in the turbulent events that occurred in Limerick between 1916 and 1923. Between 20 October 1917 and 1 November 1918, some members of the trades council wrote and circulated *The Bottom Dog*, which was the first working class newspaper ever to appear in Limerick city, and ran for about fifty issues. Casey contributed several articles and poems to this publication. In 1919, he became treasurer of the

James M. Casey
(Jim Kemmy Municipal Museum)

trades council and at the time of the Limerick Soviet (14-26 April 1919), played a leading role on the strike committee. Effectively, he was, in the words of Jim Kemmy, the 'Soviet Treasurer' and in that capacity organised the printing of the paper money issued by the strike committee. He signed thousands of them, which appeared in denominations of ten shillings, five shillings and one shilling.[139]

In 1920, Casey was returned as a Labour member of the city council and as such soon found himself in the centre of even more dramatic events. After the killing of Mayor Clancy, he served as acting first citizen of Limerick from 7 to 22 March 1921. His official title was deputy mayor. As such, he was the first member of the Labour Party (which had been founded in 1912) to head the municipal authority. During his brief tenure in office, he organised the funerals of the three victims of the curfew murders, which were attended by very large crowds and delivered the graveside oration in Mount St. Lawrence Cemetery. His bravery won him great admiration and gratitude, as his life was in danger from the Black and Tans throughout his term in office.[140]

In consequence, Casey was disappointed not to be elected mayor when Stephen O'Mara resigned on 17 October 1923, having also deputised on several occasions since his election to the council. It was not until the coming into force of the City Management Act that he was finally elected mayor, on 22 November 1934. Even then, his term of office was only until the following June, but he was then re-elected to serve a full term until June 1936. While this represented a somewhat belated tribute to his heroic role in 1921, his period in office was a great success. He turned the first sod in the Killalee Housing Scheme and performed the official opening of the St. Mary's Park Housing Scheme. He also performed the opening of the magnificent Savoy Cinema, on Bedford Row, Limerick in 1935, which was one of Ireland's finest Art Deco buildings, until its demolition some fifty years later.[142]

In the summer of 1935 serious sectarian violence occurred in Northern Ireland during the annual 'marching season', which resulted in the deaths of nine people. In consequence public opinion was inflamed throughout Ireland. On the night of Saturday 19 July, serious rioting broke out in Limerick city. A mob of around 200-300 youths charged through the streets attacking Protestant homes, businesses and places of worship. The mob attempted to burn down the Presbyterian Church on Lower Mallow Street and to stone St. Michael's Church of Ireland on Pery Square. Eventually, the Gardai, backed by soldiers from Sarsfield Barracks quelled the disturbances, and arrested five men. Mayor Casey and the city manager, J. P. Geraghty in their official capacities, visited the houses of the various Protestant clergy and on behalf of the people of Limerick offered their sympathies in connection with the riot. There were no further disturbances in Limerick.

Casey remained a member of the city council until 1942. He was very interested in sport, having been an amateur boxer in his youth. Later in life, he became national president of the Irish Amateur Boxing Union and often acted as one of its referees. He also played rugby with Garryowen RFC. For many years, he lived in Bowman Street, but in 1928 he moved to 'Emilyville', on the Shelbourne Road, which was named in honour of his wife. He was a very close friend and colleague of Michael Keyes all his life. James Casey died on 13 June 1953 and was buried in Mount St. Lawrence Cemetery.[143] He is commemorated in James Casey Walk, in Limerick's Docklands.

Dan Bourke 1936–37, 1937–38, 1938–39, 1939–40 and 1940–41.

Daniel Bourke, affectionately known as Dan, is the only figure in the eight hundred year history of Limerick Corporation to have served as mayor for five consecutive terms. He was also the first member of the Fianna Fáil Party to become mayor of Limerick. (Stephen O'Mara, Mayor in 1921–23 was a founder member of Fianna Fáil, but had held office before the party was founded). Born in 1886, Dan Bourke was a joiner by trade and was employed on the railways for a number of years, before later becoming a successful publican.

From an early age, Bourke became involved in public life. He joined the Irish Volunteers on their foundation in 1913 and when the organisation split into supporters

Dan Bourke
(Limerick City Archives)

and opponents of John Redmond, he aligned himself with the latter group. During the War of Independence, he was a member of the Mid-Limerick Brigade of the IRA (whose area of operation was the city and its environs) and saw his fair share of action. On the outbreak of the Civil War, he took the anti-Treaty side and took part in the fighting in Munster. In 1922, he was captured and imprisoned in Kilmainham and Mountjoy jails. In 1923, he was transferred to the Curragh from where he escaped through a tunnel in April of that year. Later he was recaptured and spent a further spell in prison.[144]

Bourke was first elected to the city council as part of the Sinn Féin landslide in 1920 and remained a member until his death in 1952. In 1927, he unsuccessfully contested the general election held in June but was elected to the Dáil in the general election held in September of the same year.[145] He remained a member of the Dáil until his death, thus becoming the longest serving MP or TD to represent a constituency that includes Limerick city since Charles Smyth in 1731–76. (Bourke's record was later beaten by Desmond O'Malley, who was a TD from 1968 to 2002 and by Michael Noonan and Willie O'Dea who were first elected to the Dáil in 1981 and 1982 respectively and at the time of writing continue to sit as TDs).[146]

While Bourke's record as the longest serving TD to represent a constituency that includes Limerick city has been broken, his achievement of being elected mayor of Limerick for five consecutive terms seems unlikely to be ever emulated. He held office from June 1936 to June 1941 in an age of long–serving mayors. Alfie Byrne was Lord Mayor of Dublin from 1930 to 1940 and from 1954 to 1956; Sean French was Lord Mayor of Cork from 1924 to 1930 and from 1932 to 1937 while Richard Corish was mayor of Wexford from 1920 to 1945. Dan Bourke was a popular and successful mayor. Two persons received the freedom of the city while he was in office: Dermod O'Brien (1865–1945), the distinguished artist from County Limerick who was President of the Royal Hibernian Academy and who was a pioneer in establishing an art gallery in Limerick city and William Griffin, the notorious Irish-American newspaper publisher who had played a major role in the development of a particularly salacious and sensationalist version of the tabloid press in the USA and who received the freedom only because his exploits were unknown to Bourke and his colleagues![147]

Bourke was the first mayor of Limerick since Michael Joyce in 1905–07 to simultaneously sit as an MP or TD and was a patriarchal and popular figure in the city for many years. He was also a member of the Limerick City VEC, the Harbour Commissioners and the Limerick Mental Hospital Committee. At the time of his election to the council in 1920, he was living at 43 Roxboro Road but he later resided at 10 Dominick Street, where he also ran a very successful public house. He died on 13 April 1952 at his residence and was buried in Mount St. Lawrence Cemetery. His huge funeral was attended by many dignitaries, including Eamon de Valera and the renowned veteran of the War of Independence, Dan Breen, TD, who delivered the graveside oration.[148] Bourke Avenue, off Edward Street, is named in honour of Dan Bourke.[149]

Desmond O'Malley 1941–42 and 1942–43.

Desmond O'Malley was the first public representative in a family that was destined to play a major role in the public life of both Limerick and Ireland in the twentieth century. Born in 1908, he was a son of Joseph O'Malley from Murroe, County Limerick who was an engineer and an architect. Desmond grew up in the Mill Road in Corbally but on the death of his father in 1933, the family moved to O'Connell Avenue. He was educated in the Crescent College, and later qualified as a solicitor. He returned to Limerick city in 1930 where he built up an extensive practice under the title of D.J. O'Malley and Company, Solicitors. Two future mayors of Limerick, Paddy Kiely (mayor in 1972–73) and John

Desmond O'Malley
(Limerick City Archives)

Quinn (mayor in 1992–93) were employed by him as law clerks. As a young man, Desmond O'Malley played rugby for Bohemians RFC and later became president of the club and of the Munster Branch of the Irish Rugby Football Union (IRFU). He was also an oarsman with Limerick Boat Club for several years. He had a life-long interest in greyhound racing and was legal advisor to Bord na gCon for many years. He was also a director of the Limerick Greyhound Racing Company.[150]

O'Malley was a prominent member of the Fianna Fáil Party and was elected to Limerick City Council in 1934. He served as mayor for two successive terms from June 1941 to June 1943. He retired from the city council in 1945 and was succeeded in turn by his brothers Michael, who sat on the council from 1945 to 1955 and Donogh who was a member from 1955 to 1962, and who later had a glittering ministerial career in the 1960s. Both of these also served as mayor, in 1948–49 and 1961 respectively, the only instance since 1842 of three brothers serving as mayor of Limerick.

Desmond O'Malley, who resided at River View, Corbally, became city coroner in 1957. He died on 8 December 1965 and was buried in Mount St. Lawrence Cemetery.[151] One of his sons Desmond (born 1939) was TD for Limerick East from 1968 to 2002, served in several ministerial positions between 1970 and 1992 and founded the Progressive Democrat Party in 1985 while another, Joseph is a distinguished journalist with Independent Newspapers.

James McQuane 1943–44.

Born in 1895, James McQuane was a trade union activist all his life and was, for a period, President of the Limerick Council of Trade Unions. He worked in McCarthy's Furniture store for many years. A member of the Labour Party, he sat on Limerick City Council for one term (1942–45) and served as mayor from June 1943 to June 1944. During his mayoralty, he was actively involved in recruiting volunteers for the ARP service. Throughout his life he was involved in organising pilgrimages to Lourdes. McQuane, who resided at 'Laverna', Farranshone, died on 5 February 1969 and was buried in Mount St. Lawrence Cemetery.[152]

James McQuane   2000.0071.
(Jim Kemmy Municipal Museum)

James Reidy 1944–45.

Born in 1892, James Reidy (who was often known as Jimmy or Mossie Reidy) was a prosperous coal merchant whose business premises was in Robert Street and who resided at Island View Corbally. He was a member of the Irish Volunteers and later of the IRA between 1914 and 1921 and saw active service during the War of Independence. Reidy was a member of Limerick City Council from 1925 until his death in 1963.[153] He was a member of Cumann na nGaedheal and later of Fine Gael but he was also aligned with the Progressive movement in the 1920s and early 1930s. At the time of the local elections of 1934, Reidy was classified as being one of the

James Reidy
(Limerick City Archives)

six Progressive councillors elected and he was quoted as saying that 'although belonging to Fine Gael, he did not contest the election on the political issue, as he believed politics should not enter the affairs of local councils. He hoped that politics would be reserved for their proper place'.[154] This is an interesting example of the relationship between the Progressive movement and Cumann na nGaedheal-Fine Gael at the time.

James Reidy was a member of the Dáil from 1932 to 1937 and again from 1938 to 1954.[155] He lost his seat in the 1954 General Election and subsequently became a member of the Senate from 1954 to 1957.[156] He was unanimously elected mayor of Limerick and served from June 1944 to June 1945, while simultaneously representing Limerick in the Dáil. He was the first Fine Gael mayor of Limerick and later became the second former mayor of Limerick to sit in the Senate, which had been re-established under the 1937 Constitution. Reidy was a life long friend and political associate of Patrick Donnellan (mayor 1930–33) and like him was a strong supporter of the introduction of the management system to Limerick.[157] He died on 28 November 1963 and was buried in Mount St. Lawrence Cemetery. Reidy Court and Reidy Park are both named after him.[158]

Michael Hartney 1945–46.

Michael Hartney was born in 1887 in St. Mary's Parish, Limerick city and was a printer by trade, working with the Limerick Leader from 1907 to 1960. In his youth, he was a fine oarsman and was captain of St. Michael's Rowing Club. Later he became the rowing correspondent for both the local and national newspapers for several years, under the pseudonym 'No. 7'.[159]

Michael Hartney
(Limerick City Archives)

He became involved in the Irish Volunteers and in 1916 marched with them to Killonan near Limerick city to take part in the 1916 Rising. As it happened, there was no fighting in Limerick in 1916, but Hartney later saw a great deal of action during the War of Independence. He was attached to the Mid-Limerick Brigade of the IRA and was a comrade-in-arms of Dan Bourke. Hartney was captured and imprisoned in Wormwood Scrubs Prison in London, but went on hunger strike and was released soon afterwards. On his return to Ireland, he was again active with the IRA, but was recaptured by the Black and Tans and forced to travel in their lorries as a hostage to protect them from IRA ambushes. Later he was interned in Spike Island and an unsuccessful attempt was made to rescue him and others. During this period, Hartney lived in Davis Street but his house was blown up by the Black and Tans as an act of reprisal. He then moved to 14 Prospect Villas, where he lived for the next forty years, until his death. He took the anti-Treaty side in the Civil War and in 1922, his first wife was killed during the defence of Adare against the pro-Treaty forces.[160]

With the coming of peace, Hartney became involved in politics. He joined Fianna Fáil and served as a member of Limerick City Council from 1932 to 1950. He served as mayor from June 1945 to June 1946. Perhaps the most significant event of his mayoralty was the opening of Shannon Airport for commercial air services in the autumn of 1945, an event which Hartney referred to on the roundel that he later attached to the mayoral chain.[161] He also mediated in two labour disputes and helped to bring them to an end.[162] Hartney retired from the council in 1950, but continued to work for the Limerick Leader until he was seventy-three years old. After the tragic death of his first wife, he remarried and had two daughters. Michael Hartney died on 27 June 1964 and was buried in Mount St. Lawrence Cemetery.[163]

John C. Hickey 1946–47.

Born in 1901 in Mungret Street, John C. Hickey was the proprietor of the Sarsfield Bar at 1 Rutland Street where he also lived. Two other mayors of Limerick Kevin Bradshaw (1950–51 and 1952–53) and John Quinn (1992–93) also lived on Rutland Street at this time. In 1926, John C. Hickey became a founder member of Fianna Fáil and was a member of Limerick City Council from 1928 to 1950. He was mayor of Limerick of Limerick from June 1946 to June 1947. Perhaps the most significant event of his mayoralty was the passing of a resolution by the city council on 10 December 1946, formally asking the Minister for Local Government to extend the borough boundary, thus beginning a process that culminated with the granting of the

John C. Hickey
(Limerick City Archives)

extension in 1950. Hickey was also a member of the Limerick Harbour Commissioners and VEC and was on the governing board of Barrington's Hospital. He was described as being a 'quiet spoken gentle man' and retired from public life in order to concentrate on his business interests. He died on 15 June 1976.[164]

Patrick O'Connell 1947–48.

Born in Limerick of West Clare extraction, Patrick O'Connell worked as a deliveryman with the Imperial Bakery in Sarsfield Street, the proprietor of which was Vincent Feeney, later to be mayor of Limerick from 1966 to 1967. O'Connell's granddaughter, the writer and broadcaster May Leonard described him thus: 'Wearing a buff coloured shop coat, he drove a green horse-drawn box-shaped cart that bounced along the streets with the steam of hot bread puffing out the back vents. And, oh how the smell of freshly baked bread had several children simpering after him'. She also recalls that 'everyone knew him. Men doffed their caps and women called out greetings'.[165]

O'Connell entered public life through his

Mayor Patrick O'Connell receiving the chain of
office from his predecessor John C. Hickey
(Limerick City Archives)

involvement with St. Michael's Temperance Society. He was a member of the committee for many years and later became deputy vice-president, the highest honour that a layperson could attain, as the highest positions were reserved for the clergy. He was also an active member of the drama group attached to the society and took part in numerous productions over the years. The public speaking skills that he thus acquired equipped him well for service in local politics, for he was described as being 'shrewd in his viewpoints and quite an impressive orator'.[166]

He was a founder member of Fianna Fáil and was elected to the city council in 1945, remaining a member until his death in 1959. He was mayor of Limerick from June 1947 to June 1948. One of the highpoints of his mayoralty was the opening of the Limerick City Gallery of Art on 22 March 1948. On the same day, the long serving district court judge Joseph Flood, and the renowned Limerick born artist, Sean Keating were awarded the freedom of the city in recognition of their role in establishing the art gallery. A few days later, on 24 March 1948, Seán T. O'Kelly was also given the freedom of Limerick, the only serving President of Ireland to have received it since Independence.[167] O'Connell was a member of the Harbour Commissioners, the Limerick Mental Hospital Board and the VEC. He was also a member of the Arch-Confraternity of the Holy Family and lived nearby in St. Joseph's Street. He died on 21 August 1959 and was buried in Mount St. Lawrence Cemetery.[168]

Michael B. O'Malley 1948–49.

Born in October 1916, a younger brother of Desmond O'Malley (mayor 1941–43), Michael B. O'Malley grew up in the Mill Road, Corbally, but on the death of his father in 1933, the family moved to O'Connell Avenue. He was educated at Crescent College Limerick and at Clongowes Wood College in County Kildare.[169] Like his brother Desmond, he qualified as a solicitor and practiced on his own from 1939 until 1970. In the latter year he went into partnership to form Holmes O'Malley and Sexton Solicitors, which soon became one of the largest legal firms in Ireland.[170] On his retirement in 1981, due to ill-health, his son Michael became a partner in the firm. Michael B. O'Malley was a member of Fianna

Michael B. O'Malley
(Limerick City Archives)

Fáil. He was a member of Limerick City Council from 1945 to 1955 and was mayor from June 1948 to June 1949. On leaving the city council he was succeeded by his brother Donogh. Michael B. O'Malley died on 13 September 1991 and was buried in Mount St. Lawrence Cemetery.[171]

Gerard B. Dillon 1949–50.

Born in 1905, Gerard B. Dillon was the son of Patrick Dillon, a well-known building contractor in Limerick city. In his youth, Gerard Dillon spent some time in the USA studying the latest building techniques, and put these skills to use when he began work on the family business.[172] In the early twentieth century, Limerick Corporation had some forty miles of streets and highways under its jurisdiction, but they were surfaced with limestone, which rapidly turned to mud or dust, depending on the weather conditions. Following the ending of the Civil War, the corporation undertook to change this situation, which had attracted unfavourable comment for

Gerard B. Dillon
(Limerick City Archives)

many years. The concreting of the city's streets commenced in 1924, and continued throughout the 1920s and 1930s. Between 1924 and 1931, the corporation borrowed a total of £55,351 to concrete O'Connell Street, the Crescent, Pery Square, Mallow Street, Henry Street, Denmark Street, Robert Street and others. At the same time, government grants were used to concrete Patrick Street, William Street, Mulgrave Street, the Ennis Road and other parts of the city. Limerick became Ireland's first all-concrete city and the result was the transformation of the city's streets into modern thoroughfares, equipped to handle the increasing volumes of motor vehicles using them.[173] Much of this work was carried out by Patrick and Gerard Dillon, using concrete that was called 'Dillonite' in their honour. Indeed, Gerard was nicknamed 'Paver Dillon' during his years in public life.[174]

A member of Fianna Fáil, Gerard Dillon was elected to the city council in 1945 and remained a member until his death in 1962. He was mayor from June 1949 to June 1950. The most important event that occurred during his mayoralty was the extension of the city boundary on the only occasion since 1841. On 11 January 1950, the Minister for Local Government, ex-mayor of Limerick, Michael Keyes signed the City of Limerick (Extension of Boundary) Provisional Order and brought it into effect in the Local Government Provisional Orders Confirmation Act, which became law on 30 March 1950.[175] The area under the jurisdiction of the corporation increased by 2,395 acres or nearly double the existing acreage. The city now consisted of 5,155 acres or about one fifth of its area before 1840. As a consequence of the boundary extension the membership of the city council was increased from fifteen to seventeen under the provisions of the second Limerick City Management Act, which became law on 26 July 1950.[176]

Gerard Dillon was a member of the Harbour Commissioners and the Limerick Health Authority and was a member of the Senate from 1960 to 1961. He was the proprietor of the Thomond Cinema in Nicholas Street and resided at Violet Cottage, Thomondgate. He died on 3 November 1962 and was buried in Mount St. Lawrence Cemetery.[177] His son Mr. Tony Dillon worked with Limerick Corporation/City Council for many years.

Kevin Bradshaw 1950–51 and 1952–53.

Kevin Bradshaw
(Limerick City Archives)

Kevin Bradshaw was born in 1906 and was brought up in Rutland Street near the Town Hall. John C. Hickey (mayor in 1946–47) and John Quinn (mayor in 1992–93) also lived in Rutland Street at this period. During the War of Independence Kevin Bradshaw had a distinguished record as a member of Fianna Eireann, a movement that had been founded in 1909 by Countess Markievicz and Bulmer Hobson as a kind of nationalist boy scouts and later developed into the youth wing of the IRA. As a result of his activities during the War of Independence, the teenage Bradshaw was imprisoned for seven months in Cork Jail. He maintained a lifelong interest in the boy scout movement and was a member of the Limerick Diocesan Scout Committee. He was also a senior oarsman with Athlunkard Boat Club.[178]

Kevin Bradshaw was involved in the Fianna Fáil Party for many years and was a member of the city council from 1950 to 1955. He served two terms as mayor, from June 1950 to June 1951 and again from June 1952 to June 1953. He was the first mayor to serve non-consecutive terms since Sir James Spaight did so in 1856 and 1877. Bradshaw resided at Curraghgour Cottage, Limerick and was a director of the family business, Olo Mineral Company, of Rutland Street, Limerick, which manufactured mineral water. One of his sons is Dr. Brendan Bradshaw, a Marist priest and celebrated historian, who has written much on the history of sixteenth century Ireland. Kevin Bradshaw died on 18 June 1965 and was buried in Mount St. Lawrence Cemetery.[179]

Stephen Coughlan 1951–52 and 1969–70.

Stephen Coughlan
(Limerick City Archives)

Stephen Coughlan, (usually known as Steve or Stevie) was, in the words of journalist Patricia Feehily, 'one of the most colourful and controversial figures in the political history of Limerick'.[180] He was born in Gerald Griffin Street, Limerick on 26 December 1910, the son of an accountant and in later life, he recalled that he 'was reared on religion and politics.'[181] He was educated in the Presentation Convent School and Christian Brothers School, both in Limerick and in Blackrock College, Dublin, where one of his teachers was John Charles McQuaid, later Archbishop of Dublin. After working for a time in an insurance company, he opened a public house in

St. Joseph's Street, and later became a bookmaker. He built up a flourishing business, but his political activities and generosity to the less fortunate sectors of the city's population are believed to have cost him a great deal of money over the years.[182]

Coughlan first entered politics as a member of Clann na Poblachta and became friendly with the party leader, Sean McBride, whose mother Maud Gonne had received the freedom of Limerick in 1900. Indeed, McBride was to be godfather to Coughlan's only daughter. Steve became a member of the city council in 1950. He was soon to become one of its most prominent members and was frequently involved in controversy, but was returned at four subsequent local elections and remained a member until 1979. Coughlan's first mayoralty was from June 1951 to June 1952, and he was the first of two Clann na Poblachta mayors, the other being Ted Russell. Both of them were to have the rare distinction of filling the office of mayor on more than one occasion while belonging to different political parties. Thus Coughlan was in Clann na Poblachta at the time of his first mayoralty and in the Labour Party when he held office for the second time.

In the general elections of 1954 and 1957, Coughlan stood for the Dáil as a Clann na Poblachta candidate in the Limerick East constituency, but was defeated on both occasions. By this time, Clann na Poblachta was in steep decline so Coughlan joined the Labour Party in 1960. In the 1961 general election, he was successful in securing a seat in the Dáil and having been returned at the subsequent general elections of 1965, 1969 and 1973, was to remain a member until 1977.[183] Throughout this period, he was one of the dominant figures in the political life of Limerick city and had a fierce, though friendly rivalry with Donogh O'Malley.

Coughlan was always a controversial figure and was seldom out of the news. Like many Labour TDs outside Dublin, he was more of a populist than a socialist, and held conservative views on social and religious matters. In addition, he enjoyed political combat and had a flair for publicity. He later stated that 'I relished run-ins with fellow councillors and fellow politicians. I could not stand monotony. I was always looking for change. I suppose it is fair to say that I had a great news sense and I always tried to get a good story for the press.'[184] Between June 1969 and June 1970, during Coughlan's second mayoralty when he was also a TD, these elements in his public persona reached a climax and caused a crisis in the Labour Party. In 1969, at the height of the Cultural Revolution in China, a tiny but notorious group of Irish Maoists appeared on the political scene and opened bookshops in Cork and Limerick. When the latter was attacked, Coughlan made a number of controversial statements in which he seemed to condone the incident. In December 1969, he supported the visit of a South African rugby team to Limerick and fiercely condemned the Irish Anti-Apartheid Movement. In April 1970, he made a speech in which he seemed to express approval of the Jewish Boycott of 1904. As a result of this series of episodes, many in Labour wished to see him expelled from the party, but this was opposed by the leader, Brendan Corish. As a result, a number of left-wing members, including Jim Kemmy (later to be mayor in 1991–92 and 1995–96), resigned from the party.[185]

The controversies that marked Coughlan's second mayoralty led to very serious divisions in the Labour Party in Limerick city. In the 1970s, the opposition to Coughlan within the party in Limerick came to centre around his fellow Labour councillor, Mick Lipper (mayor in 1973–74), who stood in the 1973 general election along with Coughlan, and polled very well, though he was not elected on this occasion.[186] In the local elections of 1974, Coughlan's son Thady was elected to the council and served as mayor in 1975–76, the youngest holder of the office since 1842. Steve and Thady were the only father and son to serve together on Limerick City Council since 1842. Steve Coughlan's political career came to an end between 1977 and 1979. The general election of 1977 saw Coughlan lose his Dáil seat to his arch-rival Lipper, who ran under the banner of Independent Labour but was re-admitted to the Parliamentary Labour Party soon after. Neither Steve nor Thady Coughlan stood for re-election in the 1979 local elections.

Steve Coughlan lived in retirement for the rest of his life. For many years, he resided at 3 Wellington Terrace, O'Connell Avenue. He celebrated his fiftieth wedding anniversary in June 1994 and died on 20 December 1994, a few days short of his eighty-fourth birthday. Steve Coughlan is buried in Mount St. Lawrence Cemetery.[187]

Kevin Bradshaw 1952–53.
See above under 1950–51.

John Carew 1953–54 and 1959–60.
John Carew was born in Ballymore, County Tipperary in 1901 and came to Limerick at a young age. He became a well-known figure in the business life of his adopted city and was proprietor of a thriving leather business at 55 William Street, which, at the time of writing, is still run by his family. He later became chairman of the board of directors of Irish Wire Limited, on Limerick's Dock Road.[188]

Carew was active in the public life of Limerick city for some thirty years. He was a member of the chamber of commerce and eventually became president. He was also on the governing bodies of Barrington's and

John Carew
(Limerick City Archives)

St. John's Hospitals and was active in the St. Vincent de Paul Society. He was also a member of the Harbour Commissioners and of the Limerick Health Authority (the forerunner of the Mid-Western Health Board and the Health Service Executive, this body administered the health services in Limerick city and county from 1960 to 1971).[189]

Carew was a life long member of Fine Gael. He was first elected to the city council in 1942 and was returned in five subsequent local elections, remaining a member until his death in 1968. He created a political sensation when he was elected to the Dáil in a by-election caused by the death of the long-serving TD and former mayor, Dan Bourke of Fianna Fáil.[190] The latter had headed the poll in the Limerick East constituency at both the 1948 and 1951 general elections, but Carew took the seat for Fine Gael in the by-election held on 26 June 1952. In consequence, Fine Gael had an unprecedented two TDs returned for the Limerick East constituency between 1952 and 1954: Carew and the veteran James Reidy. At the general election of 1954, Carew was again returned but Reidy lost his seat. Carew was also returned in the 1957 general election but lost his seat at the 1961 general election.[191] He served as mayor on two occasions: June 1953 to June 1954 and June 1959 to June 1960 and was simultaneously a TD for both terms of office.

Carew resided at 'Glencree' in Ballinacurra. He died on 12 July 1968 and was buried in Mount St. Lawrence Cemetery.[192] John Carew Park in Southill is named in his honour.[193]

George E. (Ted) Russell 1954–55, 1955–56, 1956–57, 1967–67 and 1976–77.

George E. Russell
(Limerick City Archives)

One of the most distinguished figures in the history of the mayoralty of Limerick, George Edward (always known as Ted) Russell was born in April 1912, the same week that the sinking of the *Titanic* occurred.[194] His family had been prominent in the commercial life of Limerick for many years and his grandfather George (1838–76) was a member of the city council in the 1870s. Ted Russell was educated at Crescent College, Limerick, Mount St. Benedict in Gorey and Stonyhurst College in Lancashire, once known as the Catholic Eton, whose past pupils included Sir Arthur Conan Doyle, the creator of Sherlock Holmes, and Herbert, Cardinal Vaughan, who built Westminister Cathedral, the largest and most significant Catholic

Church in the United Kingdom. Ted Russell returned to Limerick in 1929 and was active in the public life of the city for the next seventy-five years.[195]

Ted Russell had a lifelong interest in sport. Rugby was one of his first loves. He was on the school XV at Stonyhurst and had a long association with Bohemians RFC in Limerick. He was captain of Bohemians in 1935 and 1936, played with Munster in 1936, 1937 and 1938 and had a final trial with Ireland in 1939. It is believed that the outbreak of the Second World War prevented him from having a career as an Irish international. He was later to become president of Bohemians RFC. He had been a noted athlete at Stonyhurst, hunted with the Limerick Harriers as a young man and later became a director of Limerick Racecourse.[196]

Throughout his life, Russell played a major role in the business life of Limerick city and indeed Ireland. The Russell family owned the National Bakery with premises in Broad Street, Catherine Street and the Crescent. On his return to Limerick city in 1929, Ted worked in his uncle's business, Dan O'Connor Limited, an animal feed business then situated in William Street but which later moved to the Ballysimon Road. In the 1950s, Ted and his brother Harry founded National Rusks Limited, a food ingredients factory on the Dock Road and he founded Limerick Dairies Limited on Clare Street with Michael O'Brien Kelly. He was also involved in the establishment of Silvermines Limited of which he was chairman for thirty-eight years and later honorary life president and for many years he was chairman of Shield Insurance Company and its successor, Eagle Star Insurance Company.[195]

Ted Russell has been described as 'a merchant prince of Limerick' and 'the last of the huge benefactors of Limerick'.[196] With his wealth, patrician manner, sense of noblesse oblige and multi-faceted involvement in the life of the city, he was clearly in the tradition of such great merchant benefactors and public figures as Sir James Spaight, Alderman John Quin and the O'Mara family. He was first elected to the city council at the age of thirty in 1942, and was returned in a further six local elections, remaining a member until 1979. He was a member of the Clann na Poblachta Party from the late 1940s to 1957, an independent from 1957 to the early 1960s and a member of Fine Gael from the 1960s until his death. He stood for the Dáil for Clann na Poblachta in the general elections of 1948 and 1951 and the by-election of 1952, but was unsuccessful on each occasion, although the number of votes that he polled increased steadily. He was elected to the Dáil as an Independent in the 1957 general election but lost his seat at the 1961 general election. Subsequently, he was unsuccessful in his attempts to be returned for Fine Gael in the 1965, 1973 and 1977 general elections.[197] He was a member of the Senate on the Industrial and Commercial Panel between 1969 and 1977, and between 1976 and 1977 became the first mayor of Limerick to be simultaneously a senator. Indeed, he is the only mayor of Limerick to have been *both* simultaneously mayor and TD (for a few months in 1957) and simultaneously mayor and senator (in 1976–77). He resembled Sir James Spaight in having a glittering career as a local politician, but a less successful one at national level. However, Russell later said that 'quite honestly, I always preferred local politics', as his many business commitments took up so much of his time.[198] Nevertheless, his local and national reputation was so high that in the early 1960s, the Taoiseach, Seán Lemass, is reputed to have offered to appoint him as Minister for Industry and Commerce if he would agree to stand for the Dáil with Fianna Fáil.[199] Russell was a political figure who believed in consensus rather than confrontation and always enjoyed cross-party support and respect.

Ted Russell was one of the most distinguished mayors of Limerick in the twentieth century and held office for a total of five terms, a record only equalled since 1842 by Dan Bourke. He was also the last mayor of Limerick to date to serve three consecutive terms and the second and last mayor from the Clann na Poblachta Party. However, he was a member of Fine Gael at the time of his last two mayoralties (1967–68 and 1976–77). Two important events occurred in 1956 while he was mayor. On 16 March he revived the ancient ceremony of throwing a dart into the river in his capacity as Admiral of the Shannon and while a number of subsequent mayors have also thrown the dart, they have done so with much less ceremony.[200] On 23 June Mayor Russell hosted a dinner in Cruise's Hotel on Limerick's Patrick Street to which all former mayors of the city were invited. Alphonsus O'Mara (mayor 1918–20) was unable to attend, due to ill health but the other fifteen living ex-mayors were present. Arising from this unique gathering, all sixteen surviving former mayors presented Russell with a link for the mayoral chain, with all their signatures engraved on it, to commemorate the occasion. In 1957, Russell travelled to the USA to raise funds to pay for a proposed monument to the three victims of the 1921 curfew murders. The trip was very successful and the monument was erected in 1968 on O'Callaghan Strand near the site of the present Hilton Hotel.[201] On his resignation from the city council in 1979, he presented a gold medallion inscribed with the coat of arms of Limerick city, to be worn by the wife of the mayor on official occasions.[202] Russell's son George was a member of Limerick City Council from 1979 to 1985.

Russell served in the Local Defence Force as Assistant Company Commander from 1940 to 1945. He campaigned for many years to have a university established in Limerick. He had a very long association with the Limerick Harbour Commissioners. He was a member from 1946 until their abolition in 1997, and was chairman for what is thought to be a world record of twenty-six years, from 1966 to 1992. In 1993, the Limerick city dock was named Ted Russell Dock in his honour. On 23 June 1995, he received what he himself regarded as the greatest honour of his career when he was conferred with the freedom of Limerick, the only mayor of the city to be so honoured since the modern system of conferring the freedom was established in 1877.[203] In 2002, he received an honorary doctorate from the University of Limerick. He lived for most of his life at 'Derravoher' on the North Circular Road, the former residence of the Shaw family who had once owned one of Limerick's bacon factories. Ted Russell died on 25 November 2004 and was buried in Mount St. Lawrence Cemetery.[204] He was aged ninety-two years and was a few months older than Bryan O'Donnell (mayor from 1893 to 1895) had been at the time of his death in 1940. Consequently, Russell is, to the time of writing, the longest-lived of all the mayors of Limerick since 1842.

Christopher Keyes 1957–58.

Christopher Patrick (always known as Christy) Keyes was born on 24 December 1922, a son of Michael Keyes, who had been mayor of Limerick from 1928 to 1930. Christy was educated at St. Michael's Christian Brothers School in Limerick and in the Christian Brothers College, Marino, Dublin. By profession, he was a primary school teacher and ended his career as principal of Our Lady of Lourdes National School in Rosbrien.[205]

Christopher Keyes
(Limerick City Archives)

In 1949, Christy Keyes was co-opted to the city council to replace his father Mick, who had been appointed Minister for Local Government. Christy was re-elected at the 1950 and 1955 local elections, but lost his seat in 1960. He served as mayor of Limerick from June 1957 to June 1958. He had a lifelong interest in sport and was a member of Garryowen RFC, Richmond RFC, and Claughaun GAA Club. He was also very interested in the Irish language of which he was a fluent speaker.[206]

Christy Keyes died on 14 March 2006 and was buried in Mount St. Oliver Cemetery. He was a first cousin of Frank Leddin (mayor 1965–66 and 1997–98) and of Tim Leddin (mayor 1987–88).[207]

Joseph P. (Rory) Liddy 1958–59 and 1970–71.

A cousin of Steve Coughlan, Joseph P. (who was always known as Rory) Liddy was born at 10 Ballinacurra Terrace, Limerick in 1911, and from an early age took a prominent role in the life of the city.[208] He had a lifelong interest in the GAA and played for Claughaun GAA Club for many years. In 1929, he captained the first ever Limerick team to play in the Munster minor hurling championship, a match which was also notable for the playing debut of the legendary Limerick hurler, Mick Mackey. At the tender age of fifteen, Liddy became founder member of Fianna Fáil in 1926 and gave some sixty years of

Joseph P. Liddy
(Limerick City Archives)

service to the party. During this period he took an active part in every general election and was chairman of the Limerick city Comhairle Ceanntair for more than twenty years. He was also honorary treasurer of the Limerick East Comhairle Dáil Ceanntair for many years.[209]

Rory Liddy unsuccessfully contested the 1950 local elections but in 1952 was co-opted onto Limerick City Council to fill the vacancy caused by the death of ex-mayor Dan Bourke. Liddy remained on the council until 1974, having been successfully returned in three subsequent local elections. He was mayor on two occasions. His first mayoralty (June 1958 to June 1959) was notable for the inauguration of Eamon de Valera, Liddy's great political idol, as president of Ireland in 1959. His second term of office (June 1970 to June 1971) was notable for a number of reasons. On 18 August 1970,

Dr. Robert Wyse-Jackson, the Church of Ireland bishop of Limerick received the freedom of the city, the first non-Catholic clergyman to be so honoured. In the same year, Richard Nixon, the second ever serving American president to visit Limerick city was received by Mayor Liddy and in 1971 it was the turn of the president to receive Mayor Liddy in the White House. Liddy also held a civic reception for the three astronauts from the Apollo 13 lunar-landing mission, who survived an accident on their voyage to the moon and returned safely to Earth on 17 April 1970 (this episode was to form the subject matter of the 1995 film of the same name, directed by Ron Howard, and starring Tom Hanks). During Liddy's second mayoralty, the Watergate Housing Scheme was also opened.[210]

Rory Liddy worked for most of his life with Pan-American Airways in Shannon, and was employed as stores manager there for more than twenty years. He died on 27 August 1989 at the age of seventy-eight.[211] One of his sons, Cormac, has been a journalist with the *Limerick Leader* and latterly the *Limerick Independent* for many years. Liddy Street in the centre of Limerick is named in honour of Rory Liddy.[212]

John Carew 1959–60.

See above under 1953–54.

Patrick Kelly 1960–61.

Paddy Kelly, as he was always called, was born in Careys Road, Limerick in 1919 and lived most of his life at 51 Flood Street, Killalee. He worked for many years with CIE, and was later employed for twenty-three years as a fulltime official with the Irish Transport and General Workers Union. Kelly was also active in the Labour Party for much of his life and was a close friend and political ally of Steve Coughlan.[213] Paddy Kelly served two terms on Limerick City Council from 1955 to 1967 and was mayor

Mayor Paddy Kelly, placing a wreath on the steps of the Memorial Cross at Mount St. Alphonsus, Limerick, in honour of the Limerickmen who served in the St. Patrick's Battalion of the Papal Army in 1860. Left to Right Mr. T.J. Smalle, whose grandfather from Kilmallock fought in the campaign; Rev. Fr Michael Cagney, C.SS.R., who knew a number of the Limerickmen who fought in the Papal Army; Mayor Kelly; Mr. John F. Spencer; Capt. Frank Parker (ONE) and Mr Thomas Gough, Chairman of the Limerick Council of the Knights of Malta. Sunday 18th December 1960. (Jim Kemmy Municipal Museum)

from June 1960 to June 1961. During his term of office, Kelly became the first mayor in Ireland to organise a departure ceremony for Irish troops leaving for United Nations duty in the Congo. He was also very interested in promoting the economic development of Limerick and, along with Rory Liddy, established industrial committees to attract foreign investment to the city.[214]

Paddy Kelly died on 19 December 1990 and was buried in Mount St. Lawrence Cemetery.[215]

Donogh O'Malley 1961.

The third of the three O'Malley brothers who were successively members of Limerick City Council and mayors of the city, Donogh O'Malley was one of the most extraordinary figures in the political history of twentieth-century Ireland. He was born in Limerick city on 18 January 1921and grew up in the Mill Road Corbally and later O'Connell Avenue. He was educated at Crescent College Limerick and Clongowes Wood College, County Kildare and later attended University College Galway, graduating in 1943 with a degree in engineering.[216]

As a young man O'Malley was a prominent sportsman. He won a Munster Junior Cup medal with Shannon RFC in 1939 and had a lifelong connection the club. He played provincial

Donogh O'Malley
(Limerick City Archives)

rugby for Munster, Leinster, and Connacht, a highly unusual distinction, and narrowly missed out on playing for Ulster also when he worked for a time in Northern Ireland. He was also very interested in soccer and was president of the Football Association of Ireland at the time of his death. O'Malley also enjoyed swimming.[217]

Donogh O'Malley soon became involved in the public life of his native city. In the 1954 general election he was elected to the Dáil and took the traditional Fianna Fáil seat that had been held by Dan Bourke from 1927 to 1952. He retained his seat at the 1957, 1961 and 1965 general elections, topping the poll on each occasion.[218] O'Malley soon became one of the most colourful figures in the Oireachtas. He has been described as being a 'large, good-looking, open, cheerful, friendly' man who was also regarded as being a 'holy terror' due to his considerable capacity for heavy drinking.[219] Along with his later ministerial colleagues Charles J. Haughey and Brian Lenihan, he caroused his way around Dublin in the 1950s and early 1960s and in the process attained the status of an urban (and indeed rural) legend. The 'Three Musketeers' as they were called represented a new generation of Irish politician, who had been born since Independence and shared a very different vision of Ireland from the austere ideologies of the previous thirty years. However, behind the image of a man-about-town, O'Malley was a highly intelligent, competent and idealistic man, dedicated to modernising and improving the fabric of Irish society. He was to be one of the most striking of the new generation of Fianna Fáil ministers promoted to the cabinet by Sean Lemass in the 1960s.[220]

O'Malley was elected a member of Limerick City Council in 1955 and was re-elected in 1960. He remained a member until 1962 and unusually, was an alderman throughout his entire period on the council. While simultaneously a TD, he also served as mayor of Limerick from June to November 1961 but resigned from the mayoralty when he was appointed Parliamentary Secretary (equivalent to Minister of State) to the Minister for Finance, with special responsibility for the Board of Works. This was the first time that a mayor had resigned before the expiration of his term of office since Stephen O'Mara had done so in 1923. O'Malley remained at the Department of Finance until April 1965. It was at this time that a notorious incident occurred which changed the whole direction of O'Malley's career and arguably that of the social history of Ireland. One evening, after a drinking session, he drove the wrong way along O'Connell Street in Dublin. When a garda approached him and asked him if he had not seen the arrows, O'Malley is reputed to have replied: 'If I had seen the arrows, I'd have seen the f*** Indians!' Subsequently he was prosecuted and fined, but the garda in question was dismissed from the force a week later. O'Malley had no part in this shabby deed and was so appalled on hearing of it that he gave up drinking completely. Had he not done so, it is unlikely that his subsequent career would have been so rich in achievements.[221]

O'Malley brought about a number of changes during his period in charge of the Board of Works, and in the words of Ted Russell, 'put new life into that somewhat staid and stagnant institution'.[222] It was at this time that he began the process of alleviating overcrowding in schools by ordering prefabricated classrooms to be used, and while the 'prefabs' later acquired notoriety as a symbol of official neglect of education, his initiative won widespread praise at the time. Following the general election of 1965, O'Malley was given his first cabinet post when he was appointed Minister for Health. On 13 July 1966 he became Minister for Education, a post that he held until his death, less than two years later. His period in office was the most revolutionary in the history of Irish education since Independence. He introduced free secondary education in 1967 and a free school transport system soon after. He also planned the establishment of Regional Technical Colleges (now known as Institutes of Technology), which did not come into existence until 1970 and was a strong supporter of the new Comprehensive and Community Schools. His achievements in these areas were recognised when Letterkenny RTC, later Letterkenny Institute of Technology was named after him. O'Malley also planned to merge Trinity College and University College Dublin into one University of Dublin, but this never came about.[223]

At the height of his power and achievements, Donogh O'Malley died of a heart attack on 10 March 1968 aged only forty-seven and was buried in Mount St. Lawrence Cemetery.[224] His wife, Hilda, a medical doctor was a great beauty and was the subject of the famous poem *On Raglan Road* by Patrick Kavanagh, which was later recorded as a classic song by Luke Kelly, Van Morrison, Sinead O'Connor and other artistes.

O'Malley's son Darragh (born 1954) is a well-known actor who has appeared in several episodes of the television series *Sharpe*.

Donogh O'Malley's nephew Desmond succeeded him as TD for Limerick East in 1968 and held the seat until 2002, becoming in the process the longest serving MP or TD to represent the Limerick city area since Charles Smyth in 1731–76. Desmond held several cabinet posts between 1970 and 1992 and founded the Progressive Democrat Party in 1985. A cousin of Donogh, Tim O'Malley, sat as TD for Limerick East and served as a Minister of State at the Department of Health and Children between 2002 and 2007. Thus, an O'Malley represented Limerick East continuously in the Dáil between 1954 and 2007. O'Malley Park in Southill is named in honour of Donogh O'Malley.[225]

Frank Glasgow 1961–62.

Frank Glasgow was born in Limerick in 1901 and served in the Mid-Limerick Brigade of the IRA during the War of Independence. For a time, he was interned in Wormwood Scrubs Prison but was released following a period on hunger strike. Throughout his life, Frank Glasgow's 'first and undying love was the Irish language'.[226] He was a very prominent figure in the movement to revive the language and was among other things, an executive member of the Gaelic League and president of an organisation called Clann na h Éireann. He always spoke Irish whenever he could and used as little English as possible.[227]

A life long member of Fianna Fáil, Frank Glasgow was first elected to the city council in 1950 and was returned in the 1955, 1960 and 1967 local elections. He remained a member

Frank Glasgow
(Limerick City Archives)

until his death in 1973. He was a man of sincerity and possessed a great sense of fairness. This was demonstrated when John Carew died in 1968 while still a member of the council, and Glasgow insisted that another member of Fine Gael should be co-opted as his successor, a stance that was opposed by other Fianna Fáil councillors. When Donogh O'Malley resigned as mayor in November 1961, he was succeeded by Glasgow who served out the remainder of his term until June 1962.[228]

Frank Glasgow, who had lived in Janesboro and later at 19 Strandville Gardens, died on 30 January 1973 and was buried in Mount St. Lawrence Cemetery. Glasgow Park is named after him.[229]

Frances Condell 1962–63 and 1963–64.

Frances Condell made history for many reasons. She was the first woman to be elected mayor of Limerick (Maire O'Donovan had been deputy mayor) and was the first non-Catholic holder of the position since James Spaight in 1877. She was also the first mayor to welcome a serving president of the USA to Limerick and is to date the only woman to have served two terms as mayor.[230]

A member of the Church of Ireland, Frances Eades was born on 29 June 1916 and was educated at St. Michael's Primary School and Villiers School, both in Limerick and later in the Church of Ireland Teacher Training College and Trinity College, both in Dublin. She worked as a teacher in Villiers School for a

Frances Condell
(Limerick City Archives)

number of years and in 1937 married Robert Condell, the proprietor of an office supply business that still flourishes at 9 Roches Street, Limerick. Frances Condell soon became active in the public life of Limerick. She was a founder member of the Red Cross in the city and during the Second World War, became an area officer with the organisation. She also served as welfare officer with Shannon Development, which entailed helping families of foreign workers settle in the Limerick region.[231]

Frances Condell was a member of Limerick City Council for one term, between 1960 and 1967. She was an Independent, representing the Ratepayers Association, a body descended from similar organisations that had existed in the 1920s and 1930s. She was also the first female councillor since Maire Donovan retired in 1925 and the first non-Catholic councillor for many years. For these reasons alone, she created a sensation, but she was also, in the words of her friend Walton Empey, Church of Ireland Bishop of Limerick and later Archbishop of Dublin, 'elegant in carriage, elegant in dress, elegant in turn of phrase'.[232]

On 29 June 1962, she was elected mayor of Limerick, defeating former mayor Paddy Kelly with the assistance of the Fianna Fáil members of the council. She was to serve two terms of office until June 1964. She is the only mayor of Limerick since 1842 to have worn a ceremonial hat. Undoubtedly, the high point of her period in office was the visit of President John F. Kennedy to Limerick. Originally, Limerick had not formed part of his itinerary but following representations from Steve Coughlan TD and others, it was decided that the president would leave Ireland via Shannon Airport and include Limerick in the process. Having already visited Germany and Italy, Kennedy arrived in Dublin on 26 June 1963 and went to New Ross, Wexford, Cork and Galway, receiving the freedom of the latter three in the process. He came to Limerick in a US Army helicopter on 29 June, landing at Greenpark Racecourse where a large crowd had assembled to see him. Mayor Condell greeted him in a celebrated address that Kennedy later described as 'the best speech that I have heard since I came to Europe'. The president was then conferred with the freedom of Limerick. Soon after he travelled to Shannon and flew to Britain to continue his European tour. Frances Condell, with her elegant appearance, cultured accent and dignified manner had gained national prominence and had proved to be the best possible advertisement for the new Limerick that was emerging in the prosperous 1960s. Indeed, during the 1970s, she was mentioned as a possible candidate for the Presidency of Ireland although nothing ever came of it.[233]

Frances Condell did not contest the 1967 local elections, due to ill health. However, she remained active in public life until shortly before her death. She was a member of the Limerick Health Committee and the National Monuments Advisory Committee of Limerick Corporation and contributed regular columns to both local and national newspapers. She died after a long illness on 10 November 1986.[234] Condell Road is named after her.[235]

John Danagher 1964–65.

John (always known as Jack) Danagher was born in 1914, the son of a company sergeant major with the First Battalion of the Royal Munster Fusiliers, who had served in India for many years, and who was killed in Gallipoli in 1915. For many years, Jack Danagher was a primary school teacher in the Christian Brothers School in Sexton Street, Limerick, where one of his colleagues was Pat Kennedy (mayor in 1974–75 and 1985–86). Like Steve Coughlan and Ted Russell, Danagher was active in Clann na Poblachta and was elected to the city council on that ticket in 1955. On the dissolution of Clann na Poblachta, he joined Labour and remained active with the party until his death.[236]

Thus it was as a member of Labour that Jack Danagher was elected mayor of Limerick in June 1964, defeating former mayor Frank Glasgow by nine votes to eight. He was hampered throughout his year in office by the refusal of the Department of Education to grant his request for a year's leave of absence from his teaching post.[237] One of the high points of his mayoralty was the visit to Limerick of Kenneth Kaunda, the new president of Zambia, on 25 November 1964. On that occasion, Kaunda received the freedom of the city, the only African ever to receive it and to date is only one of four incumbent presidents (the others being Sean T. O'Kelly, John F. Kennedy and Bill Clinton) to be so honoured.

Due to work commitments, Danagher did not stand at the local elections of 1967. He lived in Pennywell for many years. Jack Danagher died on 26 April 1969 at the early age of fifty-five.[238] He is commemorated in Danagher Crescent.[239]

Frank Leddin 1965–66 and 1997–98.

Frank Leddin was born in Limerick in 1934, a son of John Leddin and Catherine Keyes, sister of Michael Keyes (mayor between 1928 and 1930). For a time, he was employed on the sales staff of Cannock and Company, but spent most of his working life with the section of the Department of Posts and Telegraphs that became known as Telecom Eireann in 1984 and was later transformed into Eircom.[240]

Frank Leddin
(Copper Reid Studio)

Frank Leddin was a life long activist with the Labour Party and was first elected to the city council in 1960. Subsequently, he was returned at three local elections and remained a member of the council until 1985. In the local elections of the latter year, he lost his seat but regained it in 1991 and remained on the council until his retirement in 1999. He was first elected to the mayoralty on 30 June 1965 by the unanimous choice of the council, and at thirty-one, was one of the youngest holders of the office since 1842.[241] His second mayoralty, from June 1997 to June 1998 saw the celebration of the eight-hundredth anniversary of Limerick's first charter and of the establishment of Limerick Corporation. On 3 October 1997, Charter Day was marked by a special meeting of Limerick City Council attended by the mayors of all the other Irish cities and the Earl of Limerick, and was followed by a civic reception, a pageant in St. Mary's Cathedral, and a Charter 800 Banquet.[242] In the same year, Frank Leddin attached a roundel to the mayoral chain, which was presented by Telecom Eireann to commemorate the meeting of the company's board of directors in Limerick in 1997. Interestingly, the interval of thirty-one years between his two mayoralties is the longest in the history of Limerick.

Frank Leddin was also a member of Limerick City VEC for forty-two years and his life long friend and colleague Frank Prendergast believed that 'his best contribution was to Limerick City VEC'. Leddin retired from the city council in 1999 and died on 15 August 2002.[243]

Vincent Feeney 1966–67.

A baker by trade, Vincent Feeney was born in Kinvara, County Galway in 1915 and came to Limerick in the 1940s to work for the National Bakery, which was owned by Ted Russell's family. Feeney was put in charge of the National Bakery premises in Broad Street but later went into business for himself and became very successful. He purchased the Imperial Bakery on 24 Sarsfield Street and later purchased the Abbey Court Bakery on Nicholas Street.[244]

Vincent Feeney
(Limerick City Archives)

Feeney was a member of Limerick City Council from 1962 to 1974. He was co-opted to replace Donogh O'Malley and was re-elected in 1967. He was a dedicated member of Fianna Fáil and in the mayoral election of June 1972, was carried into the council chamber on a stretcher to cast a crucial vote for his party colleague, Paddy Kiely (mayor in 1972–73). At the time, Feeney was a patient in Barrington's Hospital as a result of an accident, so the episode was widely reported in the national newspapers. Vincent Feeney was himself mayor from June 1966 to June 1967. He was a man of generous spirit and had a great love for his adopted city. This was evidenced by his long and close friendship with his former employer, Ted Russell and by the manner in which he staunchly and openly supported the latter in his bid to be elected to the Senate, though they were in opposing political parties. In Feeney's opinion, Ted Russell was a great Limerick man and therefore a worthy candidate.[245]

Vincent Feeney was also a long serving member of the Harbour Commissioners and of the chamber of commerce, of which he eventually became president. He was also chairman of Limerick Savings Bank and was captain and later president of Castletroy Golf Club. He resided for many years at 'Glenbrook' North Circular Road, Limerick. He died on 26 January 1988 at the age of seventy-two and was buried in Mount St. Lawrence Cemetery.[246]

George E. (Ted) Russell 1967–68.
See above under 1954–57.

Jack Bourke 1968–69, 1986–87 and 1999–2000.

Jack Bourke
(Limerick City Archives)

The only Dublin person to be mayor of Limerick since 1842, John (always known as Jack) Bourke was born in Dublin into a family steeped in nationalism and the theatre. His grandfather P. J. Bourke was a well-known actor and playwright in the culturally vibrant Dublin of the early twentieth century and wrote a number of nationalist plays, of which *When Wexford Rose* (1910) was the most popular. He formed a company of professional actors called 'No. 1 Company' that toured Ireland, including Limerick. Perhaps his most notable achievement came in 1917 when he wrote and produced Ireland's first full-length film, *Ireland, A Nation*, which was banned by the authorities after just one night's performance in the Rotunda, due to its nationalist content. Bourke lost some £10,000 on this venture. P. J. Bourke's wife was a sister of Peadar Kearney, who wrote the lyrics of the Irish national anthem. Another sister of Kearney was the mother of the writers Brendan and Dominic Behan.[247]

P.J. Bourke's son Lorcan was one of the leading figures in Irish theatre production in the mid twentieth century. He was the managing director of the Eamonn Andrews Studios and owned the Gaiety and Queens Theatres and the Masterpiece and Capitol Cinemas, all in Dublin. He also owned a company that supplied theatrical costumes and lights to theatres and drama groups all over Ireland. One of Lorcan's daughters Grainne was married to the television personality Eamonn Andrews and another Susan married Pete St. John, the singer-songwriter who composed *The Fields of Athenry and Dublin in the Rare Ol' Time*. Lorcan was also active in politics. A prominent Fianna Fáil member, he sat on Dublin City Council for many years and acted as deputy lord mayor on a number of occasions. Thus Lorcan's son Jack Bourke was heir to a vibrant tradition of family involvement in the cultural and political life of the country. Besides those already mentioned, he is related to several prominent figures in public life. The patriot Kevin Barry was a first cousin of his grandfather while the television and radio presenter Gerry Ryan is a first cousin of Jack himself.[248]

Jack Bourke was brought up in Collins Avenue Whitehall on the North side of Dublin and educated at St. Vincent's School, Glasnevin. He went to work in his father's business and came to Limerick in 1953 to manage the City Theatre, a 1,000-seat venue situated on Sexton Street, that had just been acquired by Lorcan Bourke. Under Jack's management, the City Theatre flourished for many years and for ten years was the venue for an annual ten-week festival of Irish theatre. Major figures such as Anna Manahan and Niall Toibín were among those who appeared there. Jack Bourke has also been involved in many other business ventures in the Limerick area, including a famous public house in Thomas Street and the Movieland Cinema in Roxboro. From his arrival in Limerick he became active in public life. He was the first chairman of the Limerick branch of the Variety Club of Ireland, which raised funds for needy causes. He also became a member of Shannon RFC, Castletroy Golf Club and of Shannon Rowing Club.[249]

Jack Bourke was asked to stand for the city council by Donogh O'Malley and was successfully returned in the 1967 local elections. He was re-elected in five subsequent local elections and remained a member until he lost his seat in the 2004 local elections. His unbroken thirty-seven years as a councillor is one of the longest periods of service in the history of Limerick City Council since 1842. He served as mayor for three terms: 1968–69, 1986–87 and 1999–2000. Indeed he is one of only three mayors of Limerick since 1945 to have served for three terms or more, the other two being Ted Russell and Dick Sadlier. On the first occasion, Jack Bourke was elected in highly dramatic circumstances, a mere twelve months after becoming a member of the council. Both he and his opponent Steve Coughlan received eight votes each but it was Bourke who was elected after his name was drawn from a hat by a schoolboy who was present. His second mayoralty was memorable for the manner in which urban renewal began the transformation of Limerick while he achieved lasting fame in his third mayoralty by becoming the first mayor of the new millennium.[250] Jack Bourke was a successful mayor on all three occasions, due in part to his distinguished appearance, elegant dress and fine speaking voice.

Jack Bourke was a member of the Limerick City VEC for twenty years and was a member of the Limerick Harbour Commissioners. He was also a member of the Limerick Health Authority from 1968 to 1971 and its successor, the Mid-Western Health Board from 1971 until 2004. He served as chairman of the latter from 1982 to 2000. He was also the first chairman of the board of management of the Belltable Arts Centre in Limerick, was chairman of the board of governors of Limerick Institute of Technology for five years and was on the governing bodies of the University of Limerick, University College Dublin and University College Cork. He was the first captain of Rathbane Municipal Golf Club when it was established in 1997.[251]

Jack Bourke has lived for many years in 'Roseville', Roxboro Road. His wife Monica is a cousin of the Derry-born statesman John Hume and a grandniece of Charles McHugh, the Catholic bishop of Derry from 1907 to 1926.[252]

Stephen Coughlan 1969–70.
See above under 1951–52.

Joseph P. (Rory) Liddy 1970–71.
See above under 1958–59.

Denis A. O'Driscoll 1971–72 and 1989–90.

Denis A. (always known as Gus) O'Driscoll was born on 11 January 1931 in the living accommodation overhead the Corbally Bar, in the Corbally area of Limerick city. This famous licensed premises had been established by Gus's father in 1917 and at the time of writing is still flourishing after ninety years in business. He was educated in St. Mary's Convent School, the CBS Creagh Lane (formerly the Limerick City Courthouse) and the CBS Sexton Street. In 1949, his father was killed as a result of a fall from his bicycle and Gus O'Driscoll was obliged to leave school and commence work in the family business. Over the next fifty years, he worked diligently and expanded the Corbally Bar into one of the finest licensed premises in the Limerick city area.[253]

Denis A. O'Driscoll
(Denis A. O'Driscoll)

Gus O'Driscoll is a lifelong member of Fine Gael. He was a member of Limerick City Council from 1967 to 1999, and in the latter year, retired undefeated, having been returned in five successive local elections. He served as mayor on two occasions. His first mayoralty (1971–72) coincided with the most violent phase of the Troubles in the North of Ireland. Following the killing of thirteen Civil Rights marchers in Derry by the British Army on Bloody Sunday (30 January 1972), Mayor O'Driscoll led a delegation from Limerick Corporation that travelled to Derry and attended the Requiem Mass and burial of the victims of the atrocity. Several other Irish mayors were also present on this occasion. On a less sombre note, Gus O'Driscoll was instrumental in establishing the Civic Week Festival in Limerick, which was held for the first time in March 1972 and continued to be one of the highlights of the city's calendar for the next thirty years. The highpoint of Gus O'Driscoll's second mayoralty (1989–90) was the opening of Limerick's new City Hall. It opened for business on 14 February 1990 and was officially opened by the Taoiseach, Charles Haughey on 1 June 1990. Another important event of Gus O'Driscoll's second term of office was the establishment of a twinning arrangement with Spokane in Washington State, USA.[254]

Gus O'Driscoll was also a member of the Limerick Harbour Commissioners for many years. He was a member of the board of management of Barrington's Hospital for fourteen years, and was chairman at the time of the controversial closure of the hospital on 31 March 1988. In addition to his membership of various public bodies, Gus O'Driscoll has also been active in the sporting life of Limerick. He is a lifelong member of Shannon RFC. In his youth he was a player, later he served as treasurer of the club for a quarter of a century and has been a trustee for over sixty years. He was also president of the Munster Branch of the IRFU from 1961 to 1962. As a young man he played hurling with the short-lived Corbally Hurling Club and hockey with Lansdowne Hockey Club.[255]

Gus O'Driscoll retired from Limerick City Council in 1999 but continues to take an active interest in the political, social and sporting life of Limerick city. He resides at 11 Rhebogue Avenue, Corbally, Limerick.[256]

Patrick G. Kiely 1972–73.

One of the most astute and durable figures in Limerick politics, Patrick G. (always known as Paddy) Kiely was born in Limerick city on 10 March 1935. He lived for a short time in 17 Shannon Street and then his family moved to Arthurs Quay where he resided from 1937 to 1948 before settling in Pennywell, where he still lives at the time of writing. He was educated in St. Michael's school on Denmark Street and in the CBS, Sexton Street, where one of his teachers was Jack Danagher (mayor in 1964–65). From 1950 to 1966, Paddy Kiely was employed as a law clerk with D.J. O'Malley and Company Solicitors, where his employer was Desmond O'Malley (mayor 1941–43) and one of his colleagues was John Quinn (mayor 1992–93). Later Paddy worked in the insurance business from 1966 until his retirement in 1999.[257]

It was virtually inevitable that Paddy Kiely would become involved in politics as he was related to Dan Bourke (mayor 1936–41) and he was married to Anne Marie Barry, whose father Liam had been actively involved in the IRA and mother Bridget had been a major figure in Cumann na nBan during the War of Independence. A lifelong member of Fianna Fáil, Paddy Kiely was a member of the party's National Executive from 1959 to 1975 and was a close friend and political associate of Donogh O'Malley, whom he greatly admired. Paddy Kiely first stood for the city council in 1960 but was unsuccessful. However, he was co-opted as a member in 1962 to replace Councillor Tommy Creamer. Paddy Kiely remained a member of the council until 1985, having been successfully returned at three local elections.[258]

Patrick G. Kiely
(Limerick City Library)

Paddy Kiely served as mayor of Limerick from June 1972 to June 1973. His election was notable for the manner in which Vincent Feeney (mayor 1966–67) was carried into the council chamber on a stretcher to vote for Kiely, having been brought from Barrington's Hospital, where he was a patient. Paddy Kiely saw the role of the mayor as being an ambassador for Limerick, whose task was to put the city 'on the map' and to attract business and employment at a time of economic recession. One of the high points of his mayoralty was the entry of Ireland into the European Economic Community (the forerunner of the European Union) on 1 January 1973. In connection with this, Mayor Kiely hosted a dinner in Cruises Hotel at which the ambassadors of all of the nine states that were then members of the EEC were the guests of honour. The most acute phase of the Northern Ireland Troubles coincided with Paddy Kiely's mayoralty and large numbers of refugees from the North came to Limerick at this time. Mayor Kiely personally conducted a house-to-house collection to raise funds to assist them and was actively involved in helping them find accommodation. He also played a role in averting the closure of the Clover Meats Bacon Factory in Limerick city. Mayor Kiely attended the ceremony at which President Eamon de Valera was conferred with the freedom of Cork city on 31 March 1973, but on his journey back to Limerick was involved in a road accident, in which he narrowly escaped serious injury.[259]

Paddy Kiely was a member of the Limerick Health Authority and the Mid-Western Health Board and was briefly on the Harbour Commissioners. Although retired form the city council since 1985, he is still actively involved in politics, which he describes as his sole hobby and consuming interest. He lives at 6 Pennywell Road, Limerick.[260]

Michael Lipper 1973–74.

Michael Lipper, always known as Mick, was born on 1 June 1932 and was educated at the CBS, Sexton Street and the Municipal Technical Institute, O'Connell Avenue. He worked as a train driver with Coras Iompar Eireann and during his period there became active with the ITGWU. In his youth Lipper was a well-known sportsman and was an outstanding soccer player. Like Mick Keyes (mayor 1928–30) he had a lifelong connection with Pike Rovers Soccer Club, and also played in the League of Ireland for Limerick, Transport and Sligo Rovers. In the 1950s he was one of the best-known centre-forwards in Ireland.[261]

Michael Lipper
(Limerick City Archives)

Mick Lipper's involvement with the ITGWU resulted in his joining the Labour Party at an early age. He was a member of Limerick City Council from 1960 to 1985, and was victorious in a total of four local elections. He was unanimously elected mayor in June 1973 on the nomination of Steve Coughlan and had a distinguished term in office. He had the unique distinction for a mayor of Limerick of driving the train which conveyed the Limerick senior hurling team and their supporters to and from Dublin in September 1973, on which occasion Limerick last won an All-Ireland Senior Hurling Championship. Later, Mick Lipper commemorated this event by adding a roundel to the mayoral chain.

In addition to his long service on Limerick City Council, Mick Lipper was active in national politics. He stood for Labour in the 1968 by-election caused by the death of Donogh O'Malley and came within 927 votes of Desmond O'Malley, who took the seat on the third count. He was an unsuccessful Labour candidate in both the 1969 and 1973 general elections. In the late 1970s relations between Lipper and his Labour Party colleague, Steve Coughlan, had become very strained and their rivalry culminated in the 1977 general election. Coughlan, the sitting TD was the sole official Labour Party candidate in Limerick East, but Lipper ran against him under the banner of Independent Labour. Lipper was elected and was re-admitted to the Parliamentary Labour Party soon after. He remained in the Dáil until 1981, when he lost his seat to Jim Kemmy.[262]

Mick Lipper was a member of the Mid-Western Health Board and of the Limerick City VEC for many years. He retired from the city council in 1985 and died on 18 October 1987 at the age of fifty-five.[263]

Patrick Kennedy 1974–75 and 1985–86.

Patrick (often known as Pat) Kennedy was born and reared on the Roxboro Road, Limerick and attended primary and secondary school at the CBS Sexton Street. Later he qualified as a primary school teacher after attending St. Patrick's College, Drumcondra for two years. He taught for several years at his alma mater, the CBS Primary School, Sexton Street, eventually becoming vice-principal. Later he graduated from the University of London with an Honours LLB Degree and following a period of study at King's Inns, Dublin, became a barrister-at-law.[264]

It was not surprising that Pat Kennedy became involved in politics, as his grandfather Michael Heelan had been a member of Limerick County Council from 1925 to 1945. Pat credits Frances Condell (mayor 1962–64) with bringing him into politics. He had already become involved in the Limerick Chamber of Commerce and had served as president when Frances Condell invited him to join the Limerick Ratepayers Association in 1966. Pat Kennedy became chairman of the association in 1967 and in the same year, Frances Condell who was stepping down from the city council, encouraged him to stand instead. In consequence, he was elected to the council in the 1967 local elections at the early age of twenty-nine and by topping the poll became an alderman in the process. He has been returned at all six subsequent local elections and topped the poll on every occasion except in the 1991 local elections. In 2007, he achieved the rare distinction of completing forty years on Limerick City Council, the longest period of service of any mayor of Limerick since 1842. In 2004, Pat Kennedy became the last alderman in the history of Limerick city as the title was abolished that year, under the provisions of the Local Government Act of 2001.[265]

Pat Kennedy served as mayor of Limerick on two occasions. During his first mayoralty (1974–75) he was involved in the campaign to have the Baggott Estate in the Ballinacurra area of Limerick , which eventually amounted to 100 acres, preserved as a recreational and

Patrick Kennedy meets President Bill Clinton in 1998. Looking on are former mayors Tim Leddin and Frank Leddin (Patrick Kennedy)

amenity area. Mayor Kennedy played a role in Limerick Corporation becoming the first local authority in Ireland to establish formal links with the European Economic Community, now the European Union. He was also involved in the campaign to have the venerable Model School on O'Connell Avenue (which has been destroyed by fire in 1974) rebuilt and its stone façade preserved. During his second mayoralty, he became chairman of the Urban Renewal Committee of Limerick Corporation and in conjunction with his brother-in-law John Boland, then Minister for the Environment, worked to have Merchants' Quay included in the area designated for urban renewal. This facilitated the building of the new Limerick City Hall in Merchants' Quay.[266]

As well as having a long and distinguished career in Limerick City Council, Pat Kennedy has also been active in the national arena. He stood for the Dáil in several elections between 1969 and 2002 but was unsuccessful on each occasion. However he was a member of the Senate from 1981 to 1982 and from 1983 to 1992. Indeed, during his second mayoralty between 1985 and 1986, he became only the second person to be simultaneously mayor of Limerick and senator. He also stood unsuccessfully for the Senate in 1993 and 1997. At the time of his election to the city council in 1967, he was a member of Fine Gael but he left the party in 2002 and became an Independent. At the time of writing, Pat Kennedy is the longest serving member of Limerick City Council and resides at 'Fortview', Greenpark, South Circular Road, Limerick.[267]

Thady Coughlan 1975–76.

The youngest mayor of Limerick since 1842, Thady Coughlan was born on 3 March 1951, a few months before his father Steve Coughlan became mayor of Limerick for the first time. He lived for a time in Barrington Street and later his family moved to 3 Wellington Terrace, O'Connell Avenue. He was educated in St Philomena's Primary School and St. Munchin's College, where one of his classmates was Paddy Madden (mayor 1988–89 and 1990–91). Since 1977, Thady Coughlan has been employed by Anglo-Irish Bank, now situated in 98 Henry Street.[268]

A member of the Labour Party, Thady Coughlan was a member of Limerick City Council from 1974 to 1979. His father Steve was still a councillor and this represented the only time since 1842 that a father and son were simultaneously on the council. Thady was elected mayor of Limerick on 30 June 1975 and at twenty-four years of age was a year younger than William O'Donnell (mayor in 1890) who had previously held the record for being the most youthful mayor of Limerick. His mayoralty was marked by a number of interesting events. In August 1975, he represented Limerick Corporation at the funeral of Eamon de Valera. In October 1975, he travelled to Rome for the canonisation of Oliver Plunkett and met Pope Paul VI and the future Pope John Paul II, then Archbishop of Krakow. In the same month, the kidnapping by members of the Provisional IRA of Dr. Tiede Herrema (manager of Ferenka, a factory at Annacotty outside Limerick that employed 1,400 people) resulted in Mayor Couglan becoming the centre of a lot of media attention in his capacity as first citizen of the city. Fortunately, Dr. Herrema was eventually released unharmed. The restoration of St. John's Square was also completed at this time. In March 1976, *The Late Late Show*, hosted by Gay Byrne was broadcast from the Parkway Hotel on Limerick's Dublin Road as part of Limerick Civic Week and Mayor

Coughlan was one of the panel of guests. Along with his father, Thady Coughlan did not stand at the 1979 local elections. During the 1970s, he was also a member of the Limerick City VEC and of Limerick Harbour Commissioners.[269]

Although he retired from politics in 1979 at the early age of twenty-eight, Thady Coughlan continues to be active in the public life of Limerick city. He has been involved with Shannon RFC for some forty years, first as a player and later as an administrator. He was club president in 2000–01 and was manager of the Shannon team that won the All-Ireland League in 2002. Thady Coughlan currently resides at Dalcassian House, Fanningstown, Crecora, County Limerick.[270]

The Minister for local government Mr James Tully T.D. cuts the tape to officially open the new Pairc de Valera housing scheme at Thomondgate. Also in picture from left, Mr. T.P. MacDiarmada, City Manager, Dr. Caird, Church of Ireland Bishop of Limerick, Alderman Stephen Coughlan TD, Dr. Newman, Catholic Bishop of Limerick and Councillor Thady Coughlan, Mayor of Limerick (1975-76). (Jim Kemmy Municipal Museum)

George E. (Ted) Russell 1976–77.

See under 1954–57.

Frank Prendergast 1977–78 and 1984–85.

Francis Joseph (always known as Frank) Prendergast was born in Limerick on 13 July 1933 into a family steeped in trade unionism. The Prendergasts had been involved in the bakery trade in Limerick since the late eighteenth century and were members of the

Bakers Guild. One of Frank's paternal granduncles, Michael Prendergast became the general secretary of the National Bakers Union and later helped found the Bakers Union of America. His maternal granduncle William Murphy led the Limerick Pork Butchers Society in their support for the Dublin workers at the time of the 1913 Lockout. Two of Frank's relations were elected to Limerick City Council as part of the 'Labour Party' in the 1899 local elections: his granduncle Tom who became alderman in the Glentworth ward and Tom's first cousin Michael who was a councillor in the Irishtown ward.[271]

Frank Prendergast was educated at the CBS in Sexton Street and later in life received a Diploma in Social and Economic Science from University College Cork and an MA in Industrial Relations from the University of Keele. He worked as a baker from 1950 to 1973 and became involved in

Frank Prendergast
(Limerick City Archives)

the trade union movement in 1954 when he became branch secretary of the Limerick Bakers Society. Later he served as national president of the Irish Bakers Confectioners and Allied Workers Union from 1967 to 1970. From 1973 to 1993, Frank was employed as a full time official, first with the Irish Transport and General Workers Union (ITGWU) until 1990 and then with the Services Industrial Professional and Technical Union (SIPTU) which was formed in that year as a result of the merger of the ITGWU and the Federated Workers Union of Ireland.[272]

A lifelong member of the Labour Party, Frank Prendergast was a member of Limerick City Council from 1974 to 1999, and retired undefeated in 1999, having successfully contested four local elections. He was alderman in ward one from 1979 to 1985. He served as mayor of Limerick from June 1977 to June 1978 and again from June 1984 to June 1985. He stood unsuccessfully for the Dáil in the general election of June 1981 but was successfully returned as a TD for Limerick East in the general election of November 1982. During his term in the Dáil, which lasted until he lost his seat in the general election of February 1987, Frank Prendergast achieved the rare distinction of being simultaneously an alderman, TD and mayor of Limerick between 1984 and 1985. He was an active member of the Dáil, serving as a member of the New Ireland Forum from 1983 to 1984 and chairman of the Oireachtas Committee on Commercial Semi-State Bodies, while also playing a major role in the establishment of the Joint Oireachtas Committee on the Irish Language.[273]

Like his fellow mayors Tony Bromell, Jim Kemmy and Joe Harrington, Frank Prendergast has played a notable role in the intellectual life of Limerick city and indeed Ireland for many years. A fluent Irish speaker, he was a member of An Grúpa Stiúrtha, (which is an Irish language steering group in the Department of the Environment and Local Government) from 1984 to 1999, of Comhairle Theilifis na Gaeilge (Irish language television council) from 1994 to 2000 and of the governing body of the School of Celtic Studies in the Dublin Institute of Advanced Studies from 1996 to 2000. One of his great interests is the study of Irish place names and he has been a member of An Coimisiún Logainmneacha (Irish Place Names Commission) since 1997. He is also a prolific writer and is the author of *A History of St Michael's Parish* (2000) and with Mainchin Seoighe wrote *Limerick's Glory: From Viking Settlement to New Millennium* (2002). He also contributed to *Remembering Limerick* (1997) and *Made In Limerick* Volume One (2003) and has published articles in the *North Munster Antiquarian Journal* and *The Old Limerick Journal*. For many years, he contributed a weekly column in the Irish language to the *Limerick Leader* and Anois newspapers, which were later published in book form as *Dála an Scéil* (2003).[274]

Frank Prendergast is a lifelong member of Garryowen Rugby and Claughaun GAA Clubs, and is also a member of the Thomond Archaeological and Historical Society, the Voices of Limerick Choir and the Limerick Thomond Probus Club. He resides at 'Avondonn' Mayorstone Park, Limerick city and continues to take an active part in public life.[275]

Bobby Byrne 1978–79 and 1979–80.

Patrick Robert (always known as Bobby) Byrne was born in Limerick on 3 March 1937 and spent most of his childhood in Killarney, where his father was a bank manager. He was educated at St. Mary's Convent and Presentation College, both in Killarney and in Newbridge College in County Kildare. Returning to Limerick he set up in business as a publican and was the proprietor of the Wolfe Tone Bar on 3 O'Connell Avenue for some forty years. Byrne was always interested in sport and has been a member of Limerick Golf Club since 1958. He was the first president of Rathbane Municipal Golf Club when it was established in 1997 and has been a member of Garryowen RFC all his life.[276]

A lifelong member of Fine Gael, Bobby Byrne was first elected to Limerick City Council at the 1974 local elections and was returned at three subsequent elections. He increased his vote at all four elections that he contested and retired undefeated from the council in 1999. The high point of his political career was his period as mayor from June 1978 to June 1980, and at the time of writing he has the distinction of being the last mayor of Limerick to have served two consecutive terms.[277]

The most significant event of his mayoralties was the visit of Pope John Paul II to the city on 1 October 1979. As with the visit of President Kennedy in 1963, the inclusion of Limerick in the Papal itinerary was facilitated by the Pope's departure from Ireland via

Shannon Airport and Greenpark Racecourse was used as the venue for the occasion. The visit was brief, but memorable. Some 400,000 attended Mass in Greenapark concelebrated by the Pope, eleven bishops, two abbots and thirteen priests, while 200,000 received Communion from 800 priests, a choir of 150 sang and 1,600 stewards, 600 scouts and guides, 300 soldiers and 200 members of Civil Defence were also on duty on the day.[278] Later the Pope, along with Tomás Cardinal O'Fiach, archbishop of Armagh, Dr. Gaetano Alibrandi, the Papal Nuncio and Dr. Jeremiah Newman, bishop of Limerick, received the freedom of Limerick, which was the largest number of conferrals at one ceremony since the modern system was instituted in 1877. Also, the Pope is the only monarch to have received the freedom of Limerick. Mayor Byrne was enormously impressed by the charismatic and saintly personality of the Pope, who gave him a set of rosary beads and a medallion depicting the Papal coat of arms. Other notable events of Bobby Byrne's period in office included the historic victory of the Munster rugby team over the New Zealand All-Blacks in Thomond Park, Limerick on 31 October 1978 and John Treacy winning the IAAF World Cross Country Championship in Limerick in 1979.[279]

Bobby Byrne was a member of Limerick Health Committee, Limerick City VEC and of the governing body of Barrington's Hospital. He was also a member of Limerick Harbour Commissioners for eighteen years and thus continued a family tradition, as his grandfather Thomas J. Loughrey had been a member for over a quarter of a century. Bobby Byrne resigned from the city council in 1999 after twenty-five years of unbroken service. His daughter Maria has been a member of the council since 1999. Bobby Byrne lives at 'Mannixville' O'Connell Avenue, Limerick.[280]

Clement Casey 1980–81.

The oldest living ex-mayor of Limerick at the time of writing, Clement (always known as Clem) Casey was born in Limerick city 16 March 1922 and brought up at 5 Roches Street. He was educated at CBS Sexton Street and the Good Counsel College New Ross. For virtually all of his working life, Clem Casey was the proprietor of a poultry and fish store on Roches Street and was also a wholesale potato merchant.[281]

A lifelong member of Fianna Fáil, Clem Casey was first elected to Limerick City Council in 1967 and was returned in two subsequent local elections, remaining a member until 1985. He played a notable role in the introduction of disc

Clement Casey
(Limerick City Archives)

parking to Limerick city and proposed the motion to that effect in the city council. Later he had the satisfaction of being a member of the council when disc parking commenced in 1984. Clem Casey served as mayor from June 1980 to June 1981. One of the high points of his mayoralty was the opening of the Lee Estate housing scheme. He thoroughly enjoyed the experience of being a councillor and was deeply honoured to serve as mayor. Clem Casey was also a long serving member of the Harbour Commissioners and served as chairman in the mid-1990s.[282]

In addition to his involvement in politics, Clem Casey was also a very prominent figure in the sporting life of Limerick city. Like Mick Keyes (mayor 1928–30), he has had a very long association with Young Munster RFC as both a player and a member. He joined the club committee as vice-president and served as president between 1955 and 1958.[283] Since the foundation of the club in 1895, Young Munsters had been obliged to play their home matches at various temporary locations, but during his presidency Clem Casey spearheaded the purchase of six acres of land at Rosbrien in 1958, which became their first permanent home and was later named Tom Clifford Park.[284] He was president of the Munster Branch of the IRFU in 1969–70. Clem's son Gerry Casey has also had a very distinguished career with Young Munster. He won Senior Cup Medals in 1980, 1984 and 1990, was captain of the club in 1985–86, and played in Lansdowne Road Stadium against Lansdowne in the All Ireland League in 1992. Gerry Casey followed in the footsteps of his father by becoming club president in 1995–96, the year Young Munster celebrated the centenary of its foundation.[285] To mark the occasion, the club presented a roundel to Mayor Jim Kemmy to be attached to the mayoral chain.

Pope John Paul II receiving the Freedom of Limerick at Greenpark racecourse on 1 October 1979. In the centre is Mayor Bobby Byrne and to the right is City Manager T. P. MacDiarmada.
(Veritas Publications and A.C.W. Art Publishers Ltd)

Clem Casey resided for many years at 'Mount Gerard ' O'Connell Avenue but is now living at 15 Strand Court, O'Callaghan Strand. He continues to take a lively interest in the political and sporting life of Limerick city.[286]

Thomas Allen 1981–82.

Tommy Allen was born in Limerick city in 1938 and for a time worked as a train driver with his friend Mick Lipper (mayor 1973–74). Later he was manager of Hanover Tyres and towards the end of his life set up his own printing business. He lived for much of the 1970s and 1980s in Southill, at Rose Court, Keyes Park (named in honour of a previous mayor, Mick Keyes). Southill was a vast new social housing estate with a young population and little in the way of amenities and in consequence, was afflicted by a number of social problems. A man of great energy, vision and enthusiasm, Tommy Allen soon emerged as one of the leading figures in the life of the area. He served as public relations officer for Southill

Thomas Allen
(Limerick City Council)

Community Council for many years and became editor and publisher of the area's first newsletter, *The Community Observer* which was also the first of its kind in Limerick. Indeed, there was scarcely a voluntary body or parish organisation in Southill that did not benefit from the involvement of Tommy Allen.[287]

A member of the Labour Party, Allen was elected to the city council in the local elections of 1979. He topped the poll in ward three, which included Southill, and thus became an alderman. He polled 1, 114 votes or 200 more than the quota required to be elected and received 25% of the total votes cast in the ward, the highest percentage in the city. In June 1981, he became the first resident of Southill to be elected mayor of Limerick. This was considered to be a great personal triumph for Allen and a great honour for Southill, an area that had often felt itself to be outside the mainstream of the life of the city. The most significant event of his mayoralty was the twinning of Limerick with the French city of Quimper, which was begun in 1981. Allen's mayoralty was a great success, due in no small part to the flair for publicity that he had acquired during his period as PRO of Southill Community Council.[288]

Later, Allen moved out of Southill and ward three and went to live at 50 Greenfields, Rosbrien, which was in ward four. This was believed to have been a factor in his failure to retain his council seat in the 1985 local elections, though he was only narrowly defeated for a seat in ward four. Later he joined the newly formed Progressive Democratic Party. Tommy Allen died on the 14 August 1994, aged fifty-six and was buried in Mount St. Oliver Cemetery.[289]

Tony Bromell 1982–83.

John Anthony (usually known as Tony Bromell) was born on 15 November 1932 in Chapel Street in St. John's Parish, Limerick city and was brought up in Thomondgate. He was educated in St. Munchin's CBS, and the CBS Sexton Street. A brilliant student, he was in receipt of the Limerick Corporation Primary Scholarship and the State Intermediate Scholarship, which enabled him to complete his secondary school education in the period before the introduction of free education in 1966. Later he benefited from the Limerick Corporation University Scholarship and the Department of Education University Scholarship and attended University College Galway, where he graduated with a BA in Irish,

John A. (Tony) Bromell
(Egleston Brothers Photographers)

History and Mathematics in 1954 and a Higher Diploma in Education in 1955. Between 1955 and 1968, he worked as a secondary school teacher in his alma mater, the CBS Sexton Street, where he taught Irish and Mathematics. He was heavily involved in the Association of Secondary School Teachers, Ireland (ASTI) and was national president in 1966–67 and 1967–68, one of only three individuals to have had a double presidency of the ASTI.[290]

Tony Bromell had a very long association with third-level education in Limerick. He was on the staff of Mary Immaculate College from 1968 to 1998, first as lecturer in Irish and from 1970 until his retirement as registrar. In the latter capacity, he played a major role in the life of the college at a time of enormous change and expansion. One of his most significant contributions to the public life of Limerick was his involvement with the Limerick University Project from 1957 to 1972. Since 1934, there had been sporadic attempts made by various bodies to obtain a university for Limerick city. In 1957, the campaign was revived after a lapse of ten years and in 1959 the Limerick University Project Committee (LUPC) was established to lobby for the establishment of a university in Limerick. Tony Bromell was very active in this committee and carried out a great deal of research that clearly demonstrated the need for a university in Limerick. Eventually, the campaign was successfully concluded with the opening of the National Institute of Higher Education (later to become the University of Limerick) at Plassey, near Limerick city, in September 1972.[291] As a member and as chairman of Limerick City VEC, Tony Bromell was involved in acquiring land at Moylish near the city which later became the site of the main campus of Limerick Institute of Technology. He was also a member of the governing body of Thomond College of Education which was situated on the same campus as NIHE at Plassey from its foundation in 1973, until its absorption into the University of Limerick in 1991.[292]

A lifelong admirer of Eamon de Valera, Tony Bromell became involved in the Fianna Fáil Party as a student in UCG, and was first elected to Limerick City Council in 1967.

He was returned at the local elections of 1974 and 1979, but lost his seat in the 1985 local elections. He served as mayor from June 1982 to June 1983. Later he was a member of the Senate from 1988 to 1989 on the Industrial and Commercial Panel. Ironically in view of his long academic career, he defeated Mícheál Martin and Mary Hanafin for the Fianna Fáil nomination and he defeated Niamh Breathnach in the actual Senate election, as all three were later to serve as Minister for Education![293]

In 1961, Tony Bromell married Aine Ní Thuathaigh, who won the All-Ireland Irish Dancing Championship in 1956 and the All-Ireland Traditional Singing Championship in 1957 and they had four children who are all involved in education. Una, who was the sister of the renowned Limerick-born academic Professor Gearóid O Tuathaigh of NUI Galway, died at a young age in 1988. Tony Bromell has had a lifelong interest in the Irish language and culture, particularly music, dancing and hurling and is a member of Na Piarsaigh GAA Club. In 2006, he became the first mayor of Limerick to publish his autobiography. Written in the Irish language, it is entitled *Rian Mo Chos Ar Ghaineamh an tSaoil* (My Footsteps on the Sand of Life) and gives a valuable insight into the political, social and cultural life of Limerick city since the 1930s. Tony Bromell lives at 8 Hazeldene, Ennis Road, Limerick.[294]

Terry Kelly 1983–84.

The second woman to become mayor of Limerick, Therese (usually known as Terry) Barry was born in Cork city on 5 February 1941 into a prosperous and politically prominent family. Her grandfather James J. Barry founded Barry's Tea in 1901, which by 2006 accounted for 37% of tea sales in Ireland, had an annual turnover of thirty-one million euro and employed seventy-three people. Her father Anthony Barry (1901–83) was Fine Gael TD for Cork city in 1954 –57

Mayor Terry Kelly with the Mayor of Boston Raymond (Ray) Flynn in February 1984
(Terry Kelly)

and 1961–65 and served as Lord Mayor of Cork from 1961 to 1962. Anthony Barry was also a talented photographer and a book of his photographs of Cork city was published in 2004 under the title of *No Lovelier City. A Portrait of Cork*.[295] Anthony's son and Terry's brother is Peter Barry (born 1928) who has had a very distinguished political career. He was a member of the Dáil from 1969 to 1997 and during this period held the following cabinet positions: Minister for Transport and Power (1973–76), Education (1976–77), the Environment (1981–82) and Foreign Affairs (1982–87), while he was briefly Tanaiste for a few months in 1987. Peter Barry was Lord Mayor of Cork from 1970 to 1971.[296] His daughter Deirdre Clune was a TD from 1997 to 2002 and from 2007 to the time of writing and like her father and grandfather served as Lord Mayor of Cork, in her case from 2005 to 2006.

Terry Barry was educated at St. Angela's Ursuline College and the Cork School of Art, now known as the Crawford College of Art and Design, where she studied stain glass and painting. Later in life she graduated from University College Dublin with a BA Degree. After graduating from the Cork School of Art, Terry Barry worked for two years in Dublin with Preston and Hadfield a paint manufacturing firm, before marrying John Kelly and moving to London. She lived there for ten years, and while she was a member of the British Liberal Party during this period, devoted herself fulltime to rearing her four children. In 1974, the Kelly family moved to Limerick where they became the proprietors of the Shannon Arms Hotel in Henry Street.

Despite the death of her husband in 1980 and her heavy family and business commitments, Terry Kelly took an active part in the public life of Limerick city. She was particularly interested in the women's movement and was one of the founders of Adapt, which provides accommodation and support for women and their children subjected to domestic abuse. Other areas in which she has had a lifelong interest are Northern Ireland, art and architecture and education. From 1979 to 1985, Terry Kelly was a member of Limerick City Council and served as mayor from June 1983 to June 1984. During her Mayoralty she was involved in Co-Operation North, a body that promoted reconciliation in Northern Ireland and on a number of visits to the USA spoke out strongly against the Provisional IRA. She also worked to promote Limerick at home and abroad and to enhance the co-operation between Limerick Corporation and the business community in the city.

In the local elections of 1985, Terry Kelly did not stand again for the city council. However in the following two decades she made a major contribution to the public life of the country in a variety of roles. In 1985, she moved to Dublin to take up the position of director of the Heritage Trust, which was a group of business people who wanted to make a contribution to the enhancement of the built environment in Ireland. From 1986 to 1991, she was chief executive of the Crafts Council of Ireland, which is the national design and economic development organisation for the craft industry and is a government-funded body. During this time, she was also director of the Landmark Trust, which restores vernacular buildings all over the country. Later she established her own business and was involved for a time with the Furniture College in Letterfrack, County Galway, which is a constituent college of Galway-Mayo Institute of Technology. From 1997 to 1999, she was chairperson of the Crafts Council of Ireland and during this time, its headquarters were relocated from Dublin to Kilkenny. Terry Kelly is currently residing in Donnybrook, Dublin 4.[297]

Frank Prendergast 1984–85.
See under 1977–78.

Patrick Kennedy 1985–86.

See above under 1974–75.

Jack Bourke 1986–87.

See above under 1968–69.

Tim Leddin 1987–88.

Tim Leddin was born in Limerick in 1923, and was a nephew of Michael Keyes (mayor in 1928–30), a first cousin of Christy Keyes (mayor in 1957–58) and a brother of Frank Leddin (mayor in 1965–66 and 1997–98). Tim worked for many years in the General Post Office in Limerick and very active in the trade union movement there.[298]

Tim Leddin
(Limerick City Archives)

In contrast to the other members of his family who have occupied the Limerick mayoralty, Tim Leddin was a member of Fine Gael. He contested the local elections of 1974 and 1979, and on each occasion failed to be elected by a mere handful of votes. However, displaying the determination for which he was renowned, Tim Leddin was finally elected to the city council in the local elections of 1985, and even topped the poll in ward one, becoming an alderman in the process. Two years later, he was elected mayor of Limerick in June 1987. During his mayoralty, Leddin invited the Taoiseach, Charles J. Haughey to Limerick to open the new Shannon Bridge, the first road bridge to be built over the Shannon at Limerick since 1840. On the occasion of this visit, Mayor Leddin brought the Taoiseach to see King John's Castle, which had a scheme of social housing in its courtyard at the time. It is believed that this visit resulted in Haughey sanctioning the demolition of these houses and the subsequent restoration of the castle, which was completed in 1991.[299]

Tim Leddin was re-elected to the council at the local elections of 1991. Along with his brother Frank, he retired from the council at the time of the 1999 local elections. They had created an unusual record for two brothers by serving on the council together for eight years (1991–99), while belonging to two different political parties. Tim Leddin was disappointed that his wife Kathleen was not chosen to succeed him as the official Fine Gael candidate for ward one in the 1999 local elections, but she subsequently stood as an Independent and won a seat, after a successful campaign organised by Tim. At the same election, his nephew Joe also secured a seat on the city council, representing the Labour Party. A few months later, Tim Leddin died on 24 October 1999.[300]

Paddy Madden 1988–89 and 1990–91.

Patrick (always known as Paddy) Madden was born in Limerick on 26 January 1951 and lived for many years in the Canal Bank area of the city. He was educated at St. Patrick's National School and St. Munchin's College, where one of his classmates was Thady Coughlan (mayor in 1975–76). Paddy Madden has spent virtually all of his working life in the engineering department of Cement Limited, Mungret, County Limerick. He has a life long interest in sport and played with Richmond RFC, Caledonians Soccer Club and St. Patrick's GAA Club.[301]

Paddy Madden
(Paddy Madden)

A member of the Fianna Fáil Party, Paddy Madden was first elected to Limerick City Council in 1979 and was successfully returned in 1985. He served as mayor of Limerick from June 1988 to June 1989 and again from June 1990 to June 1991. Thus he is one of only three mayors of Limerick since 1842 to have served two non-consecutive terms of office separated by one year (the other are Kevin Bradshaw in 1950–51 and 1952–53 and Dick Sadlier in 2001–02 and 2003–04). The high point of Paddy Madden's first mayoralty was the visit of President Mikhail Gorbachev of the USSR to Shannon Airport on 2 April 1989. This was the first time that a Russian head of state, Tsarist or Communist had ever visited Ireland and Paddy Madden was among the dignitaries who greeted him. As Shannon Airport is in County Clare, protocol would have decreed that Mayor Madden, strictly speaking, was not supposed to don the mayoral robe and chain for the arrival ceremony. However, he believed that as mayor of Limerick on such a historic occasion, he should represent the city in as dignified a manner as possible and wore both robe and chain as he welcomed Gorbachev to Ireland. His striking and resplendent appearance made a great impression on the Soviet party, unused to such civic elegance since the days of the Tsars. An apocryphal account of the meeting between the two men represented Gorbachev asking Mayor Madden 'What happened to Young Munster yesterday' in reference to a rugby match played the day before! During his first mayoralty Paddy Madden also welcomed Alex Ferguson and several members of the Manchester United football team to Limerick city. Indeed he was the last mayor to serve a full term in the Town Hall in Rutland Street (1988–89) and the first to be elected in the new City Hall on Merchants' Quay in 1990. His second mayoralty was notable for the Treaty 300 Festival held throughout the year 1991 to mark the tercentenary of the Treaty of Limerick. The festivities were launched on 1 January 1991 by President Mary Robinson, who opened Arthur's Quay Park on the same day.[302]

Paddy Madden remained a member of Limerick City Council until 1991 when he lost his seat in the local elections held that year. During his political career, he was also a member of the Limerick City VEC, Harbour Commissioners and the Mid-Western Health Board. While no longer a councillor, Paddy Madden is still a well-known figure in Limerick city. He currently resides at 23 Bracken Crescent, North Circular Road, Limerick.[303]

Denis A. O'Driscoll 1989–90.
See above under 1971–72.

Paddy Madden 1990–91.
See above under 1988–89.

Jim Kemmy 1991–92 and 1995–96.
Jim Kemmy was one of the leading figures in the political history of twentieth-century Limerick. He was born in the city on 14 September 1936, the son and grandson of stonemasons and was educated at the CBS, Sexton Street and the Municipal Technical Institute, O'Connell Avenue. He left school at the age of fifteen and became an apprentice stonemason. In the same year, his father had to cease working as he was suffering from tuberculosis and he died two years later. Kemmy spent much of the 1950s completing his apprenticeship but was often unemployed and on one occasion was dismissed for seeking a pay increase. After being unemployed for six months, he emigrated to Britain in 1957 and lived there for three years, working on building sites.[304] It was during this period that he first became interested in reading and, greatly assisted by the paperback revolution, embarked

Jim Kemmy
(Jim Kemmy Municipal Museum)

on a lifelong pursuit of self-instruction that resulted in his becoming, in the words of Desmond O'Malley, 'a highly educated man'.[305]

Kemmy returned to Limerick in 1960, and as a result of the economic boom of the Lemass era, was able to secure employment as a stonemason. Later he worked for Limerick

Corporation in the same capacity. He was soon drawn into the trade union movement and became branch secretary of the Brick and Stonelayers Trade Union and secretary of the Limerick Buildings Trade Group. He also became a member of the Limerick Council of Trade Unions and eventually became president.[306]

Jim Kemmy was a life long socialist, but throughout his career, his advanced views often left him at odds with many of his fellow Leftists. He joined the Labour Party in 1963 and in the 1969 general election was director of elections in the Limerick East constituency. However, he became disenchanted with Labour as a result of the controversies associated with Steve Coughlan during his 1969–70 mayoralty and what Kemmy regarded as the inadequate response of the party leadership to these events. In 1972 Kemmy and forty of his supporters resigned from the Labour Party and he remained an Independent until 1982 when he founded the Democratic Socialist Party.[307]

Kemmy was elected to Limerick City Council in 1974 and having successfully contested three subsequent local elections, remained a member until his death in 1997. During the 1970s, he became one of the most controversial figures in the public life of Limerick city. In an era when religious practice was almost universal in Ireland, Kemmy was a non-believer and opposed the still powerful influence of the Catholic Church in Irish life. In 1975, he founded the Limerick Family Planning Clinic, and in the process caused uproar at a time when artificial contraception was still banned in Ireland. Kemmy was widely criticised by the Catholic clergy and by large sections of the general public while the women who attended the clinic were dubbed 'Kemmy's Femmies' by one irate parish priest. Kemmy was also a critic of what he believed to be old-fashioned nationalist and republican attitudes to the North of Ireland and was a fierce opponent of the Provisional IRA. Consequently, he was often accused by many of having too much sympathy for the position of the unionist community in Northern Ireland.[308]

He also became a contentious figure in the city council. He was one of the first member of the council to refuse to wear the ceremonial red robe, saying that 'while some councillors act like clowns, there is no need to dress like them' and on another occasion referring to some of his colleagues as being dressed like 'Father Christmas'. His contribution to council meetings were often critical of housing conditions, poverty, the provision of family planning and other social problems, and as a result became the focus of fierce arguments that sometimes resulted in proceedings breaking up in disarray. In some quarters, Kemmy became a sort of 'hate figure' and a focus for persistent and hostile criticism. However, he was a highly intelligent, burly and formidable man, and tackled his many opponents with vigour, wit and a wide command of his subject.[309]

Inevitably, Kemmy entered the sphere of national politics and stood unsuccessfully for the Dáil in 1977. However he was first returned in the general election of June 1981 and became a figure of national prominence for the first time. In February 1982, he became the central player in the crisis that brought about the collapse of the Fine Gael-Labour Coalition administration, when he voted against the budget introduced by the then Minister for Finance, John Bruton, as it included a provision for VAT to be levied on children's shoes for the first time. In the ensuing general election, Kemmy retained his seat, and the leader of Fianna Fáil, Charles Haughey, who was attempting to put together a government, offered to support him for the position of Ceann Comhairle. Predictably, Kemmy declined. He lost his seat in the general election of November 1982, but regained it in 1987 and held it until his death, having been returned in the 1992 and 1997 general elections. In 1990, Kemmy and the Democratic Socialist Party merged with the Labour Party, of which he became vice-chairman in 1991 and chairman in 1993. However, he was disappointed to receive no ministerial position in either the Fianna-Fáil Labour administration of 1992–94, or the Rainbow Coalition administration of 1994–97.[310]

Kemmy was elected mayor of Limerick for the first time in June 1991, the year of the Treaty 300 celebrations marking the anniversary of the Treaty of Limerick in 1691. It was a belated tribute to a man who had been a councillor for seventeen years and had been elected a TD on three occasions. By this time, Kemmy's views on family planning, the role of the Catholic Church in Ireland and the Northern troubles were becoming more mainstream and he was recognised as having been far in advance of his time on these and on many other issues. The hostility and criticism that he had endured in the 1970s and 1980s was now replaced by widespread respect and affection. He was mayor for a second term in 1995–96 and on both occasions was lauded for the manner in which he filled the position, although he never wore the principal mayoral chain in public, preferring one of the smaller sheriff's chains instead. Kemmy was the last person to be simultaneously mayor of Limerick and a TD, a circumstance that is not likely to be repeated, due to the abolition of the dual mandate in 2003.[311]

Despite a long and busy political career, Kemmy found time for a varied and stimulating intellectual life. His ruling passions were the history of the Labour movement and the history of Limerick city. In the early 1970s he had founded and edited a controversial magazine entitled *The Limerick Socialist*. In 1979, along with the veteran Limerick local historian Kevin Hannan, he founded *The Old Limerick Journal*, which is still flourishing at the time of writing and which has published numerous articles by various historians (including the present writer) on the history of Limerick city and its environs. In 1996, he edited the critically acclaimed and best selling *Limerick Anthology* and an equally successful companion volume, the *Limerick Compendium* appeared shortly after his death.[312]

At the height of his political career, Jim Kemmy died on 25 September 1997 and was buried in Mount St. Lawrence Cemetery. His close friend, the distinguished Limerick-born academic Professor Gearóid O Tuathaigh of NUI Galway delivered a very stirring oration at this graveside.[313] In 2000, the Limerick City Museum was named the Jim Kemmy Municipal Museum and soon after the College of Business in the University of Limerick was named the Jim Kemmy Business School.

John Quinn 1992–93.

John Quinn was born in Limerick city on 16 September 1933 and in his youth lived in Rutland Street where John Hickey (mayor 1946–47) and Kevin Bradshaw (mayor 1950–51 and 1952–53) also resided at this period. In 1951 John Quinn moved to the new Ballynanty Estate on the Northside of Limerick where he still resides at the time of writing. He attended St. Michael's National School and the CBS in Sexton Street. On leaving school he went to work as a law clerk in D.J. O'Malley and Company, Solicitors, which was owned by Desmond O'Malley (mayor from 1941 to 1943) and in which Paddy Kiely (mayor in 1972–73) was also employed. At the time of writing, John Quinn has worked there for over fifty years.[314]

John Quinn
(John Quinn)

John Quinn has been involved in the public life of Limerick city for over half a century, particularly in community and parish work in Ballynanty. He joined the Knights of Malta in 1949 and rose to the position of area director. When the Community Games were founded in 1968, he quickly became a leading figure and has served as both chairman and president of the Limerick county executive of the Community Games. In addition he has a very long connection with the Ballynanty Residents Association and with the Gaelic League. John Quinn first became involved in politics in the 1950s. He was a member of the Fianna Fáil Party for many years and helped establish the Liam Mellows Cumann (local party branch) in Ballynanty, which eventually became one of the biggest branches in the Limerick East constituency.

He stood unsuccessfully for Limerick City Council in 1974 but was elected in 1979. He was returned in the local elections of 1985 and 1991 and retired undefeated from the council in 1999. John Quinn left Fianna Fáil and joined the Progressive Democrat (PD) Party soon after it was founded in 1985. In the 1991 local elections, he was one of three PD councillors elected to Limerick City Council and in June 1992, he became the first member of the PD Party to be elected mayor of Limerick. Interestingly, the other two members of the PD Party elected in 1991 also became mayor of Limerick: Dick Sadlier in 1994–95, 2001–02 and 2003–04 and Kieran O'Hanlon in 1996–97.[315] During his mayoralty, John Quinn opened the new Cruises Street shopping and residential project, one of the flagship projects of Limerick's urban renewal programme. He also formally welcomed to the city Dr. Richard von Weizsacker, President of Germany, the first German head of state ever to visit Limerick. On this occasion, President Mary Robinson accompanied her German colleague to Limerick. As a long-serving community activist, Mayor Quinn placed a great emphasis on visiting the various communities in Limerick, sometimes attending as many as ten functions per day. A fluent Irish speaker and lover of the language he marked the centenary of the Gaelic League by hosting a reception for the organisation in the City Hall, at which only Irish was spoken. During John Quinn's mayoralty, an additional roundel was added to the mayoral chain to commemorate the centenary of the foundation of the Irish Co-Operative Society in 1893.[316]

John Quinn was also a member of the Limerick City VEC, Limerick Harbour Commissioners, Limerick Health Committee, Mid-Western Health Board and Limerick City Enterprise Board. He has also sat on the governing bodies of St. Michael's National School and Ardscoil Rís and has been a member of several choirs. He is still involved in the Progressive Democratic Party and is currently chairman of the finance committee of St. Munchin's Parish Church. His son Niall was a member of the well-known Limerick rock band *The Hitchers* for many years. John Quinn currently resides at 38 Ballynanty Road, Limerick city.[317]

Jan O'Sullivan 1993–94.

Born in Limerick city on 6 December 1950, Janice (always known as Jan) Gale grew up in Clonlara, County Clare, just outside Limerick city. A member of the Church of Ireland, she was educated at St. Michael's National School, Pery Square, Villiers School and Trinity College Dublin, where she graduated with a BA in Modern Languages and Literature. Having obtained a Higher Diploma in Education and a Diploma in Montessori Education she worked for some years as a teacher, both in the pre-school and secondary sectors. Later, she married Dr. Paul O'Sullivan and lived for some years in Canada.[318]

On her return from Canada, Jan O'Sullivan became involved in public life. Like her predecessor Terry Kelly (mayor 1983–84), she was heavily involved in the women's movement in Limerick. She also became involved in leftwing

Jan O'Sullivan
(Limerick City Archives)

politics through the influence of Jim Kemmy, whom she greatly admired. Along with Kemmy, she became a founder member of the Democratic Socialist Party in 1982, and remained a member until it merged with the Labour Party in 1990, at which point she joined Labour. Jan O'Sullivan was elected a member of Limerick City Council in 1985, and remained a councillor until 2003, having been returned at two subsequent local elections.[319]

In June 1993, Jan O'Sullivan became the third female mayor of Limerick and only the second Protestant to have held this office since 1877 (ironically, the only other Protestant to have been mayor since that date was also female, Frances Condell). Her religion caused controversy in March 1994 when she was not permitted to read the lesson at the Mass held in St. John's Cathedral to mark the opening of the Civic Week Festival. This move, carried out on the instructions of the then Catholic bishop of Limerick, Dr. Jeremiah Newman (himself a freeman of Limerick) provoked a good deal of unfavourable comment at the time. Apart from this unfortunate incident, Jan O'Sullivan's mayoralty was a very successful one.[320] Among its high points were the opening of the University Concert Hall in 1993 and the publication of a plan to regenerate the historic King's Island. Jan O'Sullivan regarded the role of mayor as being primarily a ceremonial one of representing the city and its people and in this she was eminently successful.[321]

In addition to her career in local politics, Jan O'Sullivan has become a significant figure in the national sphere. She was a member of the Senate from 1993 to 1997, and served as leader of the Labour group there. She was the also the third and last mayor of Limerick to be simultaneously a senator. During this period, she was a member of the Forum for Peace and Reconciliation and the National Economic and Social Forum. Following the death of Jim Kemmy in 1997, a by-election was held in Limerick East on 11 March 1998, at which Jan O'Sullivan was elected to the Dáil. She was returned at the 2002 and 2007 general elections and at the time of writing is the Labour Party spokesperson on health.[322]

In consequence of the abolition of the dual mandate under the Local Government (Number 2) Act, Jan O'Sullivan resigned from Limerick City Council in 2003. She was also a member of the Limerick City VEC and of the Mid-Western Health Board. She is currently a member of the board of the Island Theatre Company, the Daghdha Dance Company, the Rape Crisis Centre and the Red Ribbon Project, and is a member of Amnesty International, CARA (Ireland) Housing Association, and the Limerick-Quimper Twinning Committee. She resides at 7 Lanahrone Avenue, Corbally, Limerick.[323]

Dick Sadlier 1994–95, 2001–02 and 2003–04.

Richard A. (usually known as Dick) Sadlier was born in Limerick city on 2 August 1950 and brought up in 3 Wickham Street, where his family had a public house. Indeed the extended Sadlier family, who have lived in Limerick for centuries, owned several licensed premises in the city at this period. Dick Sadlier was educated at the Presentation National School and at the CBS Sexton Street, where one of his teachers was Tony Bromell (mayor 1982–83). From 1968 to 1972, Dick Sadlier was a student at University College Cork, and graduated with a Bachelor of Commerce degree, and soon after he qualified as a management accountant. He worked in private practice for a number of years and for a time was also involved in running the *Limerick Weekly Echo*, a venerable and successful local newspaper. In 1980, Dick Sadlier became a lecturer in business studies in the School of Professional Studies, one of the constituent colleges of the Limerick College of Art, Commerce and Technology (Limerick CoACT), and at the time of writing is one of the longest serving staff members of what is now the Limerick Institute of Technology.[324]

Dick Sadlier
(Dick Sadlier)

Dick Sadlier has been involved in public life for virtually all of his adult life. He was involved with the Fianna Fáil Party for many years, but when the Progressive Democratic Party was founded in 1985, he became a member and was one of three members of the new party elected to Limerick City Council in the local elections of 1991. Interestingly, all three PD councillors elected in 1991 later became Mayor of Limerick: John Quinn in 1992–93; Dick Sadlier in 1994–95, 2001–02 and 2003–04 and Kieran O'Hanlon in 1996–97. In 1999, Dick Sadlier returned to the Fianna Fáil Party. He served as mayor on three occasions and is one of only three mayors of Limerick since 1945 to have served for three terms or more, the other two being Ted Russell and Jack Bourke. He is also one of the few mayors of Limerick to have filled the office on more than one occasion while belonging to different political parties, Steve Coughlan and Ted Russell being two other notable examples.[325]

Dick Sadlier's first mayoralty from June 1994 to June 1995 was characterised by the rapid progress of the city's urban renewal programme. On 23 June 1995, Dr. Edward Walsh, the founder and first president of the University of Limerick, Dr. Brendan O'Regan first chairman of Shannon Development and the driving force behind the development of Shannon Airport and Town for some 30 years and Ted Russell former mayor of Limerick received the freedom of the city, the first recipients of this honour since 1979. During Dick Sadlier's second mayoralty, the freedom was conferred on Pat Cox, MEP and president of the European Parliament on 24 May 2002. One of the highpoints of his third mayoralty was the Day of Welcomes on 1 May 2004, when ten new member countries joined the European Union. In this connection, Limerick was linked with Slovenia and an extensive programme of events were held in the city to mark the occasion, at which the prime minister of Slovenia, Anton Rop, was the guest of honour. Also in 2004, Mayor Sadlier welcomed Romano Prodi, then president of the

European Commission, and at the time of writing prime minister of Italy and Pat Cox, then president of the European Parliament, when they paid an official visit to Limerick City Hall.[326]

Dick Sadlier was also a member of the Limerick City VEC, the Mid-West Regional Authority and the General Council of County Councils. At the local elections of 2004, he lost his seat on the council, but he continues to be active in public life. He is a member of Limerick Civic Trust and is on the governing body of the Limerick Institute of Technology. He is a lifelong member of Young Munster RFC and an avid supporter of both the Limerick soccer and hurling teams. He is currently residing at 11 Plassey Grove, Castletroy, Limerick.[327]

Jim Kemmy 1995–96.
See above under 1991–92.

Kieran O'Hanlon 1996–97.

Kieran O'Hanlon
(Copper Reid Studio)

Kieran O'Hanlon was born in Limerick city on 4 June 1952 and was brought up in the Pennywell area of Limerick city, where Jack Danagher (mayor 1964–65) and Paddy Kiely (Mayor 1972–73) also lived. He was educated at St. John's Infants School, St. Patrick's Boys National School and St. Munchin's College, in which school, both Thady Coughlan (mayor 1975–76) and Paddy Madden (mayor 1988–89 and 1990–91) were a year ahead of him. Later he attended the Municipal Technical Institute, O'Connell Avenue, and became an electrician, serving his apprenticeship in Shannon Diamond and Carbide, in Shannon, County Clare. After working for a time in Cement Limited in Mungret, near Limerick city, Kieran O'Hanlon secured a position with Wyeth Nutritionals Ireland in Askeaton, where he has been employed for over thirty years.[328]

Kieran O'Hanlon came from a family with a strong political background. His grandfather fought in the War of Independence and his father was involved in Clann na Poblachta and was a friend and political associate of both Steve Coughlan and Ted Russell. Kieran himself was a lifelong friend of Jim Kemmy and canvassed for him at a number of elections. When the Progressive Democrat Party was founded in 1985, Kieran O'Hanlon became a founder member and was one of three PD councillors elected to Limerick City Council in 1991. Interestingly, all three of them later served as mayor of Limerick: John Quin in 1992–93, Dick Sadlier in 1994–95, 2001–02 and 2003–04 and Kieran O'Hanlon in 1996–97.[329]

Kieran O'Hanlon was mayor from June 1996 to June 1997, the last Progressive Democrat to be first citizen of Limerick. He was particularly honoured to be mayor in the year of the octocentenary of Limerick Corporation. Two interesting books were published to mark the anniversary: *Limerick City in Old Picture Postcards* by Jim Kemmy and Larry Walsh and *Remembering Limerick. Historical Essays Celebrating the 800th Anniversary of Limerick's First Charter granted in 1197*, which was edited by David Lee. Also an extra link, presented by Wyeth Nutritionals Ireland, was added to the mayoral chain.

One of the major themes of Kieran O'Hanlon's mayoralty was promoting peace in Northern Ireland and encouraging cross-border co-operation. He is a strong supporter of the Irish Peace Institute, based at the University of Limerick, which had been founded by Dr. Brendan O'Regan, a freeman of Limerick, in 1984. At Christmas 1996, Kieran O'Hanlon organised a peace march by candle- light through Limerick in which a large number of people, including the Catholic and Protestant bishops, participated. He also promoted peace and reconciliation and spoke against the Provisional IRA during visits to the USA. Among the highpoints of Kieran O'Hanlon's mayoralty were the opening of the Hunt Museum by Taoiseach John Bruton on 14 February 1997, and the granting of the freedom of Limerick to John and Trudy Hunt on 4 July 1997.[330]

A keen sportsman, Kieran O'Hanlon has been involved with Richmond RFC, St. Michael's Rowing Club and St. Patrick's GAA Club all his life. During his mayoralty he was delighted that the Limerick senior hurling team won the Munster final and reached the All-Ireland Final, that local club Fairview FC won the FAI Junior Cup, that Richmond RFC attained senior status and that Shannon RFC won the AIL for the third year in succession. At the time of writing, Kieran O'Hanlon is chairman of Limerick City VEC, and is a member of the Shannon Foynes Port Company. He has also served as chairman of the Mid-West Regional Authority. Kieran O'Hanlon is currently a member of Limerick City Council and resides at Rhebogue, Dublin Road, Limerick.[331]

Frank Leddin 1997–98.
See above under 1965–66.

Joe Harrington 1998–99.
The only Kerryman to have become mayor of Limerick since 1842, James Joseph (always known as Joe) Harrington was born on 16 May 1948 in Lyreacrompane, which is situated between Listowel and Castleisland and between Tralee and Abbeyfeale. He was educated at Lyreacrompane National School and the Vocational School Listowel and later worked in a variety of places, including a three-year period in Australia. After working for a period as a toolmaker in Shannon, he secured a position in the Mid-Western Health Board (which was

subsumed into the Health Service Executive in 2005) where he is currently employed as a supervisor in St. Joseph's Hospital in Limerick.[332]

Joe Harrington
(Copper Reid Studio)

From an early age, Joe Harrington was involved in the trade union movement and leftwing politics. He is a lifelong socialist. In the late 1960s and early 1970s he was a member of People's Democracy, a leftist group whose most famous members were Bernadette Devlin McAliskey and Michael Farrell and he was later involved in Trotskyite groups affiliated to the Fourth International. However he was usually classified as an Independent during his period as a member of Limerick City Council of which he was a member from 1985 to 1999. During his period as a councillor, Joe Harrington resided in O'Malley Park, Southill and continued the work begun by Tommy Allen (mayor 1981–82) in representing that area in the city council. He stood unsuccessfully for the Dáil in the general Elections of 1977, 1981, 1982 and 1992.[333]

Joe Harrington served as mayor of Limerick from June 1998 to June 1999. His priority as mayor was to make both the office of mayor and Limerick City Hall more accessible to community groups from disadvantaged areas, which in many instances, felt alienated from the local government system. As a native of rural Ireland who was also a resident in a large urban housing estate, Mayor Harrington also worked to bridge the traditional urban-rural divide and did so with considerable success, due in part to the success of his *Rambling House* radio series, which had made him a familiar figure in County Limerick. Perhaps the most notable event of Joe Harrington's mayoralty was the visit of the US president, Bill Clinton to Limerick city in September 1998. As a well-known and outspoken opponent of American foreign policy, Joe Harrington had the difficult task of welcoming the president to the city, while remaining true to his principles. However, Mayor Harrington presided over the visit with distinction and Bill Clinton was given the freedom of Limerick on 5 September 1998, in recognition of his role in the Northern Ireland Peace Process.[334]

Joe Harrington did not contest the local elections of 1999 but is still very active in public life. His main interests are traditional Irish music, folklore and local history. The *Irish Rambling House* began in the late 1980s when Joe Harrington travelled all over North Munster recording traditional singers, musicians, story-tellers and other artistes in their communities. In 1998, he began presenting a weekly *Rambling House* programme on Limerick local radio on which these recordings were broadcast and thus introduced them to a much wider audience. In March 1999, during his mayoralty, Joe Harrington produced the largest traditional Irish concert ever staged in Limerick city when 130 of the artistes from his radio series took part in a show staged in the University Concert Hall as part of the Civic Week Festival. In 2000, the Limerick Millennium Civic Week Festival was opened with a similar concert at the same venue also produced by Joe Harrington. Since then he has brought the Rambling House with a cast of between twenty and thirty artistes on tour to Irish centres all over Britain. There have also been *Rambling House* Summer shows in various hotels; concerts held all over Munster and several videos produced that have sold very well all over Ireland and Britain.[335] Joe Harrington is also the editor of the *Lyreacrompane and District Journal* which first appeared in 1990 and he is involved in many other community activities in both Lyreacrompane and Limerick.[336]

Jack Bourke 1999–2000.

See above under 1968–69.

John Ryan 2000–01.

John Ryan
(Copper Reid Studio)

John Ryan was born in Limerick city on 4 November 1959 and brought up in the Sandmall on the banks of the Abbey River. He was educated in St. Mary's National School, the CBS Sexton Street and St. Munchin's College. Later he was a student in the National Institute of Higher Education (which in 1989 became the University of Limerick), graduating in 1981 with a Diploma in Business Studies. During his period in NIHE, John Ryan was actively involved in the Union of Students in Ireland (USI) and served as national vice-president from 1980 to 1981, defeating Joe Duffy (now the well-known broadcaster) in the election for the position. Subsequently he graduated from the Open University with a BSc Degree and is currently employed as a lecturer in the Limerick Institute of Technology (where Dick Sadlier is also a lecturer).[337]

John Ryan was first elected to the city council in 1991 and is still a member, having been successfully returned in the 1999 and 2004 local elections. He was a member of the Workers Party for a number of years and when the party split in 1992, he joined the newly established Democratic Left Party. He stood as a candidate for the party in the Limerick East constituency in the general elections of 1992 and 1997 and the by-election of 1998, but was unsuccessful on all three occasions, although he was only narrowly defeated in 1997. In 1999, he became a member of the Labour Party, when Democratic Left merged with Labour.[338]

In June 2000, John Ryan became the first mayor of Limerick elected in the new millennium. One of the highlights of his mayoralty was the J.P. McManus Invitation Pro-Am Golf Tournament (an event held in Limerick every five years by the eponymous businessman and philanthropist at which huge amounts of money are raised for charity). Among the celebrities that attended in 2000 were Taoiseach Bertie Ahern and broadcaster Gay Byrne. On 4 May 2001, the freedom of Limerick was conferred on J. P. McManus and Bill Whelan, the Limerick-born composer of the music for *Riverdance*.[339]

John Ryan was chairman of the Limerick City Development Board for three years. One of his major policy interests is in education. He has been a member of the Limerick City VEC since 1991 and of the governing body of the National University of Ireland, Dublin since 2005. He has a particular interest in adult education and since 2002 has been president of Aontas, the National Association of Adult Education. From 1998, he was also a member of the European Association for the Education of Adults and is also vice-chairman of the Adult Education Board, which is a statutory sub-committee of the Limerick City VEC.[340]

Among John Ryan's principal recreations are cooking and rugby. He is currently living at 24 New Westfields, North Circular Road, Limerick.[341]

Dick Sadlier 2001–02.
See above under 1994–95.

John Cronin 2002–03.

John Cronin was born in Limerick on 19 January 1948 and was brought up in the Killeely area of Limerick city. He was educated at St. Lelia's National School, St Munchin's National School and the Municipal Technical Institute, O'Connell Avenue. He was employed for many years with the Danus Clothing Factory in Dominick Street until it closed in 1975, and then worked as a sales representative for a long period, before he obtained a post with the Mid-Western Health Board in St. Camillus' Hospital on Shelbourne Road.[342]

John Cronin
(Copper Reid Studio)

John Cronin has been very active in the voluntary sector in Limerick city for many years and has particularly involved in youth clubs. He is president of St. Munchin's Youth Exchange and has been involved in establishing links between Limerick youth clubs and their counterparts in the German town of Cloppenburg.[343]

John Cronin came from a politically aware background. His grandmother was a staunch Parnellite who still revered the memory of the fallen leader until her dying day. John has been active in the Fianna Fáil Party for many years and was elected to Limerick City Council in 1999. He served as mayor from June 2002 to June 2003. One of the highpoints of his mayoralty was the hosting by Limerick city of athletes from Slovenia who were participating in the Special Olympic World Games, held in Dublin in June 2003. In 2002, Limerick won the All-Ireland Under-21 hurling championship for the third year in succession while the Munster rugby team won the Celtic Cup in 2003, two sporting events that John Cronin recalls as being among the leading events of his mayoralty. In the field of culture, the Wagner Ring Festival that was held in the University Concert Hall in August 2002 was a remarkable event as it was only the second time ever (the first had been in 1913) that the entire Ring Cycle by Richard Wagner, the most colossal work in the history of music, had been performed in Ireland.[344]

John Cronin continues to be a member of Limerick City Council and is also a member of the Limerick City VEC and the Limerick City Enterprise Board. He is currently living at 48 Belfield Crescent, Farranshone, Limerick.[345]

Dick Sadlier 2003–04.

See above under 1994–95.

Michael Hourigan 2004–05.

Born in Limerick city, Michael Hourigan was educated at Ahane National School, near Castleconnell, County Limerick and at St. Flannan's College, Ennis, County Clare. He has worked all his life as a public servant and is currently employed in the rural economy division of Teagasc, the Irish Agriculture and Food Development Authority. He has strong roots in both Limerick city and county and is thus well placed to bridge the divide that is sometimes held to exist between urban and rural Ireland.[346]

Michael Hourigan
(Copper Reid Studio)

Michael Hourigan is a member of a family with a long and distinguished involvement in the Fine Gael Party. His cousin Paddy Hourigan was a member of Limerick County Council from 1972 to 2004 and was cathaoirleach (a position analogous to mayor) from 1993 to 1994. Paddy's brother Richard was a member of the Senate from 1983 to 1987 and from 1989 to 1992 and was a very prominent figure in the Irish Farmers Association for many years. Michael Hourigan was elected a member of Limerick City Council in 1999 and returned in the 2004 local elections. He served as mayor from June 2004 to June 2005. One of the highlights of his mayoralty was the visit of Princess Anne, the Princess Royal, to Limerick on 10 September 2004. She was the most senior member of the British Royal family to visit the city since the Prince and Princess of Wales in 1885, but in contrast to that occasion, when Mayor Stephen O'Mara and Limerick Corporation had refused to extend an official welcome to the Royal couple, Mayor Hourigan received Princess Anne in the City Hall with great cordiality and presented her with gifts of Irish Dresden china and a Munster rugby jersey. Mayor Hourigan also welcomed President Mary McAleese and her husband to the City Hall on the 28 February 2005. Another major event was the granting of the freedom of Limerick to the brothers Fr. Aengus and Fr. Jack Finucane who were honoured for their involvement in third world famine relief, and Ciarán MacMathuna the well-known broadcaster and folklorist on 21 June 2005. Mayor Hourigan was also a tireless advocate of the extension of the boundary of Limerick city and during his term of office, a formal application for an extension was made to the Minister for the Environment.[347]

Michael Hourigan continues to be a member of Limerick City Council and is also a member of the Limerick City VEC, City Development Board and Health Service Executive. He was formerly a member of the Mid-Western Health Board. He has a particular interest in the area of disability and special needs. A member of Limerick Golf Club and Na Piarsaigh and Ahane GAA Clubs, he is a strong supporter of Bohemians RFC. Michael Hourigan lives at 'Carrig Donn' Revington Park, North Circular Road, Limerick.[348]

Diarmuid Scully 2005–06.

Diarmuid Scully was born in Limerick city on 25 January 1972 and has lived virtually all of his life in Lynwood Park, situated in the Singland district of the city. He was educated at St. Patrick's Boys National School and the CBS Sexton Street. Later he attended the University of Limerick and graduated with a degree in Business Studies. While a student, he was actively involved in the Union of Students in Ireland and from 1992 to 1993, served as president of the UL branch of the Union. During this period, Diarmuid Scully also represented UL with distinction at the World Debating Championships. Following graduation,

Diarmuid Scully
(Copper Reid Studio)

he worked for five years as a technical support supervisor with Sykes Enterprise in Shannon and later became a fulltime public representative.[349]

A lifelong member of Fine Gael, Diarmuid Scully was first elected to Limerick City Council in 1999 and was re-elected in the 2004 local elections. He served as mayor of Limerick from June 2005 to June 2006, the youngest person to hold the position since Thady Coughlan in 1975–76. Appropriately enough, the youthful Mayor Diarmuid Scully did much to open the office to the young people of Limerick. During his mayoralty, the Young City Council, consisting of representatives from each secondary school in the city and from Limerick Youth Service was established and a Young City Mayor, Anthony Byrne from St. Enda's Community School elected. The Young City

Council met quarterly in the council chamber and also met with senior officials, in the same manner as the city council itself. Mayor Scully made further connections with the young people of Limerick by making weekly 'pod-casts' on matters of public interest.[350]

Diarmuid Scully also did much to promote Limerick during his mayoralty. He supported the appointment of street ambassadors to give advice and assistance to visitors to the city, worked to improve the scale and frequency of the festivals held and worked to establish twinning arrangements with various urban areas in Europe and North America. Like his predecessor, Michael Hourigan, he was a tireless supporter of the proposal to extend the city boundary. However, Diarmuid Scully describes the Munster rugby team winning the Heineken Cup on 20 May 2006 and the subsequent official welcome of the victorious team to Limerick city on the following day, at which he presided as mayor, as the highpoints of his mayoralty.[351]

Diarmuid Scully is still a member of Limerick City Council and is currently living at 19 Lynwood Park, Singland, Limerick.[352]

Joe Leddin 2006–07.

Born in Limerick on 18 June 1970, Joe Leddin lived at 47 Lansdowne Park on the city's Ennis Road throughout his childhood and youth. He attended the John Fitzgerald Kennedy Primary School and St. Nessan's Community College and having spent three years at the School of Professional Studies (which was then part of the Limerick College of Art, Commerce and Technology) graduated with a Diploma in Marketing and later studied for a year with the Marketing Institute of Ireland. At the time of writing, Joe Leddin is studying for a BA in Public Administration. From 1991 to 2005, he was employed with Cannon Office Equipment first as a sales representative and later as sales manager. In 2005, Joe Leddin was appointed parliamentary assistant to Jan O'Sullivan TD (mayor 1993–94).[353]

Joe Leddin
(Copper Reid Studio)

Joe Leddin is a member of one of Limerick's most distinguished political families. His grand uncle Mick Keyes was mayor of Limerick from 1928 to 1930, a TD from June to September 1927 and from 1932 to 1957, and was a cabinet minister from 1949 to 1951 and 1954 to 1957. Mick's son Christy was mayor of Limerick from 1957 to 1958. Two of Joe Leddin's uncles, Frank and Tim were also mayors of Limerick: Frank in 1965–66 and 1997–98 and Tim in 1987–88. Indeed members of the Keyes and Leddin families have continuously sat on Limerick City Council since 1925 and have provided the city with more mayors than any other family since the Verekers in the early nineteenth century. Given such a glittering tradition, it was not surprising that Joe Leddin became involved in politics at an early age, canvassing for his uncles. In the 1999 local elections, both Joe and his aunt Kathleen Leddin (widow of Tim) were elected to Limerick City Council. Both were also returned at the 2004 local elections.[354]

Joe Leddin was unanimously elected as mayor of Limerick and served from June 2006 to June 2007. Among the most important issues that he faced during his term of office were the extension of the city boundary, the pedestrianisation of the city centre and improvements in public transport. The highpoint of his mayoralty was the conferring of the freedom of Limerick on two famous and distinguished Limerick men on 15 June 2007: broadcaster and television personality Sir Terry Wogan and artist and former President of the Royal Hibernian Academy Dr. Thomas Ryan, RHA. In addition the magnificent Watch House Cross Library was officially opened by Mayor Leddin on 31 May 2007.[355] Joe Leddin is the most recent mayor to attach a roundel to the principal chain. It depicted the Treaty Stone on one side and the Clarion Hotel on the other symbolising the old and the new Limerick respectively. The roundel was presented by Mayor Leddin and his family, was sponsored by Leddin Finance Dublin (a business owned by his cousin and namesake Joe Leddin) and commemorated the contribution made to Limerick by the Leddin and Keyes families to the people of Limerick.

Joe Leddin is a member of Limerick City VEC, the Mid-West Regional Authority and the Southern and Eastern Regional Authority. He is a lifelong member of Limerick Boat Club, of which he was treasurer for twelve years and a staunch supporter of Young Munster RFC. He is currently living at 'Hillcrest', Summerville Avenue, South Circular Road, Limerick.[356]

Ger Fahy 2007–08.

Ger Fahy was born in Limerick on 24 October 1953 and was brought up in Marian Avenue, in the Janesboro area. He was educated in Janesboro National School and the CBS Sexton Street, the alma mater of so many mayors of Limerick over the past century. Since leaving school, Ger Fahy has spent all his working life in the hospitality industry. Between 1977 and 1994, he was involved in running the Mill Tavern (now known as Dolans) on the Dock Road and since then has worked for many years in the Spotted Dog public house in his native Janesboro.[357]

It was through his work in the bar trade that Ger Fahy first became interested in public life as he says that it gave him an insight into the minds of a wide cross-section of society over many years. A great admirer of Dr. Garret Fitzgerald, he was the first member of his family to get involved in politics and was asked to stand as a candidate for Fine Gael in the 1985 local elections, due to the resignation of former mayor Terry Kelly from politics. Ger Fahy was successful and served as a councillor for ward three (which included Janesboro) from 1985 to 1991. In the 1991 local elections, he increased his vote by 20% but still lost his seat as ward three was a particularly competitive one. Indeed the four candidates elected in ward three on that occasion– Joe Harrington, Jack Bourke, Frank Leddin and Jim Kemmy – served on the city council for a total of some 108 years and each of them occupied the mayoralty in the course of their careers. Unfortunately for Ger Fahy, the interval of eight years until the next local elections was the longest since that of 1934–42. However, he regained his seat on the council in ward three at the 1999 local elections and was re-elected in 2004 on the first count.[358]

Ger Fahy
(Egleston Brothers Photographers)

On 25 June 2007, Ger Fahy was unanimously elected mayor of Limerick to serve until June 2008. He has stated that the great respect with which the mayoralty is regarded was brought home to him in a very moving fashion when he attending Mass in his local church Our Lady Queen of Peace the following Saturday and received a round of applause from the congregation. Mayor Fahy regards accessibility and openness to the community at large as being the main priority of the mayoralty. He believes that social inclusion is one of the major challenges faced by modern Limerick but is also optimistic about the city's future. He believes that Limerick is the sporting capital of Ireland and that 'we are not shouting loudly enough from the rooftops about the major transformation in our city. We should hold our heads held high'.[359]

Ger Fahy's mayoralty commenced with a unique event when the fourth Earl of Dunraven, the only person ever struck from Limerick's roll of freedom was restored to it by unanimous vote of Limerick City Council on 2 July 2007. This was considered to be an appropriate action in view of the spectacular progress of the Northern Ireland peace process, and the notable contribution that had been made by Lord Dunraven to public life both locally and nationally.

Ger Fahy has been a member of Limerick Harbour Commissioners and is currently a member of the Mid-West Regional Authority. In December 1986, he became a founder member and continues to be a trustee of the Limerick Marine and Rescue Service, which provides a permanent professional rescue service for the city and its environs. In his youth Ger Fahy played hurling with Old Christians GAA Club and he has had a lifelong involvement with Janesboro FC soccer club, both as player and administrator.[360]

At the time of writing, Ger Fahy is the incumbent mayor of Limerick, the latest in an almost unbroken series of first citizens dating back 811 years.

Endnotes

1   For Daly's life see is O'Gríofa, 'John Daly', pp 197-204. See also Clarke, *Revolutionary Woman*, pp 11-66, 121-35.

2   O'Gríofa, 'John Daly', pp 197-99.

3   Clarke, *Revolutionary Woman*, p. 12.

4   Ibid., pp 20-23.

5   McKay, 'The Limerick Municipal Elections,' pp 3-10.

6   Herbert, 'Antiquities of the Corporation', p. 99.

7   Potter, *The Government and the People of Limerick*, p. 356-57.

8   O'Gríofa, 'John Daly', p. 203.

9   McKay, 'The Limerick Municipal Elections,' p. 8.

10 *Limerick Chronicle*, 2 August 1921.

11 Ibid.

12 CCM, 1 December 1897.

13 McKay, 'The Limerick Municipal Elections,' p. 8.

14 CCM, 20 October 1903.

15 CCM, 20 April 1904.

16 Ibid.

17 *Limerick Chronicle*, 25 September 1917.

18 O'Gríofa, 'Michael Joyce', p. 210.

19 Donnelly, 'Michael Joyce', pp 42-43.

20 O'Gríofa, 'Michael Joyce', p. 205.

21 For Joyce's electoral contests see Walker, *Parliamentary Election Results*, p. 360.

22 O'Gríofa, 'Michael Joyce', p. 209. 3

23 For Joyce and social housing, see Potter, *The Government and the People of Limerick*, p. 359-62.

24 O'Gríofa, 'Michael Joyce', p. 209-10.

25 Ibid.

26 *Limerick Chronicle*, 10 December 1932.

27 Herbert, 'Antiquities of the Corporation', p. 97.

28 *Limerick Chronicle*, 10 December 1932.

29 For the early history of the Donnellan family I am grateful to Mr. Michael Donnellan, grandson of Thomas Donnellan. For Thomas Donnellan's election to the Council see CCM, 28 November 1891.

30 McKay, 'The Limerick Municipal Elections,' p. 7.

31 Potter, *The Government and the People of Limerick*, p. 538.

32 CCM, 30 January 1920.

33 *Limerick Chronicle*, 4 March 1924.

34 Information from Mr. Michael Donnellan.

35 *Limerick Chronicle*, 8 July 1930.

36 CCM, 17 January 1905.

37 *Limerick Chronicle*, 8 July 1930.

38   Information from Mr. Tadhg Moloney.

39   *Limerick Chronicle*, 8 July 1930.

40   *Limerick Leader*, 9 September 1953.

41   *Limerick Chronicle*, 17 January 1911.

42   Crosbie, 'Era of Radicalism', pp 213-16.

43   Ibid., pp 214-16.

44   *Limerick Leader*, 9 September 1953.

45   *Limerick Chronicle*, 5 January 1920.

46   *Limerick Leader*, 9 September 1953.

47   *Who was Who 1951-1950. A Companion to Who's Who containing the Biographies of those who died during the Decade 1941-1950*, (London, 1952), p. 948.

48   For John Quin, see *Limerick Chronicle*, 13 February 1883.

49   *Who was Who 1951-1950*, p. 948.

50   Ibid.

51   McKay, 'The Limerick Municipal Elections,' pp 4-7.

52   CCM, 17 January 1914.

53   Crosbie, 'Era of Radicalism', pp 216-21.

54   CCM, 1 June 1916.

55   For this episode see Ryan, '1916 Rising-The Limerick Connection', pp 236-40.

56   Crosbie, 'Era of Radicalism', pp 219-21.

57   Ibid.

58   CCM, 18 January 1918, quoted in John O'Callaghan, 'Republican Administration of Local Government in Limerick 1920-21' in *North Munster Antiquarian Journal*, Vol. 45 (2005), p. 120.

59   *Who was Who 1951-1950*, p. 948. For streets named after Quin and his family, see Joyce, *Limerick City Street* Names, p. 46.

60   http://humphrysfamilytree.com/OMeara/contents.html.

61   Crosbie, 'Era of Radicalism', p. 221.

62   CCM, 18 January 1920.

63   Crosbie, 'Era of Radicalism', p. 221.

64   Potter, *The Government and the People of Limerick*, pp 370-74.

65   Ibid., pp 374-75.

66   *Limerick Leader*, 17 February 1958. See also http://humphrysfamilytree.com/OMeara/contents.html.

67   Jim Kemmy, 'The Killing of Michael O'Callaghan', in Lee, *Remembering Limerick*, p. 260.

68   For Kate O'Callaghan, see Sinéad McCoole, *No Ordinary Women. Irish Female Activists in the Revolutionary Years 1900-1923*, (Dublin, 2003), pp 190-91. For the Murphy sisters and their role in Mary Immaculate College, see Sister Loreto O'Connor, *Passing on the Torch: A History of Mary Immaculate College 1898-1998*, (Limerick, 1998), p. 20.

69   Ibid. See also Kemmy, 'The Killing of Michael O'Callaghan', p. 260-1.

70   CCM, 17 January 1911.

71   For O'Callaghan and the Black and Tans, see O'Connor, *Passing on the Torch*, p. 23. For the RIC raid on the Town Hall see CCM, 30 January 1920.

72   CCM, 18 November 1920.

73   Kemmy, 'The Killing of Michael O'Callaghan', p. 261. See also Ryan, 'Who Shot the Mayors?', pp 262-64.

74   Joyce, *Limerick City Street Names*, pp 41-42.

75   McCoole, *No Ordinary Women*, p. 191.

76   For Clancy see Kemmy, ' George Clancy- Murdered Mayor', pp 250-52 and 'Portrait of the Martyr as a Young Man', pp 252-60.

77   Kemmy, ' George Clancy- Murdered Mayor', pp 250-52.

78   Joyce, *Limerick City Street* Names, p. 23.

79   Kemmy, 'James Casey-Soviet Treasurer', pp 264-66.

80   http://humphrysfamilytree.com/OMeara/contents.html.

81   CCM, 22 March 1921.

82   O'Gríofa, 'Stephen O'Mara', p. 268-73.

83   CCM, 21 May 1921.

84   O'Gríofa, 'Stephen O'Mara', p. 268.

85   CCM, 30 January 1922.

86   Ibid., p. 270.

87   See Ryan, 'Armed Conflict in Limerick', pp 274-76.

88   O'Gríofa, 'Stephen O'Mara', p. 273.

89   *Limerick Leader*, 11 November 1959. See also http://humphrysfamilytree.com/OMeara/contents.html.

90   *Limerick Chronicle*, 21 January 1961. I am grateful for information on Maire O'Donovan which I have received from Mr. Eugene O'Callaghan and Fr. Brian Murphy of Glenstal Abbey, Murroe, County Limerick.

91   *Limerick Chronicle*, 21 January 1961. See also McCoole, *No Ordinary Women*, p. 190-91.

92   *Limerick Chronicle*, 21 January 1961. For the Murphy sisters and Mary Immaculate College, see O'Connor, Passing on the Torch, p. 20.

93   *Limerick Chronicle*, 21 January 1961.

94   CCM, 7 April 1921.

95   CCM, 21 May 1921.

96   CCM, 30 January 1922.

97   CCM, 5 December 1921.

98   O'Gríofa, 'Stephen O'Mara', p. 268.

99   *Limerick Chronicle*, 21 January 1961.

100 De Courcy and Cunningham, 'Bob de Courcy', P. 277.

101 Ibid.

102 CCM, 7 April 1921.

103 De Courcy and Cunningham, 'Bob de Courcy', P. 277-79.

104 *Limerick Chronicle*, 18 October 1923.

105 CCM, 30 June 1925.

106 *Limerick Chronicle*, 21 January 1961.

107 De Courcy and Cunningham, 'Bob de Courcy', P. 277.

108 *Limerick Chronicle*, 4 April 1931.

109 *Limerick Chronicle*, 9 December 1922 and 27 June 1925.

110 CCM, 30 June 1925.

111 Potter, *The Government and the People of Limerick*, p. 386.

112 T.P. MacDiarmada, City Manager and Town Clerk, *The Mayoral Chain*, (Limerick, No date of publication), p. 7.

113 *Limerick Chronicle*, 4 April 1931.

114 Information from Mr. Bryan McHugh.

115 *Limerick Leader*, 20 November 1944.

116 *Limerick Chronicle*, 25 June 1925.

117 *Limerick Chronicle*, 25 November 1944.

118 *Limerick Chronicle*, 17 November 1934.

119 *Limerick Leader*, 20 November 1944.

120 *Limerick Leader*, 9 September 1959.

121 Ibid.

122 Ibid.

123 Potter, *The Government and the People of Limerick*, p. 459.

124 Ibid., p. 539.

125 *Limerick Leader*, 9 September 1959.

126 For Keyes and the boundary extension of 1950, see Potter, *The Government and the People of Limerick*, pp 428-32.

127 *Limerick Leader*, 9 September 1959. For an interesting profile of Michael Keyes, see Niall Greene, "Mick Keyes-The Foundation of Labour in Limerick' in *Welcome to Limerick. Labour Party Conference 1995* (No place of publication, 1995), pp 37-39.

128 Information from Mr. Michael Donnellan, son of Mayor Patrick Donnellan. Sae also *Irish Times*, 15 January 1977 and *Limerick Chronicle*, 15 Janaury 1977.

129 Ibid.

130 For the MacLysaght Enquiry, see Potter, *The Government and the People of Limerick*, pp 398-401.

131 Ibid., pp 394, 416.

132 Ibid., for Donnellan's Buildings, p.392. For Donnellan and the VEC see *Limerick Leader*, 15 January 1977.

133 Ibid.

134 Information from Mr. Michael Donnellan.

135 *Limerick Leader*, 28 June 1967.

136 MacDiarmada, *The Mayoral Chain*, pp 8-9.

137 Potter, *The Government and the People of Limerick*, pp 412-13.

138 *Limerick Leader*, 28 June 1967.

139 Kemmy, 'James Casey-Soviet Treasurer', pp 264-65.

140 Ibid.

141 Ibid.

142 Ibid.

143 Ibid.

144 *Limerick Chronicle*, 15 April 1952.

145 Ibid.

146 For details of Limerick public representatives, see Potter, *The Government and the People of Limerick*, pp 458-62.

147 Ibid., p. 539.

148 *Limerick Chronicle*, 15 April 1952.

149 Joyce, *Limerick City Street* Names, p. 19.

150 *Limerick Chronicle*, 9 December 1965.

151 Ibid.

152 *Limerick Leader*, 10 February 1969.

153 *Limerick Chronicle*, 28 November 1963. I am grateful for information from Mr. Paddy Reidy, son of James Reidy.

154 *Limerick Chronicle*, 17 November 1934.

155 Browne and Farrell, *Magill Book of Irish Politics*, pp 244-45, 248-49.

156 *Limerick Chronicle*, 28 November 1963.

157 Information from Mr. Michael Donnellan.

158 For places named after Reidy see Joyce, *Limerick City Street* Names, p. 47. For his obituary, see *Limerick Chronicle*, 28 November 1963.

159 *Limerick Leader*, 4 July 1964.

160 Ibid.

161 MacDiarmada, *The Mayoral Chain*, p. 9.

162 *Limerick Leader*, 4 July 1964.

163 Ibid.

164 *Limerick Leader*, 15 June 1976.

165 Mae Leonard, 'A Dandy Man', (Unpublished article).

166 *Limerick Leader*, 22 August 1959.

167 Potter, *The Government and the People of Limerick*, pp 451-52, 539.

168 *Limerick Leader*, 22 August 1959.

169 *Limerick Leader*, 16 and 21 September 1991.

170 Ibid.

171 Ibid.

172 *Limerick Chronicle*, 3 November 1962.

173 Potter, *The Government and the People of Limerick*, p. 393.

174 *Limerick Chronicle*, 3 November 1962.

175 Act 1 of 1950.

176 Act 24 of 1950.

177 *Limerick Chronicle*, 3 November 1962. I am grateful to Mr. Tony Dillon for information on his father Gerard Dillon.

178 *Limerick Leader*, 19 June 1969.

179 Ibid.

180 *Limerick Leader*, 24 December 1994.

181 Ibid.

182 Ibid. I am also grateful for information from Mr. Thady Coughlan, son of Stephen Coughlan.

183 Browne and Farrell, *Magill Book of Irish Politics*, pp 249-51.

184 *Limerick Leader*, 24 December 1994.

185 Browne and Farrell, *Magill Book of Irish Politics*, pp 250-51.

186 Ibid.

187 *Limerick Leader*, 24 December 1994. Information from Mr. Thady Coughlan.

188 *Limerick Chronicle*, 13 July 1968. I am grateful for information from Mr. Richard Carew, son of John Carew.

189 *Limerick Chronicle*, 13 July 1968.

190 Ibid.

191 Browne and Farrell, *Magill Book of Irish Politics*, pp 249-50.

192 *Limerick Chronicle*, 13 July 1968.

193 Joyce, *Limerick City Street* Names, p. 20.

194 Mary Fennelly (ed.), *Limerick Lives*, (Limerick, 1996), p. 143.

195 Yeoman, ' George E. (Ted) Russell', p. 324.

196 *Limerick Leader*, 4 December 2004.

197 Browne and Farrell, *Magill Book of Irish Politics*, pp 248-51.

198 Fennelly, *Limerick Lives* p. 143.

199 *Limerick Leader*, 4 December 2004.

200 Yeoman, 'Throwing the Dart', pp 327-32

201 Yeoman, 'George E. (Ted) Russell', p. 324-27.

202 *Limerick Leader*, 4 December 2004.

203 Ibid.

204 Ibid.

205 Information from Mr. Frank Prendergast.

206 Ibid.

207 *Limerick Leader*, 18 March 2006

208 Mark and John Liddy, 'J.P. (Rory) Liddy', in Lee, *Remembering Limerick*, p. 355.

209 *Limerick Leader*, 28 August 1989.

210 MacDiarmada, *The Mayoral Chain*, p. 8.

211 *Limerick Leader*, 28 August 1989.

212 Joyce, *Limerick City Street* Names, p. 36.

213 *Limerick Leader*, 29 December 1990.

214 Ibid.

215 Ibid.

216 Proinsias MacAonghusa, 'Donogh O'Malley' in Jim Kemmy (ed), *The Limerick Anthology*, (Dublin 1996), p. 127.

217 *Limerick Leader*, 11 March 1968.

218 Browne and Farrell, *Magill Book of Irish Politics*, pp 249-50.

219 Proinsias MacAonghusa, 'Donogh O'Malley' in Jim Kemmy (ed) *The Limerick Compendium*, (Dublin 1997), p. 296.

220 Ibid., pp 296-98.

221 MacAonghusa, 'Donogh O'Malley' in *The Limerick Anthology* pp 127-28.

222 *Limerick Leader*, 11 March 1968.

223 Ibid.

224 Ibid.

225 Joyce, *Limerick City Street* Names, p. 44.

226 *Limerick Leader*, 30 January 1973.

227 Ibid.

228 Ibid.

229 Joyce, *Limerick City Street* Names, p. 31.

230 For Frances Condell see O'Gríofa, 'First Citizen Meets First Citizen,' pp 363-66.

231 *Limerick Leader*, 15 November 1986.

232 Ibid.

233 O'Gríofa, 'First Citizen Meets First Citizen,' pp 363-66.

234 Ibid.

235 Joyce, *Limerick City Street* Names, pp 24-25.

236 *Limerick Leader*, 26 April 1969.

237 *Limerick Chronicle*, 1 July 1965.

238 Ibid.

239 Joyce, *Limerick City Street* Names, p. 27.

240 *Limerick Chronicle*, 1 July 1965 and *Limerick Leader*, 17 August 2002.

241 *Limerick Chronicle*, 1 July 1965.

242 CCM, 3 October 1997.

243 *Limerick Leader*, 17 August 2002.

244 *Limerick Leader*, 30 January 1988.

245 Ibid.

246 Ibid.

247 *Limerick Leader*, 30 January 1988. For P.J. Bourke, see Cheryl Herr (ed.), *For the Land They Loved. Irish Political Melodramas 1890-1925*, (Syracuse, New York, 1991).

248 Information from Mr. Jack Bourke.

249 Ibid.

250 Ibid. See also Fennelly, *Limerick Lives*, p. 15.

251 Information from Mr. Jack Bourke.

252 Ibid.

253 Information from Mr. Gus O'Driscoll.

254 Ibid.

255 Ibid.

256 Ibid.

257 Information from Mr. Paddy Kiely.

258 Ibid.

259 Ibid.

260 Ibid.

261 *Limerick Leader*, 24 October, 1987.

262 Browne and Farrell, *Magill Book of Irish Politics*, pp 250-51.

263 *Limerick Leader*, 24 October, 1987.

264 Information from Councillor Patrick Kennedy.

265 Ibid.

266 Ibid.

267 Ibid.

268 Information from Mr.Thady Coughlan.

269 Ibid.

270 Ibid.

271 Inforrmation from Mr. Frank Prendergast.

272 *Who's Who in Catholic Life*, (Manchester, 2003), p. 309.

273 Ibid.

274 Ibid and information from Mr. Frank Prendergast.

275 Ibid.

276 Information from Mr. Bobby Byrne.

277 Ibid.

278 *The Visit. John Paul II in Ireland. A Historical Record*, (Dublin 1979), p. 82.

279 Information from Mr. Bobby Byrne.

280 Ibid.

281 Information from Mr. Clem Casey.

282 Ibid.

283 Michael O'Flaherty, *The Story of Young Munster Rugby Football Club 1895/96 –1995/96. A Celebration of 100 Years of Football*, (Limerick, 1995), p. 350.

284 Ibid., p. 351.

285 Ibid., dust jacket.

286 Information from Mr. Clem Casey.

287 *Limerick Leader*, 20 August 1994.

288 Ibid.

289 Ibid.

290 Information from Mr. Tony Bromell. For a detailed account of his life, see Tony Bromell, *Rian Mo Chos Ar Ghaineamh an tSaoil*, (Galway, 2006).

291 For an account of the LUPC and its predecessors, see Pat Kearney, 'Towards a University for Limerick 1934-1972' in *The Old Limerick Journal*, No 27, (Autumn, 1990), pp 45-56.

292 Information from Mr. Tony Bromell.

293 Ibid.

294 Ibid.

295 For Anthony Barry, see O'Callaghan, *The Lord Mayors of Cork*, pp 112-14.

296 For Peter Barry, see O'Callaghan, *The Lord Mayors of Cork*, pp 127-28.

297 Ibid.

298 *Limerick Leader*, 30 October 1999.

299 Ibid.

300 Ibid.

301 Information from Mr. Paddy Madden.

302 Ibid.

303 Ibid.

304 *Limerick Leader*, 27 September 1997.

305 *Limerick Leader*, 29 September 1997.

306 *Limerick Leader*, 27 September 1997.

307 Ibid.

308 Ibid.

309 Ibid.

310 Ibid.

311 Ibid.

312 Ibid.

313 For the text of Gearóid O'Tuathaigh's panegyric, see *The Old Limerick Journal,* No 34, (Summer, 1998), pp 3-4.

314 Information from Mr. John Quinn.

315 Ibid.

316 Ibid.

317 Ibid.

318 Information from Deputy Jan O'Sullivan.

319 Ibid.

320 *Irish Times,* 17 March 1994 and *Limerick Leader,* 19 March 1994.

321 Information from Deputy Jan O'Sullivan.

322 Ibid.

323 Ibid.

324 Information from Mr. Dick Sadlier.

325 Ibid.

326 Ibid.

327 Ibid.

328 Information from Councillor Kieran O'Hanlon.

329 Ibid.

330 Ibid.

331 Ibid.

332 Information from Mr. Joe Harrington.

333 Ibid.

334 Ibid.

335 For the Rambling House, see www.irishramblinghouse.com

336 See www.lyreacrompane.com

337 Information from Councillor John Ryan.

338 Ibid.

339 Ibid.

340 Ibid.

341 Ibid.

342 Information from Councillor John Cronin.

343 Ibid.

344 Ibid.

345 Ibid.

346 Information from Councillor Michael Hourigan.

347 Ibid.

348 Ibid.

349 Information from Councillor Diarmuid Scully. See also www.diarmuidscully.com

350 Ibid.

351 Ibid.

352 Ibid.

353 Information from Mayor Joe Leddin.

354 Ibid.

355 *Limerick Leader,* 2 and 16 June 2007.

356 Information from Mayor Joe Leddin.

357 Information from Mayor Ger Fahy.

358 *Limerick Independent,* 4 July 2007.

359 Information from Mayor Ger Fahy.

360 Ibid.

Shawn-a-Scoob by Desmond O'Grady

The story of Shawn-a-Scoob the most famous legend of the Limerick mayoralty is here related by Desmond O'Grady, one of Limerick's greatest writers.

When a child I associated my maternal grandfather, whom I never knew, with a story my uncle Feathereye told me of a Limerickman by the name of Shawn-a-Scoob. This was an old story also celebrated in verse by the Limerick poet Michael Hogan, the Bard of Thomond. The story has foundation in fact and the characters really lived and breathed the local fresh air, but after it got into the Bard's hands and he had done with it, his version became the one generally accepted by local storytellers.

It appears the city of Limerick was in crisis. The City Fathers had failed to elect a new Mayor. Session after session resulted in a deadlock. The Fathers could not settle on any one of themselves and no citizen would take on the responsibilities of so badgerable an office.

The crisis bulged as the deadlock held. Finally one worthy Father came up with a suggestion: the first man to cross Thomond Bridge – which led out of town to the county Clare and the western seaboard – at dawn on the following Saturday morning, whether he liked it or not, wanted, willed or wished it, would be appointed Mayor of the city. Everybody agreed that this was an astonishingly simple and acceptable solution and for the first time in a long time the weighty and wide-waisted City Fathers were of one mind.

There lived in those far off days a man who went by the nickname of Shawn-a-Scoob to all who knew or saluted him. He lived with his good wife in a wattle hut out in Cratloe Woods. His profession, if humble, was an honest one. He was a maker of brooms and brushes. All week long he toiled at cutting twigs and gathering heather, gorse and bushes which he bound to long and short wooden shafts – depending on whether he was making a broom or a brush. Early every Saturday morning – lark and linnet high in the sky, early curlew, rooking crow – he would carry strapped to his back, the week's brooms to the marketplace in Limerick city where he stood over them, his fists in his pockets, and he sold them for an honest price. This is why he was called 'Shawn-a-Scoob, or John of the Brooms', for scoob means broom or brush in the Gaelic.

And so it was Shawn was the first man to cross the river Shannon by way of Thomond Bridge that Saturday morning when the City Fathers were waiting on the alert.

Shawn was hardly the length of his big toe across the Bridge, innocently dreaming his way to market and thinking his early morning thoughts when he was accosted by the entire Council of City Fathers.

This was no small surprise for Shawn.

Before he could draw breath and give voice to his amazement – for he knew them well enough by the rich robes of office they wore – they informed him there and then, on that infamous but historical spot, that he was the first male human to cross Thomond Bridge that morning, and as such was therefore, as of this most solemn moment, Mayor of the city. All that remained was the official ceremony of swearing in the taking office. And this, they assured him, would be put into effect, carried out and dispatched forthwith and without further delay.

They transported him immediately, voiceless and bewildered, to their great, neoclassical granite Town Hall with its towering columns, formal façade and carriage arcade. Once there, crowded into the regality of the robing room they vested him in the official robes of scarlet and ermine, hung the historic gold chain about his rough neck and shoved the symbolic silver mace into the palm of his country paw.

That night, in his befuddled honour, they held celebrations all over the town with lights and coloured bulbs, luminosities and brightly foreign fireworks. Meanwhile, in the offices the lesser clerical caste made arrangements for Shawn's Mayoral Parade through the streets of his city on the following morning, the Sabbath, before the entire population.

Back in Cratloe Woods, in his husbandman's wattle hut, Shawn's healthy and honourable wife began to wonder what in the world had happened to Shawn that he had not shown his face home the Saturday night. She came to the crestfallen conclusion that he must have fallen foul of drinking company in the town and that they had got him so boneless drunk he could not make the road home. Or maybe he met a young thing, flighty and easy, who had turned his head and led him heedlessly astray against his awareness. He might well, even at this very mortal moment, be lying prone and punctured in pride and pocket in a common gutter of the town or somewhere in the ditch by the side of the open road under the indifferent moon.

So, Sunday morning, when Shawn didn't show, she threw her long black shawl about her shoulders and started down the road for Limerick.

When she reached and crossed Thomond Bridge, she found the entire populace abroad in the streets in festive mood and the town's entirety decorated like a dandy for a great parade.

And then the parade swung into sight.

There were marching soldiers and soldiers on jogging horseback all spit and polish, buckles, buttons and brass. There was a brass band with whirling drumsticks and stomping band major with moustaches. There was the easy stride of the high ecclesiastical orders about the plain purpose of their own purple and gold-embroidered authority and in the middle of all, the centre and cause of attraction, rolled the delicately sprung, open, Mayoral coach, drawn by a snow white prancing horse with the Mayor himself, no less, seated within, smiling benignly and waving graciously to the cheering, flag-waving people of his city.

The poor woman could hardly believe the two eyes in her head. There, regally enthroned in the upholstered amplitude of the Mayoral carriage, a dazzling smile of surprised success and well-being as broad as a shark's on his porkchop, country-face, benignly waving, almost Papally blessing the delirious throng, rigged out in scarlet silk and ermine fur, with gold chain entangle and weighty mace in the crook of his arm, sat her one and only, larger than life, honest husband – Shawn-a-Scoob.

Certainly the sight gave her pause. But not for long. When reality reasserted itself, she moved. She rushed forward and out. Blind and senseless to all else about her, eyes wide and fixed on the image of himself before her, as in a trance or ecstatic transportation, she broke through the cheering throng calling 'Shawn! Shawn!'

Then she was at his side. One hand grasped at the French-polished carriagework, the other stretched forward in supplication.

'Shawn', she cried. Don't you know me? Don't you know me at all?'

His attention caught by her shrill voice, his head turned a moment away from the applauding populace, his celebrating people. He looked down at her from his Mayoral height. He looked deeply into her pleading eyes. His own eyes smoked. His brows arched. He raised his Mayoral hand as if in benediction and the scarlet stuff on his robe fell silkily back from his rough wrist. His features set gravely. His gaze had the penetration of some powerful prince of the Church.

'Shawn, Shawn. Don't you know me at all?' she cried again in her desperation.

'Get away home out of that woman', said Shawn grandly in one breath. 'Can't you see I don't even know myself!'.

List of the Provosts, Mayors, Bailiffs and Sheriffs of Limerick

The title of Limerick's first citizen under the original charter of 1197 was 'prepositus' which is usually translated as 'provost' or 'reeve'. In the course of the thirteenth century, the title was changed to mayor. The two bailiffs were in effect the mayor's deputies and in 1609 their title was changed to sheriff. This list is based on the list given in Lenihan's History of Limerick, which in turn was based on material from the Arthur, Sexten and White Manuscripts. There are a number of gaps in the listing, particularly 1200–1209; 1219–1229; 1242–1254; 1256–1257; 1286–1293; 1406; 1412 and 1429. In recent times, Brian Hodkinson of the Jim Kemmy Municipal Museum has conducted research in the area and has found references in other sources to a number of mayors not included in Lenihan's list and has made other discoveries which, in general, indicate that the list is sometimes unreliable for the Medieval, Tudor and Stuart periods.

Provosts supposedly appointed before the grant of the first charter of 1197

Date	Provosts
1195	John Spafford
1196	Alexander Barrett
1197	Henry Troy

Date	Provosts/Mayors	Bailiffs
1197–98	Adam Sarvant,	John Bambery; Walter White.
1199	Thomas Cropper	
1210	Roger Maij	
1211	John Cambitor	
1212	Walter Crop	
1213	Robert White	
1214	Siward Minutor	
1215	Siwardus de Fferendona	
1216	J. Russell, alias Creagh	
1217	John Banbury	
1218	Thomas Fitz-Arthur	Nicholas Walsh; Nicholas Fitz-Hiu, A.
1219	John Avenbrugger	
1230	Reynold de St. Jacobo	Maurice Blund; Perse Russell
1231	Nicholas Fitzsimons	John Bolingford; William Mac John
1234	Geraldus Domiler	
1235	John de Hanco	
1236	John Poines	

Date	Provosts/Mayors	Bailiffs
1237	Henry Troy	John White; Philip Rainbold
1238	Richard Millesowen	
1241	Nicholas Fitz-Thos, Arthur	
1255	John White	John Moore; Richard Reymbold
1258	Thomas Crop	
1259	Adam Serjeant	
1260	Henry Troy	
1261	Robert Juvenis	
1262	Reginald de St. Jacobo	
1263	John Russell, alias Creaghe	
1264	John Banbery	
1265	Richard Troway	Aulane O'None; Owen Moore, S.
1266	Geraldus de Mulier, S.	
1267	John Hamilton	
1268	Robert Poynes (W)	
1269	Henry Troy, W.	
1270	Richard Miles Owen, W.	
1271	John White, W.	John Moore; Richard Reymbold, S.
1271	Gregory Wanybould, W.	John Danyell; John Nash, S
1273	John Banbery, W.	
1274	Gilbert Fitz-Thomas, W.	Thom Albe; John Troy, S
1275	Geraldus Millis Owen	Richard Whyte; Richard Laceye, S.
1276	Edmund Longan	Richard White; Gregory Winebald, S.
1277	Gregory Vonbonde	William de Rupe; John Danyell, S.
1278	Morris Lisborne, S.	
1279	Gerald de Murley	Anlane O'Noyne; Owen Moore, S.
1280	Maurice Blund	Anlane O'Noyne; Owen Moore, S.
1281	Richard Troy	John Walsh; John Troy, S
1282	Henry Troy	John Walsh; John Troy, S
1283	John Kildare	John Daniel; Thom. Ricolf, A.
1284	Gerald Morles	Nicholas White; Richard Longane
1285	Edward Longane	Nichols White; Gregory Wainbold
1294	Maurice Lisborn	
1295	Gerald de Morly	Anlonus O'Neonan; Owen Moore, S.
1296	Richard Troy	Nicholas Walsh; John Troy, S.
1297	Nichols Fitzsimons	
1298	Gerald Morles	
1299	Richard Troy	
1300	John Kildare	
	Gerald Domilier, W.	
1301	John de Hanco	
1302	Robert Poines	
1303	Henry Troy	John White; Philip Troy, S.
1304	Richard Milles Owen	
1305	John White	John Moore; Richard Symbols
1306	Thomas Bambury	

Date	Mayors	Bailiffs
1307	William Loung	Walter Jannell; Robert Warren
1308	Robert Juvenis or Yong	Henry Troy; Alexander Barrett
1308	Gregory Wambold	John Kildare; William Croppe
1309	Gregory Wainbold	William Clean; David Russell
1310	John Bambery	Walter White; Phillip Rainbold
1311	Rowland Troy	Robert Long; Thomas Crop
1312	John Creagh	Richard Long; Thomas Winnebol
1313	Walter White	Thomas Crop; Nicholas Ricalf
1314	John Samtone	Thomas Croppe; Nicholas Ricolfe, S.
	Robert Troy	Richard Loung; Thomas Wambold, W.
1315	Robert Juvenis	Henry Troy; Alexander Barrett, S.
	Gregory Wambold	John Dannell; John Nash, W.
1316	John White	Nicholas Fitz-Thomas Blake; William Fitz-Thomas Mouer, S
	Maurice de Lisbon	Stephen Danniel; Alanus O'Hartegan, W
1317	Thos. Blake Kildare	John Wigmore; John Troy, S.
	Gregory Wambold (White)	
1318	Nicholas White or	
	William Prendergast	
1319	Philip Rainbold	
1320	Thomas Bambery	
1321	Richard Loung	
1322	Walter White	Owen Moore; Richard Miles Owen
1323	Roger de Lisborn	
1324	John Fitz-John White	Hugo Woedfor; -, Laynach
1325	John Fitz-John le Blunt	John Hamond; Daniel Martell, A.
1326	John White	Nichols Black; William Moore, W.
1327	Gregory Wainbold	John Daniel; John Nash
1328	Henry Troy	John White; Philip Rembold
1329	Greg. Wyneband	William Blunde; David Russell
1330	Greg. Wyneband	John of Kildare; William Cropp, (A. and S.)
	John White	John Moore; John Rembold, W.
1331	Greg. Wyneband	William de Rupe; John Daniell
1332	Thomas Bambery	Thomas Tallow; John Howse
1333	Greg Wainbold	William de Rupe; John Daniel
1334	Thomas Black of Kildare	John Vignor; John Troy
1335	Richard Miles Owen	John Rembold; Richard Rembold
1336	John White	Richard Noxthine; John White
1337	Greg. Wainbold	John Daniel; John Nash
1338	John Kildare, A.W.	Nicholas Symons; John Troy, A.
1339	Thomas Kildare	Richard Troy; Nicholas Howse
1340	Richard Milles Owen	John Fleming; Laurence Daniel, W.
1341	Thomas Bambery	Thomas Taylor; John Howse, W.
1342	Robert White	John Daniel; John Nash, W.
1343	Gregory Wambold	

Date	Mayors	Bailiffs
1344	Simon Bouir	Richard Miles Owen;
	Gregory deLisborn, W.	Thomas de Rannecks, A.
1345	Nicholas Fitz-Thomas	Martin Fitz-Thomas; William More, A.
	Simon Coney	Richard Miles Owen; Thomas de Knock, W.
1346	Nicholas Fitzsymons	Nicholas Tabernator; Thomas White, A.
1347	John Croft, W.	
1348	Richard Miles Owen, sen.	Adam Moore; Richard Reymbald, A.W.
1349	Richard Miles Owen of Emly	Rd. F. Thomas; John Lofts, A.
1350	Richard Millisse of Emly	Richard Fitzthomas; John Loftus, W.
1351	Robert Creagh	John Moore; Richard Rembold, W.
1352	Nich. Fitz-Thomas	Martin Fitz-Thomas; William Moore, A.
1353	Nicholas Fitsimons	Wm. FitzAdam Moore; Maurice Fitz-Richard FitzThomas, A.
1354	John Nash (W)	Thomas Troy; Mw Howse of Hunlin, S.
1355	Nicholas Black of Kildare	John Vigoner; Richard Rembold
1356	John Kildare	Richard Fitzsimons; Thomas Troy, W.
1357	Rd. Bultingfourd	Henry Croyn; Branden Valens (A. and S.)
1358	John Crofte (S.)	
1359	Rd. Milles Owen	Rd. Fitz-Thomas; Henry Croyne (A.)
1360	Rd. Milles Owen jnr, A.W.	John Ffleminge; Laurence Daniel, A.
1361	Nicholas Bakkeear	John Wigmore; John Troy, A.
1362	Robert Creaughe, S.	
1363	John Bambery	Wm. Longe; John White S.
1364	Thos. Pill	Walter Gilbert; Roger White, S.
1365	John Fitz-Thomas Arthur	Rd. Nashe; John White, S.
1366	Thos. Bambery	Rd. Dony; Robt. Lisborne, S.
1367	John Bultingfourd	John Vigmore; Rd. Skiner, S.
1368	Gilbert Fitz-Thomas	Dominick Cricke; William Man, W.
1369	John White	Richard Nophine; John White, W.
1370	Gilbert F. Thomas Blake	John Creaugh; John Troy, A.
1371	Robert Creaugh, S.	John Arthur, W.
1372	John Arthur, S.	David Cricke; Thom White, A.
1373	Nicholas Blackader	John Wigmore; John Troy
1374	Rd. Milles Owen	John Ffleminge; Laurence Daniell, S.
1375	Wm. Bambery	Wm. Longe; John White, S
1376	Rd. Bultingfourd	Thom. Pill; Roger White, S.
1377	Thomas Kildare	Wm. Longe; Rd. Grant, S.
1378	William White	Thomas Barkley; John Man, W.
1379	Thomas Kildare	Thomas White; Thomas Spicer, S.
1380	Rd. Bultingford	Peter O'Cullen; Brandon O'Hurtigane, S.
1381	John Banbery	Wm. Longe; Thom. Taylor, S.
1382	John White	Richard Nopthyrein; John Whyte de Ballysheada, A.
1383	Richd. Troy	Nich. Woulfe; John Troy, S.
1384	Thomas Kildare	William Longe; Richard Grand, S.
1385	Thom. Pill	Mathew Long; Roger White, A.

Date	Mayors	Bailiffs
1386	Richard Bultingfourd	Nich. Gough; Nich. Scourlock, A.
1387	John White	John Spaffourd; Roger White, A.
1388	Thomas Malby	John Casey; Richard Wigmore, S.
1389	John White	Roger White; Thomas White
1390	Richard Baltingford	Pierce Callan; Brandon O'Hartigan, W.
1391	John White	John Carter; John White; Alanus O'Noyn, A.
1392	John Kildare	John Man; John Carter
1393	Thomas Kildare	John Sraws; Alanus O'Noyn, A.
1394	Thomas Kildare	John Grante; John Carter
1395	Walter Daniel, W.	John Grant; Philip Moddii, S.A.
1396	Richard Bullingfourd	Brendanus O'Hethigian; Petrus O'Cullan, A
1397	Thomas Kildare	Richard Wale; William Yonge, A.
1398	Thomas Kildare	Nicholas Walsh; Richard Mason
1399	Nicholas Black	John Vigoner; John Moody, W.
1400	John Arthur	Richard Troy; John Moddii, A.
1401	Peter Loftus	John Budston; John Fitz-Robert Crevagh, A
1402	Thomas Spicer	Thomas Comyn; John Whyte
1403	John Arthur	Thomas Comyn; Philip Lawless, A.
1404	John Arthur 27th June	
	John Spofford 6th Dec, A.	John Moddy; Peter O'Cullan, A.
1405	Thomas Kildare	Richard Troy; Nicholas Fitz-Howe, S.A.W.
1406	(Wanting in S.A.W.)	Philip Callane; John Moddy, W.
1407	Thomas Comyn	Thomas Arthur; Nicholas Walsh, A.
1408	Thomas Comyn	Thomas Arthur; Nicholas Walsh, W.
1409	Thomas Comyn	Thomas Arthur; Nicholas Walsh, A.
1410	John Bambery	William Long; John White, A.
1411	Thomas Troy, A.W.	Richard White; Nicholas Howell, A.
1412	(Wanting in S.A.W.)	Nicholas Walsh, A.
1413	Thomas Comyn	Philip Lawless; Richard White, A.
1414	Thomas White	Richard White; Peter Loftus, A.
1415	Peter Loftus	William Budston; John Crevagh, A.
1416	Thomas Comyn	John Nagle; Nicholas Walsh, A.
1417	Thomas Comyn	Richard White; Peter Loftus, A.
1418	John Gale alias Spafford	Richard White; William Harold, A.
1419	John Spafford	Nicholas Palliel; John Moddy
1420	Richard Troy	Peter Loftus; John Troy, A.
1421	Thomas Arthur	Patrick Cogan; Thomas Barton, W.
1422	Richd. Troy	Pires Loftus; John Troy, W.
1423	- Spafford	Richard Arthur; William Harold, W.
1424	Pires Loftus	John Creaugh; William Busdtone, A.
1425	Richard Troy	William Creaugh; John Borton, W.
1426	Thomas Arthur	Nicholas Walsh; John Rede, A.
1427	Nicholas Stritch	Edmond Harold; Philip Nagle, W.
1428	Thomas Comyn, W.	
1429	(Wanting in S.A.W.)	

Date	Mayors	Bailiffs
1430	Richard Troy	Patrick Cogan; Philip Russell, A.W.
1431	William Arthur	Robert Warren; John Loftus, W.
1432	John Spafford	Richard White; William Harold, W.
1433	Thomas Bambery	John Cassy; Richard Vigoner, W.
1434	William Wailsh	William Loftus; Thomas Fox, W.
1435	Richard Fox.	John Loftus; Robert Nagle, W.
1436	Nicholas Arthur, A.S.W.	John Husshie; John Cromwell, A.S.
1437	William Yong	Edmund Howell; Philip Midchael, A
1438	Thomas Comyn	Philip Russell; John Axdy, A.
1439	Walter Yong	Robert Warren; Laurence Scott, A
1440	William Arthur	Robert Waring; John Loft
1441	William Arthur	Robert Nangle; Richard Galway, A.
1442	Nicholas Arthur	Patrick Turger; Robert Warren, S.
1443	Richard Ffox	John Lofts; Robert Nangyll, A.
1444	Nicholas Arthur	John Lofts; Edmond Harold, S.
1445	Richard Arthur	John Loftus; Robert Nagle
1446	Nicholas Arthur	John Loft; Edmond Howell
1447	William Loftus, W.	
1448	William Comyn	Robert Waring; John Rede jnr., A.
1449	William Arthur	Patrick Cogane; Robert Nagle, A.
1450	Thomas Arthur	John Creagh; David Arthur, W.
1451	Richard Arthur	Edmond Howell; Robert Nangle
1452	Nicholas Arthur	John Long; Patrick Torger, A.
1453	Thomas Burthon	Patrick Vogane; Thomas Budstone, A.
1454	Nicholas Arthur	John Lofts; Edmd. Harold, S.
1455	William Longe	David Creagh; John Comyne, S.
1456	Edmond Howell	John Verdune; Willliam Whyte, A.
1457	Nicholas Arthur	John Roch; John Verdun, A.
1458	Nich. Arthur, A.W.	Maurice Roch; John Arthur, W.
1459	William Comyn	Patrick Fox; Richard Fanning, A.W.
1460	Richard Arthur	John Arthur; William Young, S.A.
1461	Patrick Torger, A.W.	Richard Stretch; Anlenus O'Neonen, A.
1462	Nich. Fitz-Thomas Arthur	Philip Troy; Walter Whyte, A.W.
1463	Nicholas Arthur, A.S.W.	Peter Arthur; John Dundon; A
1464	Nicholas Arthur	John Fitz-William Arthur; John Marshall, A.
1465	Patrick Torger	Gerald Tews; William Whyte, A.
1466	Thomas Arthur	James Creagh; John Stackpol, A.
1467	Thomas Arthur	Patrick Arthur; Richard Stretch, A.
1468	William Comyn	John Stackpoole; William Verdune, A.
1469	Thomas Arthur	John Creagh; Daniel Arthur, A.W.
1470	Henry Creagh S.	Garret Woulfe; William Whyte, W.
	David Creagh W.	
1471	John Arthur	John Comyn; John Stackpol, A.
1472	Patrick Arthur	John Waring; Thomas Woulfe, A.
1473	William Comyn	John Stackpol; John Verdon, W.
1474	John Arthur	John Stackpol; John Comyn

Date	Mayors	Bailiffs
1475	David Creagh	Edmond Arthur; William Cromwell, W.
1476	Patrick Arthur	Edward Arthur; William Cromwell, A.
1477	Daniel Crevagh	Edward Arthur; William Cromwell, A.
1478	Thomas Arthur	Edmond Torger; David Miagh, A.
1479	Thomas Arthur	John Warren; David Midchell, A.
1480	John Arthur	John Crevagh; David Arthur, A.
1481	John Comyn	George Arthur; Walter Arthur, A.
1482	David Arthur	William Comyn; David Miagh, A.
1483	John Fitz-Nicholas Arthur	John Fitz-William Comyn; William Fitz-Richard Crevagh
1484	Walter Whyte, S.A.W.	Maurice Stackpol; Philip Richford, S.
1485	William Harold	John Stackpol; Richard Stritch, W.
1486	John Arthur	William Cromwell; Myles Arthur, A.
1487	John Arthur	William Cromwell; Myles Arthur, A.
1488	David Creagh	Edmond Long; Nicholas Nangyll, A.W.
1489	Thomas Arthur, A.W.	Christopher Arthur; John Whyte, W.
1490	Patrick Arthur	George Comyn; Pierce Rice, W.
1491	David Creagh	David Roche; Christopher Arthur
1492	Maurice Stackpol	William Arthur; Edmund Nangyll, A.W.
1493	Edmond Longe	David Roche; Walter Harold; Thomas Stackpol
1494	George Fitz-Nicholas Arthur	Richard Fox; David Mcyagh
1495	Edmond Longe	David Roche; Walter Harold; Thomas Stackpol
1496	George Comyn	Richard Fitz-David Creagh; Thomas Stackpol
1497	George Comyn	Richard Fitz-David Creagh; Thomas Stackpol
1498	William Harold	Nicholas Stretch; John Fitz-William Whyte
1499	David Roche	Thomas Roche; John Stackpol
1500	Philip Stackpol	John Everard; Richard Fitz-Nicholas Creagh
1501	Christopher Arthur	Robert Stackpol; Edmond Comyn
1502	John Creagh	Richard Harrold; Thomas Cromwell
	Mayors	Bailiffs
1503	Nicholas Stretch	Robert Roche; Nicholas Bonevyle
1504	Nicholas Stretch	Nicholas Lawless; Nicholas Fitz-John Arthur; John Lewis or Lawless
1505	William Harold	Nicholas Creagh; Nicholas Rochford
1506	William Arthur	Richard Whyte; Richard Sergeant
1507	William Creagh	Nicholas Harold; Nicholas Ryce
1508	Nicholas Fitz-Patrick Fox	Thomas Yong; Richard Sergeant
1509	Nich. Thos. Fitz-W. Arthur.	David Comyn; Richard Boneovle
1510	Nicholas Stretch	Walter Rice; Richard Fanning
1511	Thomas Roch	Patrick Fanning; Thomas Rochfort
1512	Robert Harrold	David Whyte; Peter Comyn
1513	Robert Stackpol	James Stretch; Christopher Harrold

Date	Mayors	Bailiffs
1514	Richard Fox	Christopher Creagh; James Fitz-Edward Arthur
1515	Thomas Comyn	William Long; William Arthur
1516	Nicholas Harrold	Richard Milonis (Fitz-Milo) Arthur; Galfridus Stretch
1517	Nicholas Harrold	James Harrold; Peter Walter Arthur
1518	David Comyn	George Stretch; Peter Fitz-William Creagh
1519	John Rocheford	Edmond Harrold; Daniel Fitz-John Arthur
1520	Walter Ryce	Stephen Creagh; Thomas Woulfe
1521	David Comyn	William Fanning; Andrew Harrold
1522	David Whyte	John Ryce; Thomas Arthur
1523	David Roche	James Creagh; Stephen Comyn
1524	Christopher Arthur	Peter Creagh; Patrick Everard
1525	James Harrold	Richard Comyn; Patrick Everard
1526	Thomas Yong	Nicholas Fitz-Thomas Creagh; John Nangyll
1527	Nicholas Creagh	John Fitz-Nicholas Arthur; Peter Fitz-Christopher Arthur
1528	Nicholas Stretch	William Creagh; Leonard Creagh
1529	Patrick Fanning	Nicholas Comyn; Patrick Long
1530	Stephen Creagh	William Verdun; Richard Stackpol
1531	Edmond Harrold	John Harrold; Roland Arthur
1532	Daniel Fitz-Nicholas Arthur	George Creagh; Wm. White
1533	Thomas Yong	David Ryce; Thomas Long
1534	John Fitz-Nicholas Arthur	Bartholomew Stretch; John Fitz-John Stretch
1535	Edmond Sexten	Dominick Whyte; Ocunepherous Fitz-Christopher Arthur.
1536	Bartholomew Stretch	John Comyn; Jasper Fanning
1537	Nicholas Comyn	William Yong; Patrick Ryce
1538	Wm. Fanning	James Fox; James Roche
1539	Leonard Creagh	Wm. Stretch; Thomas Creagh
1540	Dominick Whyte	David Creagh; James Loftus
1541	Patrick Everard	Walter Harold; Dominick Comyn
1542	George Crevagh	Wm. Stretch; James Stackpol
1543	David Whyte	Wm. Creagh; Wm. Yong
1544	James Harrold	Andrew Harrold; Hector Fitz-James Arthur
1545	Dominick Whyte	Patrick Long; George Rochfort
1546	Stephen Creagh	Wm. Verdun; Myles Stretch.
1547	John Fitz-Nicholas Arthur	Thomas Arthur; John Stackpol
1548	Wm. Stretch	Peter Whyte; James Creagh
1549	John Fitzgeorge Stretch	John Harrold; Christopher Creagh
1550	James Fox	James Stretch; Edward Fitz-Daniel Arthur
1551	James Creagh for 1 month James Fox for 2 months	Clement Fanning; Nicholas Harrold
1552	William Stretch	Roland Harold; Philip Rochford

Date	Mayors	Bailiffs
1553	Willaim Verdune	Nicholas Whyte; John Creagh
1554	James Stretch	William Fox; Richard Fanning
1555	John Stackpol	David Comyn; Thomas Creagh
1556	James Comyn	Peter Fitz-Leonard Creagh; George Roche
1557	Clement Fanning	Richard Arthur; John Everard
1558	Edward Fitz-Daniel Arthur	Stephen Whyte; Dominick Creagh
1559	Daniel Comyn	Dominick Fanning; Thomas Fitz-Peter Creagh
1560	Peter Fitz-Leonard Creagh	Thomas Fitz-Patrick Creagh; Richard Young
1561	Richard Fanning	Patrick Rochford; David Cromwell
1562	Nicholas Whyte	Nicholas Woulfe; Patrick Fox
1563	Nicholas Harrold	John Comyn; John Fanning
1564	George Roche	George Fanning; Thomas Harrold
1565	Thomas Fitz-John Arthur	Patrick Creagh; William Creagh
1566	Roland Harrold	Roger Everard; Stephen Fanning
1567	Christopher Creagh	James Creagh; John Wolfe
1568	Dominick Fanning	Thomas Fitz-Arthur; Richard Cromwell
1569	Philip Rochford	Nicholas Price; Stephen Whyte
1570	John Fitz-Stephen Comyn	Dominick Everard; Daniel Fitz-Daniel Arthur
1571	Geo. Fitz-William Fanning	George Fitz-Daniel Arthur; George Comyn
1572	Richard Stretch	Philip Comyn; Jordan Roche
1573	Thomas Fitz-John Arthur	Thomas Stretch; Milo Fitz-Eustace Arthur
1574	Thomas Harrold	George Cromwell; Nicholas Whyte
1575	Roger Everard	Stephen Fitz-Dominick Whyte; David Rochfort
1576	Stpn. Fitz-Dominick Whyte	William Fitz-John Arthur; Patrick Fanning
1577	Thomas Fitz-John Arthur	Walter Fitz-Patrick Ryan; Nicholas Stretch
1578	John Woulfe	John Stretch; Peter Stretch
1579	Nicholas Fitz-Bw. Stretch	Thomas Stretch; Arthur Creagh
1580	Jordan Fitz-Gerald Roche	Andrew Creagh; Edward Fitz-Hector Arthur
1581	James Fitz-John Galway	Thomas Yong; George Harrold
1582	John Fitz-Bw. Stretch	Peter Fitz-Dominick Creagh; Peter Oenopherous Arthur
1583	Nicholas Comyn	Oliver Harrold; Nicholas Bourke
1584	James Fanning	Nicholas Harrold; Patrick Midchell
1585	Stephen Sexten	Patrick Woulfe; Oliver Bourke
1586	Thomas Yong	Roberty Whyte; James Cromwell
1587	George Fanning	Stephen Roche; Edmond Comyn
1588	Jordan Roche	Martin Creagh died; Walter Ryce, and Patrick Woulf
1589	Nicholas Bourke	William Fitz-Wm. Creagh; Thomas Stackpol
1590	Thomas Fitz-Wm. Stretch	Thomas Woulf; Nicholas Fox
1591	Oliver Bourke	Edmond Fox; Richard Woulfe

Date	Mayors	Bailiffs
1592	Nicholas Fitz-Thomas Arthur	John Fitz-Andrew Comyn de Parke; David Woulfe
1593	Peter Fizt-Dominick Creagh	Bartholomew Fitz-Jas. Stretch; Ed. Fitz-Stephen Whyte
1594	John Fitz-Bw. Stretch	Dom. Fitz-John Arthur; Edward Stretch
1595	James Whyte died 1st month Peter Fitz-John Creagh	John Fitz-John Arthur; Clement Fanning
1596	Robert Whyte	Bartholomew Stackpol; Robert Bourke
1597	Dominick Fitzjordan Roche	Wm. Fitz-Thos. Arthur; Jas. Fitz-Stephen Whyte
1598	James Cromwell	Philip Roche; Thomas Bourke
1599	Wm. Fitz-John Stretch	David Fitz-Nicholas Whyte; Michael Waters
1600	Galfridus (Sir Geoffrey) Galway	Simon Fanning; Robert Arthur
1601	Stephen Roche	William Fitz-Thomas Stretch; Jas. Fitz-Edward Arthur; David Fitz-Walter Ryce
1602	Philip Roch	James Fitz-James Whyte; Wm. Myeagh
1603	Nicholas Bourke	Thomas Fitz-Philip Comyn; Thos. Fitz-Patrick Creagh
1604	James Galway	David Fitz-Milo Comyn; Thos. Fitz-Patrick Creagh
1605	Edmund Fox	Dominick Fitz-Peter Creagh ; James Woulf
1606	Edmund Sexten	Christopher Arthur; P. Creagh
1607	Nicholas Arthur	Nicholas Whyte; William Hally
1608	Patrick Arthur	Wm. Creagh; Geo. White

(Title of Bailiff changed to Sheriff in 1609).

Date	Mayors	Sheriffs
1609	David Whyte	William Myeagh; Dominick Creagh
1610	Clement Fanning	Walter Whyte; Jasper Whyte
1611	David Comyn Edmund Sexten	David Fitz-Geoffrey Ryce; Christopher Creagh; Patrick Lysaght
1612	Wm. Myeagh Christopher Creagh	Patrick Fitz-Henry Whyte; John Skeolan George Fitzjames Creagh; John Lyseiaght
1613	Dominick Fitz-Peter Creagh William Haly,	John FitzJohn Arthur; George Woulfe David Bourk; Thomas Power
1614	Michael Walter	Nicholas Fitz-Nicls. Stretch; Wm. Roch de Cahiravahalla
	James Fitz-James Whyte James Galway Fanning; Christopher Fitz-D. Arthur	William Rochford; Peter Fitz-Peter Creagh David Bourke; Thomas Power, Arthur

Date	Mayors	Sheriffs
1615	William Stretch	James White Fitz-Henry;
		Walter Fitz-Richard Arthur;
	Simon Fanning;	George Sexten; George Rochford;
	David Comyn;	Nicholas Fitz-Henry Whyte; Geo. Rochford
1616	James Galway	James Fitz-John Stretch; Geo. Rochford
	Christopher Creagh	Patrick Leyseaght; James Fitz-John Stretch
	Dominick Roche	John Fitz-john Stretch; Richard Lawless
1617	John Fitz-John Stretch	George Fitz-James Creagh; Peter Harrold
1618	Dominick Roche	
	Peter Fitz-Peter Whyte	Edward Sexten; David Roch
1619	Edward Sexten	Edward Sexten; Philip Ronane
1620	Henry Barkley	
1621	Dominick Roche	James Lawless; Robert Lawless
1622	John Fitz-John Stretch	Peter Harrold; Philip Ronane
1623	Edward Sexten	George Fitz-James Creagh; Patrick Lawless
1624	David Fitz-Nicholas Comyn	James Sexten; Edward Barkley
1625	Henry Barkley	Nicholas Fanning; John Meyeagh
1626	James Fitz-Nicholas Bourke	James Fitz-Bw. Stackpol; George Bourke
1627	James Fitz-John Stretch	Andrew Fitz-Andrew Creagh;
		Peter Fitz-Oliver Harrold
1628	Peter Fitz-Peter Creagh	Dominick Fitz-Bw. Whyte;
		Edward Skeolane
1629	Dr. Domk. Fitz-David Whyte	Peter Fitz-Andrew Creagh;
		William Fitz-Stephen Roch
1630	Nicholas Fanning	Stephen Fitz-James Whyte; Robert Hally
1631	Andrew Fitz-Andrew Creagh	Stephen Stretch; Dominick Tyrry
1632	James Lawless	James Fitz-Stephen Whyte;
		Francis Fanning
1633	John Meyeagh	James Fitz-Ed. Fox; Peter Fitz-Peter Creagh
1634	Peter (or Pierce)	John Fitz-Thomas Bourk;
	Creagh Fitz-Andrew	William Fitz-Peter Creagh
1635	Thomas Fitz-Martin Arthur	Daniel Nihell; James Fitz-Water Ryce
1636	Sir Domk. Fitz-Bw. Whyte	Luke Stretch; William Leyseaght
1637	James Fitz-James Whyte	James Fitz-John Creagh; James Hackett
1638	Robert Lawless	James Fitz-David Whyte;
		Nicholas Fitz-Ed. Fox
1639	Jordan Roch (the younger)	David Fitz-David Whyte;
		Wm. Fitz-Wm. Stretch
1640	William Fitz-Ed. Comyn	John Fitz-Jasper Comyn; Henry Cassy
1641	Dominick Fitz-Simon	Thomas Fitz-James Whyte;
		George Fitz-Patk.
	Fanning (third time)	Rochfort
1642	Peter Fitz-Pierce Creagh	Laurence Whyte; Laurence Ryce
1643	Dominick Fitz-David Whyte	Thomas Fitz-David Comyn;
		James Sarsfield
1644	Francis Fanning	James Mahowne; Patrick Meyeagh

Date	Mayors	Sheriffs
1645	John Fitz-Thomas Bourk	Thomas Fitz-Patrick Stretch; Edmund Fitz-Stephen Roch
1646	Dominick Fitz-Stephen Fanning	David Fitz-Peter Creagh; James Fitz-Geo. Sexten
1647	Peter (Pierce) Creagh Fitz-Andrew	Bartholomew Fitz-David Ryce;, Patk, Woulfe
1648	Sir Nichs. Fitz-David Comyn	Patrick Fitz-Oliver Arthur; Andrew Bourk
1649	John Fitz-Wm. Creagh	David Rochefort; James Bonefield
1650	Thomas Fitz-Patrick Creagh	Martin Fitz-Andrew Creagh; Nicholas Ronan
1651	Peter Fitz-Peter Creagh	Stephen Fitz-David Skeolan; Wm. Fitz-David Creagh

(Limerick Corporation abolished by Cromwellian Regime 1651–1656)

Date	Mayors	Sheriffs
1656	Colonel Henry Ingolsby	John Comyn; Peter Ash
1657	Captain Ralf Wilson	John Comyn; Peter Ash
1658	William Yarwell, Esq.	Jeremy Heywood; Christopher Keyes
1659	Wm. Hartwell, Esq.	Robert Passy; John Crabb
1660	Thomas Miller	Henry Price; Robert Shutt
1661	John Comyn	James Banting; Wm. Pope
1662	Henry Bindon	Henry Salfield; Wm. Joint
1663	Sir Ralph Wilson	Thomas Martin; John Burn
1664	Sir Ralph Wilson	John Lence; Samuel Foxon
1665	Sir William King	Henry Price; John Symmes
1666	Samuel Foxon	John Backner; John Arthur
1667	Sir Ralph Wilson	Wm. York; Anthony Bartlett
1668	Sir Ralph Wilson	Edward Clock; John Bennett
1669	E. Werendoght	Rowland Bonton; Henry Clinton
1670	R. Studdendoght	Francis Whittamor; George Bockendoght
1671	John Bourin, chirugeon	Danile Hignett; John Hart
1672	Sir Geo. Ingoldsby	John Beer; John Halpin Halpin replaced by James Philips
1673	Wm. York	Robert Higgins; Bartholomew Ast.
1674	Wm. York	Thomas Rose; Robert Smith
1675	Edward Clarke	George Roche; Wm. Craven
1676	Capt. Humphrey Hartwell	Pierce Graham; Edward Waight
1677	Capt. Humphrey Hartwell	Richard Lyllis; Wm. Clifford
1678	Wm. York Sir William King	Thomas Long; John Bond
1679	Sir William King	Wm. Allen; Moses Woodroff
1680	Anthony Bartlett	Richard Ingram; Thomas Meagher
1681	Fras Whitamor	John Craven; Nathaniel Webb
1682	Wm. Gribble	Edward Clark; Giles Spencer
1683	Wm. Gribble	Richard Allen; John Ford

Date	Mayors	Sheriffs
1684	Robert Smyth	Daniel Bowman; Simon White
1685	George Roche	Thomas Breveter; Samuel Bartlett
1686	George Roche	John Young; James Robinson
1687	Robert Hannan	Thomas Harrold; Peter Monsell
1688	Robert Hannan	Francis White; Philip Stackpole
1689	Thomas Harrold	Thos. Creagh; Richard Harrold
1690	John Power	James Arthur; Nicholas Murrough
1691	George Roche	John Young; Jas. Robinson
1692	John Craven	Zachary Holland; Bartholomew Lee
1693	John Foord	Wm. Davis; Abraham Bowman
1694	Edward Waight	Henry Chaplain; Charles Atkins
1695	Thomas Rose	Richard Sexton; George Roche
1696	Simon White	John Vincent; Pierse Piersy
1697	John Young	Thomas Flaxon; John Higgins
1698	James Robinson	Tock Roche; Raudal Holland
1699	Robert Twigg	Richard Craven; Ezechias Holland
1700	Richard Pope	Walter Parker; George Robinson
1701	Wm. Davis	Railly Colpoys; Robert Wilkinson
1702	George Roche (younger)	Redmond Fitz-Maurice; Isaac Moth
1703	John Vincent	Wm. Grimes; George Bridgeman
1704	Richard Lyllis	George Sexton; James Jacques
1705	Tock Roch	John McCall; Wm. Medcaff
1706	John Higgins	Wm. Butler; Richard Chinnery
1707	Randel Holland	Henry Exham; Wm. Franklin
1708	Richard Craven	Francis Sargent; John Seamor
1709	Rawly Colpoys	David Davis; James Yeamans
1710	Pierse Piercy	John Murray; Thomas Cash
1711	Edward Waight	Paul Terry; Wm. Carr
1712	Wm. Butler	Christopher Carr; Robert Palmer
1713	Ezechias Holland	Joseph Phibbs; Michael Abjohn
1714	Wm. Franklin	Benjamin Barrington; Edmond Vokes
1715	George Sexten	Charles Coply; John Carr
1716	Francis Sergeant	Joseph Wilson; David Bendon
1717	George Bridgeman	John Busshery; Wm. Buxton
1718	Wm. Medcaff	Arthur Vincent; Richard Moore
1719	Richard Davis	Joseph Hartwell; John Graves
1720	John Seamor	Wm. Norris; Isaac Clampett
1721	George Roche MP	Thomas Mason; Wm. Turner
1722	Joseph Wilson	Christopher White; Richard Roch
1723	Tock Roche	George Wright; Wm. Parker
1724	Tock Roche	Thomas Vincent; Joseph Franklin
1725	John Carr	Samuel Mounsell; Wm. Gardiner
1726	Lieut.-Gen. Thos. Pierse	Philip Rawson; Wm. Jessop
1727	John Vincent	George Ross; Richard Chester
1728	Arthur Vincent	James Seamor; George Sexton
1729	Walter Parker	John Wright; Benjamin Barrington

Date	Mayors	Sheriffs
1730	Wm. Carr	Richard Seymour; Joseph Roch
1731	Philip Rawson	Thomas Roch; John Ingram
1732	Charles Smyth MP	John Bull; Mark Scaly
1733	Wm. Wilson, Esq.	John Shepherd; Simon Burton
1734	Richard Maunsell	Peter Sargent; Arthur Roche
1735	George Wright	James Sargent; William Roch
1736	Thomas Vincent	Henry Long; William Robinson
1737	The Lord Thos. Southwell, Peer	John Franklin; Zachary Davis
1738	George Sexton	Richard Graves; David Roche
1739	Isaac Clampett	John Long; John Gough
1740	Joseph Roche Thomas Vincent	Robert Cripps; John Davis George Waller
1741	John Wight	James Smyth; Wm. Vokes
1742	John Robinson	John Jones; Walter Seymour
1743	Arthur Roche	Henry Ivers, Esq.; Thomas Maunsell
1744	Henry Long	James Robinson; Thomas Brown
1745	Robert Cripps	Wm. Davis; Zachary Johnson
1746	Henry Ivers, Esq.	Henry Holland; Frederick Gore
1747	John Ingram	Richard Nash Esq.; Francis Sargent
1748	John Jones	George Vincent; Robert Hallam
1749	David Roch	John Smyth; John Bull
1750	Capt. Henry Southwell	Andrew Shepherd; Joseph Cripps
1751	James Smyth, Esq.	John Weakly; John Tavernor
1752	John Sheppard	Thomas Palmer; Joseph Barrington
1753	Peter Sargent	Sexten Bayly; Dr. John Barrett
1754	John Gough	George Sexton; Christopher Carr
1755	Stepney Rawson Stepney	Edward Villiers; Joseph Johns
1756	Arthur Roch	Andrew Welsh; Exham Vincent
1757	Andrew Shepherd	Christopher Briston; Wm. Goggins
1758	Sexten Baylee	John Parker; Wm. Gubbins
1759	Francis Sargent	Walter Widenham; Thomas Pearse
1760	Arthur Roche	Thomas Vokes; Eaton Maunsell
1761	George Vincent	John Monsell; Francis Sargent
1762	Edward Villiers, Esq.	Eyres Evans Powell, Esq.; Thos. Vereker
1763	Robert Hallam	John Prendergast Smyth; John Verker
1764	Thos. Smyth, Esq.	Alexander Franklin; John Tonnadine
1765	George Sexton, Jnr.	Samuel Johns; Francis Sargent
1766	Joseph Cripps.	Henry Wm. Bindon; John Shepherd jnr
1767	Thomas Vereker, Esq.	Wm. Smyth; Raleigh James
1768	Dr. John Barrett, MD	Wm. Gabbett; Richard Harte
1769	John Vereker, Esq.	Edmond Morony; Thomas Ewer
1770	Exham Vincent	John Creaghe; John Atkinson
1771	Christr. Carr Christopher	Bryan Mansergh; Wm. Piercy
1772	Arthur Roche George Roche	Wm. Stamer; Pierse Piercy

Date	Mayors	Sheriffs
1773	Joseph Johns	Thomas Carpenter; Miles Jackson
1774	Richard Hart	Philip Smyth; Burton Bindon
1775	Wm. Gabbett	Wm. Fitzgerald; Joseph Gabbett
1776	Thomas Smyth MP	Christopher Knight; Thomas Vincent
1777	Walter Widenham	Charles Sargent; Francis Russell
1778	Philip Smyth	John Gabbett; Amos Vereker
1779	Eaton Maunsell	Hugh Gough; John Harrison
1780	F. Sargent James	Edward Parker; John Ferrar, historian
1781	Thomas Carpenter	Wm. Fosbery; John Frederick Furnell
1782	George Smyth	George Tomkins; Hugh Brady
1783	Alexander Franklin	John Fitzgerald; Wm. Russell
1784	Thomas Pearse	Wm. Wallace; Michael Blood
1785	Sir Christopher Knight, Kt.	Joseph Sargent; Arthur Vincent
1786	Wm. Fitzgerald, Esq.	Wm. Percy; Henry Rose
1787	John Creagh	Robert Wallace; Samuel Hunter
1788	Richard Maunsell	John Cripps; Wm. Hunt
1789	Joseph Gabbett, Esq.	Henry D'Esterre; Thomas Moroney
1790	John Minchin	John Augustine Ievers; Bryan McMahon Michael Furnell
1791	Rev. Thomas Shepherd	George Sargant; David Dwyer
1792	Benjamin Frend, Esq.	Ralph Westrop; Henry Brady
1793	Henry D'Esterre, Esq.	George Davis; Thomas Edwards Philip Russell
1794	Henry D'Esterre, Esq.	Robert Briscoe; Joseph Cripps
1795	Thos. Gabbett, Esq.	Nicholas Mahon; Frederick Price
1796	John Harrison, Esq. Joseph Cripps	Robert Briscoe; Andrew Watson
1797	Joseph Cripps	Francis Lloyd; Richard Webb
1798	Frederick Lloyd	Andrew Watson; Henry Pierce Carroll
1799	Frederick Lloyd	Francis Lloyd; Richard Webb Philip Russell
1800	Ralph Westropp	Philip Russell; Henry Collis
1801	Ralph Westropp	Ed. Morony; Thos. E. Wilkinson
1802	Joseph Sargent	Abraham Russell; Henry Collis
1803	Arthur Vincent	Henry Pierce Carroll; Colclough Stritch
1804	Robert Briscoe	Henry Pierce Carroll; Colclough Strich
1805	Wm. Fosbery	Ab. Colclough Strich; Bryan McMahon
1806	Richard Harte	Henry P. Carroll; D.F.G. Mahony
1807	Kilner Brooke Brasier	Edmond Morony; Thomas Westropp
1808	John Cripps	Edmond Morony; Thomas Westropp
1809	Francis Lloyd	Edmond Morony; Thomas Westropp
1810	Francis Lloyd	Edmond Morony; Thomas Westropp
1811	William Hunt	D.F.G. Mahony; Henry Watson
1812	Andrew Watson	Henry Collis; Arthur Brereton
1813	Thos. S. Wilkinson	Henry Collis; Arthur Brereton
1814	Edmond Moroney	Henry Collis; Arthur Brereton

Date	Mayors	Sheriffs
1815	John Vereker	Henry Collis; Arthur Brereton
1816	John Vereker	Henry Collis; Arthur Brereton
1817	John Vereker	Henry Collis; Arthur Brereton
1818	Joseph Gabbett	W.M. Jackson; J. McAlister Taverner Wm. Taylor
1819	Joseph Gabbett	W.M. Jackson; Wm. Taylor
1820	Sir Chris. Marrett, Knt.	W.M. Jackson; Wm. Taylor
1821	Thos. Orsmby	W. Taylor; Andrew James Watson
1822	D.F.G. Mahony	W. Taylor; Andrew James Watson
1823	Henry Watson	John Piercy; Henry Rose
1824	Henry Watson	Wm. Hunt; Wm. Percy
1825	Henry Watson	John Harrison; John Westropp
1826	Nicholas Mahon	A.J. Watson; Richard Franklin, Jnr.
1827	Thos. Jervis	John S. T. Piercy; Edmond Moroney, Jnr.
1828	Vere Hunt	Wm. Gibson; John Standish
1829	Henry Rose	Wm. Piercy; George Lloyd
1830	John Cripps	Andrew James Watson; Henry Mahon
1831	Hon. J.P. Vereker	Edmond Moroney jnr; Ralph Westropp Brereton
1832	Hon. J.P. Vereker	Richard Franklin; George Sexten
1833	John Vereker, Jnr.	Wm. Piercy; Samuel Moore Watson
1834	John J. Piercy	George Lloyd; Francis Philip Russell
1835	Wm. Gibson	Edmond Moroney, jnr.; Ralph W. Brereton
1836	Alderman J. Vereker, Jnr.	Henry Mahon; Hughes Russell
1837	Edmond Moroney	Richard Franklin; Henry Vereker
1838	Garret Hugh Fitzgerald	George Lloyd; James Sexten
1839	Richard Franklin, M.D.	Robert Hunt; Thos. F.G.Sexton
1840	Henry Vereker Lloyd	Ralph Westropp Brereton; Thomas Lloyd
1841	Hon. C.S. Vereker	Robert Ringrose Gelston; Arthur V. Watson

(New reformed Limerick Corporation came into existence due to Municipal Corporations (Ireland) Act of 1840. Number of Sheriffs reduced to one).

Date	Mayors	Sheriffs
1842	Martin Honan	Robert Ringrose Gelston
1843	Martin Honan	John Norris Russell
1844	Pierse Shannon W.J. Geary	Samuel Dickson
1845	W.J. Geary	Wm. Roche
1846	E.F.G. Ryan	Henry Watson
1847	Thomas Wallnutt	Richard Russell
1848	Michael Quin	Henry Maunsell
1849	John Boyse Laurence Quinlivan	David Leahy Arthur
1850	Laurence Quinlivan	Wm. Spaight
1851	Thaddeus McDonnell	P.A. Shannon
1852	Thomas Kane, MD	Wm. Gabbett

Date	Mayors	Sheriffs
1853	Wm. H. Hall	James Spaight
1854	Henry Watson	Major George Gavin
1855	Henry O'Shea	Francis Grene
1856	James Spaight	Helenus White
1857	Thomas Kane, MD	Captain Michael Gavin
1858	Edmund Gabbett	Thomas Kane, MD
1859	Michael R. Ryan	Andrew V. Watson
1860	Wm. Fitzgerald	Edward Murphy
	T. McDonnell	
	John T. McSheehy	
1861	John T. McSheehy	Thompson Russell
1862	Wm. Lane Joynt	Robert Hunt
1863	Robert MacMahon	Thomas Boyse
1864	Eugene O'Callaghan	H.C. Smyth Vereker
1865	John Richard Tinsley	John Thomas McSheehy
1866	Peter Tait	Eugene O'Callaghan
1867	Peter Tait	Eugene O'Callaghan
1868	Peter Tait	Lawrence Quinlivan
	Thomas Elliot Carte	
1869	Thomas Boyse	John Quin
1870	William Spillane	John MacDonnell
1871	Robert McDonnell	John MacDonnell
1872	John Watson Mahony	John Howley
	John J. Cleary	
1873	John J. Cleary	Michael Robert Ryan
1874	John J. Cleary	Robert McDonnell
1875	Ambrose Hall	John McDonnell
1876	John Francis Walker	Thomas Enright O'Brien
1877	James Spaight	Charles Dawson
1878	Stephen Hastings	William I. Hunt
1879	Michael O'Gorman	Charles McDonnell
1880	Michael O'Gorman	Maurice Lenihan, historian
1881	Thomas George O'Sullivan	Octavius Wallace
1882	Jerome Counihan	William Boyd
1883	Jerome Counihan	William Boyd
1884	Maurice Lenihan, historian	Stephen Dowling
1885	Stephen O'Mara	Stephen Dowling
1886	Stephen O'Mara MP	Lawrence O'Keeffe
1887	Francis A. O'Keeffe	James O'Mara
1888	Francis A. O'Keeffe MP	Stephen O'Mara
1889	Francis A. O'Keeffe MP	W.J. O'Donnell
1890	W.J. O'Donnell	Wm. M. Nolan
1891	Patrick Riordan	Patrick E. Bourke
1892	Denis F. McNamara	Thomas McMahon Cregan
1893	Bryan O'Donnell	Michael Spain
1894	Bryan O'Donnell	Patrick Kenna

Date	Mayors	Sheriffs
1895	Bryan O'Donnell	Patrick Kenna
	William Nolan	
1896	William Nolan	J.P. Gaffney
	M. Cusack	
1897	M. Cusack	Stephen B. Quin
1898–99	M.Cusack	Thomas H. Cleeve
1899–1900	John Daly	Thomas H. Cleeve
1900–01	John Daly	Seamus F. de Barra
1901–02	John Daly	Patrick McDonnell
1902–03	James F. Barry	Patrick McDonnell
1903–04	Michael Donnelly	James Flynn
1904–05	Michael Donnelly	James Flynn
1905–06	Michael Joyce MP	E.J. Long
1906–07	Michael Joyce MP	E.J. Long
1907–08	John Kerr	Thomas H. Cleeve
1908–09	Thomas Donnellan	Thomas H. Cleeve
1909–10	Thomas Donnellan	W.L. Stokes
1910–11	Timothy Ryan	William Holiday
1911–12	Timothy Ryan	Charles McDonnell
1912–13	Timothy Ryan	Charles McDonnell
1913–14	Philip O'Donovan	Stephen O'Mara
1914–15	Philip O'Donovan	Stephen O'Mara
1915–16	Philip O'Donovan	Thomas S. Lawlor
1916–17	Sir Stephen Quin	Thomas S. Lawlor
1917–18	Sir Stephen Quin	James H. Roche
1918–19	Alphonsus M. O'Mara	James H. Roche
1919–20	Alphonsus M. O'Mara	Maurice P. O'Riordan
1920–21	Michael O'Callaghan	Maurice P. O'Riordan

(Office of Sheriff discontinued and later abolished by Irish Free State Government in 1926)

1921	George Clancy (murdered 7/3/21)
	J.M. Casey (Deputy Mayor to 22/3/21)
1921–22	Stephen O'Mara (elected for rest of year)
1921–22	Maire O'Donovan (Deputy Mayor 21/5/21 to 30/1/22 due to absence of O'Mara in the U.S.A.)
1922–23	Stephen O'Mara
1923	Stephen O'Mara (resigned 1/10/23)
1923–24	R.W. de Courcy (elected for rest of year)
1924–25	R.W. de Courcy
1925	R.W. de Courcy (resigned 30/6/25.).

(Date of election of Mayor changed from January to June)

Date	Mayors
1925–26	Paul A. O'Brien
1926–27	Paul A. O'Brien
1927–28	John George O'Brien
1928–29	Michael J. Keyes
1929–30	Michael J. Keyes
1930–31	Patrick Donnellan
1931–32	Patrick Donnellan
1932–33	Patrick Donnellan
1933–34	Patrick F. Quinlan
1934	Patrick F. Quinlan

(Limerick City Management Act comes into effect. Term of Office terminated on 22/11/1934)

Date	Mayors
1934–35	J. M. Casey (elected for rest of year)
1935–36	J. M. Casey
1936–37	D. Bourke TD
1937–38	D. Bourke TD
1938–39	D. Bourke TD
1939–40	D. Bourke TD
1940–41	D. Bourke TD
1941–42	Desmond O'Malley
1942–43	Desmond O'Malley
1943–44	James McQuane
1944–45	James Reidy TD
1945–46	Michael Hartney
1946–47	John C. Hickey
1947–48	Patrick O'Connell
1948–49	Michael B. O'Malley
1949–50	Gerard B. Dillon
1950–51	Kevin Bradshaw
1951–52	Stephen Coughlan
1952–53	Kevin Bradshaw
1953–54	John Carew TD
1954–55	George E. Russell
1955–56	George E. Russell
1956–57	George E. Russell TD
1957–58	C.P. Keyes
1958–59	Joseph P. Liddy
1959–60	John Carew TD
1960–61	Patrick Kelly
1961	Donogh B. O'Malley, TD (Resigned November 1961)
1961–62	F. Glasgow (elected for remainder of term)
1962–63	Frances Condell
1963–64	Frances Condell
1964–65	John Danagher
1965–66	Frank Leddin

Date	Mayors
1966–67	Vincent Feeney
1967–68	George E. Russell
1968–69	Jack Bourke
1969–70	Stephen Coughlan TD
1970–71	Joseph P. Liddy
1971–72	Denis A. O'Driscoll
1972–73	Patrick G. Kiely
1973–74	Michael Lipper
1974–75	Patrick Kennedy
1975–76	Thady Coughlan
1976–77	George E. Russell, Senator
1977–78	Frank Prendergast, PC
1978–79	Bobby Byrne
1979–80	Bobby Byrne
1980–81	Clement Casey
1981–82	Thomas Allen
1982–83	Tony Bromell
1983–84	Terry Kelly
1984–85	Frank Prendergast, PC, Alderman, TD
1985–86	Patrick Kennedy, PC, Alderman, Senator
1986–87	Jack Bourke
1987–88	Tim Leddin
1988–89	Paddy Madden
1989–90	Denis A. O'Driscoll
1990–91	Paddy Madden
1991–92	Jim Kemmy, TD
1992–93	John Quinn
1993–94	Jan O'Sullivan, Senator
1994–95	Dick Sadlier
1995–96	Jim Kemmy, TD
1996–97	Kieran O'Hanlon
1997–98	Frank Leddin
1998–99	Joe Harrington
1999–2000	Jack Bourke
2000–01	John Ryan
2001–02	Dick Sadlier
2002–03	John Cronin
2003–04	Dick Sadlier
2004–05	Michael Hourigan
2005–06	Diarmuid Scully
2006–07	Joe Leddin
2007–08	Ger Fahy

List of Abbreviations. A. Arthur Manuscript, S. Sexten Manuscript, W. White Manuscript

The Principal Mayoral Chain

Mayoral chains were uncommon in Britain and Ireland before the eighteenth century and there is no reference to the wearing of ceremonial chains by the mayor and sheriffs of Limerick Corporation before 1820, which would seem to indicate that the custom only commenced in that year. In 1820 four gold chains of office were purchased. Two were for the mayor and the other two were for each of the sheriffs. After the establishment of the Reformed Corporation in 1841, the two sheriffs' chains were worn by the town clerk and the city treasurer. Nowadays, the two mayoral chains continue to be used but the two sheriffs' chains are no longer worn. The mayor's principal chain is only worn on major ceremonial occasions due to its great weight. Instead the mayor generally uses the second chain, which consists of fifty-one plain links and is much easier to wear.

From 1822 onwards many of the mayors added extra roundels or links to the principal chain inscribed with their name, year of office and (after 1841) details of the events of their mayoralty. The last such link was added by Mayor Joe Leddin in 2007, to make a total of seventy-six. The following is a full listing of the roundels on the principal mayoral chain.

1.   D.G.F. Mahony. Esqr., Mayor, Year 1822.

2.   Henry Watson, Esq., Mayor. Years 1823, 1824, 1825.

3.   Nichs. (Nicholas) Mahon. Esqr., Mayor, Year 1826.

4.   Thomas Jervis, Mayor of Limerick, 1st October, 1827.

5.   Vere Hunt. Mayor of Limerick, October 1st 1828.

6.   Henry Rose, Esq., Mayor of Limerick, Year 1829.

7.   John Crips, Esq., Mayor of Limerick, 1831.

8.   The Honble (Honourable) J.P. Vereker, 1832–1833.

9.   Alderman John Vereker 1833.

10.   Alderman John J. Piercy 1834.

11.   Garrett Hugh Fitzgerald, Esqr., Mayor of Limerick, October. 1st. 1838.

12.   Sir Richard Franklin, M.D., Mayor of Limerick, 30th September, 1839.

13.   Honble (Honourable) Charles Smyth Vereker - Mayor 1841.

14.   Martin Honan, Mayor for the years 1842–1843. The Municipal Reform Act became Law in Limerick, Nov. 9th, 1841.

15.   Pierce Shannon, Corbally House, Mayor. Jany. 1st 1844. Died in his Mayoralty June 6th. 1844.

16.   William J. Geary, M.D. Mayor of Limerick, 1844–45. First arch stone of the Abbey River Bridge laid 29th Nov., 1845.

17.   Edmd. F-G Ryan. Mayor 1846. Floating Docks commenced. Total failure of potatoe (sic) crop. £5,000 collected in the city for the poor.

18. Thomas Wallnutt, Esq., Mayor of Limerick, 1847. The Liberator died at Genoa 15th May. Genl. Election, John O'Brien and John O'Connell, the son of the Liberator, returned.

19. Michael Quin, Mayor. 1848. Got possession of the Island Bank for the citizens. Railway communication opened 9th May between Dublin and Limerick.

20. Alderman John Boyse, J.P., Mayor of Limerick, 1849. Presented the Corporation Address to Her Majesty at Levee, Dublin. Laid the foundation stone of the Floating Docks, on which occasion he was presented with a silver trowel.

21. Laurence Quinlan, (Quinlivan) Esqr., Mayor. 1850. Presided at banquet of the citizens to Genl. Lord Gough on his Lordship's return from India 16th May. Attended Lord Mayor of London's Banquet to Prince Albert and the Mayors of the United Kingdom in furtherance of the Great Industrial Exhibition of all nations.

22. Thaddeus McDonnell, Esq., J.P. Mayor 1851. The Earl of Arundel and Surrey elected M.P. for the City.

23. Wm. (William) Henry Hall Mayor of Limerick, 1853. Great Munster Fair, new Corn Market, Floating Dock opened by Earl St. Germains.

24. Henry Watson, Esq., Mayor. 1823, 1824, 1825, 1854. War against Russia declared. Irish Militia embodied. The Mayor this year traversed land and water boundaries of the Corporation Municipality.

25. Henry O'Shea, Esq., Mayor 1855. Public fountains erected for the poor of the City.

26. James Spaight, Esq., Mayor 1856. Visit and entertainment of the Earl of Carlisle, Lord Lieutenant. Laid foundation stones of St. John's Cathedral and Sailor's Home. Peace with Russia. 1877 Opened People's Park. Reformed Night Watch.

27. Thomas Kane, J.P., M.D. mayor of Limerick 1852/57. General Election: Robert Potter & Francis William Russell Esqrs., Esqs. Returned members for Limk. The O'Connell statue inaugurated 15th August. General Election: Francis William Russell and Sergeant O'Brien elected 1857.

28. Edmond Gabbett, Esq., Mayor 1858. Visit of H.R.H. Prince Alfred, 26 June. James Spaight, Esq., returned M.P. For Limerick. Russian guns placed on Wellesley Bridge.

29. Michael Robert Ryan, J.P., Mayor of Limerick, 1859. General Election 4th May. F.W. Russell elected third time, Major Gavin elected second time Members of Parliament for the City. Silver cradle presented to Mrs. Ryan by Town Council and Corporation Officers in accordance with ancient custom of the city, to commemorate the birth of a son and heir, on 30th January in year of Mayoralty.

30. Alderman William Fitzgerald, Mayor. 1860. Died during his Mayoralty, 26 October, aged 34 years.

31. John Thomas MacSheehy Esq., J.P. Shannon Lawn, Mayor of Limerick for the year 1861. Presented by the citizens with a valuable silver testimonial on leaving office. Civil War broke out this year in the hitherto United States of America. Prince Consort died 14th December in this year. £1,100 collected for the purchase of fuel for the poor of the City.

32. Alderman William Lane Joynt, Mayor 1862. Appointed Clerk of the Crown for County Limerick. Great distress in Lancashire consequent on the Civil War in America.

33. Robert McMahon, J.P., unanimously elected Mayor of Limerick, 1st December, 1862 for year 1863. New Church of St. Alphonsus dedicated 7th same month. Prince of Wales married 10th March and address of congratulation presented by Mayor at Marlboro' House. Mayor presented at Queen's Levee, St. James Palace, 8 June. Slob lands at Corkanree transferred by the Crown to Corporation on 20th Nov.

34. Eugene O'Callaghan, J.P. Mayor of Limerick 1861 (actually he was Mayor in 1864). Presented address to Lord Wodehouse on his assuming Lord Lieutenancy of Ireland. Birth of a son to Prince of Wales. The Corporation Gas Works renovated. Bill for Corkanree Embankment promoted by the Corporation.

35. Alderman John R. Tinsley, J.P. Mayor of Limerick, 1865. General Election, Russell and Gavin re-elected for the City. £3,000 expended on sewerage. Distress among working classes and outdoor relief obtained. £500 expended on City Gaol. £500 obtained for Corkanree Embankment and work began. Ancient Treaty Stone raised on pedestal. Jubilee Fountain erected in St. John's Parish. Tait Testimonial Tower begun.

36. Thomas Boyse, J.P. Mayor of Limerick, 1869. The judges of Assises attended Mass in state at the Cathedral with the Mayor and Corporation in their robes, being the first occasion of the kind since the Reformation. Election petition against City members defeated. The Protestant Church disestablished in Ireland.

37. William Spillane, Esq., J.P. Mayor 1870. President of the Limerick Athenauem and School of Art, Public Free Library and Limerick Boat Club, unanimously elected to each office. Declaration of war between France and Prussia, July 15th. Irish Land Act became law, Aug. 1st. Corcanree Embankment opened Oct 14. First Public Free Library in Limerick opened Dec. 15.

38. Robert MacDonnell Esq., J.P. mayor of Limerick, 1871. Siege and surrender of Paris and termination of Franco-Prussian War. Visit of H.E. (His Excellency) Earl Spencer, Lord Lt. (Lord Lieutenant) 10th June and presentation of address at Town Hall. Presentation of Address by Mayor and Corporation to Col. (Colonel) W. Monsell M.P. for County Limerick, at Tervoe, Jan. on his appointment as Postmaster-General. John McDonnell, J.P. Father of Mayor High Sheriff, City of Limerick 1870–1871.

39. J.J. Cleary, Mayor of Limerick, 1872. Visit of Earl and Countess Spencer, Lord Lieutenant. Address presented from the Corporation. Resignation of Ministry. Formation of Conservative Government by Mr. Disraeli.

40. J.J. Cleary. Unanimously re-elected Mayor 1873. Vote by Ballot Act becomes law in Ireland. Opening of Graving Dock by Earl Spencer, Lord Lieut. May 14th. Over 300 citizens invited by Mayor to accompany his Excellency and Countess Spencer to Scattery Island de jeuner on board steamer. Ashantee war broke out. Irish Eight won shield at Wimbledon.

41. J.J. Cleary, Mayor of Limerick. Re-elected for the third time, 1874. Mayor attended the banquet, June 3rd of the Lord Mayor of London. Gladstone Ministry resigned. First Parliamentary election under the Ballot Act. Isaac Butt, Q.C., Richard O'Shaughnessy returned Feb. 8th. Address of congratulation to his Grace the Duke of Abercorn presented by the Mayor and Deputation for the Corporation at the Viceregal Lodge. First sod of the Peopl's Park raised by Mayor Oct. 26. Silver spade and trowel presd (presented). Silver cradle presented to Mayoress by the Corporation and citizens, value 250 guineas.

42. Ambrose Hall declared Mayor for the year 1875 by Right Hon. Justice Keogh after trial on petition in Court of Queen's Bench. International rifle match between America and Ireland. Frightful inundations in France, Hungary, England, Ireland, &c. International Municipal Festivities in London. O'Connell centenary celebration. Fancy charity ball organised by Mayor, by which £120 was realised for the poor.

43. John Francis Walker, Mayor 1876. Thomas E. O'Brien Esqr., South Hill, First Catholic High Sheriff elected by the Reformed Corporation. Opening of Catholic Institute. The laying of the foundation stone of the Tower and Spire of the Redemptorist Church, Mount St. Alphonsus with a grand peal of bells. All being the gift of Alderman John Quin, ex High Sheriff.

44. Stephen Hastings, Mayor 1878. Elected unanimously 1st Dec. 1877. Death of His Holiness Pius IX in the 32nd year of his Pontificate. Congratulatory address to Leo XIII on his accession. Treaty of Berlin signed July 13th. Invasion of Afghanistan.

45. Michael O'Gorman, Mayor 1879 and re-elected 1880. 1879 St. Alphonsus Tower completed & bells blessed. Mayor and Corporation attending ceremony. Isaac Butt, M.P. for the City died. Prince Imperial of France killed in Zulu War. Water arbitration held in Limerick. 1880, Limerick Gas Company's works acquired by Corporation. General Election. Resignation of Lord Beaconsfield. Gladstone appointed Prime Minister. Address of welcome to His Excellency, Earl Cowper, Lord Lieut. (Lieutenant) presented by the Mayor & deputation of the Corpn. Foundn. (foundation) stone of Clock tower at Dock laid by Miss O'Gorman, daughter of Mayor. Great agtn (agitation) for Reform of Land Laws thro (through) Ireland.

46. Alderman Jerome Counihan, Mayor, 1882–1883. Address of welcome presented by Mayor and Corporation in Dublin to Earl Spencer on appointment as Lord Lieutenant. Opening of Dublin Exhibition attended by Mayor and Mace Bearers. New Church of St. Michael's built and St. John's Cathedral Spire finished. Most Rev. Dr. Butler, Lord Bishop. First tree of Military Road planted by Mayor. Wellesley Bridge opened free of toll. Gold key presented to Mayor by Harbour Board. Royal Agricultural Society Show and Art Exhibition opened during visit of Lord Lieutenant and Countess Spencer. Bill passed to free Athlunkard Bridge from toll. Water works purchased and taken over by the Mayor.

47. S. O'Mara, Mayor of Limerick, 1885. Failure of Munster Bank. Visit of Prince of Wales to Railway Station. Not received in City by Mayor or citizens. Resistance to Police Tax brought to a successful issue. First Mayor elected as Nationalist.

48. S. O' Mara, Mayor of Limerick. (1886). Elected M.P. Queens County Ossory Division. Home Rule Bill introduced by W.E. Gladstone. Right Rev. Dr. G. Butler, Bishop, died. Rev. Dr. E.T. O'Dwyer consecrated Bishop.

49. Francis A. O'Keeffe, Solicitor, Mayor of Limerick for three years 1887, 1888, 1889. Elected Member of Parliament for the City of Limerick, 18th April, 1888. Introduced Public Libraries Act into Limerick. Turned first sod of New Waterworks, 5 Sept 1888. Corporation Artisans dwellings first erected. Re-elected M.P. for the City at contested elections 1892, 1892.

50. Wm. (William) J. O'Donnell, J.P., Mayor 1890. Sheriff 1889. The youngest Mayor of Limerick on record. 1890.

51. Alderman P. Riordan, Mayor, 1891. The Leader of the Irish People, Chas. S. Parnell died Oct. 6th 1891.

52. Denis F. McNamara, Mayor, 1892. Cardinal Manning died January 14th 1892. Gladstone elected to power on the Home Rule Ticket.

53. William M. Nolan, High Sheriff 1890. Mayor 1895 to 1896. Chairman, Committee "Garryowen" Fete, opened by Countess of Dunraven, and realised £3,000 for Barrington's Hospital. Mayoress presided at "Colleen Bawn" Stall. Nolan's Cottages built. Scheme for Technical Instruction for City initiated. Mayor went with deputation to Lord Lieutenant re endowment for Technical Education. Trade & Labour Congress in Limerick attended by Mayor in state. Band Stand in the People's Park inaugurated by Mayor. Garryowen Football Club won Munster Cup. Presented by Mayoress.

54. Seaghan O Dalaigh do daoradh than ceann treasuin cumh braigdeanas pionuis le linn a saoghail, 1884. Do sgaoileadh soar as carcar Phortland 1896. Do toghad d'eanguth na Meire e 1899 agus 1900. Do bhuadhuigh ar an d-teoruidhe an Ridire Tomas de Cliobh 1901.

55. James F. Barry 1902. Seamus F. de Barra, I. Na S. abhi 'na Ard Sirram Meire Luimnighe 1902.

56. John Kerr. 1907. Opened All Ireland Industrial Conference in the Town Hall. Nov. 28. Opened the Tuberculosis Exhibition in the Athenauem, Nov. 30. Attended the consecration of the Most Rev. Dr. Boylan as Bishop (of) Kilmore in Cavan Cathedral with sword and mace bearers, also Alderman McNiece & J.H. Roche Esq., J.P.

57. Alphonsus O'Mara, Mayor of Limerick, First Sinn Féin Mayor in Ireland. Refused Oath of Allegiance to the British Crown in 1918–19. Freedom of the City conferred on American delegates – Michael P. Ryan, Edward S. Dunne, Frank P. Walsh, 7th May, 1919.

58. Miceal O'Ceallachain, Meire, 1920. Go stuama calma stiuraigh se gnothai na cathrach bliain ba deine comhrach agus ba mho uafas I gCogadh na Saoirse, bliain glormhara a cruthaigh do claoideacht agus co-anntracht Gael. I gcoimh na h-oiche, Marta 7, 1921, ina thig fein dunmarbhaoidh e ag Gallaibh I lathair a bancheile. Beidh buan-cuimhne ar a oide I measc na ndaoine, 1879–1921.

59. Cuimnighid ar Luimnig. Do buanu cuimne Sheoirse Mhic Fhlannchadha. Oglach agus Oifigeach d'arm na Poblachta. Meire Luimnighe 1921, a dunmarbhuoidh le Gallaibh na thig fein I lathair a bean-ceile an 7u Marta, 1921.

60. Stiophain M. O'Meara, Meire Luimni 1921–23. Torcaire Dáil Éireann sna Stait Aontaithe 1921. Fe glas I gcampa Droichead Nua 1922–23. Ball de'n Coirle Stait. Stephen O' Mara, Mayor Limerick 1921–23. Trustee Dáil Éireann 1921. Special envoy to U.S.A. 1921. Interned Newbridge 1922–23. Member of Council of State. Appointed by President de Valera 1959.

61. Paul A. O'Brien, 1925–27. Archbishop Mannix made Freeman, Aug. 1925. Shannon Hydro El. (Electric) Scheme started Aug. 1926. A.B.C. (Athlunkard Boat Club) Boat House completed Dec. 1925. Dominicans celebrate 700 years in Limerick Jan. 1926. Bohs R.F.C (Bohemians Rugby Football Club) win first Munster Cup, April, 1926. G.A.A. acquire Ennis Road Grounds, April, 1926.

62. P.F. Quinlan. Co. (Councillor) P.F. Quinlan elected Mayor of Limerick 24th June 1933. Inaugurated poor children's excursion to Youghal 30th July 1933. Pres. (President) de Valera opened Civic Carnival 2nd October, 1933. Entertained Atlantic flyers Capt. Pond (and) Lieut. Stabelli 17th May 1934 who conveyed Mayor's Petition to Holy Father, Pope Pius XI. Turned sod Limerick's largest housing scheme (380 houses) Island Field, 7th June '34. Messrs. P. Molloy & Sons and M. Doyle & Son, Builders. Entertained French Engineers 3rd July, 1934. Unanimously re-elected Mayor 9th July, '34. Apostolic Benediction received from Holy Father Pope Pius XI 13th July, 1934. Mayoral Banquet 25th Oct. '34 to Limerick's team on victory All-Ireland Hurling Final. G.A.A. Jubilee year. Limerick City Management Act became Law, 6th Sept. 1934.

63. Alderman James M. Casey elected First Mayor under the Limerick City Management Act, 1934–36. Alderman James M. Casey acted as Deputy Mayor from 7th to 22nd March, 1921, after the murder of the Mayor by British Crown Forces.

64. Ald. (Alderman) Michael Hartney, Mayor 1945–46. Commandant Mid Limerick Brigade Old I.R.A. Commercial Air Services from the United States of America to Shannon Opened October 24th, 1945.

65. Miceal B. O'Maille, Meire, 1948–49. Dligheadoir.

66. This link was presented to Seoirse E. Ruiseil Mayor of Limerick 1954–55, 1955–56, 1956–57, by the sixteen surviving former Mayors of Limerick. G.B. Dillon, J.C. Hickey, A. O'Mara, Michael B. O'Malley, Michael J. Keyes, Stephen O'Mara, P. F. Quinlan, Patrick O'Connell, B.C., P.C., John Carew, James Reidy, Michael Hartney, K. Bradshaw, P.J. Donnellan, Des. J. O'Malley, Stephen Coughlan, James McQuane.

67. Vincent V. Feeney, Mayor of Limerick 1966–67. Aiseirí na Cásca 1916–1966.

68. Joseph P. Liddy, Mayor of Limerick. 1958–59 – Consecration of Bishop Murphy. Inauguration of President de Valera. 1970–71 – Freedom of the City conferred on Bishop Wyse-Jackson. Received President Nixon in Limerick. Enthronement of Bishop Caird. Civic Reception for Apollo 13 Astronauts James Lovelle, Jack Swigert, Fred Haise. Visit to U.S.A. received by President Nixon at White House. 50th Anniversary of deaths of Civic Leaders O'Callaghan, Clancy, Wall and Vol. (Volunteer) O'Donoghue. Attended funeral of Cardinal Michael Browne, O.P. visit of Lord Mayor and Mayoress of London, Sir Peter and Lady Studd and Party. Opened Watergate Housing Scheme.

69. Michael D. Lipper, 1973–74. Mayor of Limerick.

70. An Comhairleoir Tony Bromell Méara Luimní 1982/83
A bhean Áine is a gclann
Úna, Déaglán, Fionnuala, Eamonn
Cláraitheoir Choláiste Mhuire gan Smál
Briathar Dé Mo Lóchrann.

71. Maurice Lenihan Historian
1884 Mayor of Limerick
Presented by J.J. Kenneally & Sons Jewellers Limerick 1992
1691–1991 Limerick Treaty 300
Mayor Jim Kemmy and Mayor Paddy Madden.

72. Presented to Clr. John Quinn Mayor of Limerick
1st February 1993
By ICS Liam Ahern Chief Executive Irish Co-op Society Limerick
ICS 1893–1993

1893	-	Chairman	-	1993
Sir Horace Plunkett				W.R. Nagle

73. Ald. J. Kemmy Mayor of Limerick
A.I.B. Bank
Y.M.R.F.C.
G. Casey President 1995
Young Munster R.F.C. Centenary 1895–1995.

74. Kieran O'Hanlon Mayor 1996/97
Marking 800th Anniversary of Charter
Presented by Wyeth Nutritionals Ireland.

75. Frank Leddin Mayor 1997/98
Marking Telecom Eireann Board Meeting in Limerick
Presented by Bord Telecom Eireann Plc.

76. Cllr. Joe Leddin Mayor of Limerick 2006/2007
Marking The Contribution By The Leddin & Keyes Families
To The People of Limerick
Presented by Joe Leddin & Family
Leddin Finance Dublin

List of persons who received the Honorary Freedom of Limerick

Name	When Admitted	Mayor at the Time
Isaac Butt, M.P. for Limerick City	January 1, 1877	James Spaight
Richard O'Shaughnessy, M.P. for Limerick City	January 1, 1877	James Spaight
Charles Stewart Parnell, M.P. for Cork City	July 14, 1880	Michael O'Gorman
Michael Davitt	April 14, 1884	Maurice Lenihan
Edward Dwyer Gray, M.P. for County Carlow	April 14, 1884	Maurice Lenihan
Charles Dawson, M.P. for Carlow Town	April 14, 1884	Maurice Lenihan
William Ewart Gladstone, M.P. for Midlothian	October 4, 1886	Stephen O'Mara
William O'Brien, M.P. for the South-East Division of Cork	June 13, 1887	Francis A. O'Keeffe
The Most Noble Geo. Fredk. Samuel, Marquis of Ripon, K.G.	February 3, 1888	Francis A. O'Keeffe
John Morley, M.P. for Newcastle-on-Tyne	February 3, 1888	Francis A. O'Keeffe
The Right Revd. James F. Corbett, D.D., Roman Catholic Bishop of Sale, Australia	December 23, 1889	Francis A. O'Keeffe
The Hon. Ishbel Maria Countess of Aberdeen, Wife of his Excellency the Earl of Aberdeen, Governor-General of Canada His Eminence Cardinal Logue, Cardinal Archbishop of Armagh;	June 8, 1894	Bryan O'Donnell
Primate of All-Ireland	June 14, 1894	Bryan O'Donnell
Thomas J. Clarke	March 2, 1899	John Daly
James F. Egan	May 10, 1900	John Daly
Thomas Myles, M.D., F.R.S.I., President of the Royal College of Surgeons in Ireland	June 16, 1900	John Daly

List of persons who received the Honorary Freedom of Limerick

Name	When Admitted	Mayor at the Time
Maude Gonne	December 13, 1900	John Daly
Andrew Carnegie	October 20, 1903	M. Donnelly
Joseph O'Mara	October 2, 1908	T. Donnellan
The Right Hon. The Earl of Dunraven	December 7, 1908	T. Donnellan

(Lord Dunraven was struck off the Roll of Freemen on 2 May 1918 during the Mayoralty of Alphonsus O'Mara, and restored on 2 July 2007, during the Mayoralty of Ger Fahy)

Name	When Admitted	Mayor at the Time
Douglas Hyde, LL.D., DR.LIT., President of Gaelic League	June 5, 1909	T. Donnellan
Capt. Edward O'Meagher-Condon	September 13, 1909	T. Donnellan
His Lordship, the Most Rev. Dr. E.T. O'Dwyer, Bishop of Limerick	August 3, 1916	Stephen Quin
Mrs. Thomas Clarke	September 5, 1918	A. O'Meadhra
Eoin MacNeill	September 5, 1918	A. O'Meadhra
E. de Valera	September 5, 1918	A. O'Meadhra

Freedom granted as a protest against the action of the British Government in proclaiming certain Irish Nationalist Associations of which Mrs. Clarke, Mr MacNeill and Mr. De Valera are representatives, viz; Cumann na mBan, Gaelic League and Sinn Féin.

Name	When Admitted	Mayor at the Time
Michael P. Ryan	May 7, 1919	A. O'Meaghra
Edward S. Dunne	May 7, 1919	A. O'Meadhra
Frank P. Walsh	May 7, 1919	A. O'Meadhra

Members of Irish-American Delegation to Peace Conference.

Name	When Admitted	Mayor at the Time
His Grace Most Rev. Dr. Mannix, Archbishop of Melbourne	August 5, 1925	Paul A. O'Brien
His Eminence Cardinal Van Rossum, C.SS.R., Cardinal Prefect of Propaganda, Rome	July 21, 1928	M. J. Keyes
Most. Rev. Dr. Patrick Murray, Superior-General of Congregation of the Most Holy Redeemer, Rome	July 21, 1928	M. J. Keyes
His Excellency Most Revd. Monsignor Paschal Robinson, O.F.M., Apostolic Nuncio, Irish Free State, Dublin.	July 21, 1928	M. J. Keyes

Name	When Admitted	Mayor at the Time
His Grace Most Revd. Dr. Richard Downey, Ph.D., Lord Archbishop of Liverpool, England	April 21, 1932	P. Donnellan
Dermod O'Brien, Esq., Hon. President, Royal Hibernian Academy	February 27, 1936	J. M. Casey
William Griffin, Editor and Publisher of the New York Enquirer	January 14, 1937	Dan Bourke
Joseph Mary Flood, B.L.	March 22, 1948	Patrick O'Connell
John Keating, R.H.A.	March 22, 1948	Patrick O'Connell
His Excellency Sean T. O Ceallaigh, Uachtaran na h-Éireann	March 24, 1948	Patrick O'Connell
His Eminence John Cardinal Dalton, D.D., Archbishop of Armagh and Primate of All-Ireland	September 25, 1953	John Carew
His Excellency Most Revd. Gerald Patrick O'Hara, J.U.D., Archbishop, Bishop of Savannah-Atlanta, U.S.A. Apostolic Nuncio to Ireland	June 25, 1954	John Carew
His Eminence Michael, Cardinal Browne	August 15, 1962	Frances Condell
His Excellency John Fitzgerald Kennedy, President of the United States Of America	June 29, 1963	Frances Condell
Dr. Kenneth David Kaunda, President of the Republic of Zambia	November 25, 1964	John Danagher
His Eminence William, Cardinal Conway, Archbishop of Armagh and Primate of All-Ireland	April 12, 1966	Frank Leddin
Most Rev. Joseph B. Whelan, C.S.Sp., Bishop of Owerri	April 2, 1970	Stephen Coughlan
Rt. Rev. Robert Wyse-Jackson, Bishop of Limerick	August 18, 1970	Joseph P. Liddy
His Holiness, Pope John II, Supreme Pontiff of the Roman Catholic Church and Bishop of Rome	October 1, 1979	Bobby Byrne
His Eminence, Tomás, Cardinal O Fiaich, Archbishop of Armagh and Primate of All-Ireland	October 1, 1979	Bobby Byrne

Name	When Admitted	Mayor at the Time
His Excellency, the Most Rev. Gaetano Alibrandi, D.D.,U.J.D., Titular Archbishop of Binda, Apostolic Nuncio to Ireland	October 1, 1979	Bobby Byrne
His Lordship, the Most Rev. Jeremiah Newman, D.D., Bishop of Limerick	October 1, 1979	Bobby Byrne
G.E. Russell	June 23, 1995	Dick Sadlier
Dr. Brendan O'Regan	June 23, 1995	Dick Sadlier
Dr. Edward M. Walsh	June 23, 1995	Dick Sadlier
John Hunt	July 4, 1997	Kieran O'Hanlon
Trudy Hunt	July 4, 1997	Kieran O'Hanlon
His Excellency William Jefferson Clinton, President of the United States of America	September 5, 1998	Joe Harrington
J.P. McManus	May 4, 2001	John Ryan
Bill Whelan	May 4, 2001	John Ryan
Pat Cox, M.E.P., President of the European Parliament	May 24, 2002	Dick Sadlier
Fr. Aengus Finucane, C.S.Sp	June 21, 2005	Michael Hourigan
Fr. Jack Finucane, C.S.Sp	June 21, 2005	Michael Hourigan
Ciarán Mac Mathúna	June 21, 2005	Michael Hourigan
Sir Terry Wogan	June 15, 2007	Joe Leddin
Dr. Thomas Ryan, RHA	June 15, 2007	Joe Leddin

Bibliography

MANUSCRIPT SOURCES

Limerick City Archives
Minutes of Limerick Corporation 1769–1796.
Minutes of Limerick Corporation (fragments) 1807–1809.
Minutes of Limerick Corporation 1841–1972.
Minutes of Limerick Corporation Committees 1841–1972.
Two lists of Freemen 1730s to 1836.
Court of Claims Register 1823–1841.
Register of Admissions 1832–1841.
Oath Book 1798–1892.
Paying Orders of Council 1777–1801.
City Manager's Orders 1934–1959.

Limerick City Library.
Minutes of Limerick Corporation/City Council 1972–2007.
City Manager's Orders 1960–2007.
Jim Kemmy, A History of the Limerick City Library and Granary, (Unpublished manuscript, 1985).
Robert Potter, Limerick Corporation Index 1843

National Archives, Dublin.
Department of the Environment and Local Government. Files relating to Limerick Corporation.

National Library, Dublin.
Mss. 16092–16093. Poll book for Limerick city in general election of 1761.

British Library, London.
Additional Mss.19859. Acts and Orders of the General Assembly and Common Council of the City of Limerick, Sept., 1672 to Oct., 1680.
Additional Mss.19865. Papers of the Sexton family of Limerick.
Additional Mss.31885. Papers of the Arthur family of Limerick.
Additional Mss.31886. The annals of the city and diocese of Limerick (from the earliest times) to 1768, compiled by the Rev. James White. A transcript of the original manuscript by Maurice Lenihan, 1865.
Additional Mss.31888. Poll book for Limerick city bye-election of 1731.

Knight of Glin, Glin Castle.
Viscount Gort, Notes on the Gort Family (unpublished manuscript).

PUBLISHED MATERIAL

Newspapers.
Freemans Journal
Irish Independent
Irish Times
Limerick Chronicle
Limerick Echo
Limerick Herald
Limerick Leader
Limerick Reporter
Munster News

Irish Parliament Publications (Eighteenth Century).
Report of His Majesty's Attorney and Solicitor General upon the Bill for better regulating the Corporation of Limerick, (Dublin, 1762).
Statutes of the Irish Parliament.

Irish Government Publications.
Acts of the Oireachtas.
Central Statistics Office. *Census of Population, 1986–2002.*
Report of Mr. J. MacLysaght, B.L., Local Government Inspector into the Powers, Duties and Obligations of the Limerick Corporation and the Limerick County Borough Board of Health, (Dublin, 1932).

British Government Publications.
Report from the Select Committee on the Limerick Election Together with the Special Report from the Said Committee, H.C. 1820 (229).
Report from a Committee of the Irish House of Commons, on Petition from Freemen of Limerick, &c. 23rd December, 1761, H.C. 1820 (270).
Report from the Select Committee on Petitions Relating to the Local Taxation of the City of Limerick, H.C.1822 (617), vii.
Reports of the Commissioners Appointed to Enquire into Municipal Corporations in Ireland. H.C. 1835 (27).
Reports and Instructions by Lord Lieutenant, with Reference to Boundaries and Divisions of Cities, Boroughs and Towns Corporate in Ireland, H.C. 1837 (301) xxix.
Report from the Select Committee on Local Government and Taxation of Towns (Ireland); together with the Proceedings of the Committee, Minutes of Evidence and Appendix, H.C. 1877 (357), xii.
Second Report of Commission on Municipal Boundaries, H.C. 1881 (3089), 50.
Statutes of the British Parliament.

Limerick Corporation/City Council Publications.
Abstract No.7. Receipt and Expenditure of the Corporation of the Borough of Limerick, from 1st March 1848 to 1st March 1849, (Limerick, 1849).
Corporation of Limerick. *List of the Mayors and Sheriffs of the City from 1197 to the Present Day* (Limerick 2001).
County Borough Council of Limerick. *Return of the Average Weekly Expenses of the Different Departments of the Corporation,* (Limerick, 1902).
Limerick City Council, *Proposal for a City Boundary Extension. Prepared in Accordance with the Local Government Act, 1991 and Regulations made thereunder,* (Limerick, October 2004. Amended October 2005).
Limerick Corporation/City Council *Annual Reports, 1991–2006.*
Limerick Corporation *City Hall. Limerick Celebrates* (June 2 1990).
Limerick Corporation *Yearbook and Diary 1989.*
Limerick. Official Guide to the City of Limerick, (Limerick, 1976).
Limerick. Official Guide to the City of Limerick, (Limerick, 1990).
T.P. MacDiarmada, City Manager and Town Clerk, *The Mayoral Chain,* (Limerick, No date of publication).
Report of the Local Government Auditor, Yearly Abstracts of Accounts and Explanatory Schedules for the Years 1891, 1892, 1893 & 1894, (Limerick, 1896).
Report of Robert Potter, Esq. Law Agent to the Corporation, (Limerick, 1844).

Other Printed Primary Sources.

William Bassett, *Limerick City and County and the Principal Towns in the Counties of Clare, Tipperary and Kerry, Directory, 1880–1,* (Limerick, 1880).

Calender of the Carew Manuscripts Preserved in the Archiepiscopal Library at Lambeth, 6 Vols, (London, 1867–73).

Calender of Patent Rolls, (London 1891–1971).

Calendar of State Papers Relating to Ireland, 24 Vols. (London, 1860–1912).

The Crescent College Review, No. 1, (Midsummer, 1897).

E. Curtis and R. B. MacDowell (eds.), *Irish Historical Documents,* (London, 1943).

John Ferrar, *Ferrar's Directory of Limerick,* (Limerick, 1769).

G.E.C. (ed.), *The Complete Baronetage,* 6 vols, (Exeter, 1900–09).

General Directory of Cork for 1867 with which is Incorporated Wynne and Co's Business Directory of the Principal Towns in the Province of Munster, (London, 1867).

J. H.Gilbert (ed.), *Historical and Municipal Documents of Ireland,* (London, 1870).

The Irish Fiants of the Tudor Sovereigns during The Reigns of Henry VIII, Edward VI, Philip and Mary, and Elizabeth I, 3 Vols, (Dublin 1994).

Charles Mosley (ed.), *Burke's Peerage and Baronetage,* 2 Vols. (106th edition, Crans, Switzerland, 1999).

Nealon's Guide to the Dáil and Seanad, (Dublin, 1973–2002).

Slaters Directory of Munster (1846).

H. S. Sweetman, *Calender of Documents Relating to Ireland, Vol. 2, 1252–84,* (London, 1877).

Brian M. Walker (ed.), *Parliamentary Election Results in Ireland, 1801–1922,* (Dublin, 1978).

Who's Who in Catholic Life, (Manchester, 2003).

Who was Who 1951–1950. A Companion to Who's Who containing the Biographies of those who died during the Decade 1941–1950, (London, 1952).

Books, Pamphlets, Reports and Articles.

David Abulafia (ed.), *The New Cambridge Medieval History. Volume 5 c1198–c1300,* (Cambridge, 1998).

M. S. Anderson, *Europe in the Eighteenth Century,* (Oxford, 1979).

Anonymous (Dean Charles Massy), *A Collection of Resolutions, Queries, &c. Wrote on Occasion of the Present Dispute in the City of Limerick,* (Limerick, 1726).

Anonymous, *A Descriptive and Historic Guide Through St. Mary's Cathedral, Limerick,* (3rd edition, Limerick, 1887).

Anonymous, *Limerick City and the Great Hunger,* (Limerick, 1997).

Anonymous, *A True State of the Present Affairs of Limerick Shewing the Rise and Progress of the Disputes in that City with Some Remarks on the Dangerous Consequences which must Attend the Investing Military Men with the Civil Powers of Corporations,* (London, 1726).

Anonymous, *The Visit. John Paul II in Ireland. A Historical Record,* (Dublin 1979).

William F. Bailey, *Local and Centralised Government in Ireland. A Sketch of the Existing Systems,* (Dublin, 1888).

T.C. Barnard, *Cromwellian Ireland, English Government and Reform in Ireland 1649–1660,* (Oxford, 1975).

Toby Barnard, *The Abduction of a Limerick Heiress. Social and Political Relations in Mid-Eighteenth Century Ireland,* (Dublin, 1998).

Rev. John Begley, *The Diocese of Limerick,* 3 Vols, (Dublin 1906–38).

Peter Borsay, *The English Urban Renaissance, Culture and Society in the Provincial Town, 1660–1770,* (Oxford, 1989).

D. George Boyce, *Nationalism in Ireland,* (London, 1982).

John Bradley, 'The Medieval Towns of Tipperary' in D.W. Nolan and T. McGrath (eds), *Tipperary History and Society, Interdisciplinary Essays on the History of an Irish County,* (Dublin, 1985).

Brendan Bradshaw, 'Fr. Wolfe's Description of Limerick City, 1574' in *North Munster Antiquarian Journal,* Vol. XVII, (1975).

Brendan Bradshaw, *The Irish Constitutional Revolution in the Sixteenth Century,* (Cambridge, 1979).

Brendan Bradshaw, S.M., 'The Reformation in the Cities: Cork, Limerick and Galway, 1534–1603' in John Bradley, (ed.), *Settlement and Society in Medieval Ireland. Studies presented to F. X. Martin, O.S.A.,* (Kilkenny, 1988).

Tony Bromell, *Rian Mo Chos Ar Ghaineamh an tSaoil,* (Galway, 2006).

Vincent Browne and Michael Farrell, *The Magill Book of Irish Politics,* (Dublin, 1981).

James Burke, 'Limerick in the Golden Age of Siege Warfare' in Bernadette Whelan (ed.), *The Last of the Great Wars. Essays on the War of the Three Kings in Ireland 1688–91,* (Limerick, 1995).

R.A. Butlin (ed.), *The Development of the Irish Town,* (London, 1977).

R.A. Butlin, 'Irish Towns in the Sixteenth and Seventeenth Centuries,' in R.A.Butlin (ed.), *The Development of the Irish Town,* (London, 1977).

R.A. Butlin 'Urban and Proto-Urban Settlements in Pre-Norman Ireland', in R.A.Butlin (ed.), *The Development of the Irish Town,* (London, 1977).

Joseph Byrne, *Byrne's Dictionary of Irish Local History,* (Cork, 2004).

Bibliography

Liam Cahill, *Forgotten Revolution. Limerick Soviet 1919. A Threat to British Power in Ireland,* (Dublin, 1990).

Mary Rose Callaghan, *'Kitty O'Shea', The Story of Katherine Parnell,* (London, 1989).

Mark Callanan, 'The Role of Local Government' in Mark Callanan and Justin F. Keogan (eds.), *Local Government in Ireland Inside Out,* (Dublin, 2003).

Mark Callanan and Justin F. Keogan (eds.), *Local Government in Ireland Inside Out,* (Dublin, 2003).

Nicholas Canny, *From Reformation to Restoration: Ireland 1534–1660,* (Dublin, 1987).

Nicholas Canny, *The Elizabethan Conquest of Ireland: A Pattern Established 1565–76,* (Hassocks, 1976).

Raymond Carr, *Spain 1808–1975,* (second edition Oxford, 1982).

Basil Chubb (Ed.), *A Source Book of Irish Government,* (Dublin, 1964).

City and County Management 1929–1990. A Retrospective, (Dublin, 1991).

Aidan Clarke, 'The Irish Economy, 1600–60' in Art Cosgrove (ed.), *A New History of Ireland, Volume II, Medieval Ireland 1169–1534.* (Oxford, 1987).

Howard B. Clarke (ed.), *Irish Cities,* (Cork and Dublin, 1995).

Kathleen Clarke, *Revolutionary Woman. Kathleen Clarke 1878–1972 An Autobiography. Edited by Helen Litton,* (Dublin, 1991).

Peter Clarke, David Michael Palliser and Martin J. Daunton (eds), *The Cambridge Urban History of Britain, Volume II, 1540–1840,* (Cambridge, 2000).

Art Cosgrove (ed.), *A New History of Ireland, Volume II, Medieval Ireland 1169–1534.* (Oxford, 1987).

Virginia Crossman, *Local Government in Nineteenth Century Ireland,* (Belfast, 1994).

L. M. Cullen, 'Economic Development, 1691–1750' in T.W. Moody and W.E. Vaughan (eds.), *A New History of Ireland, Vol. IV, Eighteenth-Century Ireland 1691–1800,* (Oxford, 1986).

L. M. Cullen, 'Economic Development, 1750–1800' in T.W. Moody and W.E. Vaughan (eds.), *A New History of Ireland, Vol. IV, Eighteenth-Century Ireland 1691–1800,* (Oxford, 1986).

L. M. Cullen, 'Economic Trends, 1660–91' in T.W. Moody, F.X. Martin and F.J. Byrne, (eds.), *A New History of Ireland, Vol.III, Early Modern Ireland 1534–1691,* (Oxford, 1991).

Judith Crosbie, 'The Era of Radicalism: Limerick's Mayors During World War One' in David Lee (ed.), *Remembering Limerick. Historical Essays Celebrating the 800th Anniversary of Limerick's First Charter granted in 1197,* (Limerick, 1997).

Heather Cunningham, 'Civic Peacocks' in David Lee (ed.), *Remembering Limerick. Historical Essays Celebrating the 800th Anniversary of Limerick's First Charter granted in 1197,* (Limerick, 1997).

Robert Cussen, 'Caleb Powell, High Sheriff of County Limerick, 1858, sums up his Grand Jury' in Etienne Rynne, (ed.), *North Munster Studies. Essays in Commemoration of Monsignor Michael Moloney,* (Limerick, 1967).

William Dalrymple, *White Mughals,* (London, 2002).

Mary E. Daly, *The Buffer State. The Historical Roots of the Department of the Environment,* (Dublin, 1997).

Martin Daunton (ed.), *The Cambridge Urban History of Britain, Volume III, 1840–1950,* (Cambridge, 2001).

Rene David and John E.C. Brierley, *Major Legal Systems in the World Today,* (London, 1978).

Padráig de Bhaldraithe and Padráig Og de Bhaldraithe, 'The Nolans and Costelloes of Listowel, Limerick and Calgary' in *The Old Limerick Journal,* No. 27, (Autumn, 1990).

John W. de Courcy and Heather Cunningham, 'Bob de Courcy – The Republican Engineer' in David Lee (ed.), *Remembering Limerick. Historical Essays Celebrating the 800th Anniversary of Limerick's First Charter granted in 1197,* (Limerick, 1997).

David Dickson, 'Catholics and Trade in Eighteenth-Century Ireland: an Old Debate Revisited' in T.P. Power and Kevin Whelan (eds.), *Endurance and Emergence: Catholics in Ireland in the Eighteenth Century,* (Dublin, 1990).

David Dickson, 'Large-Scale Developers and the Growth of Eighteenth-Century Irish Cities' in P. Butel and L.M. Cullen, (eds.), *French and Irish Perspectives on Urban Development, 1500–1900,* (Dublin, 1986).

David Dickson, *New Foundations: Ireland 1660–1800,* (Dublin, 1987).

Richard Doherty, *The Williamite War in Ireland, 1688–1691,* (Dublin, 1998).

Michael Donnellan, 'Limerick's Water Supply' in David Lee (ed.), *Remembering Limerick. Historical Essays Celebrating the 800th Anniversary of Limerick's First Charter granted in 1197,* (Limerick, 1997).

Brian Donnelly, 'Michael Joyce: Squarerigger, Shannon Pilot and M.P.' in *The Old Limerick Journal,* No. 27, (Autumn, 1990).

Kevin Donnelly, Michael Hoctor and Dermot Walsh, *A Rising Tide. The Story of Limerick Harbour,* (Limerick, 1994).

Barry M. Doyle, 'The Changing Functions of Urban Government: Councillors, Officials and Pressure Groups' in Martin Daunton (ed.), *The Cambridge Urban History of Britain, Volume III, 1840–1950,* (Cambridge, 2001).

William Doyle, *The Old European Order 1660–1800,* (Oxford, 2nd edition, 1992).

R. Dudley-Edwards, 'The Beginnings of Municipal Government in Dublin' in Howard Clarke (ed.), *Medieval Dublin. The Living City,* (Dublin, 1990).

Steven G. Ellis, 'Historical Revision XIX: The Irish Customs Administration under the Early Tudors' in *Irish Historical Studies,* Vol. XXII, No. 87, (March, 1981).

Stephen G. Ellis, *Ireland in the Age of the Tudors 1447–1603. English Expansion and the End of Gaelic Rule,* (Harlow, 1998).

Mary Fennelly (ed.), *Limerick Lives,* (Limerick, 1996).

Laurence Fenton, 'A Riot in Limerick, 1848' in *The Old Limerick Journal,* No. 40, (Winter 2004).

John Ferrar, *History of Limerick, Ecclesiastical, Civil and Military from the Earliest Records to the Year 1787*, (Limerick, 2nd ed. 1787).

Diarmaid Ferriter, *'Lovers of Liberty?' Local Government in 20th Century Ireland*, (Dublin, 2001).

Francis Finegan, S.J, *Limerick Jesuit Centenary Record*, (Limerick, 1959).

Francis Finegan, S.J., 'Maurice Lenihan- Historian of Limerick, Part One', in *The Old Limerick Journal*, No 17, (Winter, 1984).

Francis Finegan, S.J., 'Maurice Lenihan- Historian of Limerick, Part Two', in *The Old Limerick Journal*, No 18, (Winter, 1985).

Francis Finegan, S.J., 'Maurice Lenihan- Historian of Limerick, Part Two', (in reality Part Three) in *The Old Limerick Journal*, No 19, (Summer, 1986).

Francis Finegan, S.J., 'Maurice Lenihan- Historian of Limerick, Part Four', in *The Old Limerick Journal*, No 20, (Winter, 1986).

Elizabeth Fitzpatrick and Raymond Gillespie (eds), *The Parish in Medieval and Early Modern Ireland. Community, Territory and Building*, (Dublin, 2006).

P. Fitzgerald and J.J. McGregor, *The History, Topography and Antiquities of the County and City of Limerick; with a Preliminary view of the History and Antiquities of Ireland*, 2 Vols, (Dublin, 1826-7).

John Fleming and Sean O'Grady, *St. Munchin's College Limerick 1796-1996*, (Limerick, 1996).

Juliet Gardiner and Neil Wenborn (eds.), *The History Today Companion to British History*, (London, 1995).

John Garrard, *Bureaucrats Rather Than Bureaucracies: The Power of Municipal Professionals 1835-1914*. Occasional Papers in History and Politics No.33, (Salford, 1993).

John Garrard (ed.), *Heads of the Local State: Mayors, Provosts and Burgomasters since 1800*, (Aldershot, 2007).

John A. Garrard, 'The History of Local Political Power-Some Suggestions for Analysis' in *Political Studies*, Vol. 25, No.2, (1977).

John Garrard, *Leadership and Power in Victorian Industrial Towns 1830-80*, (Manchester, 1983).

John Garrard, 'The Mayoralty since 1835' in *Proceedings of the Lancashire and Cheshire Historical Society*, Volume 90, (1994).

John Garrard, 'The Middle Classes and Nineteenth Century and Local Politics' in John Garrard, David Jary, Michael Goldsmith and Adrian Oldfield (eds), *The Middle Classes In Politics*, (Farnborough, Hants, 1978).

John Garrard, 'Urban Elites, 1850-1914: The Rule and Decline of a New Squirearchy?' in *Albion*, Vol. 27, No.3, (Autumn, 1995).

M.E. Gleeson, 'Dr. John Geary and Dr. Wm. John Geary: 1779-1853' in *The Old Limerick Journal, Barringtons' Edition*, No. 24 (Winter, 1988).

Mike Goldsmith and John Garrard, 'Urban Governance: Some Reflections' in Robert J. Morris and Richard H. Trainor (eds), *Urban Governance. Britain and Beyond Since 1750*, (Aldershot and Burlington, 2000).

B. J. Graham, 'The High Middle Ages: c. 1100 to c. 1350' in B. J. Graham and L. J. Proudfoot (eds.), *An Historical Geography of Ireland*, (London and San Diego, 1993).

B.J. Graham, 'The Towns of Medieval Ireland' in R.A.Butlin (ed.), *The Development of the Irish Town*, (London, 1977).

B. J. Graham and L.J. Proudfoot (eds), *An Historical Geography of Ireland*, (London and San Diego, 1993).

B. J. Graham and L.J. Proudfoot, *Urban Improvement in Provincial Ireland, 1700-1840*, (Athlone, 1994).

Brian Graham, 'Urbanisation in Ireland during the High Middle Ages, c. 1100 to c. 1350' in Terry Barry (ed.), *A History of Settlement in Ireland*, (London and New York, 2000).

Niall Greene, 'Mick Keyes-The Foundation of Labour in Limerick' in *Welcome to Limerick. Labour Party Conference 1995*, (No place of publication, 1995).

J. Grene-Barry, 'The Liberties of Limerick' in *Journal of the North Munster Archaeological Society*, Vol. 2, No. 4., (January, 1913).

Charles Gross, *The Gild Merchant. A Contribution to British Municipal History*, 2 vols., (Oxford, 1890).

Simon Gunn, 'Ritual and Civic Culture in the English Industrial City, c. 1835-1914' in Robert J. Morris and Richard H. Trainor (eds), *Urban Governance. Britain and Beyond Since 1750*, (Aldershot and Burlington, 2000).

M. M. Xavier Gwynn, SHCJ, *From Hunting Field to Cloister*, (Dublin, 1946).

Kevin Hannon, *Limerick. Historical Reflections*, (Limerick, 1996).

Kevin Hannan, 'The Rich Inheritance of a Limerick Mayor' in David Lee (ed.), *Remembering Limerick. Historical Essays Celebrating the 800th Anniversary of Limerick's First Charter granted in 1197*, (Limerick, 1997).

Kevin Hannan, 'Sir Peter Tait' in *The Old Limerick Journal*, No. 31, (Winter, 1994).

David Harkness and Mary O'Dowd (eds.), *The Town In Ireland*, (Belfast, 1981).

William Henry, *Roll of Honour. The Mayors of Galway City 1485-2001*, (Galway, 2002).

Robert Herbert, 'The Antiquities of the Corporation of Limerick' in *North Munster Antiquarian Journal*, Vol. 4, No. 3, (Spring, 1945).

Robert Herbert, 'The Chairing of Thomas Spring Rice' in *North Munster Antiquarian Journal*, Vol. 4, No. 4, (Autumn, 1945).

Cheryl Herr (ed.), *For the Land They Loved. Irish Political Melodramas 1890-1925*, (Syracuse, New York, 1991).

Dilys M. Hill, *Democratic Theory and Local Government*, (London, 1974).

Judith Hill, *The Building of Limerick*, (Cork, 1991).

Judith Hill, *Irish Public Sculpture*, (Dublin, 1998).

Judith Hill, 'Reputations: Nineteenth-Century Monuments in Limerick' in *The Old Limerick Journal*, No. 33, (Winter, 1996).

Judith Hill, 'The Use of the Castle of Limerick: Seal and City Motif' in David Lee (ed.), *Remembering Limerick. Historical Essays Celebrating the 800th Anniversary of Limerick's First Charter granted in 1197*, (Limerick, 1997).

Brian J. Hodkinson, 'Edmund Sexten: The First Irish Mayor of Limerick' in David Lee (ed.), *Remembering Limerick. Historical Essays Celebrating the 800th Anniversary of Limerick's First Charter granted in 1197*, (Limerick, 1997).

Bibliography

Brian Hodkinson, 'Lenihan's Mayoral List' in *North Munster Antiquarian Journal*, Vol. 41 (2001).

Brian Hodkinson, 'The Medieval City' in Liam Irwin, Gearoid O'Tuathaigh and Matthew Potter (eds) *Limerick History and Society* (forthcoming 2008).

Brian Hodkinson, 'The Topography of Pre-Norman Limerick' in *North Munster Antiquarian Journal*, Vol. 42 (2002).

Eric Hobsbawm, *The Age of Revolution*, (Oxford, 1962).

J.J. Hogan, *From Small Beginnings. The Story of the Limerick School of Art and Design 1852–2002*, (Limerick, 2004).

Joanna Innes, 'The Local Acts of a National Parliament: Parliament's Role in Sanctioning Local Action in Eighteenth-Century Britain', *in Parliamentary History*, Vol. 17, No. 1, (1998).

Liam Irwin, 'Introduction to the 1991 Edition' in Maurice Lenihan, *Limerick, its History and Antiquities, Ecclesiastical, Civil and Military, From the Earliest Ages*, (Dublin, 1866. Reprinted Cork, 1991), pp ix-xiii.

Liam Irwin, 'Lords President of Munster and Connacht, 1569–1672' in T.W. Moody, F.X. Martin and F.J. Byrne, (eds.), *A New History of Ireland, Volume IX, Maps, Genealogies, Lists. A Companion to Irish History, Part 2*, (Oxford, 1984).

Liam Irwin, 'Sarsfield: The Man and the Myth' in Bernadette Whelan (ed.), *The Last of the Great Wars. Essays on the War of the Three Kings in Ireland 1688–91*, (Limerick, 1995).

Liam Irwin, 'Seventeenth Century Limerick' in David Lee (ed.), *Remembering Limerick. Historical Essays Celebrating the 800th Anniversary of Limerick's First Charter granted in 1197*, (Limerick, 1997).

Liam Irwin, 'The Suppression of the Irish Presidency System', in *Irish Historical Studies*, XXII, (1980–81).

Liam Irwin, Gearóid O'Tuathaigh and Matthew Potter (eds) *Limerick History and Society* (forthcoming 2008).

E. M. Johnston-Liik, *History of the Irish Parliament 1692–1800: Commons, Constituencies and Statutes 1692–1800*, 6 vols, (Belfast, 2002).

Gerry Joyce, *Limerick City Street Names*, (Limerick, 1995).

Pat Kearney, 'Towards a University for Limerick 1934–1972' in *The Old Limerick Journal, No 27*, (Autumn, 1990).

Sir David Lindsay Keir, *The Constitutional History of Modern Britain Since 1485*, (9th Edition, London, 1968).

Cornelius Kelly, *The Grand Tour of Limerick*, (Allihies, Beara, Co. Cork, 2004).

Maria Kelly, *A History of the Black Death in Ireland*, (Stroud, Gloucestershire, 2001).

Jim Kemmy, 'A Changing City-A Personal View', in David Lee (ed.), *Remembering Limerick. Historical Essays Celebrating the 800th Anniversary of Limerick's First Charter granted in 1197*, (Limerick, 1997).

Jim Kemmy, 'The Death of a Cabin-Boy' in Jim Kemmy (ed.), *The Limerick Anthology*, (Limerick 1996).

Jim Kemmy, 'George Clancy- Murdered Mayor' in David Lee (ed.), *Remembering Limerick. Historical Essays Celebrating the 800th Anniversary of Limerick's First Charter granted in 1197*, (Limerick, 1997).

Jim Kemmy, 'James Casey-Soviet Treasurer' in David Lee (ed.), *Remembering Limerick. Historical Essays Celebrating the 800th Anniversary of Limerick's First Charter granted in 1197*, (Limerick, 1997).

Jim Kemmy, 'The Killing of Michael O'Callaghan' in David Lee (ed.), *Remembering Limerick. Historical Essays Celebrating the 800th Anniversary of Limerick's First Charter granted in 1197*, (Limerick, 1997).

Jim Kemmy, 'Portrait of the Martyr as a Young Man' in David Lee (ed.), *Remembering Limerick. Historical Essays Celebrating the 800th Anniversary of Limerick's First Charter granted in 1197*, (Limerick, 1997).

Jim Kemmy and Larry Walsh, *Limerick in Old Picture Postcards*, (Limerick, 1997).

Liam Kenny, 'Local Government and Politics' in Mark Callanan and Justin F. Keogan (eds.), *Local Government in Ireland Inside Out*, (Dublin, 2003).

Dermot Keogh and Andrew McCarthy, *Limerick Boycott 1904: Anti-Semitism in Ireland*, (Cork, 2005).

Colin Knox, 'Mayoralty in Northern Ireland: Symbol or Substance?' in John Garrard (ed.), *Heads of the Local State: Mayors, Provosts and Burgomasters since 1800*, (Aldershot, 2007).

Patricia Lavelle, *James O'Mara a Staunch Sinn Féiner 1873–1948*, (Dublin, 1948).

H. G. Leask, 'The Ancient Walls of Limerick' in *North Munster Antiquarian Journal*, Vol. 2, No. 3, (Spring, 1941).

David Lee, 'Limerick-Magnet of Liberty' in David Lee (ed.), *Remembering Limerick. Historical Essays Celebrating the 800th Anniversary of Limerick's First Charter granted in 1197*, (Limerick, 1997).

David Lee, 'Limerick's Viking Democracy' in David Lee (ed.), *Remembering Limerick. Historical Essays Celebrating the 800th Anniversary of Limerick's First Charter granted in 1197*, (Limerick, 1997).

David Lee (ed.), *Remembering Limerick. Historical Essays Celebrating the 800th Anniversary of Limerick's First Charter granted in 1197*, (Limerick, 1997).

David Lee and Debbie Jacobs, *James Pain Architect*, (Limerick, 2005).

Maurice Lenihan, *Limerick, its History and Antiquities, Ecclesiastical, Civil and Military, From the Earliest Ages*, (Dublin, 1866).

Colm Lennon, *Sixteenth-Century Ireland: The Incomplete Conquest*, (Dublin, 1994).

Colm Lennon, *The Lords of Dublin in the Age of the Reformation*, (Dublin, 1989).

Colm Lennon, *The Urban Patriciates of Early Modern Ireland: A Case-Study of Limerick*, (Dublin, 1999).

Denis Leonard, 'Provosts and Mayors of Limerick, 1197–1997, in David Lee (ed.), *Remembering Limerick. Historical Essays Celebrating the 800th Anniversary of Limerick's First Charter granted in 1197*, (Limerick, 1997).

Mae Leonard, 'A Dandy Man', (Unpublished article).

Mark and John Liddy, 'J.P. (Rory) Liddy', in David Lee (ed.), *Remembering Limerick. Historical Essays Celebrating the 800th Anniversary of Limerick's First Charter granted in 1197*, (Limerick, 1997).

Alexander Llewellyn, *The Decade of Reform: the 1830s* (New York, 1971).

David Luscombe and Jonathan Riley-Smith (eds.), *The New Cambridge Medieval History Volume 4, c 1024–c 1198, Parts 1 and 2*, (Cambridge 2004).

J.F. Lydon, *The Lordship of Ireland in the Middle Ages*, (Dublin 1972).

Kathleen Lynch, Roger Boyle, *1stEarl of Orrery*, (Knoxville, 1965).

Proinsias MacAonghusa, 'Donogh O'Malley' in Jim Kemmy (ed) *The Limerick Anthology*, (Dublin 1996).

Proinsias MacAonghusa, 'Donogh O'Malley' in Jim Kemmy (ed) *The Limerick Compendium*, (Dublin 1997).

Muiris MacCarthaigh and Mark Callanan, 'The Mayoralty in the Republic of Ireland' in John Garrard (ed.), *Heads of the Local State: Mayors, Provosts and Burgomasters since 1800*, (Aldershot, 2007).

Sinéad McCoole, *No Ordinary Women. Irish Female Activists in the Revolutionary Years 1900–1923*, (Dublin, 2003).

Oliver McDonagh 'Ideas and Institutions 1830–45' in W.E. Vaughan (ed.), *A New History of Ireland Volume V Ireland Under the Union, I, 1801–70* (Oxford, 1989).

R.B. McDowell, 'Administration and the Public Service, 1800–70' in W.E. Vaughan (ed.), *A New History of Ireland Volume V Ireland Under the Union, I, 1801–70* (Oxford, 1989).

R.B. Mc Dowell, *Ireland in the Age of Imperialism and Revolution, 1760–1801* (Oxford, 1979).

R.B. Mc Dowell, 'Ireland in 1800' in T.W. Moody and W.E. Vaughan (eds.), *A New History of Ireland, Vol. IV, Eighteenth-Century Ireland 1691–1800*, (Oxford, 1986).

R.B. McDowell, *The Irish Administration, 1801–1914*, (London, 1964).

Eamonn McEneaney (ed.), *A History of Waterford and its Mayors from the 12th to the 20th Century*, (Waterford, 1995).

Eamonn McEneaney, 'The Golden Age. Roger le Lom, Mayor- 1284–85' in Eamonn McEneaney (ed.), *A History of Waterford and its Mayors from the 12th to the 20th Century*, (Waterford, 1995).

Eamonn McEneaney, 'Mayors and Merchants in Medieval Waterford City, 1169–1495, in William Nolan, Thomas P. Power and Des Cowman (eds.), *Waterford History and Society*, (Dublin, 1986).

Eamonn McEneaney, 'Origins' in Eamonn McEneaney (ed.), *A History of Waterford and its Mayors from the 12th to the 20th Century*, (Waterford, 1995).

Jonathan McGee, 'The Mayoralty and the Jews of Limerick' in David Lee (ed.), *Remembering Limerick. Historical Essays Celebrating the 800th Anniversary of Limerick's First Charter granted in 1197*, (Limerick, 1997).

Enda McKay, 'The Limerick Municipal Elections, January 1899' in *The Old Limerick Journal*, No. 36, (Winter, 1999).

Eileen McMahon, 'Robes of Office' in David Lee (ed.), *Remembering Limerick. Historical Essays Celebrating the 800th Anniversary of Limerick's First Charter granted in 1197*, (Limerick, 1997).

James McMahon, Limerick Athenaeum. *If Walls Could Talk. The Story of an Irish Theatre*, (Limerick, 1996).

Sarah McNamara, *Development of Limerick by Honan Merchants. The Unfolding of a Hidden History*, (Limerick, 2003).

Gearóid MacNiocaill, *Na Buirgeisi*, XII-XIV Aois, 2 Vols, (Charraig Dhubh, 1964).

Gearóid MacNiocaill, 'Socio-Economic Problems of the Late Medieval Irish Town' in David Harkness and Mary O'Dowd (eds.), *The Town In Ireland*, (Belfast, 1981).

A.P.W. Malcomson, 'Speaker Pery and the Pery Papers' in *North Munster Antiquarian Journal*, Vol. XVI, (1973–74).

Alan Mansfield, *Ceremonial Costume*, (London, 1980).

Robert Millward, 'The Political Economy of Urban Utilities' in Martin Daunton (ed.), *The Cambridge Urban History of Britain, Volume III, 1840–1950*, (Cambridge, 2001).

Arthur Mitchell, Labour in *Irish Politics. The Irish Labour Movement in an Age of Revolution*, (Dublin, 1974).

T.W. Moody, F.X. Martin and F. J. Byrne, (eds.), *A New History of Ireland, Vol.III, Early Modern Ireland 1534–1691*, (Oxford, 1991).

T.W. Moody, F.X. Martin and F.J. Byrne (eds), *A New History of Ireland, Vol. IX, Maps, Genealogies, Lists. A Companion to Irish History, Part 2*, (Oxford, 1984).

T.W. Moody and W.E. Vaughan (eds), *A New History of Ireland, Vol. IV, Eighteenth-Century Ireland 1691–1800*, (Oxford, 1986).

Jennifer Moore, 'Newtown Pery- the Antithesis to Corporation Corruption and the Birth of a New City in Eighteenth Century Limerick' in *History Studies*, Volume V, (2004).

Robert J. Morris and Richard H. Trainor (eds), *Urban Governance. Britain and Beyond Since 1750*, (Aldershot and Burlington, 2000).

Thomas J. Morrissey, *Bishop Edward Thomas O'Dwyer of Limerick, 1842–1917*, (Dublin, 2003).

Charlotte Murphy, 'A Corporation Minute Book- 1769–1796' in *Old Limerick Journal*, Vol. 6 (Spring 1981).

Charlotte Murphy, 'Gleanings from the Meetings of the Corporation of Limerick, 1809–1823' in *North Munster Antiquarian Journal*, Vol. 18, (1976).

C.M. Murphy, *Limerick City. An Architectural Guide*, (Limerick, 1986).

James H. Murphy, *Abject Loyalty. Nationalism and Monarchy in Ireland During the Reign of Queen Victoria*, (Cork, 2001).

Bibliography

The *New Encyclopaedia Britannica*, Volume 7, Micropaedia, (London, 1988).

Jeremiah Newman, Bishop of Limerick, 'Scattery: an Unknown Part of the Diocese of Limerick' in *North Munster Antiquarian Journal*, Vol. 34 (1992).

David Nicholas, *The Growth of the Medieval City from Late Antiquity to the Early Fourteenth Century*, (London, 1997).

David Nicholas, *The Late Medieval City 1300–1500*, (London, 1997).

Kenneth Nicholls, *Gaelic and Gaelicised Ireland in the Middle Ages*, (Dublin, 1972).

Alan Norton, *International Handbook of Local and Regional Government. A Comparative Analysis of Advanced Democracie*s, (London, 1994).

Antóin O'Callaghan, *The Lord Mayors of Cork 1900 to 2000*, (Cork, 2000).

John O'Callaghan, 'Republican Administration of Local Government in Limerick 1920–21' in *North Munster Antiquarian Journal*, Vol. 45 (2005).

Mrs. O'Callaghan, Mrs. Clancy and others, 'The Limerick Curfew Murders of 7th March, 1921' in *Limerick's Fighting Story. Told by the Men who Made it*, (Tralee, no date of publication).

John O'Connor, *On Shannon's Shore. A History of Mungret Parish*, (Mungret, 2003).

Sister Loreto O'Connor, *Passing on the Torch: A History of Mary Immaculate College 1898–1998*, (Limerick, 1998).

Patrick J. O'Connor, *All Ireland is in and about Rathkeale*, (Newcastle West, County Limerick, 1996).

Patrick J. O'Connor, *Exploring Limerick's Past. An Historical Geography of Urban Development in County and City*, (Newcastle West, Co. Limerick, 1987).

Dáibhí O'Cróinín (ed.), *A New History of Ireland. Vol.I. Prehistoric and Early Ireland*, (Oxford, 2005).

Dáibhí O'Cróinín, *Early Medieval Ireland 400–1200* (London, 1995).

John O'Donovan (ed), *Annals of the Kingdom of Ireland by the Four Masters. From the Earliest Period to the Year 1616*, 7 Vols., (Dublin, 1856. Reprint, 1990).

Eamon O'Flaherty, 'Three Towns: Limerick Since 1691' in Howard B. Clarke (ed.), *Irish Cities*, (Cork and Dublin, 1995).

Eamon O'Flaherty, 'The Urban Community and the State 1590–1690' in Bernadette Whelan (ed.), *The Last of the Great Wars. Essays on the War of the Three Kings in Ireland 1688–91*, (Limerick, 1995).

Eamon O'Flaherty, 'Urban Politics and Municipal Reform in Limerick 1723–62' in *Eighteenth Century Ireland*, VI, (1991).

Michael O'Flaherty, *The Story of Young Munster Rugby Football Club 1895/96 –1995/96. A Celebration of 100 Years of Football*, (Limerick, 1995).

Ciarán O'Gríofa, 'First Citizen Meets First Citizen. Frances Condell and the Visit of John F. Kennedy, June, 1963' in David Lee (ed.), *Remembering Limerick. Historical Essays Celebrating the 800th Anniversary of Limerick's First Charter granted in 1197*, (Limerick, 1997).

Ciarán O'Gríofa, 'John Daly, the Fenian Mayor of Limerick', in David Lee (ed.), *Remembering Limerick. Historical Essays Celebrating the 800th Anniversary of Limerick's First Charter granted in 1197*, (Limerick, 1997).

Ciarán O'Gríofa, 'Limerick During the Emergency' in David Lee (ed.), *Remembering Limerick. Historical Essays Celebrating the 800th Anniversary of Limerick's First Charter granted in 1197*, (Limerick, 1997).

Ciarán O'Gríofa, 'Michael Joyce-Maritime Mayor' in David Lee (ed.), *Remembering Limerick. Historical Essays Celebrating the 800th Anniversary of Limerick's First Charter granted in 1197*, (Limerick, 1997).

Ciarán O'Gríofa, 'Stephen O'Mara and the Limerick Crisis, March 1922' in David Lee (ed.), *Remembering Limerick. Historical Essays Celebrating the 800th Anniversary of Limerick's First Charter granted in 1197*, (Limerick, 1997).

Ciarán O'Gríofa, 'Structures of Municipal Government in Limerick 1841–1934,' in David Lee (ed.), *Remembering Limerick. Historical Essays Celebrating the 800th Anniversary of Limerick's First Charter granted in 1197*, (Limerick, 1997).

Eunan O'Halpin, 'The Origins of City and County Management' in *City and County Management 1929–1990. A Retrospective*, (Dublin, 1991).

The Old Limerick Journal. Famine Edition, No. 32, (Winter, 1995).

Chris O'Mahony, 'Limerick Night Watch 1807–1853' in *The Old Limerick Journal*, No. 21, (Autumn, 1987).

Celie O'Rahilly 'Medieval Limerick: The Growth of Two Towns' in Howard B. Clarke (ed.), *Irish Cities*, (Cork and Dublin, 1995).

Denis O'Shaughnessy, *How's your Father? Stories of Limerick*, (Limerick, 2002).

Katherine O'Shea, *Charles Stewart Parnell: His Love Story and Political Life*, 2 Vols., (London, 1914).

Micheal O'Siochru, *Confederate Ireland, 1641–1649. A Constitutional and Political Analysis*, (Dublin, 1998).

M.D. O'Sullivan, *Old Galway. The History of a Norman Colony in Ireland*, (Cambridge, 1942).

Terry O'Sullivan, 'Local Areas and Structures' in Mark Callanan and Justin F. Keogan (eds.), *Local Government in Ireland Inside Out*, (Dublin, 2003).

Gearóid O'Tuathaigh, *Ireland Before the Famine 1798–1848*, (Dublin 1972).

Gearóid O'Tuathaigh, 'Words Spoken at the Grave of Jim Kemmy, Mount St. Lawrence Cemetery, Limerick, 29 September, 1997', in *The Old Limerick Journal*, No. 34, (Summer, 1998).

A.J. Otway – Ruthven, *A History of Medieval Ireland*, (London, 1968).

J. Otway-Ruthven, *Liber Primus Kilkenniensis*, (Kilkenny, 1961).

D.M. Palliser (ed.), *The Cambridge Urban History of Britain, Volume I, 600–1540,* (Cambridge, 2000).

Seamus Pender (ed.), *Census of Ireland, c. 1659,* (Dublin, 1939).

Colin Platt, *The English Medieval Town,* (London, 1976).

Matthew Potter, *The Government and the People of Limerick. The History of Limerick Corporation/City Council 1197–2006,* (Limerick, 2006).

T.P. Power and Kevin Whelan (eds.), *Endurance and Emergence. Catholics In Ireland in the Eighteenth Century,* (Dublin, 1990).

Frank Prendergast, 'The Limerick Soviet- A Review Article' in *North Munster Antiquarian Journal,* Vol. 34, (1992).

Frank Prendergast, 'Medieval Borough Boundaries' in David Lee (ed.), *Remembering Limerick. Historical Essays Celebrating the 800th Anniversary of Limerick's First Charter granted in 1197,* (Limerick, 1997).

l. J. Proudfoot, *Property Ownership and Urban and Village Improvement in Provincial Ireland, ca. 1700–1845,* (London, 1997).

L.J. Proudfoot, 'Spatial Transformation and Social Agency: Property, Society and Improvement, c. 1700 to c. 1900' in B.J. Graham and L.J. Proudfoot (eds), *An Historical Geography of Ireland,* (London and San Diego, 1993).

David B. Quinn, 'Anglo-Irish Local Government 1485–1534', *Irish Historical Studies,* I (1938–9).

D.B. Quinn, '"Irish" Ireland and "English" Ireland' in Art Cosgrove (ed.), *A New History of Ireland, Volume II, Medieval Ireland 1169–1534.* (Oxford, 1987).

Padge Reck, *Wexford - A Municipal History,* (Wexford, 1987).

Susan Reynolds, *An Introduction to the History of English Medieval Towns,* (Oxford, 1977).

Anthony Riordan, 'A nineteenth-Century Citizen' in *The Old Limerick Journal,* No. 18, (Winter 1985).

Desmond Roche, *Local Government in Ireland,* (Dublin, 1982).

Dick Roche TD, 'The Experience of Ireland in Europe' in *Administration,* Vol. 52, No. 3 (Autumn, 2004).

George Rudé, *Europe in the Eighteenth Century. Aristocracy and the Bourgeois Challenge,* (London, 1972).

Des Ryan, 'Jewish Immigrants in Limerick- A Divided Community' in David Lee (ed.), *Remembering Limerick. Historical Essays Celebrating the 800th Anniversary of Limerick's First Charter granted in 1197,* (Limerick, 1997).

Des Ryan, '1916 Rising-The Limerick Connection' in David Lee (ed.), *Remembering Limerick. Historical Essays Celebrating the 800th Anniversary of Limerick's First Charter granted in 1197,* (Limerick, 1997).

Des Ryan, 'Who Shot the Mayors?' in David Lee (ed.), *Remembering Limerick. Historical Essays Celebrating the 800th Anniversary of Limerick's First Charter granted in 1197,* (Limerick, 1997).

P.J. Ryan, 'Armed Conflict in Limerick' in David Lee (ed.), *Remembering Limerick. Historical Essays Celebrating the 800th Anniversary of Limerick's First Charter granted in 1197,* (Limerick, 1997).

Anthony Sheehan, 'Irish Towns in a Period of Change 1558–1625' in Ciaran Brady and Raymond Gillespie, (eds.), *Natives and Newcomers. Essays on the Making of Irish Colonial Society 1534–1641,* (Dublin, 1986).

Anthony J. Sheehan, '*The* Recusancy Revolt of 1603: A Reinterpretation' in *Archivium Hibernicum,* XXXVIII 1983.

Robert C. Simington, *The Civil Survey A.D. 1654–1656 County of Limerick Vol. IV. ,* (Dublin, 1938).

J.G. Simms, The Restoration, 1660–85' in T.W. Moody, F.X. Martin and F.J. Byrne, (eds.), *A New History of Ireland, Vol.III, Early Modern Ireland 1534–1691,* (Oxford, 1991).

Sir Leslie Stephen and Sir Sidney Lee (eds.), *The Dictionary of National Biography,* (London, 1908–09), 23 Vols.

John Stevens, *Journal of John Stevens, 1689–1691,* edited by R.H. Murray (Oxford, 1912).

Howard A. Street, *The Law Relating to Local Government,* (Dublin, 1955).

Rosemary Sweet, *The English Town, 1680–1840. Government, Society and Culture,* (Harlow, Essex, 1999).

Clodagh Tait, 'A Trusty and Well-beloved Servant. The Career and Disinterment of Edmond Sexton of Limerick, d.1554' in *Archivium Hibernicum,* Vol. 56, (Maynooth, 2002).

James Tait, *The Medieval English Borough. Studies on its Origins and Constitutional History,* (Manchester, 1936).

Avril Thomas, *The Walled Towns of Ireland,* 2 Vols., (Dublin, 1992).

Fr. Mark Tierney, 'Citizen Kane, Mayor of Limerick' in David Lee (ed.), *Remembering Limerick. Historical Essays Celebrating the 800th Anniversary of Limerick's First Charter granted in 1197,* (Limerick, 1997).

Robert Tittler, 'The Incorporation of Boroughs, 1540–1558' in *History,* LXII, (1977).

Nora-Ann Toomey and David Lee, 'The General Strike as a Political Weapon-Limerick, 1918–20' in David Lee (ed.), *Remembering Limerick. Historical Essays Celebrating the 800th Anniversary of Limerick's First Charter granted in 1197,* (Limerick, 1997).

Thomas Toomey and Harry Greensmyth, *An Antique and Storied Land. A History of the Parish of Donoughmore, Knockea, Roxborough and its Environs in County Limerick,* (Limerick, 1991).

Richard H. Trainor, 'The "decline" of British urban governance since 1850: a reassessment' in Robert J. Morris and Richard H. Trainor (eds), *Urban Governance. Britain and Beyond Since 1750,* (Aldershot and Burlington, 2000).

Victor Treadwell, 'The Establishment of the Farm of the Irish Customs 1603–13' in *The English Historical Review,* Vol. XCIII, (1978).

Victor Treadwell, 'The Irish Customs Administration in the Sixteenth Century' in *Irish Historical Studies,* Vol. XX, (1976–77).

Bibliography

John Van Der Kiste and Bee Jordaan, *Dearest Affie- Alfred, Duke of Edinburgh, Queen Victoria's Second Son*, (London, 1995).
W.E. Vaughan (ed.), *A New History of Ireland Volume V Ireland Under the Union*, I, *1801–70* (Oxford, 1989).

John C. Waite, *Peter Tait. A Remarkable Story*, (Little Norton, 2005).
Joseph Frazer Wall, *Andrew Carnegie*, (Second edition, Pittsburgh, 1989).
Maureen Wall, *The Penal Laws, 1691–1760*, (Dundalk, 1967).
Larry Walsh, 'Abolition and Reinstatement of the Limerick Night Watch, 1898–1899' in *The Old Limerick Journal*, No. 36, (Winter, 1999).
Larry Walsh, 'The Mayoral Myth' in David Lee (ed.), *Remembering Limerick. Historical Essays Celebrating the 800th Anniversary of Limerick's First Charter granted in 1197*, (Limerick, 1997).
Laurence Walsh, *Historic Limerick, The City and Its Treasures*, (Dublin, 1984).
John J Webb, *Municipal Government in Ireland: Medieval and Modern*, (Dublin, 1918).
Sidney and Beatrice Webb, *Statutory Bodies For Special Purposes*, (London, 1922).
Martin Weinbaum, *The Incorporation of Boroughs*, (Manchester, 1937).
Bernadette Whelan (ed.), *The Last of the Great Wars. Essays on the War of the Three Kings in Ireland 1688–91*, (Limerick, 1995).
Kenneth Wiggins, *Anatomy of a Siege. King John's Castle, Limerick, 1642*, (Bray, Co. Wicklow, 2000).
Kenneth Wiggins, *King John's Castle. Bridging the Centuries*, (Limerick, 2004).
Liz Wood, 'Charles Stuart' in Colin Matthew, Brian Harrison and Laurence Goldman (eds), *Oxford Dictionary of National Biography* (Oxford, 2004–07) consulted online at www.oxforddnb.com

Anne Yeoman, 'George E. (Ted) Russell, Mayor of Limerick, 1954–55, 1955–56, 1956–57, 1967–68, 1976–77, Freeman of Limerick' in David Lee (ed.), *Remembering Limerick. Historical Essays Celebrating the 800th Anniversary of Limerick's First Charter granted in 1197*, (Limerick, 1997).
Anne Yeoman, 'Throwing the Dart' in David Lee (ed.), *Remembering Limerick. Historical Essays Celebrating the 800th Anniversary of Limerick's First Charter granted in 1197*, (Limerick, 1997).

Unpublished Theses

Pat Collins, 'Labour, Church and Nationalism in Limerick 1893–1902', (Unpublished MA thesis, University College Cork, 1984).
Liam Irwin, 'The Lord Presidency of Munster 1625–72' (Unpublished MA thesis, University College Cork, 1976).
Sarah Johnson, 'By Crafty Means: Edmund Sexton and the Politics of Patronage in Sixteenth Century Ireland', (Unpublished MA thesis, St. Hugh's College, Oxford, 2005).
Kenneth Milne, 'The Irish Municipal Corporations in the Eighteenth Century', (Unpublished Ph.D. thesis, Trinity College, Dublin, 1962).
William Patrick Mulligan, 'The Enemy Within; The Enemy Without. How the Wealthier Class Manipulated Local Government in Nineteenth Century Limerick'. (Unpublished MA thesis, University of Limerick, 2005).
Matthew Potter, 'A Catholic Unionist: the Life and Times of William Monsell, first Baron Emly of Tervoe 1812–1894,' (Unpublished Ph.D thesis, National University of Ireland, Galway, 2001).
Jennifer Ridden, 'Making Good Citizens': National Identity, Religion and Liberalism among the Irish Elite, c. 1800–1850 (Unpublished Ph.D. thesis, London University, 1998).

Dr. Matthew Potter Biography

Dr. Matthew Potter is a graduate of the University of London (BA) and NUI Galway (Ph.D). He is on secondment from Limerick City Council to the University of Limerick where he is an IRCHSS Postdoctoral Fellow in the History Department. In 2006 *the book The Government & People of Limerick. The History of Limerick Corporation/City Council 1197-2006* was published. He is married with two children and lives in Limerick.

Index

Note: Page number in **Italics** indicate photographs or illustrations.